D1528465

Life among the Indians

Studies in the Anthropology of North American Indians Series

Editors
Raymond J. DeMallie
Douglas R. Parks

Life among the Indians

First Fieldwork among the Sioux and Omahas

Alice C. Fletcher

Edited and with an introduction by Joanna C.
Scherer and Raymond J. DeMallie

University of Nebraska Press | Lincoln and London

In cooperation with the American Indian Studies Research
Institute, Indiana University, Bloomington

© 2013 by the Board of Regents of the University of Nebraska

All rights reserved

Manufactured in the United States of America

Library of Congress Cataloging-in-Publication Data

Fletcher, Alice C. (Alice Cunningham), 1838–1923.

Life among the Indians: first fieldwork among the Sioux and Omahas / Alice C. Fletcher;

edited by Joanna C. Scherer, Raymond J. DeMallie.

pages cm.—(Studies in the anthropology of North American Indians)

Includes bibliographical references and index.

ISBN 978-0-8032-4115-2 (cloth: alk. paper)

1. Fletcher, Alice C. (Alice Cunningham), 1838–1923. 2. Women anthropologists—Great

Plains—Biography. 3. Dakota Indians—Social life and customs. 4. Omaha Indians—Social

life and customs. I. Title.

GN21.F54A3 2013

301.092—dc23   [B]

2013020503

Set in Lyon by Laura Wellington.

Designed by J. Vadnais.

Dedicated to the memory of Margaret C. Blaker (1924–2008), archivist
of the Bureau of American Ethnology (later National Anthropological
Archives) from 1958 to 1972, who gave us both our first introduction to
the rewards and necessary rigor of archival research;

and to

the memory of Marjorie Sue Abramovitz (1942–2007),
lifelong friend of Joanna C. Scherer

Alice C. Fletcher seated at her desk, probably in Washington DC at her Temple Hotel residence, in February or March 1889. The photographer is unknown, and the photo is dated based on the February 15, 1889, issue of *Science* on Fletcher's desk. Smithsonian Institution, National Anthropological Archives, Bureau of American Ethnology collection (gn-04510).

Contents

Illustrations

Figures

Original field sketches by Alice C. Fletcher, 1881

Musical Scores

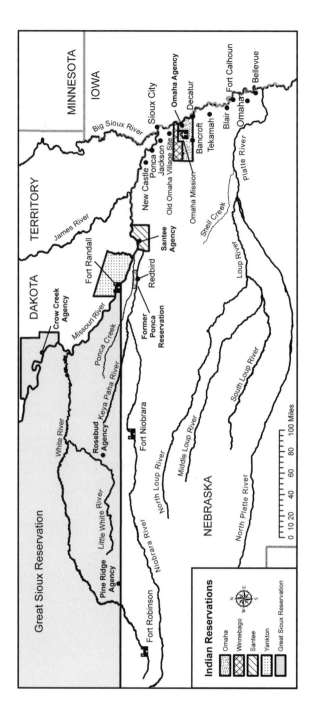

Alice Fletcher's travels in Nebraska and Dakota Territory, 1881–82.

Introduction

Joanna C. Scherer and Raymond J. DeMallie

Alice Fletcher's "Life among the Indians"

In a letter dated June 26, 1886, to her friend Electa Sanderson Dawes, wife of Henry L. Dawes, the Massachusetts senator who chaired the Senate Committee on Indian Affairs,[1] Alice Fletcher described a manuscript she was writing about her first experiences in anthropological fieldwork among the Omaha and Sioux Indians in fall 1881. She wrote from the Temple Hotel in Washington DC, where she rented rooms when she returned to the capital from her travels. She was suffering from inflammatory rheumatism, which had first flared up during her 1881 field trip.

> Temple Hotel
> My dear Mrs. Dawes,
> My visit to you was about the last thing I did. I have been confined to my room and am still. I think I can say I am better, for the fever is about gone but the bad old knee is very naughty. I must have strained it. I can't use it and when I am not lying down I get round my room on crutches, not using that bad leg at all. Isn't it fortunate that I didn't start with you. I would have been worse than any domestic or foreign domestic!
> In spite of sickness I've kept at the book and I put in the chap-

ter you and Miss Dawes thought needful. Those completed are as follows.

Over the Border
Reporting
The Welcome
The Chief's Entertainment
The White Man's Shadow
A Religious festival [crossed out]
Acting out a Vision
An Outline Chapter
Indian Women
The Woman's Society
... (1)
The Ghost Lodge
Journeying with the Indians
... (2 or 3)
Among the Omahas
The Young Mother
An Indian Story
... (2 or 3)
Hunting

These will make about 170 printed pages. The breaks indicate where chapters are to go in. And it will take about 4 after Hunting making about 25 or 26 chapters and 300 or 325 pages. Isn't that doing pretty well for 25 days work & sick beside.

Now for the title. I have tried on the Ethnological Journey. Most people think it will scan. I like it, but this book is not for me so I have been thinking—what do you think of this?

The Domestic Alien
A Study from Nature

I may express the whole thing to you but just yet I have to keep it in hand.

I so wish I could see you both, but I am a fixture for a time &

how long I don't know. My knee is to be pronounced upon in a few days but I hope to get it back again before very long.

I hope you are all right and Miss Dawes better.

My love to both you and her.

Ever Affectionately,

Alice C. Fletcher

June 26, 1886.

Fletcher eventually titled her manuscript "Life among the Indians." The prologue (printed in the present volume) is dated February 15, 1887, eight months after her letter to Mrs. Dawes. Her book, Fletcher wrote, was based on "scenes and incidents that were always recorded at the time of happening, although for the purposes of grouping in the following chapters no attempt has been made to preserve the actual chronological order." The field notebooks in which she recorded her observations are now housed in the Smithsonian Institution's National Anthropological Archives.[2]

"Life among the Indians" offers a view of daily life among the Sioux and Omahas only five years after the 1876 defeat of Lt. Col. George Armstrong Custer's Seventh Cavalry on the Little Big Horn River, the battle popularly known as "Custer's Last Stand." The media represented Indians either as bloodthirsty savages or childlike noble savages. Indians were generally considered to be both racially and intellectually inferior to whites. Following the social evolutionary rhetoric of the day, reformers like Dawes and other "friends of the Indian" believed that Indians were destined to lose their tribal ways, the survivors eventually to assimilate into mainstream American society.

In her manuscript Fletcher depicts both the Indians and the Euro-American settlers who lived side by side in the 1880s, separate and unequal under U.S. law. Her dispassionate observations lead readers to compare their contrasting lifestyles. One of Fletcher's goals was to reveal to non-Indian readers the uniqueness, complexity, and diversity of Indian cultures. She situated Sioux and Omaha social institutions and individual personalities as she experienced them on their reservations, presenting Indians' and whites' common humanity as a way of countering prejudice and convictions of racial inferiority. She expressed it in these words (at the end of chapter 3): "as I lay within the lodge, sharing the bosom of mother earth with my Indian friends, the thrill of a common humanity came over me as I recalled the welcome of the stranger and the care bestowed upon her." By stressing their common humanity, Fletcher sought to win her readers over to a sympathetic perspective on American Indians and to raise public support for Indian reform.

Another of Fletcher's goals for the manuscript was to contribute to the ethnographic record of these tribes. She wrote in chapter 2, "Reporting," that her motivation for engaging in this field trip was "the desire to see Indian life from the other side, and to try to get at its meaning; to seek for the springs of the Indian's religious thought and ceremonies; to trace out the lines common to the human race; and to do my share toward preserving the record of the people who were native to our country." She desired above all else to "let the Indian paint his own picture, no matter how different it might be from the supposed reality" (chapter 6, "An Outline Chapter").

Indeed, "Life among the Indians" includes a wealth of cultural detail gained through participant observation. In chapter 6, for example, she details her observations on fundamental social institutions: kinship, which was the basis for Indian society; naming practices and the importance of names for social organization; etiquette, for example, where and how to sit inside a tipi; the importance for men of the accumulation of honors and property that could not be inherited but must be earned by each individual; the significance of the office of chief and how it was determined; a variety of religious practices; and perspectives on illness and the ways of treating ailments. In chapter 7, "The Indian Woman," she describes the position of power and honor accorded to women in Sioux society. In chapter 9, "Acting out a Vision," she details the Sioux Elk Society[3] and describes how Sioux women raised a tipi. In chapter 13, "The Ghost Lodge," she recounts this powerful Sioux ceremony associated with death and mourning.

In her ethnographic descriptions Fletcher reveals Indian lifestyles that would have greatly surprised late nineteenth-century readers. When she is invited to a women's society feast (chapter 8, "The Woman's Society") her hostess bids her to bring her own dishes, explaining that this was common courtesy among the Sioux because "[n]o person would have enough dishes for so many people." In chapter 7 she describes the many insults the Sioux were forced to endure, including those from white traders and even from visiting whites, some of whom, for example, would mimic Indian dress. Chapter 14, "Beef versus Men," concludes the part of the book devoted to the Sioux and reveals her dawning realization that the reservations are "places . . . not safe or helpful toward manly progress."[4]

Turning to her experiences among the Omahas, in chapter 17, "An Indian's Story," she describes how Omaha women built earth lodges. In chapter 18, "Child Life," she describes the naming of children, their distinctive clan haircuts, learning gender-appropriate skills, and the vision quest. In chapters 19 and 20, "Hunting" and "Winter and War," she details the appointment of Omaha buffalo-hunt leaders and their hunting prowess and recounts stories told her around the fire about war exploits and daily life. She experiences spring among the Omahas and describes courtship, friendship, and marriage. Chapter 22, "The Make-Believe White Men," is devoted to the then-current state of assimilation of some of the Omahas, the mission schools, their new homes, the men's experiences in farming, and the development of cash crops. Throughout the manuscript, in ethnographic descriptions of both the Omahas and the Sioux, she displays an acceptance of Indian life and an open-mindedness that foreshadow the anthropological concept of cultural relativism.

The experiences Fletcher wrote about in many of these chapters reveal an intimacy and everyday understanding of the life of the Omahas and Sioux. She later revised and expanded some of this material for inclusion in her magnum opus, coauthored with Francis La Flesche, *The Omaha Tribe* (1911). For example, the description of buffalo hunting in chapter 19 of "Life among the Indians" can be compared with the more detailed account in *The Omaha Tribe* (pp. 215, 276–83). The latter includes specification of roles within subgentes (subclans, to use the modern anthropological term), the precise order in which hunt activities occurred, the Omaha terms for the articles used to perform the rites needed for a successful hunt, and the punishments for hunters who frightened away game. The manuscript, on the other hand, includes stories of human interest remembered by individual Omahas concerning events that occurred on specific hunts. Thus while the 1911 publication is a more definitive ethnographic account, it does not supplant the 1887 manuscript.[5]

Although the manuscript describes her actual experiences, Fletcher in most cases preserves the anonymity of her subjects. She stayed in the home of the Omaha leader Joseph La Flesche (Iron Eyes) but simply calls him "the father."[6] She traveled on this first field trip with one of La Flesche's daughters, Susette (Bright Eyes),[7] and her non-Indian husband, Thomas Henry Tibbles, but does not mention them by name. She also met another daughter, Rosalie, and relates some of Rosalie's mission school experiences but does not identify her either.[8] Likewise, she does not name the Rosebud Indian agent, John Cook, who received her with arrogance and condescension on October 12, 1881, nor does she identify the Sioux family (that of chief Milk) with whom she told the agent she planned to visit and live. Since much of her manuscript relates serious problems that faced individual Omahas and Sioux, the omission of personal names was likely a way of protecting those individuals from possible reprisal by government officials.

Fletcher's approach in this manuscript may be characterized as literary realism, a style that values first-person observation of group-based differences.[9] The flow of the narrative was fictionalized; most of the events described are based on her experiences in 1881, but she included as well some events that occurred during the following year. Her accounts are all based on firsthand observations and preserve ethnographic accuracy, but by exaggeration and omissions she presents herself as the lone and intrepid heroine venturing into the heart of Indian country where her sophisticated eastern friends warned her not to go.

By setting the stage for her readers to anticipate the otherness of American Indians, the example of her personal experiences on the reservations served to counter the prejudice. Her narrative transforms the Indians into wronged protagonists who are fettered by the corrupt and dehumanizing reservation system. Conflicts are drawn in which the Indians' humanity is thwarted by the system into which they find themselves locked. Fletcher empathizes with Indian life and expresses a cultural relativism and tolerance far ahead of her time. For example, she writes sympathetically about polygyny and the harmonious relationship that existed among multiple wives, an opinion that likely would have shocked readers of the 1880s.[10] She describes many occasions when she witnessed wisdom and humor in her Indian hosts' actions and lives, which foreground their humanity for the reader. She details the joy and fun the Sioux women share in their society circle and how it compares with Euro-American women's clubs to which she herself belonged. She describes the Indian women's curiosity about her clothing and the way they criticized the quality of the sewing on her dress, while approving—and adopting—the innovation of pockets in the skirt. She opines that in Indian culture, as in Euro-American, bringing up girls properly was not an easy thing to do.

"Life among the Indians" was not written in the ethnographic present, which was the professional standard of the day, but was presented in the past tense as a narrative appropriate for general readers. With it she intended to convey her sense of adventure and the immediacy of her experiences. Two articles that Fletcher published in 1884 for the children's magazine *Wide Awake* are very similar in content and form.[11] Titled "The Carlisle Indian Pupils at Home" and "Camping among the Sunflowers," these articles were solicited and encouraged by the publisher, D. Lothrop and Company. In a letter of March 16, 1882, the editors wrote to Fletcher, "We in common with many Boston people, are much interested in your travels and stay among the Indian peoples of the far West; and we have thought that your studies of Indian home life and etc. would by and by shape themselves into a book which would be very popular and valuable. Should you write such a volume, we should like to confer with you regarding its publication."[12]

Such an open invitation may have been the impetus for Fletcher to write "Life among the Indians." She described the project to Professor Frederic Ward Putnam, her mentor at Harvard University, who was the director of the Peabody Museum.[13] The letter is dated June 27, 1886, the day after she had sent the outline of the manuscript to Mrs. Dawes:

My dear Prof. Putnam,

. . . I have a book well on toward completion that I wish you could see. It is a series of pictures and takes in my life among the Indians. Those who have heard it say words of praise, but you know about puddings. Will the public eat it, is the question. Scribners are thinking of it. They asked me to write such a book a year and a half ago and I wrote them about it. If I could only have your word of judgment I should feel better. The pictures are true, but I think some of them will be doubted. I have had fun writing it, it is far easier than the ethnological or historical work.[14]

Fletcher intended the manuscript to present her perspectives on American Indians in a form that would appeal to a popular audience. Still, she worried about her lack of credentials and whether readers would find her material credible. On July 4, 1886, she wrote to Putnam,

> I have a favor to ask of you. Will you permit me to dedicate my new book to you? I hope it will be granted. I owe so much to you that shall be glad to make any acknowledgement possible. May I date my preface from the Museum. I don't believe people will credit my practice, but they are true to the letter and I would like to hail from the only place that knows me, the dear old Museum. You can refuse both my requests. You are free to do so & I beg of you to do what ever is best for you.[15]

We have not found Putnam's reply, but it was undoubtedly positive. The prologue to the manuscript, dated February 15, 1887, identifies her affiliation as Peabody Museum, Cambridge.

Correspondence in the files of Charles Scribner's Sons in New York indicates that Fletcher was hoping that they would publish her book. The publisher recommended on May 10, 1886, that she write a "narrative of your life among the Indians," and on June 4 suggested that "there would be a greater popular interest in a narrative of personal experiences among the Indians."[16] It seems likely that based on this encouragement Fletcher titled her book "Life among the Indians." On July 28, 1886, Fletcher wrote to Mrs. Dawes, "I have not yet heard from the book. Mr. Scribner is away but will return this week & then it will be yea or nay. I am so sorry not to read the proof for one can make so many changes for the better when the MS is cool in print."[17] However, there is no record of Fletcher's manuscript being received or rejected by the publishing company. Whatever Scribner's reaction might have been, it clearly did not discourage Fletcher from continuing to polish her manuscript.

Fletcher's diary reveals that she visited Putnam early in 1887. On February 14 she wrote,

reached Boston 6 p.m.
strike Cambridge cars
worn out
Prof. and Mrs. Putnam very kind—read ms.

On February 15 her diary states,

Over to the museum
had talk Mr. Carr
Prof. P[utnam] and others
very bad reaction
In eve read book
left all ms. with Prof Putnam.[18]

On March 11, 1887, Fletcher wrote an apologetic note to Putnam: "After I left you I felt sort of wicked. I felt as though I had been like a child that gathers up all its broken playthings and pours them at her father's feet for care and mending. I had burdened you with all my mss. . . . I am only as a child to you in ability. I hope it has not worried you for if it was naughty to do it, it was also nice. The world is a cold place, and the museum my only home."[19] The "very bad reaction" to which Fletcher referred may explain why the manuscript was never published. Had it been published when it was written, it would have been the first work by a female ethnologist to be based on fieldwork using the method of participant observation.

It is important to understand the intellectual climate in which Fletcher attempted to publish a popular volume about American Indians. At the time there was a widespread prejudice against promoting popular science and therefore against writing for nonacademic circles. Joseph Henry, secretary of the Smithsonian from 1846 to 1878, believed that "if anthropology in America were ever to transcend the realm of hobbyists, students had to forego the lures of public acclaim and subject their methods and results to the scrutiny of the small group of persons—the 'learned few'—capable of judging their work in the 'regular channels of scientific communication.'"[20] That Fletcher pursued publishing for a wider audience probably reflected, at least in part, her need for income to support herself during this first decade of her anthropological career.

Whatever Putnam's reaction might have been—presumably a recommendation to revise the manuscript rather than abandon it—Fletcher continued to plan for its publication. She noted in her diary on May 23, 1887, "At Mrs. Lander's, Mrs. Blair there, read ms. think I should write a novel and work in all my material."[21] In July 1887 she mentioned to Putnam, "As to the ms. I read some of it to Mrs. Senator Blair and Mrs. Lander. From them I rec'd valuable suggestions. I can make the book very much better if I can work on it a little."[22] Although Fletcher became caught up in other work, in March 1891 she was still considering publishing the manuscript. Her friend and companion Jane Gay[23] wrote to Putnam on Fletcher's behalf: "Miss F. thinks that sometime she may make a book of camp sketches and Indian studies—& wants to be free to use parts of *all* her articles—& if she wants to—In this case arrangement might be made with the Century Co. but everything ought to be understood."[24]

While writing "Life among the Indians" in 1886 and 1887 Fletcher considered a number of titles. Initially she called it "The Domestic Alien." This title appears on her manuscript but was later crossed out in pencil and above it is written "Life among the Indians." The manuscript comprises two parts. The first is titled "Camping with the Sioux." The second part was titled "Life among the Omahas," but that is crossed out and replaced with, in pencil, in Fletcher's hand, "The Omahas at Home." At the bottom of this title page, in pencil, she wrote, "Mem. As the first plan was to publish these papers in two volumes under one title, a preface will have to be written for this volume if the plan should be followed of publishing these sketches in two separate volumes." That she changed the title from one referring to the Indian as "the domestic alien" suggests a deemphasis of the Indians' political status—since the Dawes Act in 1887 provided not only for the allotment of lands to individual Indians but also granted them U.S. citizenship—and a focus instead on her own experiences among the Indians.

Fletcher, as a scientific researcher, is the main character throughout the manuscript, demonstrating the practice of ethnography and the methods used to record and interpret the data firsthand.[25] She portrays herself during her first field trip as essentially ignorant of the government's treatment of American Indians and its many failures to uphold treaty obligations. Fletcher presents herself as the outside observer, the authoritative professional, who gives voice in the first person to the scenes that she witnesses.

For comic relief, Fletcher time and again pokes fun at herself and her ignorance of Indian etiquette. She describes her inability to walk on soft ground in her boots and the obvious advantages of moccasins; her awkwardness in entering a tipi; her inability to eat at multiple feasts, for which her hostess bailed her out by carrying away the uneaten food; the difficulty of riding in a wagon loaded with supplies, the usual place for women; her initial fear of the wildness of Indian song and dance; and the questions she asks that elicit shock and often laughter from Indian women, such as when (in chapter 8) she asked whether those who were invited to join a woman's society were selected on the basis of their husbands' prestige and was told, "White people ask such queer questions! If a woman is bad what difference does it make who her husband is?" The narrative is created from the details of her own extraordinary behavior, her account of just being there. The manuscript develops no other plot.

A few details in the manuscript of "Life among the Indians" were left unfinished. For example, she left blank the footnote reference to the *Annual Report of the Commissioner of Indian Affairs* in which she intended to document the wrong done to the Sioux when the Black Hills were overrun by non-Indian prospectors searching for gold, in violation of the 1868 treaty (chapter 5). A notation indicates that she intended to include the musical score for the prayer a twelve-year-old Omaha boy chanted during his first religious sojourn (chapter 18). She also intended to add musical scores for the songs used in the Omaha ceremony of the sacred pipes that she was privileged to study after her long illness and recovery (chapter 26). Two manuscript musical scores kept with the manuscript are inserted.

At some point, probably after Fletcher's death in 1923, Francis La Flesche intended to prepare Fletcher's manuscript for publication. He began drafting a foreword (reprinted in this volume) and made the typewritten transcript of parts of her field notebooks that is preserved in the Smithsonian Institution's National Anthropological Archives, available on their website.[26]

In 1884, prior to writing "Life among the Indians," Fletcher published a number of academic articles in the *Annual Reports of the Trustees of the Peabody Museum of American Archaeology and Ethnology* that include more detailed ethnographic material than her unpublished manuscript. For example, her article on the Oglala Sioux Ghost Lodge provides detailed descriptions and diagrams and was intended for a more academic audience than was the corresponding chapter in her unpublished manuscript (chapter 13, "The Ghost Lodge").[27] That chapter, however, complements and expands on the scientific description. It exemplifies the way in which Fletcher makes the reader feel the authenticity of a scene by using the conventions of representational realism. Through her eyes we experience the deaths of Sioux sons and the tribute to them made by enacting the Ghost Lodge, which kept the family focused on the deceased for two years. In this chapter we also see how cautious Fletcher was as an ethnographer. She longed to know what was going on in the lodge of the deceased but respectfully kept her distance: "How long I lay watching the lodge that I did not like to enter I cannot tell.... I turned back to the tent where I was visiting, filled with sympathy for the mourning ones, and turning over in my mind as to what could be the meaning of the ceremonies I had seen at a distance."

Fletcher was acutely respectful of the Indians' sensibilities. In chapter 19 of her manuscript she wrote, for example,

When I talked of past ceremonies and customs, only a few were ever present.... Such themes as the inaugurating of chiefs, the ceremonials of the hunt, the religious festivals, the honors and duties connected with war, the tribal organizations, and kindred subjects were never discussed in the presence of a company....The willingness of certain persons to discuss these topics with me came only after a tried experience. To some of the leading men I made known my wish to secure for preservation as much as possible of the past history of the Omahas, to prepare a faithful record of their traditions, myths, and customs while yet they remained in memory or practice. It was also understood that I would publish nothing without their knowledge and permission. The rich results of my research among them are largely due to their acquiescence in my plan, and cordial cooperation.

She also wrote in a footnote to her article about the Sioux Elk Society,

> Concerning the private forms of religious observance, the Indians
> are very reserved. It was long before I was trusted with the facts
> mentioned concerning their children and the ritual chant when fast-
> ing. It required much persuasion to be allowed to write down the
> music or obtain permission to tell "the white people." The unvary-
> ing reply was, "The white people do not understand us. They laugh
> at our sacred things, and they will laugh at these things which they
> did not know before." I plead that the laugh came from ignorance
> and a better understanding would secure better treatment. On these
> terms I obtained consent to make public many of the facts set forth
> in this paper; for, although a close observer, I was not a spy among
> my trusting friends.[28]

During the mid-1890s Fletcher published a number of articles for popular audiences in *Century Illustrated Monthly Magazine* that include material taken from her unpublished manuscript.[29] "Personal Studies of Indian
Life: Politics and 'Pipe-Dancing'," (1893) and "Home Life among the Indians: Records of Personal Experience" (1897), in particular, include entire
sections taken from "Life among the Indians." By this time she probably
had come to accept that "Life among the Indians" would not be published
as a book and she therefore incorporated parts of it into these articles.

What else might have influenced Alice Fletcher to write "Life among
the Indians"? She was acquainted with the Smithsonian anthropologist
Frank Hamilton Cushing and must certainly have been familiar with the
three-part series "My Adventures in Zuni" that he published in 1882–83
in *Century Illustrated Monthly Magazine*. Cushing's account was the first
to bring before the general public the new government-sponsored research
on Native American life. He portrays himself as a reporter and interpreter
whom the Zunis incorporated into their social world. "My Adventures in
Zuni" is as much about Cushing's struggles as a researcher to record ethnographic information as it is about the Zuni people themselves. His experiences, such as receiving a Zuni name and incurring the Zunis' anger and
resistance to his writing and sketching, mirror some of Fletcher's experiences among the Omahas and Sioux.[30]

From the beginning of his stay in 1881, Cushing lived in the house of the governor of Zuni, one of the most influential men in the pueblo, who helped him become a Zuni by teaching him to speak the Zuni language while Cushing was convalescing from illness. Speaking the native language provided him a much better entrée into the culture than Fletcher experienced. Though Cushing's goal was scientific study of the Zuni, by publishing in *Century Magazine* for a general audience he publicized his research and sought financial support to further his studies. Fletcher's personal narrative is similar in presentation to Cushing's account.[31] They both focus on themselves as ethnographers and on the difficulties and rewards of the field experience. Both were scientists yet served at the same time as spokesmen for the tribes they studied.[32] Cushing's articles may well have served as a model for Fletcher as she prepared her manuscript for publication.

Some differences between Cushing's and Fletcher's experiences may also be noted. First and foremost, Cushing was employed by the Smithsonian Institution. In 1879 Smithsonian secretary Spencer Baird assigned Cushing, who was twenty-two years old, to accompany Col. James Stevenson's expedition to Zuni, where he remained for four and a half years. Fletcher, on the other hand, was an independent researcher under Putnam's guidance at Harvard's Peabody Museum. She was forty-three years old when she began her field studies in 1881; she had to pay her own way and struggled to maintain herself on an income derived from lecturing and time-consuming government contracts. It was only in October 1890 that Fletcher was awarded a fellowship under the umbrella of Harvard's Peabody Museum that allowed her to undertake ethnology full time.[33]

Second, Cushing learned the Zuni language, which allowed him to understand the culture more thoroughly. Perhaps because Fletcher came under the influence of Joseph La Flesche's family, whose members embraced an ideology of accommodation and acculturation, she never needed to become fluent in the Omaha language. The La Flesche family would not have been inclined to speak to her in Omaha while she was convalescing from her illness; moreover, her close association with Francis La Flesche made it unnecessary for her to learn to speak it fluently. She did, however, appreciate the importance of learning Omaha and in an 1887 letter to Putnam she wrote, "I am making headway with the Omaha language and it will greatly strengthen my work."[34] In her publications she frequently explored in depth the significance of terms in the native language as a method for understanding subtleties of culture. "Notes on Certain Beliefs Concerning Will Power among the Siouan Tribes" (1897) is a good example in which she focused on "certain words, customs, and ceremonies" that provide insight into Omaha concepts of the mind, individual agency, and supernatural power. Fletcher argues that together these concepts reveal "the dominance of the idea of 'Personality.'"[35]

Third, as a private citizen, Fletcher was free to become a spokesperson for the Omahas and to help them in their struggle to retain their lands. Cushing, on the other hand, learned that his role as tribal spokesman was incompatible with his status as a government employee. When he attempted to help the Zunis retain their water rights he brought down the wrath of local politicians who had clout with Congress and eventually had him recalled to Washington.[36]

While Fletcher worked on "Life among the Indians" from May 1886 to July 1887, another massive project competed for her time. A Senate resolution on February 23, 1885, directed the Bureau of Education of the Department of Interior to prepare a "study of progress of Indian education and civilization."[37] Fletcher became the compiler and final author of this work. In transmitting the manuscript to the secretary of the interior on July 16, 1887, Bureau of Education Commissioner N. H. R. Dawson wrote, "I have the honor to forward the accompanying report prepared by Alice C. Fletcher, partly from material collected by this Office and partly from the results of her own wide and varied knowledge of the subject. . . . I beg to invite special attention to the zeal, industry, and judgment shown by Miss Fletcher in the preparation of this material and the treatment of these important topics, qualities which do credit to the author and render this document of great value to the Government and the people of the country."[38]

The Victorian customs of Fletcher's day were not supportive of the development of women professionals. In general there was a great divide between the domestic and public domains, a hierarchy that relegated women to the home in their role as wife and mother. The Victorian ideal emphasized that God had given women nurturant qualities and that biologically women were weaker in mind and in physical strength than men. As a consequence, women were believed to be unsuited for professional work but ideally suited for their domestic role as the mainstay of their children's upbringing. Otis T. Mason's "Woman's Share in Primitive Culture" (1889) offers a contemporary justification of this position based on comparative anthropological study.

Nonetheless, some anthropologists were beginning to recognize the value of women's participation in fieldwork. The English anthropologist Edward B. Tylor, in a talk before the Anthropological Society of Washington in October 1884, observed that the wife of Col. James Stevenson, Matilda "Tilly" Coxe Stevenson, was a definite asset in collecting first-hand observations on women's daily life while her husband collected information on men's roles:

> [I]t was interesting at Zuni to follow the way in which Col. and Mrs. Stevenson were working the pueblo, trading for specimens, and bringing together all that was most valuable and interesting in tracing the history of that remarkable people. Both managed to identify themselves with the Indian life. And one thing I particularly noticed was this, that to get at the confidence of a tribe, the man of the house, though he can do a great deal, cannot do all. If his wife sympathizes with his work, and is able to do it, really half of the work of investigation seems to me to fall to her, so much is to be learned through the women of the tribe, which the men will not readily disclose. The experience seemed to me a lesson to anthropologists not to sound the "bull-roarer", and warn the ladies off from their proceedings, but rather to avail themselves thankfully of their help.[39]

Anthropology was in its infancy and Fletcher was knowingly in the vanguard of participant-observation fieldwork, which became the central practice of academic anthropology. Because she was a single woman her fieldwork itself challenged then-current assumptions concerning what females were capable of doing on their own. Yet she challenged the status quo under cover of the nineteenth-century tradition of feminine service and moral superiority, often acting in the role of a protective mother to her wards.[40]

Fletcher's "Life among the Indians" is a personal account by a woman who overcame both cultural and personal handicaps to become a valued and energetic force in the new field of American anthropology. No attempt is made here to present a full biography of Fletcher. Both her personal and her professional life—especially as they relate to her dedication to the allotment of Indian lands—have been ably explored by Joan Mark in *A Stranger in Her Native Land: Alice Fletcher and the American Indians* (1988).

In this introduction we focus on Fletcher's entry into anthropology and her first fieldwork with the Sioux and Omahas that culminated in her writing, then abandoning, "Life among the Indians." We follow her career through 1887, the year she completed writing "Life among the Indians," provide a discussion of her involvement in Indian reform, and end with a brief overview of her professional career as a whole.

Historians of anthropology are intrigued by the literary forms and constructions of early anthropological writing. Fletcher's first-person narrative was an experimental form of popularization that can be constructively compared to her original field notes, as well as to her professional publications, in terms of subjects, substance, and style.

Fletcher's Early Life

Alice Cunningham Fletcher was born in Cuba on March 15, 1838. Her father, Thomas Gilman Fletcher, a lawyer by training, suffering from ill health, had moved there with his second wife, Lucia Adeline Jenks, shortly before their daughter Alice was born. The family also included his seven-year-old son Francis (Frank) Hopkins Fletcher from his previous marriage. They returned to New York the summer Alice was born. The next year her father died in New Jersey.

Subsequently, Alice's mother settled in Brooklyn Heights. There, in 1846, she enrolled eight-year-old Alice in the Brooklyn Female Academy, which had just opened its doors. The school taught Latin, geography, history, arithmetic, natural history, and natural philosophy and quickly found a following among the more prominent families and those wishing to provide good English and classical education to young women. The school became known as the Packer Collegiate Institute. Alice must have graduated in the early 1850s; the date is uncertain because the building burned in 1858 and most of its records were destroyed. When Alice was about twelve her mother married Oliver C. Gardiner, who was listed on the 1850 census as an "editor," although later business directories identify him as a lawyer, merchant, and broker. During her adolescence, family problems, the details of which have gone unrecorded, prompted her to leave home and take a position as a governess to the children of a wealthy hardware merchant, Claudius Buchanan Conant.[41]

During the 1860s Fletcher worked first as a governess and later as a teacher in the New York City area and in Boston. When she was in her early thirties (plate 1) she became active in women's clubs, particularly Sorosis, which was founded in 1868 and brought together East Coast women intellectuals—poets, journalists, writers, and scientists—who were denied membership in similar men's professional clubs. Fletcher was invited to join in 1870 and in 1873 was listed as the club's secretary.[42] In 1873 the Association for the Advancement of Women (AAW) was founded, modeled after the mainly all-male American Association for the Advancement of Science (AAAS, founded in 1848). Many of the leaders were suffragists, but the association's scope was considerably wider. In 1875 the AAW organized six committees that reflected its breadth of interest: science, statistics, industrial training, reform, art, and education.

Fletcher became one of the first secretaries of the AAW and was the chair of the Committee on Topics and Papers in 1877 and 1879–81. In this capacity she was in charge of planning the annual congresses of the AAW. The members presented papers on a wide variety of topics, including prison reform, income distribution within the family, cooperative housekeeping, the legal status of women in regard to property, and subjects of more literary and cultural interest.[43] The 1881 meeting (the last one Fletcher organized) was particularly significant in that one of the papers read there was authored by Susette La Flesche, an Omaha woman. Titled "Home Life of an Indian Woman," it presented "an inside view, such as is not often obtained, of many of the domestic and social points of Indian life and etiquette. A letter on the same subject had been received from Miss Alice Fletcher, who is at present among the Indians, visiting a friendly tribe."[44] The AAW report noted that both communications described features of Indian women's lives that were not altogether different from those of Euro-

Plate 1. Alice Fletcher at age thirty. At this period she was active in such wom-
en's organizations as Sorosis and the Association for the Advancement of
Women. Ferrotype by Marcus Ormsbee, New York City, 1868, size of original 2.3
x 3.5 in. The gallery label affixed to the back of the image indicates that eighteen
vignette ferrotypes could be purchased for seventy-five cents. Smithsonian
Institution, National Anthropological Archives (83-11264).

American women. Neither Fletcher nor Susette La Flesche was present at the 1881 meeting, which was held in Buffalo, New York; they were together in Nebraska, where Fletcher was beginning her fieldwork.

During the latter part of the 1870s and throughout the 1880s, out of financial necessity, Fletcher became a public lecturer.[45] She gave presentations mainly to women's clubs in the East and Midwest: New Jersey, Rhode Island, Massachusetts, Ohio, Wisconsin, and Minnesota. The topics included personal experiences, such as her impressions of books she had read and events of her childhood, as well as presentations on history, religion, geography, botany, philology, ethnology, and archaeology. She did extensive research to prepare her lectures, for which she charged an entrance fee of one dollar.[46] Among her anthropological topics were "The Moundbuilders," "Arts of the Moundbuilders," "Antiquities of the Coast," "The People of the Pueblos," "Earliest Traces of Humankind," and "Value of Anthropological Study."[47] Maps, watercolor paintings, drawings, and specimens illustrated many of her presentations. She realized that by lecturing on American archaeology she would reach a wide audience of natural historians who might have found or collected Indian artifacts. Her concern regarding such artifacts led her to contact the secretary of the Smithsonian Institution, Spencer F. Baird, in October 1879, asking for some printed circulars to give to prospective donors who might have "Indian relics" that would be of interest to the Smithsonian. He replied in the affirmative.[48] Returning home from her first field experience in December 1882 she gave a talk in Boston titled "Life among the Omahas."[49] Fletcher's lecture experience greatly aided in her future public outreach and her work with Indian rights associations.

Fletcher was remarkably reticent about her past and her personal life. In 1890, when a Miss E. F. Lander asked permission to write an illustrated article about her, Fletcher wrote to Putnam, "Now I don't want to offend her or do anything to cool her ardor toward the Museum but I do hate publicity and I dislike exceedingly to be written up. What shall I say and do in this matter?"[50] Her desire for privacy led her ultimately to destroy much of her personal correspondence. Very little of a personal nature is preserved in her papers in the National Anthropological Archives. Insights, such as they are, are to be found in her friends' diaries and letters.

Becoming an Anthropologist

When Fletcher turned from her career as a lecturer to prepare herself as an anthropologist she had few role models. In the United States, anthropology as a distinct field of study had only begun to develop during the mid-nineteenth century, focused largely on American Indians. Fieldwork with the specific purpose of describing American Indian life began with Lewis Henry Morgan, who studied the Iroquois of western New York in the 1840s and traveled up the Missouri River to record kinship systems of the Plains tribes from 1859 to 1862. Morgan's *Ancient Society* (1877), a textbook on social evolution, articulated the theory that peoples advanced from more primitive states of "savagery" and "barbarism" to "civilization." In particular, Morgan saw the development of private property as critical to progressive advancement along the social evolutionary scale. Social evolution became the dominant theory in anthropology until about 1920, when it was replaced by the culture-historical approach championed by Franz Boas.

John Wesley Powell, director of the Geological and Geographical Survey of the Territories, began in 1878 to plan for a government bureau devoted to anthropology. He embraced Morgan's evolutionary theory enthusiastically and developed it into the explanatory principle for describing American Indians. That year he hired James Owen Dorsey to begin field study with the Omaha Indians and Albert Gatschet to do so with Indians in Oregon. In 1879 Congress approved the establishment of the Bureau of Ethnology within the Smithsonian Institution, which rapidly expanded to become the most visible center for anthropological research in the United States.[51] Like Powell, Fletcher's perspective on American Indian tribes was shaped by social evolutionary theory. Her later vision of improving Indian life through the allotment of tribal lands to individuals, leading eventually to private ownership of land—complemented by the critical importance of Euro-American education for Indian children—was the outcome of this influence.[52]

Fletcher's introduction to anthropology came not from the Smithsonian but from the Peabody Museum of American Archaeology and Ethnology, founded at Harvard University in Cambridge, Massachusetts, in 1866.

In 1878 a new building was constructed that became the first museum in the United States devoted entirely to anthropology. Fletcher's initial correspondence with Frederic Ward Putnam, the museum's director (plate 2), is dated September 9, 1879, asking to purchase copies of the museum's reports and inquiring whether there were other institutions devoted to American archaeology and ethnology.[53] Putnam suggested that she come to the museum in order to gain firsthand experience with artifacts. Historian Ralph Dexter writes, "Already, Putnam had established an important research collection. . . . When the new building was opened the Museum contained some 30,000 specimens. A printed announcement, *Archaeological Research in America*, proclaimed that 'students may come for special investigations, with the assurance that, so far as American archaeology is concerned, they have access to the most important collections that have been brought together.'"[54] Fletcher's association with Putnam and his staff, and especially with Lucien Carr, Putnam's assistant curator, brought her into contact not only with ethnological and archaeological artifacts but also with the methods and concerns of museum anthropology.

Putnam encouraged Fletcher's interest in anthropology. He invited her to join the Archaeological Institute of America, founded in 1879, and to study in the museum. At this time there were no degree programs in anthropology. Instruction was by correspondence and tutoring. Putnam did not initiate graduate coursework in anthropology at Harvard until 1890, when George A. Dorsey and John G. Owens enrolled for graduate study with him, despite the lack of a formal anthropology curriculum. During the first few years Putnam offered only research courses, with emphasis on archaeology and the museum's artifact collections, and it was only in 1894–95 that the first general anthropology courses were offered at Harvard.[55] No female students were accepted at Harvard, even in the late 1890s. The Women's Anthropological Society of America, founded in Washington in 1885, was the sole professional organization to which women aspiring to participate in the new field could belong.[56] Fletcher was involved in the formation of the society and became its president in 1890.[57] That she never formally enrolled as a student of anthropology at Harvard was the result of the barrier against women. She sought instead an apprenticeship to achieve comparable experience. Putnam

Plate 2. Frederic Ward Putnam (1839–1915), director of the Peabody Museum of American Archaeology and Ethnology at Harvard University, Cambridge, Massachusetts. Putnam was a teacher and mentor to Fletcher. The photographer and date are not recorded. Reproduced as the frontispiece in *Putnam Anniversary Volume: Anthropological Essays Presented to Frederic Ward Putnam in Honor of His Seventieth Birthday, April 16, 1909*, ed. Franz Boas et al. (New York: G. E. Strechert, 1909).

became Fletcher's mentor, and for many years, at least through 1903, she continued to seek his approval for her academic projects.

First Fieldwork with the Sioux and Omahas

The impetus that apparently propelled Fletcher to undertake fieldwork with the Omahas and Sioux occurred in 1879 when she met Thomas Henry Tibbles, then assistant editor of the *Omaha Herald*; Susette La Flesche, an Omaha Indian; and Susette's half brother, Francis La Flesche (plate 3). They were in the East on a speaking tour with Susette's uncle, Standing Bear, a Ponca chief, to aid the cause of the Poncas, who had been forcibly removed from their reservation in Nebraska to Indian Territory in 1877, but who fled back north in January 1879.[58] Francis, only nineteen or twenty at the time, came as a chaperon for Susette. There was extensive publicity for the tour and Boston was one of their stops. The event caught Fletcher's attention. Tibbles later recalled,

> While we were in Boston in 1879, a lady [he does not mention Fletcher by name] told me that after studying ethnology for years in books and museums she now wished to visit Indian tribes in their own lodges, living as they lived and observing their daily customs herself—especially the women's and children's ways. . . . I found it hard to take her plan seriously. She, a thorough product of city life, was evidently nearing her forties. I could not imagine her leaving all her home comforts to go out to the far frontier and live among the Indians in an Indian lodge. Still, she was so earnest that I reluctantly agreed to take her someday with our group for the trip she wished. Circumstances kept her from coming to us in 1880, but on September 1, 1881, she arrived in Omaha with letters of high praise from the Secretary of War, the Secretary of the Interior, the Postmaster General, and many scientific men.[59]

Fletcher was, in fact, forty-three years old when she made her first trip west. She chose as her initial research topic the role of Indian women, one to which she must have felt her gender would give her entrée. Moreover, her previous involvement with women's clubs made it logical that she would be interested in Indian women's social groups. As her correspon-

Plate 3. Francis La Flesche and his sister, Susette La Flesche, also known as Bright Eyes, of Omaha, Ponca, and French ancestry. This photograph was taken about 1879, probably during the La Flesches' tour with their uncle, the Ponca chief Standing Bear. Smithsonian Institution, National Anthropological Archives, Bureau of American Ethnography collection (NAA INV 0689800 enhanced).

dence reveals, she was unsure of herself, naive, and almost subservient in her outreach to the established academic community. These letters reflect a preprofessional moment in anthropology and the lack of any defined place for women in the new discipline.

On February 24, 1881, Fletcher wrote to Putnam to arrange a meeting with Susette La Flesche: "I hope it will be convenient to you to see Miss La Flesche (Bright Eyes) on Friday between 11 and 12 A.M. It is the first moment I could get her and the only day when both of us could wait and go to Cambridge. I have asked Mr. Tibbles to be of the party. He is very familiar with Indian life and has the confidence of Indians and is much among them. It is therefore not impossible that he may serve you in some way."[60] In the same letter she told Putnam that she had "a proposition made to me that I desire to lay before you and ask your counsel." This was her first solicitation for Putnam's guidance and advice and may have been her initial outreach to him regarding the possibility of her doing fieldwork in the West.

On August 3, 1881, writing from the Manhattan Beach Hotel, Coney Island, New York, Fletcher addressed a letter to Lucien Carr, Putnam's assistant at the Peabody Museum. She had worked with him informally and he had shared with her the archaeological perspectives of the day.

Please fancy you are at your table in the Museum and I in the seat which you so kindly assigned me, for I want much to ask some questions, and if you will drop into the part, I shall not feel it needful to apologize for troubling you with a letter.

After my long confinement incident to my fall, holding me prisoner for more than four months, I am at last on the road to health.[61] The sea air and baths have won back some of my power to work. Within a day or two the way has opened for me to go west and study the life of Indian women. I am going out to journey for a few months with Bright Eyes and her husband Mr. Tibbles, and after I leave them push on further and in different directions if possible. I do not care to say much about this for two reasons. First, Mr. Tibbles is in ill odor with the Gov't. and that might prejudice my obtaining an open letter from the Sec'y of War & Sec'y of Interior, which I desire if possible to procure. Second, I am not versed in original research, and therefore shall have to learn and experiment at the same time.

I want to ask your help in two ways, if you will permit me. I would be grateful for any suggestions as to how I could procure the letters from the Depts., and also for any letters of introduction you might be willing to give me to persons interested in Anthropology, living west. And my second request is, that you will be so kind as to give me some directions as to the points I should aim to discover in Indian life. You know what will be valuable & what is already known, far better than I, and what it is possible for me, as a woman, to ascertain, which will add to the sum of knowledge.

If you will chart out my work I shall be very, very thankful. Had I not been stricken down I should have seen you and talked with you, but until the past fortnight I had almost despaired of my future usefulness.

I know that what I aim toward is difficult, fraught with hardship to mind and body, but there is something to be learned in the line of woman's life in the social state represented by the Indians that if truthfully set forth will be of value not only ethnographically but help toward the historical solution of "the Woman Question" in our midst. Is it not so?

I regret I have not a year for careful preparation, but I must go now, and so if you will tell me what to study at once—en route to the Sioux—you will help me. Even if you tell me that I "aim my arrows at the sun" I must earnestly reply I must still aim.[62]

Fletcher corresponded with many individuals who might have been able to give her information and the introductions she needed to undertake ethnological fieldwork. On August 10, 1881, she wrote from New York to John Wesley Powell in Washington, head of the U.S. Geological Survey and of the Bureau of [American] Ethnology:

I am about starting for the far west to devote myself to the investigation of the life of Indian women. Shall begin among the tribes on the upper Missouri—how far I shall go will depend on opportunity,

&c. Will you kindly send me copy of the instructions issued by the Smithsonian Inst. for the study of Indian peoples, and any other directions that you are inclined to add will be gratefully rec'd.

You will hardly recollect me altho. we met in Boston last year when I told you that I hoped to undertake this work and you generously offered to aid me. I wish to get at Indian women's lives from the inside, and as the segregation of the sexes is marked among barbarous people, I trust that being a woman I may be able to observe & record facts & conditions that are unknown or obscure owing to the separation of the male & female life.

Mr. Lucian [sic] Carr has given me a letter to the Hon. Sec'y. of War. I desire if possible to obtain an open letter from the Dept. of War & Dept. of Interior that I may have proper credentials to present should I need at any time shelter or assistance. I enclose my circular to show you the kind of work I have done & the line of study which I have followed for some years.

I shall be at the Scientific Ass. on Monday & Tuesday Aug. 22 & 23d & hope I shall have the pleasure of meeting you personally.

Any points you would specify as particularly desirable to search out or seek for I shall be indebted to you for mentioning them.[63]

The letter to Powell was not an easy one for her to write. To Putnam, also on August 10, 1881, she confided, "I am en route for the Indians. I want very much to have a half hour with you to receive some instructions as to my work in observing the life of Indian women. . . . I wish I did not feel so shy of Maj. Powell. I can't trust him. I want letters to Agents etc. I want an open letter from the War Dept. and Interior Dept. so that I can present credentials in case of need. The one thing I desire of you, my Teacher, is direction."[64] Then, on August 23, 1881, she wrote to Garrick Mallery of the Bureau of Ethnology, "If it is not too much to ask will you favor me with any suggestions or directions for my work among Indian women."[65] There is no record of his reply.

Fletcher's fieldwork began September 16, 1881. This trip was crucial to her professional development and resulted in an important study of the Sioux and ultimately in a comprehensive study of the Omahas. She traveled with Tibbles and Susette La Flesche, who had recently married. The party also included Wajepa, an Omaha (plate 4).[66] After October 2 they were joined by Buffalo Chip, an Omaha who also spoke the Sioux language, and his wife Gaha;[67] after October 10, a Sioux named Thigh, together with his wife, joined the travelers.

Early in the trip they spent several days with Susette's family on the Omaha Reservation. There Fletcher was taken under the wing of the La Flesche family and developed an immediate friendship with Rosalie La Flesche,[68] who was seven years younger than Susette. The patriarch, Joseph La Flesche, the son of a French Canadian trader, had been educated in St. Louis. By all accounts he was an intelligent, generous, and thoughtful individual, and he shared with Fletcher his deep concern over the precariousness of the Omahas' ownership of their lands. He had long advocated the adoption by the Omahas of Euro-American education and economic lifestyles. He spoke Canadian French, not English, and required his children to attend school. The results were the significant academic achievements of his family.[69] Although Joseph La Flesche represented only one faction of the tribe, those who strove for accommodation with the white people, Fletcher took up his cause and forged a strong bond with him.

During this trip Fletcher also got to know Francis La Flesche, Joseph's eldest surviving son. He was to become central to her for the remainder of her life, both intellectually and emotionally. He later recalled that first visit on September 18, 1881: "Miss Fletcher met many of the members of this tribe and made friends with a number of the prominent men and women. She was quick to observe their peculiar dress and manners, their mode of living and their jovial spirit, and she even began to write their language."[70]

Fletcher's first fieldwork experiences are detailed in her notebooks and in Francis La Flesche's unfinished foreword to "Life among the Indians," included in this volume. Unfortunately, his draft covers only the period from September 16 to October 2. Starting from the Omaha Reservation, Fletcher and company traveled through the Winnebago Reservation to the Santee Sioux Reservation, where they visited the Congregational Mission. Leaving the Santees, Fletcher's party passed through the former Ponca Reservation, where a warm welcome awaited them, probably because Tib-

Plate 4. Wajepa, an Omaha also known as Ezra Freemont, who traveled with Fletcher, Susette La Flesche, and La Flesche's husband, Thomas Henry Tibbles, on Fletcher's first field experience. Photographed in Washington DC, probably about 1881. Smithsonian Institution, National Anthropological Archives, Bureau of American Ethnography collection (gn-03935-a).

bles was among the party. After a brief stop at Fort Niobrara, they arrived October 11 on the Great Sioux Reservation at the camp of Spotted Tail (son of the famous chief of the same name who recently had been murdered).[71]

In "Life among the Indians" Fletcher relates that she had been invited to visit at Rosebud by a student friend she had met in the East. It is likely that the student was Daniel Milk, who attended the Carlisle Indian Industrial School in Pennsylvania from 1879 to 1882. This would explain why, in Spotted Tail's camp, Fletcher stayed in the lodge of Asanpi (Milk), a Brule chief, and was feasted by members of his band.[72] Chapter 3, "The Welcome," relates the story of that memorable night when she was invited to partake of four meals, one after the other.[73] On October 12 she went to the Rosebud Agency, where she met with the Indian agent, John Cook. At Spotted Tail's camp she met White Thunder and Swift Bear and witnessed her first Indian dance, a funeral, and the issue of government rations, including the beef distribution. The party left Rosebud Agency on October 19, heading for Fort Randall. Fletcher became ill with what she describes as "a nervous chill, my cough hard and lungs painful."[74]

Fletcher's notebooks are filled with personal observations about her companions. The physical display of affection between the Tibbleses, newlyweds to be sure, made her uncomfortable and irritable. On October 23 she confided in her notebook, "On my right Wajapa lies wrapped up in his comforter, head and all—his dirty legs showing above his moccasins. Further on Ga-ha is putting two ragged pairs of stockings on one over the other—sometimes the holes match! Hands still show signs of baking. To my right, S[usette] with her cooking apron on—brushing dander out of Mr. T[ibble's] head which lies on her lap. The unheeded visitor [referring to herself] by the tent door. The pot hanging by a rope over the fire with the soup boiling & the storm pelting out[side]!!!"[75]

Wajepa piqued her curiosity; she found his behavior interesting but fraught with exotic frailties. She greatly admired the women—Buffalo Chip's wife, Gaha, and Thigh's wife (whom she does not name)—for their ability to cope so efficiently in the wilderness. That the rigors of camping did not cause her to retreat from her goal testifies to her tenacity, her need to make a place for herself, and her ultimate commitment to help people whom she found needed her. This field experience gave Fletcher a renewed purpose and established the connections with the La Flesche family that sustained her for the remainder of her life.

On October 25 they reached Fort Randall, where she had several meetings with Sitting Bull, the Hunkpapa Sioux chief who, with his band of 168 people, was being held at the fort as a prisoner of war. He appealed to Fletcher to write a letter to the secretary of war relating the condition of his band. She did so.

She noted on October 26, "In the P.M. had a little trouble with Mr. T. which was afterward settled—a misstatement." While we do not know what this disagreement was about, the Tibbleses and Fletcher parted company on October 29.[76] The next day Fletcher joined the newly arrived inspector general, Maj. William Wilkins Sanders, who was making rounds of some Indian agencies. She went with him to the Yankton Agency and then back to Fort Randall, where she had "a pleasant talk with Insp. Gen. about Sitting Bull and ethnography."[77]

Returning to the Santee Reservation, Fletcher enjoyed the hospitality of the Congregational Mission. There she received mail and had the opportunity to write and send correspondence. In a letter to Putnam dated November 7, 1881, she reported on her field experiences:

My dear Prof. Putnam,
        Thanks for the paper—and your many past kindnesses—being in the wilderness makes friends more valuable.
        While at Fort Randall I was the guest of Mrs. Col. Andrews and she bade me tell you I had "stayed with Emily Oliver."[78] A lovely lady—a lovely home—a complete oasis in the midst of desolation & barbarous meagerness. I wish I had time to tell you of her flowers, her gracious hospitality—and the real New England aroma of her home—but it would take long. [Fig. 1]
        My experiences have been many and varied. I have taken such "a header into barbarism" as a friend of mine puts it, as I would not advise any lady to attempt. For over two months I have been nearly all the time living with Indians, as far as possible. Like one of them. I think I can pass a sort of Indian muster! The hardships and horrors of it are not to be told—but from a scientific point of

view, the experience has been valuable. I have worked myself round to where the Indian stands—and looked at his life and ways as he does—this in a good measure. People who have lived among the Indians all their life, like Rev. John Williamson[79] & the elder & young Mr. Riggs[80] tell me I have got at it.Now comes the test, using the knowledge I have gained. I have I think got at some points—to work at these & be sure of them. I shall be here, for how long a time I cannot tell, here among the Santees & also among the Yanktons some 40 or 50 miles away. I have been out to Spotted Tail's. I was the guest of Asanpi—and also of 3 other chiefs— White Thunder, Standing Elk, and Young Spotted Tail. The latter gave me a dance. I saw the Indian in full undress, paint & feathers; have been with Standing Elk at the death of one of his principal men, witnessed the killing of the horse, the dog, the denuding of the family; have met the naked runner of destiny and bowed my head as he put his cold hand on me; have been danced to by the women & "feasted"(!) to my torment. I know just how they live and act. Have been at councils & spoken! And lastly won the friendship of Sitting Bull—but of that I shall write Mr. Goddard.[81]

I am going for a month to the Omahas. Have traveled 800 miles in open wagon, suffered from fire, frost, and flood, been carried across rapid rivers on the back of an Indian & forded & been pulled by Indians! Have been entirely alone with wild painted men & women & here I am un-hurt, un-harmed—but with many a friend back among the red folk. The women gather about me put their babies' hands in mine & say "Our friend." My name is Ma-sha-há-the meaning the high soaring of the eagle that sees the new day, as it were. The name was given me with much expression of practical sentiment, for I was the first lady to come alone among them to be their friend & know them in their home. Some wanted to call me Tce-sa-mi, the eldest born, but Ma-sha-há-the, prevailed. . . .

I am at work on the women.[82]

A few days later, on November 14, she wrote to Jane Smith, Putnam's secretary:

Fig. 1. "From Mrs. Andrews' side window parlor, Ft. Randall, Oct. 28, 1881."
"Reached Fort Randall about 2 P.M. Called on the Commander of the Post, Col.
George L. Andrews. After a little conversation, Mrs. A. appeared. A New England lady. She graciously received me, and I became their guest. The rest were
camped on Stony Point, a pretty spot near to water and the pasturage fair for the
horses" (Fletcher, 1881 Notebook 2, 142). Original field sketch (p. 150) enhanced.
Smithsonian Institution, National Anthropological Archives (ms. 4558).

I have ventured in taking a fresh lease of an old favor and given
the Museum as my permanent address. My own movements are
likely to be such that no letters could be sure of catching me
except at intervals. The Museum address I have only given to persons interested in American study and who would not be likely to
write me except at long periods of time. If you will be so kind as to
forward such letters to me to the points I will notify you of I shall
be greatly obliged. Until Jan. anything sent to care of Rev. A. L.
Riggs, Santee Agency, Nebraska will find me.[83]

On November 16 Fletcher wrote again to Major Powell, hoping for some
guidance from the Bureau of Ethnology:

It was quite a disappointment not to receive the promised letter indicating points you would think it well for me to particularly observe in Indian home life. The sad events which have over shadowed the nation necessarily eclipsed all minor matters. While the sadness remains the work of life goes on, and I trust that the duties of your department will permit you to send me a few words of counsel.

For nearly three months I have been living, nearly all the time, with Indians, in their tepees, or log-houses. I have been introduced into Indian homes by Indians and have conformed as far as possible to Indian life. The inside view has been open to me and I have tried to see it from the Indian standpoint, to get at the Indian way of thinking. Much valuable information I have already secured, but my work is still of course in its beginning. I have been looking up the various Societies among the Indian women. Can you tell me where I can get the observations of others on this point? If there is anything published will you send it to me. I can return it.[84]

Powell, however, was ill at the time and did not respond to this letter either. At the end of November Fletcher received a short note from James Pilling, chief clerk of the Bureau of Ethnology, saying that he knew of no previous research on Indian women's societies. Fletcher was at the forefront of a new research method in anthropology—fieldwork.

Fletcher returned to the Omaha Reservation in November and remained there for four months. All in all, her first field experience was both exhilarating and exhausting, but with a singular mind she found time to complete a paper on Indian women for the annual AAW Congress.[85] Her field notebooks record ethnographic observations that she later reported in her publications. But her academic focus was soon interrupted by Joseph La Flesche and other Omahas, who beseeched her to help them obtain legal protection for their land. As she wrote in chapter 19 of "Life among the Indians," "What right had I to be enjoying working out the sociology of the people, getting at their inner life and thought, when their sore troubles, from the greed of my own race were so plainly discernible. . . . But what could I, a woman, do against this trend of wrong? To get rid of these wearying thoughts, I strove the harder at my ethnological work."

The Omaha Reservation had been created by treaty in 1854 and under its terms, continued by a subsequent treaty in 1865, after the eastern portion was finally surveyed in 1872, some 350 allotments had been assigned to heads of families and single adult males. The Omahas built houses and some began to farm in the belief that they were the rightful owners of their allotments. In 1879, however, when their close relatives the Poncas were removed from Nebraska to Indian Territory, the Omahas became worried about the security of their own lands. They discovered that Congress had never ratified the allotments and therefore they had no legal ownership of them.[86]

During December Fletcher worked on a petition to the commissioner of Indian affairs on behalf of Joseph La Flesche and other Omahas who believed that the only way to secure their lands was through individual ownership. The men who signed the petition acknowledged that they did not speak for the whole tribe.[87] The petition asked Congress to approve allotments only for those who wanted them, which Fletcher estimated as about one-third of the tribe. Fletcher wrote in an accompanying letter dated December 31, 1881, addressed to Senator John T. Morgan of Alabama, an enthusiastic supporter of allotment and American Indian assimilation,[88]

> Today I mail a package . . . the petition of 53 Omaha Indians asking that titles be given them to the lands on which they have worked and practically homesteaded. . . .
>
> How it comes about that a woman should lend her hand to this cause is told in a few words. Scientific study connected with the home life of the Indians brought me here. To accomplish my work I had to live among the people, become their friend. The living cry of those with whom I found myself so claimed my ear and heart that I felt I must do something to help.[89]

Fletcher's interest in the reform of Indian policy and her active involvement in it were the direct result of her fieldwork experience. She had intended to continue her research during the winter in Indian Territory and travel up the Pacific coast before returning to the plains, but instead she remained with the Omahas during the winter of 1881–82, waiting for responses from government officials. She began to teach reading, writing, and geography at the Omaha Mission (plates 5 and 6), and after numerous adults began to attend the lessons the school added adult night classes to its curriculum.[90]

In a letter to Putnam dated February 4, 1882, Fletcher described the new perspective she had developed during this first field trip to the Sioux and Omahas:

> The Indian character, particularly among those I have lived [with], is wonderfully misunderstood. So too are many of the peculiarities of Indian life. It is strange for me now to read the books that have been written about the people. The white man sees only himself. He has attributed his faults and some of his virtues to the Indian. I have taken much pains to get at the Indian ideas of property, of the use and occupation of land. Owning it, they never dreamed of, save as they have now been taught by removals. They would as soon thought of owning air & rain. And also the Indian idea that comes nearest to our notion of law. The family relation is very hard for a white person to understand without imposing his own hereditary & trained thought upon it. I've worked hard on that & have sometimes succeeded in twisting round to the Indian view. Polygamy as represented to us as practiced in the East, is not found by me. I have stayed in families where there are several wives. I know well many such families, women as well as men. I have watched them closely, talked with them about many things that would throw side lights on the subject. To talk with them directly upon the subject would be most foolish. They are an unawakened, or undeveloped people & have never thought upon topics pertaining to sociology. Their lack of thought upon these matters is in itself a factor in the solution of their condition. Licentiousness has little or nothing to do with plurality of wives. Licentiousness involves a species of consciousness & that the Indian have not even got. This fact bears directly upon the life of the woman, but the topic is too large for this page.[91]

Plate 5. Alice Fletcher (seated in the middle of the bottom row) with Indian and Anglo women at the Presbyterian Mission on the Omaha Reservation, Walthill, Nebraska. The photograph was taken between 1883 and 1884 by an unknown photographer. Smithsonian Institution, National Anthropological Archives, Bureau of American Ethnology collection (gn-04473).

In April 1882, when the Omaha petition was introduced in the Senate, Fletcher returned to the East to lobby in Washington, although her home base was still in New York City.[92] In her attempt to secure the Omahas' title to their lands she courted politicians and made friends with their wives, including Mrs. Henry Dawes. She appealed to the secretary of the interior, the commissioner of Indian affairs, and other influential Washington bureaucrats. She enlisted the support of the Women's National Indian Association and of Capt. Richard Henry Pratt, who in 1879 had founded Carlisle Indian Industrial School in Pennsylvania. She met with John Wesley Powell, now able to approach him as a fellow anthropologist. In the end, Fletcher succeeded in her cause by drafting an addendum to a bill providing for the sale of a portion of the Omaha Reservation that was already making its way through Congress. While Fletcher's draft called for allotment only to those Omahas who had shown initiative in working their land, Congress made allotment compulsory and universal. All Oma-

Plate 6. Omaha Mission school, Walthill, Nebraska. The woman standing on the far right in the shade is identified as Mary E-la-hon-h. This photograph, possibly by Fletcher, was taken about 1882–84. Smithsonian Institution, National Anthropological Archives, Bureau of American Ethnography collection (gn-04472).

has, whether they wanted it or not, would be assigned allotments and most of the remaining lands opened to non-Indians.[93]

Among the many people Fletcher sought out during this time in Washington, none was more important to her future than Joseph La Flesche's son, Francis, who had been appointed to a position as clerk in the Office of Indian Affairs in 1881. They had in common both a commitment to helping the Omaha people and a deep interest in American Indian ethnology. On May 10, 1882, shortly before Fletcher left Washington to continue her field studies, Frank Hamilton Cushing brought a man from Zuni Pueblo to meet them.[94] Fletcher recorded the occasion in detail. With Cushing translating, the Zuni and La Flesche found much in common between their tribes' hunting techniques. The record of this meeting suggests that Fletcher and La Flesche had already begun the collaborative work that would continue through four decades, until Fletcher's death.

Fletcher returned to the field in June 1882, having been commissioned by Pratt to escort forty-one Sioux and Omaha children who were on their way home from Carlisle. She kept an informal journal of this trip and later wrote about her experiences, parts of which she included in letters to Pratt that were published in the *Morning Star*, the official Carlisle Indian School paper, in October 1882.[95] She returned the Sioux children to their agencies and arranged to witness the Sun Dance at Pine Ridge Agency in early July, which Indian Agent Valentine T. McGillycuddy heralded as the last great Sun Dance.[96] At Pine Ridge she also witnessed the performance of an Elk dreamer and the ceremony of the Ghost Lodge. In July she witnessed the Hunkpapa White Buffalo ceremony performed by Sitting Bull's band at Fort Randall and the Santee Four Winds ceremony at Santee, Nebraska. In August 1882 she visited the Omahas and celebrated with them the passage of legislation on the seventh of the month that provided for the allotment of reservation lands. She also arranged for a number of young Omahas to attend school at Hampton Institute[97] and Carlisle and returned east with them in fall 1882.[98] She summed up her philosophy in an article published in May 1883 titled "On Indian Education and Self-Support": "[T]here is no safety for any people except in education, law and freedom."[99] Toward this goal she resumed her lecturing to help raise money to send additional Indian students to school and she continued to draw attention to the cause of Indian education.

Allotting the Omahas

After her return to the Peabody Museum in the fall of 1882 Fletcher was officially listed as a special assistant in ethnology.[100] On November 24 she wrote exuberantly to Mrs. Dawes, on Peabody Museum stationery:

> The train was 2 hours late into Boston. . . . Professor [Putnam] and Mr. Carr say words of commendation. Today the great blessing has come. Money to take me to my work and I hope to start next week. This is as you know what I have most desired and the Lord has granted it to me. I shall now be connected with the Museum & hope I can do good work and bring honor to those who look to me. It is a happy and a solemn day—for original work demands a power of self control, pluck, and dedication that well nigh makes one timid. Still on one must go.[101]

In her new position she wrote a paper on the Pine Ridge Sun Dance that she read at the 1883 AAAS meeting in Minneapolis and published in their *Proceedings*. She also wrote detailed accounts of the Sioux and Omaha ceremonies that she witnessed, which Putnam published in the museum's 1884 annual report.

In 1883, however, practical concerns again interrupted Fletcher's anthropological studies. That April Commissioner of Indian Affairs Hiram Price appointed Fletcher as allotment agent for the Omahas. Every head of family would receive 160 acres, every unmarried adult 80 acres, and every child 40 acres, to remain tax-free and held in trust for twenty-five years.[102] Francis La Flesche was to serve as the official interpreter. For Fletcher the assignment offered the potential to combine her concern for the Omahas' welfare with ethnology. "Good will come of it to the people," she wrote to Putnam, and, "[i]f you approve, next year, if I live, you can have a complete exposition of one tribe's life & customs." In a postscript she added, "[O]ff to the wild life—& unknown future , where the unknown past may find a voice." Another postscript reads, "Frank is detailed to go with me & we may be together for 6 mos. on the Reserve."[103]

On May 12, 1883, Fletcher and La Flesche arrived at the Omaha Agency.[104] The work of surveying and assigning land and preparing the legal allotment papers continued through June, but in July Fletcher became severely ill. She first identified her malady in September 1883 as inflammatory rheumatism but by July 20, 1884, she described her medical condition as "inflammation of the covering of the thigh bone, the inflammation had extended to & involved the large muscles and injudicious treatment had resulted in adhesion. There is no anchylosis of the joint & the muscular adhesions are not so that they cannot be broken up, & that probably without a surgical operation. . . . The surgeon says I will walk & that without cane or help & have a serviceable if not a perfectly limber leg."[105] She recovered slowly in the home of George W. Wilkinson, the Indian agent for the Omahas and Winnebagos. Omaha women visited her frequently and she continued her work, with Francis's help.[106] During her recovery, on January 20, 1884, she wrote to Caroline Dall,

Now for the changes in me. I've grown old, have lost my hair which was hard to see go. . . . I look 20 years older but that can't be helped.

The most serious part of the change is that I shall be a cripple. The disease necessitated such absolute quiet that I have a stiff leg, within a few days, there is a ray of hope in favor of motion so that I may yet walk, though I may be lame. It has been hard to face the fact of being a cripple for it would seem to close my ethnological career, but it is all in God's hands and I submit. . . . The marvel of my sickness has been the kindness of the people to me. Dr. and Mrs. Wilkinson are just as kind to me today as when I was carried into their parlor 5 months ago. And my nurse, a white woman married to an Indian, has taken care of me 5 months often sleeping little.[107]

Fletcher and La Flesche completed the allotment work for the Omahas by June 1884. They had assigned land both to those who willingly accepted allotments and to those who opposed them. Fletcher made a complete census of the tribe and came to know many of the Omahas personally. Before they left, the Omahas acknowledged the importance of her work on their behalf by honoring her with a calumet ceremony, using the Omaha sacred pipes. La Flesche wrote about this event in his obituary of Fletcher:

When she was about to begin her work [as allotment agent] the older members of the tribe came together for consultation as to how they could best express their gratitude for what she had done for the tribe. They decided to perform for her the ancient calumet ceremony, although it was not customary to give it informally. A notice was given to the people to come, and on the day appointed many came and assembled in an earth lodge. The calumets were set up in their sacred place, and when Miss Fletcher entered as the honored guest the house became silent. Three men arose and took up the symbolic pipes (the calumets) and the lynx skin on which they rested; then, standing side by side, they sang softly the opening song. At the close the three men turned, and facing the people, who sat in a wide circle, sang a joyful song as they moved around the circle, waving the sacred pipes over their heads. Song after song they sang for their friend, of the joy and happiness that would follow when men learned to live together in peace. When the evening was over they told Miss Fletcher that she was free to study this or any other of their tribal rites.[108]

Joseph La Flesche made a set of the ritual objects used in the calumet ceremony to be given jointly to his son Francis and Fletcher. They were presented to them in May 1884, the two pipes with their pendant fans of golden eagle feathers, two gourd rattles, a wildcat skin, and a tobacco pouch made of a bladder. Later Fletcher displayed them prominently on the wall over the piano in her home (plates 7, 8, and 9).[109]

Fletcher's Developing Career and the Writing of "Life among the Indians"

Fletcher left the Omaha Reservation in mid-June 1884 and returned to Washington DC, where she moved into the Temple Hotel, a residence hotel comprising two row houses across from the Patent Office. When La Flesche returned to Washington in September he took rooms in the same hotel, but in the adjacent building.[110] Although Fletcher's knee continued to be painful, leading her to consult numerous doctors in both New York City and Washington, she nonetheless managed to persevere in her ethnological work. On July 28, 1884, Fletcher wrote to Putnam about the upcoming AAAS meeting: "To Phila. I must go & shall if it is to go in as crippled a condition as I am now & I want to give a paper."[111]

In September she and La Flesche both presented papers to the anthropology section of the AAAS on the Omaha calumet ceremony, bringing the sacred pipes to Philadelphia and demonstrating their use.[112] Fletcher also presented a paper titled "Lands in Severalty to Indians; Illustrated by Experiences with the Omaha Tribe," in which she uses a first-person narrative to offer a scientific perspective on her work as allotment agent. Following the dominant social evolutionism of the day, she argues, "Prosperity and social growth depend largely upon the stability and security of the family." With the demise of the old tribal social order after settlement on reservations, a new order must prevail. "It is clear beyond cavil that the Indian must die or become absorbed in the body of citizens." This was impossible in the isolation of reservations. "What the Indian needs is that which every man needs: opportunity for experience, the freedom to make mistakes and suffer from them, the urgency of necessity to stimulate and secure individual and social growth."[113]

Later that month Fletcher also gave her first talk to the Conference of

Plate 7. Alice Fletcher and Francis La Flesche at the piano, date not recorded. The Omaha sacred pipes and associated items given to Fletcher and La Flesche in May 1884 are on the wall. They were made specifically for the ceremony called Wawan ("to sing for someone"), which would create a bond between two unrelated parties, thus bringing peace. In a letter to F. W. Putnam detailing the gifting of the sacred objects, Fletcher writes, "This was astonishing & they showed much feeling in doing it they said they did it that I might help them to preserve the pipe." She adds, "Frank LaF. says that these pipes are not in any museum he has seen & he does not think any other white person has them. The Indians certainly hold them as most precious & I think he may be true in what he says. I am surprised at what has opened to me" (Fletcher to Putnam, May 13, 1884, Harvard University Archives, Peabody Museum General Correspondence, UAV 677.38, box 5, folder "1884 C–F," Fletcher Letters). On the piano is a plucked dulcimer of a type made and used by Pennsylvanian Germans in the late nineteenth century (personal communication, Stacey Kluck, Division of Music, Sports, and Entertainment, Smithsonian, April 21, 2009). Smithsonian Institution, National Anthropological Archives (NAA INV 006891.00 enhanced).

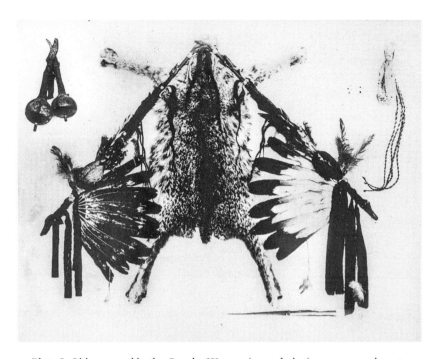

Plate 8. Objects used in the Omaha Wawan (sacred pipe) ceremony, given to
Alice Fletcher and Francis La Flesche in 1884. *Top left*: two gourd rattles; *top right*:
bladder tobacco pouch; *center*: wildcat skin with two pipes of ash. The pipe on the
left is painted blue, representing the masculine element, and is decorated with a
fan-shaped arrangement of mature golden eagle tail feathers representing the
feminine; the pipe on the right is painted green, representing the feminine element, and decorated with young golden eagle tail feathers, representing the masculine. It is possible that a crotched stick is also shown in this image—it was made
of hardwood, painted red, and in the crotch the mouthpieces of the two pipes
would have rested (Fletcher, "The 'Wawa*n*,'" 310; published in Fletcher and La
Flesche, *Omaha Tribe*, fig. 87). According to the Peabody Museum accession
records, these items were collected by La Flesche in 1883 (an apparent error in
the early record, for surely this was in 1884) and donated to the museum. These
objects were returned to the Omahas on September 18, 1990, except the crotched
stick, which was returned on July 12, 1989, and the wildcat skin, which is apparently still in the Peabody collections. Smithsonian Institution, National Anthropological Archives, Bureau of American Ethnology collection (gn-04048-b-9).

62

The peace pipe which are two—the tobacco bag—gourd rattle—corn painted green fastened to stick—wildcat skin—& crotch stick—

x bands are green on the bag & rattle

1 Peace pipe
2 Tobacco bag
3 Gourd rattle
4 Corn on stick corn green stick red
5 wildcat skin
6 crotch stick painted red

Plate 9. A field sketch of the Wawan articles from Fletcher's 1882 field notebook. Fletcher's caption reads, "The peace pipe which are two—the tobacco bag— gourd rattle—corn painted green fastened to stick—wildcat skin—& crotch stick. 1 Peace pipe/ 2 Tobacco bag/ 3 Gourd rattle/ 4 Corn on stick corn green stick red/ 5 Wildcat skin/ 6 crotch stick painted red/ 'x' bands are green on the bag & rattle" (Fletcher, "Omaha Field Diaries," 1882, 62). Smithsonian Institution, National Anthropological Archives, Bureau of American Ethnology collection (ms. 4558, box 20, p. 62 enhanced).

the Friends of the Indian at Lake Mohonk, New York.[114] The Friends of the Indian, a lobbying association established in the previous year whose annual meetings were held at a resort lodge in the Hudson River Valley, was dedicated to Indian reform. Committed to ending the reservation system and assimilating Indians into mainstream America, the participants lauded Fletcher's work with the Omahas. Moreover, because she had lived on reservations and was personally familiar with the daily realities of reservation life, the reformers accepted her as an authority whose opinion carried considerable weight.

Among the topics that the Lake Mohonk conferees discussed during their three-day meeting was citizenship for Indians. A summary appears in the official proceedings: "The debate on this topic resolved itself at first into a consideration of the bill passed by the Senate last winter, and known as the Coke, or Dawes, Bill. This bill gives a tribe inalienable title to its reservation for twenty-five years, and permits granting of lands in severalty if the President deems it advisable and two thirds of [the adult male members of] the tribe vote in favor—but any individual can have lands assigned in severalty and his title inalienable for twenty-five years if he so elects. The bill does not include citizenship."[115] The conference had already gone on record concerning their opposition to continuing to recognize tribes: "*Resolved*, That the organization of the Indians in tribes is, and has been, one of the most serious hindrances to the advancement of the Indians toward civilization, and that every effort should be made to secure the disintegration of all tribal organizations."[116] For this reason, a number of the conferees—including Richard Henry Pratt and Fletcher—opposed the bill. Fletcher argued that patenting land to the tribes was "the wrong principle." Moreover, she commented that it was "useless to expect to get two-thirds of a tribe to vote in favor of allotting lands in severalty," noting, "[e]ven among the Omahas more than two-thirds were originally opposed to it." In short, Fletcher argued, "the work must be done for them, whether they approve or not." She also proposed that the trust period be shortened to ten years and that education be made compulsory.[117]

During 1883–84, while Fletcher was engaged with the Omaha allotment, she continued to write to Putnam and Carr at the Peabody Museum on ethnological matters. She had photographs of Omahas and Sioux made in front and profile positions and recorded body measurements as contributions to physical anthropology, one of Putnam's interests.[118] She studied Omaha personal names, associated them with clans, and recorded clan customs, such as boys' symbolic haircuts.[119] She and La Flesche were also instrumental in having important tribal religious artifacts preserved at the Peabody Museum. The objects accompanying one of the Sacred Tents of War were transferred in June 1884[120] and the Sacred Pole in 1888.[121]

After completing the Omaha allotment Fletcher continued to work as a special agent of the Bureau of Indian Affairs. At the request of the bureau's commissioner of education she developed an exhibit for the World's Industrial and Cotton Centennial Exposition held in New Orleans in 1885, "setting forth the progress and present status reached by the Indians, by showing their past life and their present condition." Fletcher used photographs to contrast the story of Omaha life before allotment and the results derived from education. She arranged for a photographer to go to the Omaha Reservation and she asked her Omaha friends to pose in "old time costumes" and "to be photographed in acts indicative of their past customs."[122] Fletcher herself became an integral part of the New Orleans exhibit, explaining to visitors the problems the Omahas were facing. She was asked to give "Noon Talks" that were apparently well attended and were reported in the news media. She also produced a booklet titled *Historical Sketch of the Omaha Tribe of Indians in Nebraska*, which included engravings of sixteen photographs and several sketches and maps that were part of the display.[123] It was distributed at the exposition to those who expressed interest in Indian advancement and copies were also circulated to Indian rights associations and to individuals interested in Indian reform.

After her work in New Orleans was over Fletcher was commissioned to complete a report for the secretary of the interior in response to a Senate resolution of February 23, 1885, on the progress of Indian education and civilization. Published in 1888, the report is a comprehensive survey of relations between the U.S. government and Indians. The first part included summaries of the history and organization of the Indian Office and listings of the population and distribution of Indians within the United States, the property they controlled, the school population of each reservation, and the cost to the government of supporting the schools. The second part was a historical review of relations between Euro-Americans and Indians from the sixteenth century to the 1880s.[124] This part included a history of Indian reservations by state or territory, a summary of the treaties with the tribes, and a summary of nineteenth-century missionary work.

While preparing the report Fletcher took time to attend the 1885 AAAS meeting in Ann Arbor, Michigan, where she presented two papers. One dealt with Omaha war customs and the Sacred Tent of War, which she and La Flesche had just unpacked at the Peabody Museum. The other, "An Average Day in Camp among the Sioux," was particularly successful. The journal *Science* reported, "In a most racy and vivid manner the common incidents of such a day were given, and with the zest which comes from actual experience."[125] The paper was published in *Science* that summer, along with a companion piece titled "An Evening in Camp among the Omahas."[126] The positive reception of these ethnographic memoirs may have been a major factor in her decision to write "Life among the Indians" the next year.

In October 1885 Fletcher attended the third Lake Mohonk Conference, where she gave an address on the government's record of fulfilling treaty obligations in which she argued that commitments for annuities, food, and clothing were carried out as promised—in part because it was profitable for general commerce—while commitments for education went unfulfilled.[127] In November she also attended the Indian Rights Convention in New Haven, Connecticut, where Senator Dawes (plate 10) was the main speaker.[128]

Fletcher's political activism on behalf of the Omahas, and in particular her opposition to allowing Indians to lease their allotments to local white settlers, further strained her relationship with Thomas Henry Tibbles; enmity developed between them. During the winter of 1885–86 verbal attacks and slander against her, initiated by Tibbles, proliferated.[129] Fletcher was accused of having had a financial interest in the Omaha allotments and of impropriety in her relationship with Francis La Flesche. Herbert Welsh, corresponding secretary of the Indian Rights Association, took it on himself to investigate. He wrote to Martha Le Baron Goddard,

Plate 10. Henry L. Dawes (1816–1903), Massachusetts senator, 1875–93. Senator
Dawes recognized Fletcher as a source of firsthand information about Native
Americans. Both his wife, Electa Sanderson Dawes, and his daughter Anna L.
Dawes were personal friends of Fletcher. At the request of Joseph La Flesche
and other Omaha Indians, Fletcher lobbied Senator Dawes to help pass the
Omaha Act of 1882 that allotted Omaha tribal lands. Dawes was also instrumental in passing the General Allotment Act in 1887. This act permanently
altered the lives of Native Americans, establishing a system of land allotted to
individuals in an attempt to assimilate the members of the tribes. Photograph
by Samuel Montague Fassett, 925 Pennsylvania Ave. NW, Washington DC, albu-
men silver point, taken about 1876. National Portrait Gallery, Smithsonian
Institution (NPG.77.173).

a newspaper columnist in Worcester, Massachusetts, and outlined the allegations against Fletcher. Her reply to Welsh, dated August 2, 1886, laid the matter to rest:

> Your letter of July 28 has just come to me from Manchester. I write you as confidentially as you wrote me. I shall destroy your letter at once. I have heard all these stories in their worst form. I have no evidence by which I can prove or disprove their truth. . . . The land business is complicated. I do *not* believe that *A* had made money out of this. I do *not* believe that her relations with her Indian friend are improper. She is enthusiastic, unconventional & very emotional. She has fallen into a wretched sentimental way of calling the Omaha her children—her babies & such pet names—this is well enough in private talk with a friend—no, not well enough but still not bad, but it is mischievous as a habit & in public—petting acts follow petting words, and *A* is frankly foolish about her heavy, burly, twice married "boy,"[130] but I think there is no wrong. . . . It is true that when A. was so ill on the Reservation, she was nursed chiefly by Frank La Flesche. The Indians thought it indecent. She saw no harm in it, & speaks of him with boundless gratitude. In Washington she made a point of taking him everywhere, & introducing him to all her friends. She knows that there has been some malicious gossip about this, but she laughs at it as too absurd to notice. I honestly believe that there is no need to be disturbed about her relations with any man, excepting as a matter of taste.[131]

Fletcher experienced a relapse of her health problems in spring 1886, perhaps brought about by the stress from malicious gossip. Privately, she wrote to Samuel C. Armstrong, head of Hampton Institute, to explain Tibbles's campaign against her:

> All the imps of darkness have been dancing about. Mr. Tibbles is an unfortunate man. . . . He has refused to confront me. He knows that his talk won't stand fire that is why I suppose. The Commis. refused to listen to him except in my presence even when the talk was about the Omahas. The character of the man is well known to the

Nebraska delegation here and the Indians have entered a protest against him. He made charges concerning me . . . and the Indians refuted all the charges. I said nothing only to lay bare all evidence & let the story tell itself. The facts are there. Mr. Tibbles is heavily in debt. He suggested to certain real estate men on the border that he would come East, stir up the Boston people, raise money, open up the Omaha reservation to the white people and by this service to the land business get discharged from debt and also make something himself. He had meetings in Bancroft & elsewhere and the papers said "a boom on the reservation" was to be expected.[132]

It was during this unsettling period, while she was recovering from fever and a flare-up of her inflammatory rheumatism, that she wrote "Life among the Indians." She was well enough by the end of July to attend the Indian Rights Association meeting in Newport, Rhode Island, where she read a paper on Indian gender roles.[133]

In 1886 Fletcher was commissioned to undertake a survey of Alaskan Natives and to propose how an educational initiative might be developed there (plates 11, 12, and 13). That fall, during a three-month trip, she visited both Alaskan and Canadian Native communities, witnessing the cultural disruption brought about by missionaries and the deleterious influence of traders. It was a welcome diversion for Fletcher; she collected some artifacts for Putnam and, importantly, was able to regain her health.[134]

Fletcher returned to Washington in December 1886. Although she became a long-time resident there,[135] a member of several Washington-based professional societies, and a frequent associate of Smithsonian ethnologists, and although she and La Flesche eventually published their joint study of the Omahas in the Bureau of American Ethnology annual reports series, she was never an employee of the Smithsonian. Throughout her life she maintained her affiliation with the Peabody Museum in Cambridge.

On February 8, 1887, the Dawes Severalty Act or General Allotment Act became law. Fletcher called it "the Magna Charta of the Indians of our country."[136] Individual property ownership was the heart of the act; after twenty-five years the land was to be released to the owners under fee pat-

Plate 11. *Left to right*: Alice Fletcher, Mrs. Frances A. Reigart, Rev. Sheldon Jackson, and Isaac Newton Wyckoff, several weeks before Fletcher began writing "Life among the Indians." During the fall of 1886 Fletcher was commissioned to travel to Alaska with Jackson, the first superintendent for education in Alaska, to help survey the mission schools serving the indigenous population. Reigart and Wyckoff were employed by the Bureau of Education, Department of the Interior, in Washington DC; Reigart was a copyist in the Division of Statistics and Wyckoff was a clerk for the Division of Records. The photograph was taken by an unidentified photographer in Washington DC in March 1886. Presbyterian Historical Society, Presbyterian Church (USA), Philadelphia PA (RG-239-11-22). (The color and contrast of the photograph have been adjusted for publication.)

ents.[137] The Lake Mohonk Friends of the Indian applauded the passage of the bill. In an editorial printed in the Carlisle Indian School newspaper, the *Morning Star*, Fletcher described four ways in which the passage of the bill benefited Indians. First, it provided them with their own homesteads; second, it substituted individual ownership of land for tribal ownership; third, it placed the Indian landowners under the civil and criminal laws of the states and gave them citizenship; fourth, it provided, with the consent of the Indians, for the opening to non-Indian settlement of the surplus lands that remained after allotments had been made.[138] Since education was a cornerstone of the allotment policy, Fletcher proposed to provide

22. Cabin to Steam Schooner "Leo," Sitka, Alaska.

Plate 12. "Cabin to Steam Schooner 'Leo,' Sitka, Alaska." *Left to right*: James William Keene, master and pilot of the Steam Schooner *Leo*; probably George Kostromentinoff, the official interpreter to the District of Alaska; Kate Foote; Fletcher; and Reverend Jackson. This photograph was taken while Fletcher accompanied a survey of Alaska with Jackson, several months after she completed "Life among the Indians." Fletcher's Alaska notebook for November 8, 1886, notes, "De Groffs took our pictures on the boom & in the cabin" (Fletcher, 1886 Field Notebook 2, Smithsonian Institution, National Anthropological Archives, ms. 4558, box 18). De Groffs, a commercial photographer, actively advertised the Native American photos he took in Alaska in the 1880s, but his promotion of photos never listed the two he took of Fletcher and company; he must have considered them too personal to place on sale. Photograph by Edward de Groffs, November 8, 1886, courtesy of Hampton University Archives.

assistance in building frame houses for newly educated, married Indian couples who returned to their reservations from boarding school.[139]

In the spring and summer following the passage of the Dawes Act Fletcher revised and finalized the manuscript of "Life among the Indians." The timing seemed right for a popular book that would expose the corruption and inequities of the reservation system, as well as the humanity of the Indians, scientifically, from the vantage point of anthropology. The combination of activism and science was Fletcher's distinctive con-

Plate 13. On the deck of the *Leo*. *Left to right*: Kostromentinoff, Keene, Reverend Jackson, Fletcher, and Foote. Photograph by Edward de Groffs, November 8, 1886, Smithsonian Institution, National Anthropological Archives (55,376).

tribution. It is unclear why the manuscript was not published in 1887; perhaps its concerns seemed outdated given that Congress had, in theory, resolved the Indian problem by legislating allotment and the eventual dissolution of reservations. In any case, the commissioner of Indian affairs appointed Fletcher allotting agent for the Winnebagos whose lands bordered on those of the Omahas. She left for Nebraska in August 1887, and "Life among the Indians" was filed away.

The Aftermath of Allotment

The allotment policy had far-reaching effects on American Indians, but the reformers' vision of a smooth transition from tribal peoples to independent landowners failed utterly. As early as February 1887 an article titled "Miss Fletcher Sadly Disappointed" appeared in *Council Fire*:

> During the recent conference at the Riggs House Miss Alice Fletcher was called upon to report on the progress of her protégés, the Omaha Indians, whose lands she divided in severalty three years ago. At the conference, a year ago, she was full of hope, and thought she had

done a great thing for those Indians. This year she was almost in despair. She said "I have recently visited the Omahas, and I am sorry to be obliged to report that in some cases they are not doing as well as I had hoped. Indeed they are doing very badly. They seem utterly at a loss how to get along. They don't seem able to work their lands themselves, and they can't let white men work them for them. White men are anxious to get leases, and almost all the Indians would lease their lands if they could."[140]

In addition to pointing out the negative effects of leasing reservation lands, Fletcher was adamantly opposed to perpetuating the reservation system itself, believing that mismanagement had created a class of demoralized people. In an article published in 1888 in the *Southern Workman* titled "The Indian and the Prisoner," she aptly describes the negative aspects of the reservation system and gives voice to the importance of Indians maintaining their "Indianness" as long as that meant individual freedom rather than tribal oversight of the individual's actions.

Again, in September 1889, writing from the field camp in Idaho where she was allotting lands to the Nez Perce Indians, she cautioned attendees at the Seventh Annual Lake Mohonk Conference: "Each year I am more deeply convinced that neither the government nor the friends of the Indians as yet realize the changes that are at hand, and already here, under the working of the act of Feb. 8, 1887. These changes nothing can deter, and they bring much trouble and distress that could be averted, were they anticipated and suitable action taken to prepare the Indian to meet them."[141]

To make matters worse, in February 1891 Congress amended the Dawes Act to allow leasing of Indian-owned lands under certain conditions, arguing that it would provide a flow of income from rental land to individual Indians and to the tribes from residual communal landholdings.[142] In fact, the amendment catered to the interests of non-Indian settlers who were anxious to lease Indian lands at bargain rates.

Nonetheless, Fletcher continued to support the Dawes Act and the land allotment policy. In 1892 at the Lake Mohonk Conference she said, "[T]he bill, after working under it for six seasons, rouses more interest and enthusiasm in my mind than when I began." She now argued that land ownership was not as foreign to Indians as people generally believed. She observed that for the Omahas in prereservation times the use and occupancy of land established a claim of right to possess the tract from which an individual derived substance. Nevertheless, land was never bought, sold, or inherited and home was wherever the extended family resided. The Dawes Act presented "land" to the Indian in a new way, "as a bit of individual property that shall be not only a source of revenue to him, but something that is to remain with him and pass in a given line to his heirs, and also as something which must be looked at from a mercantile point of view, as to trade and the nearness to market. All this is new."[143]

In 1892 Fletcher already was cautioning that Indian allotment was not a failure simply because many Indians did not want to become farmers. From her perspective, a family's allotted land was a "site for a home and the division of inherited property."[144] She saw the home itself and adoption of the Euro-American cultural values of legal, monogamous marriage and domesticity as key to Indian evolutionary progress.

On August 23, 1897, Fletcher returned to the Omaha Reservation with La Flesche and stayed until September 9. They visited with members of the La Flesche family and a number of other Omaha families.[145] This was her first visit in seven years and what she found confirmed some of her concerns. Since Omaha men were not farmers by tradition and the women farmed only their small garden plots, it was no wonder that they had begun to lease their allotments to non-Indians. It was the leasing of land, not allotment itself, that both Fletcher and Francis La Flesche saw as a negative outcome of the Dawes Act. La Flesche summed this up in an address he gave at the Lake Mohonk Conference in 1900 when he described the example of an Omaha man who maintained his landholdings while his Indian neighbors

one by one, including the returned Hampton students, . . . left their lands to the use of white men and returned to the poorest part of the reservation. . . . Last summer when I was visiting my home this man came to see me. Said he: "I wish to send a message by you to the white people, to any of them who might wish to help us. The leasing business is ruining the Omahas in every way. . . . Nearly all of the land is leased, and most of the Indians have scarcely a thing to show for the rent they receive. . . . So long as the system of indiscriminate leasing exists, work among the people will be almost an impossible thing. Cannot the friends of the Indians relieve us of this curse in some way?"

I have delivered my message.[146]

In *The Omaha Tribe* (published in 1911 but completed in 1909), the culmination of Fletcher and La Flesche's collaborative studies, they simply write, "[T]he twenty-five-year 'period of trust' has been fraught with many experiences, not all of which have been happy. . . . the act [of August 7, 1882 granting land to individual Omaha Indians] has not been altogether evil nor has it been wholly good for the people."[147]

Fletcher had become a major force in lobbying for the Indians. She wanted to make them self-sufficient and equal under the law. But for the Omahas, the allotment of land in severalty had a cataclysmic impact and was disastrous to their traditional way of life. That the Omahas had been deeply concerned over the potential loss of all their reservation lands in Nebraska, and that some of them had asked Fletcher for her help, did not lessen the blow.

In fact, the deterioration of the economic situation of the Omahas resulting from the quagmire of fractionated inheritance was not fully realized until after Fletcher's death in 1923. The Meriam Report of 1928 clearly showed that the attempt to force Native Americans to accept Euro-American land values through the homestead requirement was a failure.[148]

Margaret Mead carried out anthropological fieldwork among the Omahas from June to October 1930 and observed the devastating effects of allotment firsthand. Using the pseudonym "Antlers" to provide anonymity for the tribe, she wrote, "Since 1920, conditions have been getting steadily worse on the reservation. Those who received fee patents to their lands have, almost without exception, sold them . . . and spent all their money." Although the allotments were expected to provide the economic base for future generations of Omaha farmers, in fact, as Mead observed, "No attempt was made to deal with the problems of inheritance. . . . The original allotments have been divided and subdivided in a fashion utterly incompatible with western farming . . . [T]he land, given to their grand-fathers as a perpetual economic basis for their existence, is irretrievably lost and nothing remains in its place."[149]

Fletcher's Career in Perspective

In the nineteenth century it was a remarkable decision for an unmarried woman to venture alone to the West for the purpose of gaining firsthand knowledge about American Indians. Fletcher's pioneering field studies were thus significant in several ways: because of her gender, because she did fieldwork without the support of a spouse, and because she was test-ing the uncharted new field of ethnology, for which fieldwork was the pri-mary means of gaining information.[150] Although her initial research was to be on women's lives, she quickly expanded her research interests. Her notebooks and publications reflect concern for detail in ethnographic descriptions of rituals and the minutia of daily life. She gathered plants and pressed them in her notebooks for correct species identification to complement her drawings and verbal descriptions. Fletcher was well aware that she was a pioneer in the field. She wrote to Jane Smith, Putnam's sec-retary, on November 14, 1881,

> I should be glad to know how many white women have spoken in Indian Counsels [sic]. Perhaps Mr. Carr can tell & also whether any lady has done similar work to mine, among them, Mrs. Smith's is different. I can't find [a] trace of it, and I would really like to know. It is nearly three months that I have most of the time been living with Indian families as one of them. I know their inside life pretty well. The Indian is not the character he is usually drawn, at least the Indians I know best and these are the Omahas, Poncas, Santees, Yanktons & some Bands of the Ogallalas & Brule. . . . It is certainly a mistake to measure a race solely by the standard of the Anglo Saxons or modern Western European types. It takes some hard thinking, at least it did so with me, to get around to the Indian's own aspect of life. And now that I have done so in a degree, daily I make discoveries of their reasons why in their social customs & their home habits. It is profoundly inter-

esting & reflects much light on our own social advancement as well as our social questions and problems. Often these comparative studies keep me awake the better part of the night.[151]

Earlier in the same letter she mused, "My scientific work is of course fraught with fearful hardships, how hard I do not care to tell. But for all that I am not daunted & shall push on. Already I have many warm friends among the Indians, several of them chiefs & prominent men and women. My close and friendly relations have opened up to me aspects of the modern 'Indian Question' that appeal strongly to my sense of justice and humanity. One day I may feel that I must tell what I know and have seen."

Fletcher's work helped pave the way for the development of anthropology. She was in the forefront of the process by which anthropology was transformed from an avocation to a professional science. She aided the efforts of archaeological research by participating in excavations as well as by helping to raise funds and petition Congress for the preservation of sites.[152] She was one of the founders of the School of American Archaeology (now the School of Anthropological Research) in Santa Fe, New Mexico. She experimented with methods in physical anthropology, reporting the results in *Science*. She participated in the physical measurement of Nez Perces using instruments and instructions given to her by Franz Boas and regretted "not getting more measurements for Dr. Boas."[153] Using composite portraits of Sioux men and women, Fletcher attempted to create a visual representation of an ethnic "type" by combining their physical features.[154] Ultimately, the intention was to determine psychological and cultural characteristics from physiological appearances.

Fletcher was always concerned about linguistic accuracy and the subtleties of translation. In 1894 she purchased a Graphophone, a phonograph that used wax cylinders, and began to record Indian songs and ritual texts at her home in Washington, bringing consultants there. She described her success with this new technology in a letter to Putnam on February 13, 1895: "I have bought a Graphophone, and already have taken important records. Monday night I had here 3 Otoe Indians and took down on the cylinders 22 songs, words and music and got at some very interesting material. It is my purpose when I have exploited the cylinders to file them in the museum for future reference. You would be surprised how well I can record language and it occurred to me that it would be a good thing to secure such records of the different languages."[155]

By the turn of the twentieth century Fletcher was recognized as a major contributor to American anthropology. In 1903 she was requested to write articles for the Bureau of American Ethnology's *Handbook of American Indians North of Mexico*, under the editorship of Frederick W. Hodge.[156] Over the next three years she wrote some ninety-seven entries, many brief, on a staggering variety of topics (see the list in the bibliography). Among her more important articles are those on "Music and Musical Instruments," "Property and Property Right," and "Wakonda" (the concept of the sacred). For many of her topical articles she drew heavily on her studies of the Omahas.

Since Fletcher's original intention in undertaking fieldwork was to learn about Indian women's lives, one might well ask about the results of her planned study. While she, too, doubtless saw what appeared to outsiders as evidence for the inferior position of Indian women, she also discovered something else, something that must have challenged her thinking about the way in which women were conceptualized as second-class citizens in her own society.[157] The Omaha and Sioux women she visited were independent. They owned property, including the house (whether earth lodge or tipi) as well as its contents, and they earned their own status. In September 1888, writing to Gen. Eliphalet Whittlesey, chairman of a committee of the Lake Mohonk Friends of the Indian, in her capacity as a member of the committee to report on the Dawes Act, she keenly observed, "The imperfection of our laws regarding women are very clearly brought out in dealing with the Indian women under the Severalty Act."[158] In terms of property rights and status, Indian women lost more under allotment than did the men.

Despite her professional success, it would be difficult to characterize Fletcher as a feminist. She collaborated and competed with men on equal terms, prompting Joseph La Flesche to characterize her on first meeting as "a remarkable woman; in thought and expression she is more like a man than a woman."[159] In 1891, when she was elected an honorary and corresponding member of the Woman's Branch of the World Congress

Auxiliary during planning for the 1893 World's Columbian Exposition, she wrote to Putnam, "I have accepted but I don't see anything for me to do. I don't believe in trying to disintegrate work according to sex, but many do."[160] After the exposition she traveled to Europe and wrote to Putnam from Dresden, Germany, in October 1894: "I am sometimes tempted when I think of the museum & of what I could possibly do there, to wish that I never did wish, to be a man! I am aware that being a woman I am debarred from helping you as I otherwise could—but the bar is a fact."[161] Her enthusiasm for anthropology was tempered by the realization that she could never achieve an appointment in either a museum or a university. Ironically, although Fletcher did not hesitate to question the fairness of Indian policy she seems never to have taken an active role in questioning the position of women in American society.

Despite her frustration in being blocked from a regular appointment, Fletcher held an enviable position in that she had complete freedom to choose whatever she wished to study. Her life as an independent scholar was made possible by the award in 1890 of the Thaw Fellowship, established under the auspices of the Peabody Museum by Mary Thaw, a private philanthropist, to support Fletcher's work.[162] Harvard University's acceptance of the Thaw Fellowship was an important milestone in two ways. It recognized the scholarship of a woman, even though the university did not yet admit women to its faculty or student body, and it recognized anthropology as an academic discipline, even though there were as yet no universities that offered a degree in anthropology.

In 1891 Mrs. Thaw even arranged for Fletcher to purchase a small house in Washington, on Capitol Hill, at 214 First Street, SE. Fletcher moved there on January 14, 1892, and noted in her diary, "[B]rought my goods and I moved in. First night in house. Very happy and grateful."[163] On August 16, 1892, La Flesche also moved into the house, occupying a room that Fletcher had prepared for him.[164] This would be her home for the rest of her life, one that she would share periodically with La Flesche.

Continuing to rely on Putnam's direction and encouragement, Fletcher developed her career in many directions. In the end, she made contributions to all four fields of anthropology and foreshadowed the development of the discipline.

Fletcher's use of anthropology to highlight contemporary social issues and to influence government Indian policy qualifies her, as Margaret Mead and Ruth Bunzel noted, to be regarded as "America's first applied anthropologist."[165] She struggled with the conflict between devoting herself strictly to scientific research and ignoring the conditions under which the Indians lived or becoming an activist on behalf of those peoples whom she studied. She chose the latter. Her enthusiasm for reaching a broad popular audience through public speaking, women's organizations, and popular writing set her apart from most of her male colleagues. She deemphasized Indian exoticism and described Indian life in a matter-of-fact and unsensational manner. Her articles in *Century Magazine* brought anthropology to the attention of a wider audience and introduced readers to the concept of cultural relativism.[166] It was a theme in many of her writings, such as the essay "Ethics and Morals," published in the *Handbook of American Indians North of Mexico*:

> It is difficult for a person knowing only one code of morals or manners to appreciate the customs of another who has been reared in the knowledge of a different code; hence it has been common for such a one to conclude that the other has no manners or no morals. Every community has rules adapted to its mode of life and surroundings. . . . [I]t is clear from all that is known of the natives of this continent that there existed among them standards of right conduct and character. . . . [T]ruth, honesty, and the safeguarding of human life were everywhere recognized as essential to the peace and prosperity of a tribe, and social customs enforced their observances; the community could not otherwise keep together.[167]

Nonetheless, Fletcher never gave up on the social evolutionary view of progress as exemplified by Euro-American civilization and the conviction that through education and the ownership of land any Indian could become a productive American citizen. At the same time, as she wrote to Lucien Carr before beginning her field studies, she believed that an understanding of "woman's life in the social state represented by the Indians" might shed light on "the Woman Question" in civilized society.[168] There were important lessons to be learned from the study of earlier evolutionary periods.

In her popular writings, especially in the *Southern Workman* (published at Hampton Institute), Fletcher also tried to dispel persistent stereotypes about Indians. In an 1899 article titled "Indian Speech" she wrote about the "many [popular] delusions, among them the notion that there is one Indian language understood by all the tribes."[169] In another article she addressed the misconception that all Indians were nomadic and therefore had no attachment to the land. She also addressed the widely believed stereotype that Indian women were held in degraded positions within their tribes, countering that the women's role in tribal society "had always been one of honor rather than one of slavery and degradation."[170] The process of allotting land to the Omahas clearly revealed to her the conflicting worldviews of the Omahas and Euro-Americans. In a letter to Commissioner of Indian Affairs Hiram Price in June 1884 she pointed out,

> In connection with this close personal superintendence in allotting the lands, the laws of property and legal descent were explained to the people, a matter difficult for them to fully comprehend owing to their previous customs and modes of thought. This difficulty was marked in regard to the rights of children to their deceased parents' property, such claims being secondary to those of lateral relationship in Indian society; and, also the absorbing of the wife's rights to land in that of her husband's, it seeming unjust to the Indian that the wife should not possess land distinctive from her husband, she being as responsible as he regarding the family.[171]

Fletcher took a humanistic perspective to bring to public attention the inequities of the Indian situation. She exposed the poverty, suffering, and illegal and unjust application of laws under which the Indians were forced to live and helped bring much-needed attention to the late nineteenth-century reservation system. Her position as an activist for Indian land rights was pressed upon her by the Omahas with whom she collaborated. They appealed to her to help them in their struggle for ownership of their lands and she did not ignore their appeal. As Fletcher wrote in chapter 20 of "Life among the Indians," she sensed the urgency of the charge:

"Speak for them! You can do it, for you know them as no white person ever did before."

Fletcher was extremely successful in applying her scholarship, personal contacts, and political networks to promote laws and policies that she hoped would aid American Indians and to secure land title for them. In this she worked within the accepted theories of the anthropology of her time. That the results were not as successful as predicted should serve as an object lesson for applied anthropologists today.

Reformer

Fletcher was a central figure in the reform of Indian policy during the decade of the 1880s. This was a period during which humanitarian interests, based primarily in New England, sought to deal with the "Indian problem" once and for all. Frederick Hoxie presents a cogent analysis of that movement, which was motivated by the multiple disasters of 1879.[172] In January a starving group of 149 Northern Cheyennes led by Dull Knife broke out of their prison at Fort Robinson, Nebraska, and more than half of them were shot down—men, women, and children—by the army troops stationed there. Their crime was in leaving the reservation in Indian Territory to which they had been removed two years earlier and attempting to return to their homelands in the north. In March a group of sixty-five Poncas, led by Standing Bear, also fled from the reservation in Indian Territory to which they had been removed in 1877 and returned to their homeland in Nebraska. Arrested and tried, Standing Bear was released in May; that fall he began an eastern speaking tour, arranged by Thomas Henry Tibbles, that brought the disenfranchisement of American Indians to public attention. In September Nathan C. Meeker, Indian agent for the Utes, was murdered by his charges when he called in troops. The trouble started over the agent's insistence that the Utes take up farming and ended in the short-lived "Ute War," in which a number of soldiers, agency employees, and Indians were killed. Finally, in December Commissioner of Indian Affairs Ezra A. Hayt was charged with financial wrongdoing on a reservation in Arizona to protect his personal business interests; the revelation led to his resignation. All these events, clustering in a single year, drew inescapable attention to the failure of the government's Indian reservation system.

Introduction   65

At the same time settlers and entrepreneurs in the West, as well as railroad interests in the East and Midwest, sought to abolish Indian reservations altogether and let the native people adapt or die. Given the belief—backed by government statistics—that the Indians were, in any case, a dying race, western politicians resented the money spent on supporting the reservations and begrudged the Indians the lands that they retained.

The reform movement sought to treat the remaining Indian population in a moral and humanitarian manner, protecting them from twin evils—the corruption of the government's reservation system and the greed of western settlers for Indian land. The solution, to be implemented humanely over time, as tribes were prepared for it, was to abolish the reservations and the tribal structures, absorbing the Indians as individuals into the increasingly multiethnic fabric of the United States, just as—in theory—was happening with the blacks who had formerly been slaves. To ensure the likelihood of success required granting lands to individual Indians to enable them to become farmers and educating their children in English, teaching them the principles of American democracy as well as the arts of domesticity and useful manual skills.

Senator Henry Dawes of Massachusetts emerged as the political leader of Indian reform. A long-term Republican politician, Dawes in 1879 was looking for a minimally controversial issue to champion to prove his leadership and protect his Senate seat from the challenge of younger party members. As Hoxie writes, "It would seem that the senator's sudden involvement in Indian affairs in late 1879 saved his career."[173] The impetus for his adoption of the cause of Indian reform was the much-publicized visit of Standing Bear and his party to Boston.

Whereas Dawes saw political opportunity in his meeting with Standing Bear and his party, Fletcher, by her own account, saw ethnographic opportunity. She planned a trip west to study Indian women. In the meantime, she continued her lecturing to earn an income, met Frederic Putnam, allied herself with the Peabody Museum, and begin to identify, at first informally, with the field of anthropology. When Tibbles and Susette La Flesche returned to Boston in 1881, Fletcher gave them a tour of the Peabody and asked them to help her initiate what would be her first field trip.[174]

As Fletcher settled in to her work with the Omahas she was under the patronage and protection of the influential La Flesche family, whose mixed-blood ancestry, conversion to Christianity, and dedication to living in the white men's way on individual farms, separated from tribal ties, put them and other like-minded Omahas at odds with more traditional tribal members. She was moved by their fear that, as with the Poncas, the government would decide to remove them from their traditional location in the rich farmlands of eastern Nebraska to Indian Territory. The members of the progressive faction wanted the security of landownership and Fletcher, though she would have preferred simply to carry out her ethnological studies, could not refuse their appeal. That fall she worked on a petition that was signed by fifty-three Omaha men, asking Congress to grant them individual title to their lands. When mailing the petition seemed to produce no results, she went to Washington to lobby for it. With the aid of Senator Dawes the Omaha bill was passed in 1882, mandating the allotment of land not only to the petitioners but to the entire Omaha tribe.

In 1882 Fletcher agreed to work for Richard H. Pratt to recruit students for Carlisle Indian School. This paid her a small wage and allowed her to return to the Sioux that summer to continue her fieldwork. On her way west she accompanied a group of Sioux and Omaha students who were returning from Carlisle, and on her way east she escorted new students destined for Carlisle and Hampton.

In 1883 Fletcher accepted the job of carrying out allotment for the Omahas. Despite a painful illness she completed the work in 1884. At the same time she carried out ethnographic studies, and at the conclusion of her allotment work the Omahas rewarded her with a pipe dance, after which she was given permission to study and record anything she wished about their traditional culture. In fall 1884 she attended for the first time the Lake Mohonk meeting of Friends of the Indians, speaking about the Omaha allotment.

For the next few years Fletcher continued to be supported by special appointments from the Office of Indian Affairs, including her studies of Indian education (1885–87) and—following the passage of the General Allotment Act in 1887—the allotment of reservation lands for the Winnebagos (1887–88) and Nez Perces (1888–92). Throughout the fieldwork required for allotment she continued her ethnographic studies. In 1890, during a visit to Pittsburgh, the philanthropist Mary Thaw told Fletcher that she was wasting her talent on government work and eventually established a fellowship through the Peabody Museum that would allow her to devote herself to her ethnological studies full time. Once she finished with the Nez Perce allotment (the paperwork dragged on until 1894) she was free of the need to accept government contracts.

In 1895, reflecting on the American Indian situation, Dawes wrote, "It is true that we have not yet assimilated the Indians, but it is also true that we have already absorbed the Indian." He compared them to Bohemians in Chicago and Polish Jews in New York, who "are absorbed into our civilization, though they speak no English or live in squalor."[175] For Dawes, "absorption" was the necessary first step to assimilation. With this, one suspects, Fletcher agreed. Despite its terrible human costs, Indian reform had saved the Indians from extinction and allowed them to preserve at least some of their lands. Education had brought some Indians into the mainstream. Moreover, after the 1890 census, the Indian population, which had fallen steadily throughout the nineteenth century, began to rise.

Fletcher became a political activist only at the request of the Omahas whose traditional culture she was studying. For more than a decade she subordinated her work as a scholar to her work with the practical affairs of Indian people in terms of education and allotment. On a return visit to the Omahas in 1897 she was presented firsthand with the failures of the allotment system. The imagined prosperity of the Omahas living on small family farms, interspersed with those of their white neighbors, failed to match reality. She blamed the failure, at least in part, on the decision of Congress to allow Indians to lease their allotments, which most Omahas preferred, rather than attempting to farm them. But she was not prepared to publically condemn the allotment system as a complete failure. However, as Joan Mark observes, after 1897 she began to express a change of attitude. Whereas previously she felt the necessity of severing Indians from their past and plunging them into American civilization, she now began to argue a more moderate stance: "There is much in his [the Indians'] past that should be conserved, for no people can be helped if they are absolutely uprooted."[176] It seems that, at last, Fletcher the ethnologist had merged with Fletcher the reformer.

Subsequent historians' treatment of Fletcher has been less balanced than Mark's. Writing from the perspective of postcolonial theory and attempting to force Fletcher into a protofeminist mold, they have portrayed her as a scheming architect of ill-advised reform.[177] They condemn Fletcher for her advocacy of allotment and for her involvement in sending children to boarding schools, both seen as maternalistic meddling in the lives of Indian people. Moreover, Fletcher has been gratuitously accused of using her position as an agent of reform to extort cultural information for her scientific purposes and tribal artifacts for the Peabody Museum. Such historical judgment, written on the basis of present-day standards and with the benefit of knowing the ultimate effects of the reform movement in terms of lost lands and abused and psychologically traumatized children, operates from a series of postulates, assumed to be fact: that allotment was an unmitigated evil, the ultimate goal of which was to alienate Indians from their land; that boarding schools, which forcibly separated children from their families and forced them to learn English and the ways of mainstream American life, were likewise an unmitigated evil; and that ethnology itself, as another expression of colonialist mentality, dispossessed Indian people even of their cultures. Little wonder that, arguing from these premises, Fletcher is portrayed as an arrogant meddler—no matter how well intentioned—doing irreparable harm to Indian people.

These twenty-first-century judgments are informed by knowing the extent of the disaster caused by the allotment policy and the anguish caused by sending children away from their families to boarding school. Looking at the political realities of the 1880s, however, it is important to consider the alternatives. The reservation system had failed to protect the Indians' interests and to prepare them to live in the rapidly modernizing world. It is a romantic notion that they could have been allowed to continue traditional ways of life—there was little game left to hunt—or to develop tribal- or community-based herding or farming operations—there was no capital to fund such enterprises. Moreover, reservations were surrounded by land-hungry whites who had little or no regard for Indian rights and who were a perpetual threat. Like the Northern Cheyennes and the Poncas, other tribes faced the real possibility of removal to Indian Territory. Children could have been allowed to grow up without the benefit of education or understanding of English. However, without education there would have been no tribal members to develop into leaders in the twentieth century, men and women who could look after their people's welfare by using their ability in English and the skills learned in school to become intermediaries between their people and the U.S. government. Tribal leaders routinely requested that their children be educated, but reservation schools—with the exception of some church-run boarding schools on or near reservations—were poorly staffed and underfunded. Government-supported boarding schools appeared to be the best solution.

Given the constraints faced by tribes, reformers like Fletcher used their best judgment to devise strategies for ensuring the survival of Indian people and their integration into U.S. society. In the light of hindsight, it is easy to condemn Fletcher for her maternalism, her reformist zeal, and her role in promulgating the allotment program and off-reservation boarding schools. Yet situating Fletcher and the reform movement within the context of their times and within the bounds of their knowledge and experience offers a far more complex understanding. She put her own ethnological work to the side for over a decade in the attempt to give the people who asked for her help the assistance they requested. She sought to right the wrongs she had observed on her first visits to Indian reservations in Nebraska and Dakota Territory, the subject of "Life among the Indians," in which she vividly describes her efforts. When her reformer's work was done she returned full time to her scientific pursuits, which ultimately blossomed from superficial observation to insightful understanding of the nuances of Indian cultures.

Ethnologist

Fletcher was among the first anthropologists to recognize that Indian cultures were not static, that Indian peoples had the ability to refit themselves to both the radical social contact with Euro-Americans and contact with neighboring tribes. Her 1890–91 articles on the spread of a syllabary from the Sauks and Foxes to the Winnebagos and on the Ghost Dance movement are clear statements of the process in action.[178] Similarly, in her 1892 article "Hae-thu-ska Society of the Omaha Tribe" she elaborated on the presence of the same men's society among the Otoes, Iowas, Pawnees, and Sioux. The dance and songs of this society were, she observed, incorporated by the Sioux as the Omaha Dance or Grass Dance. Over time, despite periodic warfare between the Sioux and Omahas, Fletcher noted that the dance passed from one tribe to another:

> There are many signs of transplanting rather than of an indigenous growth in the dance as seen in these other tribes. It is social rather than historical. . . . It is an interesting fact that to-day, when the Omaha Indians are within the fold of United States citizens . . . that among the most progressive and industrious of the men, there should have been a revival of the Hae-thu-ska Society. . . . [I]n citizens' or white man's dress, these Omaha farmers meet during the winter evenings in an old earth lodge. . . . [T]hese industrious descendants of warriors meet and rehearse the songs and dramatic dances of their forefathers.[179]

That she appreciated the ability of Indian culture to incorporate new traits from without cannot be doubted, yet, as she keenly observed, while such trappings as clothing may change, this did not hinder the continuation of deeper cultural traits.

Fletcher's ethnographic studies included Indian ceremonies, dances, rituals, myths, kinship systems, and women's lives, but above all she was interested in Indian music. "A Study of Omaha Indian Music" (1893) was the first ethnographic presentation of the music of an American Indian tribe and was published with credit on the title page to her Omaha assistant, Francis La Flesche.[180] Fletcher's interest in Omaha music originated with her first fieldwork experience. She continued to record Omaha songs with La Flesche both in the field and at their home in Washington; for example, George Miller, an Omaha student at Hampton Institute in Virginia, contributed to their song collection in May 1888.[181] Fletcher was among the first anthropologists to use a Graphophone. Her music recordings included not only Sioux and Omaha, but also Arapaho, Cheyenne, Chippewa, Kiowa, Nez Perce, Osage, Otoe, Pawnee, Plains Ojibwa, Ponca, Potawatomi, Wichita, and Winnebago songs.[182]

In addition to her groundbreaking studies of Indian music, Fletcher was keenly interested in material culture. She collected the ritual objects used in the Sioux Sun Dance, including a painted buffalo skull and a sacred pipe.[183] Similarly, she and La Flesche were instrumental in obtaining the Omaha Sacred Pole and Tent of War for the Peabody Museum. Her essay on porcupine quillwork, which includes detailed descriptions of quilling techniques, attests to her close study of this art form.[184]

The development of Fletcher's anthropology was greatly influenced by her relationship with Francis La Flesche. When they began their collaboration, Fletcher considered him both interpreter and consultant. Then, appreciating La Flesche's talent as a writer, she encouraged him to pursue a career in literature, leaving the scientific writing to herself. She was instrumental in brokering the publication of La Flesche's *The Middle Five: Indian Boys at School* (1900), a literary success that established him as a major American Indian writer.[185] Although La Flesche continued his creative writing, despite Fletcher's plan for him, his interests were in anthropology. By 1907, as the manuscript of *The Omaha Tribe* was at long last coming together, Fletcher had come to rely on La Flesche as a coauthor. Writing to Putnam on the progress of the manuscript, Fletcher explained, "Francis and I are at work on the plan. He will do [a] considerable part of the book. He will have to write it for I want it to have the true Omaha flavor & not be diluted thro me."[186]

Fletcher's attention to the native language in her writings was always integral to her work. As early as 1884, in her article on the Omaha Pipe Dance (*Wáwą* 'to sing for someone') she incorporated the ritual song texts in the Omaha language.[187] Throughout her writings, close semantic analysis of fundamental Omaha concepts was a hallmark of her ethnography, a trait that now makes Fletcher seem far ahead of her time. The linguistic sophistication of her analysis was possible because of La Flesche's intuitions as a native speaker of Omaha and an ethnographer himself. Like her, he was dedicated to preserving not just a description but an interpretation of Omaha culture.

Although Fletcher's anthropology is rooted in the now-discredited social evolutionary theory of the nineteenth century, in other ways her work foreshadowed twentieth-century developments of ethnoscience, symbolic anthropology, and reflexive anthropology. If the massive study of the Omahas that she coauthored with La Flesche can be criticized as homogenized, normative, and overly intellectualized, it nonetheless offers a coherent ethnography from an Indian point of view. It is, in a very concrete sense, a memorial to the Omahas, a summing up of a culture that was, for the authors, a thing of the past. Today *The Omaha Tribe* stands as a prototype of collaborative ethnography, an approach popular once again in the twenty-first century.

It seems incongruous that a proper Victorian woman, at middle age, would turn to anthropology and devote the remainder of her life to the study of American Indians. It is even more remarkable that she succeeded in her major endeavors: she became the most vocal activist among the anthropologists of her generation in lobbying for the reform of government Indian policy and in advocating for Indian education; she was an important force pressing for legislation to protect archeological sites; and she carried out field studies and published some of the most detailed and nuanced ethnographies of Plains Indians, particularly their rituals, of the late nineteenth and early twentieth centuries. Moreover, she nurtured the career of her Omaha protégé, Francis La Flesche, who became one of the first Native American anthropologists.

"Life among the Indians," written near the beginning of Fletcher's anthropological career and reporting her first experiences of ethnographic fieldwork, reveals her fears and uncertainties but never wavers in the conviction that the purpose of her trip was to experience life firsthand from the Indians' point of view. She was protected in her endeavor by official letters from the Departments of War and the Interior, but her only tools for achieving her goal were her pencils and notebooks and her genuine interest in and empathy for the people she was visiting. How she should go about getting information and what information should be recorded in the name of science were questions she had to resolve as she went about daily life while living with the Sioux and the Omahas. The particular value of this manuscript is the extent to which it reveals Fletcher in the process of doing ethnographic fieldwork, working out through trial and error the methods of the anthropologist's craft. She loses no opportunity to make fun of herself and to imagine how she appears in the Indians' eyes.

Because the manuscript was written for a popular audience at a time when Fletcher had to earn money through her writings to support herself, she felt free to alter the chronology and omit details in the interest of narrative. Most of her Indian hosts go unnamed, as does the Indian agent whose rudeness so offended her. Rather, the work focuses on her and her experiences, with the Indians seen through her eyes or telling their stories as she jots them down in her notebook. Such a participatory account, revealing how information was gathered in the field, was at odds with the ethnographic practice of the day as exemplified by the publications of the Bureau of Ethnology. The positivist idea of science as the accretion of facts separate from any prejudice or value judgment precluded the intrusion of the ethnographer's voice into published ethnographies.

When Fletcher first went to the field, the idea of reflexive anthropology was still a century in the future. It is tempting, therefore, to see her as far ahead of her time. However, there is an important difference. Fletcher conceptualized "Life among the Indians" as a literary work, not a scientific one—a distinction we would not make so definitively today.

During her first field trip Fletcher depended on her Indian companions to translate for her. She does not seem to have attempted to record much material in the Lakota or Omaha languages, with the exception of personal and place-names and song lyrics. This underscored her identity as an outside observer. Although her object was to grasp the Indian point of view, she had no notion of trying in any sense to become Indian herself. She remained firmly committed to civilization and to the importance of Indians achieving civilization through formal education. While she was clearly fascinated by tribal cultures she had no doubt that they must pass away in order for Indians to survive in the modern world. Thus she resists setting up tribal society as a literary foil to expose the problems of modern American life.

"Life among the Indians" portrays Fletcher grappling with what she would later characterize as the "perplexities" of field research: "There is the difficulty of adjusting one's own mental attitude, of preventing one's own mental atmosphere from deflecting and distorting the image of the Indian's thought. . . . Explications of his beliefs, customs and practices have to be sought by indirect rather than by direct methods, have to be eliminated from a tangle of contradictions, and verified by the careful noting of the many little unconscious acts and sayings of the people, which let in a flood of light, revealing the Indian's mode of thought and disclosing its underlying ideas."[188] Quaint as the wording strikes us today, Fletcher's "perplexities" are shared by modern-day ethnographers. In her autobiographical narrative we can watch her as she first encounters and learns to meet the challenges of fieldwork. This is a remarkable account by a remarkable pioneer anthropologist. The manuscript has languished overlong in archival obscurity. Its publication at last brings Alice Fletcher's voice and an appreciation of her contribution to the development of the field to new generations of anthropologists, both as inspiration and as a cautionary tale.

A Note on the Editing

"Life among the Indians" is written in ink on lined paper, eight x fourteen inches. Since Fletcher's intention was to publish the two parts separately, the pages of part 1 are numbered 1–157 and part 2, 1–148; the chapters in part 1 are numbered 1–14 and in part 2, 1–12. For publication here we have renumbered the chapters 1–26. Most of the manuscript is written in the hand of a copyist, although the prologue, half of chapter 9, and chapters 14 and 24–26 are entirely in Fletcher's hand. Throughout the manuscript are frequent corrections, editorial changes, and additions by Fletcher. Our goal is to present the manuscript faithfully while preserving historical and ethnographic detail. In her editing for publication Fletcher occasionally struck out material that we considered significant; these phrases and sentences have been restored to the text in square brackets. Punctuation, spelling errors, and the occasional obvious slip of the pen have been corrected silently. Footnotes added by Fletcher are printed at the bottom of the page, with our editorial additions in square brackets; our editorial notes appear at the end of the book.

Acknowledgments

The project to publish Fletcher's "Life among the Indians" began in the late 1960s, when Scherer was employed in the National Anthropological Archives and DeMallie worked there on summer internships. We had the privilege of working under the supervision of archivist Margaret C. Blaker, a rigorous professional who taught us to appreciate archives and how to use them effectively. This book has taken far longer to see publication than either of the editors had expected, and they have accumulated a large number of debts to many individuals and institutions. These are best expressed by the editors individually.

Joanna C. Scherer's Acknowledgments

It was during my tenure in the National Anthropological Archives (December 1966–1970) that I became interested in Fletcher's "Life among the Indians" and began transcribing the handwritten manuscript as time allowed. Using a manual typewriter, the transcription took me years to complete (during which time I raised three daughters and worked as illustrations researcher on fourteen volumes of the Smithsonian's *Handbook of North American Indians*, among other things). Once I retired from the *Handbook* project in 2006 I began to finalize the Fletcher manuscript and to draft an introduction. From day one Raymond J. DeMallie had taken a keen interest in the project, read every transcribed page, and kept me going when my energy lagged. He edited and made additions to the introduction and wrote the majority of the endnotes for the Fletcher manuscript. The project has been in every sense a collaborative effort.

During the research in preparation for writing the introduction, archivists, librarians, and dedicated researchers have made my work far easier than I imagined it would be. I would like to thank the staff of the National Anthropological Archives for providing me with much of the original source material for this project. Mary Frances (Morrow) Ronan, archivist, National Archives and Records Administration, fielded many queries relating to the Bureau of Indian Affairs records. Barbara Landis, Carlisle Indian School biographer, helped search through the Carlisle Indian papers, now at the Cumberland County Historical Society, to identify the Sioux student Fletcher visited on her first field trip. At Hampton University, Donzella Maupin, assistant to the archivist, was helpful during my research visit.

I am also grateful for the generosity of many scholars for help on specific subjects. The research of Nicole Tonkovich (University of California, San Diego, Department of Literature) concerning the years Fletcher spent on the Nez Perce Reservation meshed, but did not overlap, with my work on Fletcher among the Sioux and Omahas. We shared transcribed correspondence between Fletcher and Putnam that benefited both of our projects. Francis Flavin (research historian, Office of Federal Acknowledgment, Assistant Secretary—Indian Affairs), provided assistance on a number of historical points. Curtis M. Hinsley (Northern Arizona University, Department of Comparative Cultural Studies) kindly shared his talk from the American Anthropological Association Annual Meeting in 2009, "Frank Hamilton Cushing." Our good friend and colleague Karen Blu (retired professor of anthropology, New York University), gave invaluable help during a research trip to Princeton.

We are indebted to my husband, Noel P. Elliott, for the many hours he spent enhancing Fletcher's field sketches. They have faded with time, bled through the paper, and bear stains from rusty paper clips but are primary evidence of the visual subjects that caught Fletcher's attention during her first fieldwork.

I have saved for last a note of my appreciation to the research assistants who contributed to this project, many of whom were interns working at the Smithsonian for a semester. They are listed with dates of participation and, if applicable, the university with which they were associated. To each one I say thanks for your help. I couldn't have done it without you.

Bev Byrne—May 1998
Roy Wortman—June 1998
Monika Carothers—1998-2000
Rebecca Bloom—October 1998-April 1999
Marie Wisecup, Mary Baldwin College—Summer-Fall 2004
Julianna La Bruto, Smith College—Fall 2005
Brieanne Waltnam, George Washington University—Fall 2005-Spring 2006
Alex Antram, George Mason University—Spring 2006
Helen Lapedes, George Washington University—Summer-Fall 2006
Sarah Montana Hodge—December 2006-June 2007
Hannah Maier, University of Michigan—Summer 2007

Rebecca Simon, Pennsylvania State University—August 2007–April
   2008
Mary Ecker, George Washington University—Summer–Fall 2007
John Ulrich, researcher/Harvard University—2008–10
Erin Gorman, Wittenberg University—Spring 2008
Michaela Haber, Goucher College—Summer 2008
Abigail Xerxa, University of California, Davis—Fall 2008
Justine Benanty, George Washington University—Spring 2009
Emma LeClerc, Ithaca College—Spring 2009
Savannah Fetteroff, Columbia University—Summer 2009
Ceilidh Galloway-Kane, Smith College—Fall 2009
Madeline Johnson, George Washington University—Fall 2009
Kaden Triffilio, George Washington University—Spring 2010
Mattie Wong, American University—Spring 2010
Kelin Flanagan—Summer–Fall 2010
Alicia O'Brien, George Washington University—Fall 2010
Kayleigh Stack—Spring–Summer 2011
Erin Beasley, George Washington University—Spring 2012
Amy Kelch, New York University—Summer 2012
Zara Browne—Spring 2013

Raymond J. DeMallie's Acknowledgments

My interest in Fletcher began in 1966 when I was the recipient of a National
Science Foundation Summer Undergraduate Research Participation grant
in the Office of Anthropology at the National Museum of Natural History,
Smithsonian Institution. At that time Rachel Penner, assistant to Margaret C. Blaker, the departmental archivist, was completing arrangement of
the Fletcher–La Flesche collection. Rachel's enthusiasm for the collection
was contagious. The notebooks documenting Fletcher's fieldwork among
the Sioux, with their delicate pencil sketches, especially captured my imag-
ination. In subsequent summers as a student and during the academic
year 1971–72 as a postdoctoral fellow, I continued to work with manu-
scripts and photographs in the archives, alongside Joanna C. Scherer. Our
collaboration dates back to 1967.

   It is therefore a pleasure to express my indebtedness to the Smithsonian Institution for the financial support that helped me to transform my youthful interest in American Indians into a profession as a historically minded anthropologist. Margaret C. Blaker played a major role in my education, through instruction and example as well as generous support of many kinds.

I am grateful to linguists Robert L. Rankin, John Koontz, and Kathleen Shea for retranscribing and translating Fletcher's rendering of words in the Omaha language.

Thanks are also due to the staff of the American Indian Studies Research Institute at Indiana University and especially to our computer technician, Travis Myers, for his help finalizing the book for publication.

Finally, we wish to express our gratitude to Marshall Goldberg, husband of the late Marjorie Abramovitz, for financial assistance that allowed this work to be published.

Life among the Indians

By Alice Cunningham Fletcher

Foreword

Francis La Flesche

For some time Miss Fletcher had been studying archaeology and ethnology under the instruction of Prof. F. W. Putnam, Curator of the Peabody Museum of Harvard, Cambridge, Mass. There was no lack of interest for Miss Fletcher in either of these studies but as her work progressed she became more and more inclined toward her ethnological work. Then there came a time when she made up her mind to carry on that study in earnest and to begin her work among the North American Indians. She had already taken many notes from books written by travelers and by men who had been engaged in that particular study, but the idea of compiling a book from the publications of other writers did not appeal to her. She believed that the most satisfactory way of studying the Indians was by personal contact and observation. She made known to Prof. Putnam her determination to go to the homes of the Indians to study their tribal and home life in all their phases. From the very start the Professor tried to discourage her by picturing to her the crudity of the savage life, the hardships and the privations she would have to undergo. Other friends offered their kindly protests against her taking such a course but none of them could persuade her to turn aside from the path she had already marked out for herself.

The departure from Cambridge and the separation from her fellow workers at the museum, Miss Fletcher seldom mentioned but she often spoke of those friends with tender affection.

According to a journal kept by Miss Fletcher, she arrived in the city of Omaha in the early part of September 1881, where she visited "Bright Eyes" and her husband Mr. T. H. Tibbles. Knowing that the lady was on her way to visit the Indians of northern Nebraska and Dakota for the purpose of studying Indian life, the two offered to accompany her.

Before beginning her travel to the western country, Miss Fletcher wisely obtained the following letters of introduction from the Secretary of the Interior and from the Secretary of War:

Department of the Interior,
Washington September 3rd, 1881.
To Indian Agents.

Miss A.C. Fletcher visits the region of the Upper Missouri in the interest of science, with a view to obtaining certain facts bearing upon points of Ethnological interest. I recommend her to the courtesy of the officers of this Department and request that she may receive such facilities as can be properly granted without detriment to the service, or cost to the United States.
Respectfully,
S. J. Kirkwood,
Secretary.

War Department
Washington City
August 12th, 1881
To Officers of the United States Army.

This will introduce to you Miss Alice C. Fletcher, of New York, who intends spending some time in the region of the Upper Missouri, with the view of studying the character and mode of life of Indian women.

Officers of the Army within whose commands she may happen to come will extend to her proper courtesies, and render such aid and assistance as she may require, not inconsistent with the interests of the military service.
H. T. Crosby,
Chief Clerk,
For the Secretary of War, in his absence.

Miss Fletcher presented to General Crook, the Commandant at Fort Omaha, the letter of the Secretary of War. Gen. Crook became interested in Miss Fletcher's work and he arranged to have her and her companions carried as far as the Omaha Indian reservation, a distance of about eighty miles.

On the morning of the 16th of the month, in rain and mud, the three began their journey northward, following an old trail that lay along the western banks and bluffs of the Missouri River, a trail that was used by the Omaha and Otoe Indians, long before the country was settled by white people.

The first stop made by the travelers was at a little place called Fort Calhoun. This locality is known to this day by the Omahas as "The land where Te-soń lies buried." Te-soń was one of the old Omaha chiefs.[1] At a time when the Omahas happened to be in this part of their country the chief died and they buried him on the top of a hill among the bluffs.

At seven o'clock in the evening of the 17th day of the month Miss Fletcher and her companions came to the little town of Tekama where they stopped for the night. [Fig. 2] About three miles east of the town is a spot called by the Omahas, "The place where Village-maker's camp was attacked." In December 1846 the Omahas were camped in the woods along the banks of the Missouri River. Village-maker was the only chief in the camp, the rest of them had gone with most of the men toward the west to hunt buffalo. One morning the camp was attacked by the Yankton and Santee Sioux and many men, women and children were killed. At the time Miss Fletcher passed through this place she did not know this bit of Omaha history but in later years she recorded it in her book on "The Omaha Tribe."

At 1:15 on the afternoon of the 18th day of September 1881 Miss Fletcher and her companions entered the Omaha reservation. This Reservation was established by a solemn treaty between the United States and the Omaha tribe in 1854. At that time the Omahas were living in a village about five miles south of the present site of Omaha City. In 1855, the tribe removed to this reservation where they have since lived to the present time. The three travelers remained on the Omaha Reservation for two days. During this short stay Miss Fletcher met many of the members of

Fig. 2. "1881, Sept. 17, 11 AM. Blair, Neb." "Blair is a thrifty little town, two principal streets cross each other at right angles. One going over the R.R. track &
branching off on either side stretching into the farms beyond. The well built
street lying parallel to the R.R. mostly two stories & one story houses with flam-
ing signs" (Fletcher, 1881 Notebook 1, 17). The town of Tekamah, where they
stopped for the night on September 17, was just north of Blair. Original field
sketch (p. 16) enhanced. Smithsonian Institution, National Anthropological
Archives (ms. 4558).

this tribe and made friends with a number of the prominent men and
women. She was quick to observe their peculiar dress and manners, their
mode of living and their jovial spirit, and she even began to write their
language. She was tempted to remain among them and to begin her work
there, but she reluctantly prepared for her journey to the Ponca and the
various Sioux tribes and to carry out her original plan.

On the morning of the 21st of September 1881, the travelers continued
the journey, in a conveyance of their own, toward the Santee Reservation
in Northern Nebraska. They were driving along the Omaha creek, which
runs through both the Omaha and the Winnebago reservations, when
they were overtaken by Wajepa, one of the prominent men of the Omaha

tribe, who joined them and accompanied them throughout the journey. [Fig. 3] As they were passing through the ancient Omaha village site, about 18 miles north of the Omaha agency, Wajepa pointed out the place with the remark, "Here I was born." Bright Eyes' father, a cousin of Wajepa, was also born there. On May 12, 1811, John Bradbury, an English botanist, visited this old Omaha village when it was still occupied by the people, as he was traveling up the Missouri River to pursue his botanical studies.[2] The travelers stopped at this place for dinner and to rest the horses. To their right they could see the little hill that was named by the Omaha "The Tiny Graves," because on the top of the hill were buried many of the Omaha children who died in an epidemic. Miss Fletcher made a sketch of the place. [Fig. 4] They pushed on and in the evening camped for the night at a place they called "Mosquito Camp." [Fig. 5] It was the first time Miss Fletcher camped out, a strange experience for her.

On the morning of September 22, 1881, at about eight o'clock the travelers broke camp and again moved northward. (It was on this day that I happened to come home from Washington to my father's house on some business. The first thing he said to me was, "Your sister has gone up to the Sioux with a white woman. They went yesterday and you have just missed them by a day. Your sister's friend is a remarkable woman; in thought and expression, she is more like a man than a woman.") They plodded on over the muddy road and came to a little town called Jackson. To the Omahas the place was known as "The Cut River Bluff," which means that at this place the Missouri River cut over its banks and made a new channel. Up to this place the travelers were never out of sight of the river but now they turn almost directly west to make a cut across the great bend of the river. They pushed on through rain and mud and at 1:30 arrived at a little town called "Ponca City." Wajepa explained that the land on which this town is located was at one time the home of the Iowa Indians, and that here these Indians planted corn, and the place was called "The Iowa Farms." Here the plucky little woman was saddened by the news of President Garfield's death. The party camped among the trees for the night. Miss Fletcher made sketches of the tent and the trees. [Fig. 6]

Friday, September 23, 1881. Miss Fletcher was the first to rise in the morning and was greeted by "a glowing sky." As all were enjoying break-

Wajapa Omaha Tribe
Oct. 5, 1881.

Fig. 3. "Wajapa, Omaha Tribe, Oct. 5, 1881." "I sketched Wajapa's profile. When I said I was going to, he sprang up & said in his hearty, impulsive loud voice, 'I will go & wash my face', I laughed thinking it a joke but it was not, he returned & his face glossy his hair combed & shining & sat down by me. That was queer to experience" (Fletcher, 1881 Notebook 1, 114). Wajapa's Omaha name was *Wajé·pʰa* 'Herald'; his English name was Ezra Freemont. Original field sketch (p. 110) enhanced. Smithsonian Institution, National Anthropological Archives (ms. 4558).

Fig. 4. "Hill of the Graves—Me-ha-pach-he." September 21, 1881. "On the right the site of an old Omaha village—mud lodges built about a circle high hill on left, the place where the dead were buried" (Fletcher, 1881 Notebook 1, 22). La Flesche's list identifies the place as Homer, Nebraska. The Omaha name is *Míxe ppahé* 'Cemetery Hill'. Original field sketch (p. 22) enhanced. Smithsonian Institution, National Anthropological Archives (ms. 4558).

fast she suddenly burst out with a hearty laugh and was later obliged to explain that it was the thought of the contrast between the camp life and the city life she was accustomed to from childhood that provoked the laugh. They hitched up and began the day's journey but had to wait for a time in the little town on account of threatening storms. While waiting the members of the party gave to each other new names in a spirit of fun, and Wajepa gave to Miss Fletcher the Omaha name, Ma´-she-ha-the, which means, The motion of the Eagle as he sweeps high in the air.[3] The name was one of the sacred names belonging to the old man's family and gens.

At 8:45 they again started and, as usual, the monotony of travel was relieved by discussions of literature, the roadless country, the onward march of civilization, by the three English-speaking members, and Indian folklore and traditions by Wajepa, whose knowledge of English did not go beyond "watermelon." The country over which they traveled this day is described

Fig. 5. "Oo-hay-a-ta, Sept. 21, 1881. Wednesday night." "We did not camp on the old Winnebago ground because Mr. T[ibbles] who had rode on ahead to find a place, saw that under the mats it was full of fleas. A mile or so beyond, we stopped at a clump of trees. Here we camp—Mosquito Camp—Susette calls it. The fire was built—supper of bacon and coffee. The hammock was slung. Mr. and Mrs. T. slept on the ground at my head, Wajapa beside the fire. Mosquitoes were many to the inch. Slept with our hats over our heads but about midnight we all wakened. Mr. T. said he had not slept at all. S. had, so had I. Mr. T. built two fires. There was no wind—one tall fire near us, one low one further away. The smoke drove out the mosquitoes and we slept till dawn" (Fletcher, 1881 Notebook 1, 26–27). According to La Flesche this was the first night that Fletcher camped out in Nebraska. On La Flesche's listing he translates Oo-hay-a-ta as 'ford'. The Omaha name is apparently *Uhé·a·tʰq·tʰe* 'Bridge Creek'. Original field sketch (p. 35) enhanced. Smithsonian Institution, National Anthropological Archives (ms. 4558).

Fig. 6. "Camp in Ash Grove on bank of creek Tanda-Hoi-a—(Smells bad) Ponca
City, Neb. Sept. 22." "Reach Ponca city at 1.30. Turn into Ash Grove—Wajapa
pitches tent, lights fire. . . . Dry myself by the fire, determine to camp out & take
the luck of camp life. Conclude to think of going direct to Spotted Tail agency
from Santee. To camp here all night & push on early in the a.m." (Fletcher, 1881
Notebook 1, 31–32). The Omaha name may be *Ttɑ̨de xwiⁿ* 'soil stinks'. Original
field sketch (p. 32) enhanced. Smithsonian Institution, National Anthropological
Archives (ms. 4558).

by Miss Fletcher as "desolation, no trees, only yellow, billowy land, miles and miles, and miles again; seemed to have no beginning or end, to come from no where to go no whither." Now and then they pass the wreck of an abandoned home with "gapping windows," the owners discouraged perhaps by nostalgia. In the afternoon the weary travelers came to Bow creek, a stream called by the Omahas Ta´-wa-ne, Village Creek, because it was on this creek their village was located many decades ago.[4] The beauty of the little stream with trees on its banks delighted Ma´-she-ha-the (Miss Fletcher), after the drive over "miles and miles" of treeless land. Here they camped and in the evening Wajepa spoke of the life of the Omaha when they lived on the Ta´-wa-ne and of the stories that came down from them, of his travel to the Indian Territory, and of the threatened removal of the tribe to the "Hot Country" (Indian Territory) by the government. Their rest was disturbed by a heavy thunderstorm in the night. [Fig. 7]

In the morning, September 24, 1881, they went on again. At 5:30 or 6 o'clock the travelers arrived at a place called by the Omaha, "The Hidden Grove," where they camped for the night. The talk about the camp was serious. The future struggles of the Indians. It was a wakeful night for the brave lady for the air was cold, the dew heavy and the ground hard.

September 25, 1881. After a breakfast of corned beef and coffee, and some struggle with a balky horse, followed by a series of mishaps the travelers pushed on again. As they moved over hills and gullies Wajepa pointed out to Ma´-she-ha-the (Miss Fletcher) a spot along the banks of a creek where, when he was a little boy, the Omahas had camped. A great rain storm came in the night and overflowed the creek, carried away many of their belongings beside two little girls. They passed over sand hills which the lady called "desolation let loose," then suddenly they came in sight of the bluffs of the Missouri River. They met a wagon load of Indians who tried to talk to Wajepa but could not make him understand, they were Santee Sioux. The government and mission buildings ahead was a welcome sight to all and in particular to Miss Fletcher. She speaks of the Santee Sioux as "a fine looking race of men," in describing the appearance of the men and women.

The party remained at the Santee Mission for about four days during which they witnessed the work of the teachers and their Indian scholars.

Fig. 7. "Camp Dta-wa-ne (Village Creek) white man [named it] Big Bow. Sept.
23." "Thought to stop on a level just beyond the bridge but the mosquitoes were
dense, pushed on past a log house where 'a widder woman lived', to another
space when Mr. T. said he 'would camp anyhow'. . . . The fire was started, the
horses lariated just over the bridge on the other side of the stream where the
pasture was fine. A supper of fried potatoes, hardboiled eggs & black coffee &
biscuit partaken of with a relish made us feel fine. The wagon had been drawn
up near the fence and the tent spread over it & the intervening space made available by putting poles from the wagon to the top board, we had a comfortable,
low, studded bedroom, the harness, dishes &c. were packed under the wagon &
while supper was preparing I made my bed & combed & braided my hair.
Wajapa said we would have rain" (Fletcher, 1881 Notebook 1, 54–56). The
Omaha name is Ttą́·wą nį 'Village Creek'. Original field sketch (p. 53) enhanced.
Smithsonian Institution, National Anthropological Archives (ms. 4558).

Miss Fletcher was much impressed with the work being done by Doctor
and Mrs. Riggs among the Santee Sioux.

On the morning of September 30, 1881, the travelers bade goodbye to
their hosts and resumed their journey. They slowly moved over the muddy
road along the Missouri River, toward the Ponca Reservation. Miss Fletcher
and "Bright Eyes" got out of the wagon and walked when they came to

steep hills in order to save the strength of the horses. In the afternoon they arrived at the Niobrara River and camped along the eastern bank opposite the Ponca agency and the Indian village. [Fig. 8] The evening sky was perfectly clear and as the travelers sat in the open air talking of Indian life, Wajepa pointed to the group of stars commonly called by the whites "Great Dipper" and told Miss Fletcher that his people spoke of it as Wa´ba-ha (travois), a frame for carrying the sick or the wounded. The stars that formed the handle of the dipper, he said, were the three horses that dragged the Wa´baha, that the cup was the frame in which sat the wounded propped up with robes and pillows.[5] He also pointed out a perfect circle of stars (Corona Borealis) which he said was called Hu´-thu-ga, the Camp Circle.[6]

October 1, 1881. Our brave little woman writes in her journal. Rose early. Saw the sun rise. I finished my article on Indian women for the Women's Congress. Buffalo-chip and friend came over. Will go with us. We were just stepping into the boat to go to Standing Bear's when Wajepa called out, "Here come the Poncas." So they did, in wagons, ox carts and horseback, galloping along the bank. Then she gives a description of the gay costumes of the men, women and children, and their ornaments, and remarks, parenthetically: The women had the seam of the hair painted red. Years later, in the course of her study of Indian customs, she learned that this little red line symbolizes the path of the sun that arches over the earth from east to west, and also life eternal.

This little body of men and women who with their children hastened in this impetuous fashion to welcome their visitors were a part of the people of the Ponca tribe who, in the year 1877, were dispossessed of their lands and forcibly removed to the Indian Territory. Standing Bear and his followers could not endure the indignity or to live under restraint so they broke away from the tribe, defying governmental authority and made for their old home at the mouth of the Niobrara. They were arrested and they appealed to the court. The Judge decided that, "no rightful authority exists for removing by force any of the prisoners to the Indian Territory" and ordered their release. The prisoners then resumed their journey unmolested to their old home.

After the greetings the little Ponca tribe conducted their visitors to the village, fording the two swift channels with considerable excitement. Hav-

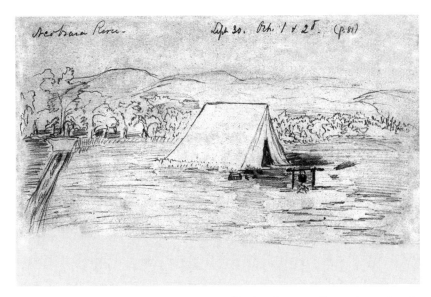

Fig. 8. "Niobrara River, Sept. 30, Oct. 1 & 2ᵈ" After the council meeting at Standing Bear's encampment on October 1, Fletcher and her traveling companions made a difficult journey over the Niobrara River back to their camp to find it in flames. Everything burned except their tent. Original field sketch (Fletcher, 1881 Notebook 1, 81) enhanced. Smithsonian Institution, National Anthropological Archives (ms. 4558).

ing safely reached the opposite shore, the procession moved on to Standing Bear's tent where all the afternoon the Poncas and their guests discussed tribal affairs and the future welfare of the people. [Figs. 9, 10, and 11] Miss Fletcher and her companions got back to their camp just in time to save their tent from destruction by fire.

The morning of October 2, 1881, was drizzling but the travelers broke camp, got into their wagon and made their way toward the Rosebud reservation over a rough and muddy road, following the Niobrara River. The number of the party had increased to six, Buffalo-chip and his wife having been invited to go along. [Fig. 12]

Fig. 9. "Standing Bear's Tent. Oct. 1, 1881." "Went to Standing Bear's tent—see picture—the stove stood in the middle, beds at the left of entrance, trunks, bags of grain at the back edge, rocking and two chairs" (Fletcher, 1881 Notebook 1, 86). Standing Bear was the leading Ponca chief. Original field sketch (p. 81). Smithsonian Institution, National Anthropological Archives (ms. 4558).

Fig. 10. Council on the Ponca Reservation, October 1. "After dinner a council held. Standing Bear in chair—3 chairs at his left, Mr. T. [Thomas Henry Tibbles] S. [Susette La Flesche] & I. First Buffalo-chip arose—shook hands, Mr. T. S. & me & spoke—Each speaker shook hands with us. Mr. T shook hands with all before he spoke, I spoke after the general talk. After my speech, which S. interpreted, we shook hands all around & bade goodbye" (Fletcher, 1881 Notebook 1, 86–93). Her notebook reports the substance of speeches by Buffalo-chip, Standing Bear, Old Smoke, Brave Heart, and Jack Paniska (see Fletcher, *Camping with the Sioux*). Original field sketch (p. 92) enhanced. Smithsonian Institution, National Anthropological Archives (ms. 4558).

Fig. 11. "Yellow Horse Tent." October 1, 1881. Yellow Horse, a Ponca, was a member of Standing Bear's band (Fletcher and La Flesche, *Omaha Tribe*, 56). The date is from La Flesche's list of sketches. Original field sketch (Fletcher, 1881 Notebook 1, 82) enhanced. Smithsonian Institution, National Anthropological Archives (ms. 4558).

Fig. 12. "Ga-haege-pah-he Creek (Ponca). Where they picked out chiefs. Sunday Oct. 2, 1881, 2:30 P.M." The Omaha name is *Gahí·ge·ppahé* 'Hill of the Chiefs'. Original field sketch (Fletcher, 1881 Notebook 1, 97) enhanced. Smithsonian Institution, National Anthropological Archives (ms. 4558).

Prologue

The sketches contained in this volume are taken from the field notebooks of the writer and set forth actual scenes and incidents that were always recorded at the time of happening, although for the purposes of grouping in the following chapters no attempt has been made to preserve the actual chronological order. The conversations are not fanciful; many of them, and all of them relating to the relations between the Indians and the White men, are copied literally from notes taken as the men talked. The statements made by the Indians can be substantiated by other evidence. It is only just to the people herein described to make this explanation as the Indian's point of view and his home life are little known to members of our own race.

It is not within the purpose of these books to show the difficulties which beset the Indian agent and the general administration of Indian affairs. How great and manifold these are cannot be appreciated unless one has followed their growth and manifestation during the colonial period and since our existence as a nation. Precedents and regulations have come about by an accumulation of makeshifts, born of passing exigencies in the development of the country, and these are frequently stumbling blocks in the path of progress and delay and impede the practical application of beneficial legislation.

A study of Indian sociology and customs reveals that the aborigines of America possess traits of character worthy of our respect. Today, in spite of many debasing influences which have encompassed them, they still claim of us the right of being regarded and treated as men. The following glimpses of Indian life as it exists in thousands of Indian homes may help toward a better understanding between the two races and show that there is something to forgive and to admire in both peoples.

Peabody Museum of American Archaeology and Ethnology
Cambridge, Mass.
Feb. 15, 1887.

PART ONE

Camping with the Sioux

ONE

Over the Border

Precisely at 9 A.M. by the hotel clock in one of the towns on the upper Missouri the sleek mules drew up under the dripping trees, and the wagon stood waiting for an adventure.[1] The rain poured as we piled bundles and bags, blankets and pillows, kettles and boxes, and all the needed camp outfit in and around the capacious vehicle. The driver, a tall, clean, pleasant man, was handy from his frontier experience, but no amount of skill could obviate the unmistakable peddler look of the carriage. The driver lifted me bodily until I could catch at the step and swing into the vehicle; then he closed the door with a clamp, leaving me in a dull, yellow gloom, for little light came through the oiled and closely fastened curtains. Perched high on bundles I struggled for equilibrium as we dipped and plunged along the muddy roads. It was needful to stop at the store to gather up the full supply of provisions. All the canned articles were tightly boxed, but the sugar and flour were in large paper packages, and had to be stowed under the boot, and take the chance of turning to syrup and paste. Once more the mules responded to the snap of the lash, and we were off to try life among the Indians.

We passed the fairgrounds just outside the town. There lay the track, now gullied with rivulets over which a woman had ridden ten miles in twenty minutes, leaping from one tired horse to a fresh one in order to make her time and distance. Soaking desolation possessed the place and was reflected on the faces of the petty hucksters who cowered in the corner of their shanties when the least rain fell and hardly looked at us as we dashed along through the blinding rain, throwing mud and water far out on either side of the road.

A score or so of miles on our line of travel lay all that remained of a projected town. A railroad had been prophesied, vantage points along the route selected, town lots laid out, and in this instance, a hotel built and newspaper started, but the railroad took another turn and the town became a phantom. We had hoped to reach this place early in the day and find there shelter and refreshment. Toward noon I peered around the edges of the curtains, but only miles on miles of early summer verdure were to be seen. Late in the afternoon three houses were discerned. These were the town.[2] On a paper nailed to the hotel door was scrawled, "Closed up." Nearby was a sort of store, and every lower pane of the window framed the face of a towheaded child. Of the few loungers at the store none were able to give us entertainment nor were our offers to camp in the empty hotel accepted. In the midst of the questioning a long man swung up toward us, the rain swashing around the rim of his broad hat, and without any particular interest expressed in his face or tone, he remarked, "Miss Jones, a mile an' half on the road, takes travelers—there's a barn for animals."[3]

Thanking our benefactor, we started on in the chilling rain, up the steep hills. On the summit we could see the bluffs on the other side of the Missouri, blue and hazy in the storm, and the river winding like a broad, leaden band among the wooded patches and stretches of bottomlands. On we went, one mile, two miles, two miles and a half, and still not a house to be seen. Another mile and a ploughed field came in sight, then an orchard, and beyond at a distance back from the road stood a good-sized house with large outbuildings. We turned toward the haven, the mules plucked up fresh courage as they waded to their fetlocks in the oozy muddy grass, and the coach bent and bowed like an old-time gallant saluting his lady. We stopped at the trim picket fence, beyond which honeysuckles and roses were in full bloom and crystalled by the rain. The tap at the door was answered by a tall woman dressed in black. She wore her gray hair banded over the ears and her silver-bowed spectacles resting across the top of her head. Her face was comely, but firm, and she scanned us steadily from her deep-set eyes as we asked hospitality. This was granted, and we entered through the door into the sitting room, with its three rocking chairs, red-covered divan, tall bureau, and looking glass flanked on either side by a pyramid of books. Shutting the door after us our hostess called a man to "come and put up a heating stove." While this was in process and the fire kindled, I took from the right-hand book pyramid *Maxims of Worth and Wealth*, and was edified thereby.[4]

The hostess soon returned, bringing a wooden bowl of apples, and seating herself beside me began paring the fruit, the peel curling in long ribbons from her dexterous fingers while questions fell as rapidly from her lips. Where did I come from? Had I been there long? Where was I going? What was my business? A pause followed my answer. Then came slowly the query, "What is ethnology?" As I struggled to give the desired definition, she interrupted, "Just tell me, how are you going to work?"

After supper the old lady gossiped of her early days and pioneer life, of her thrifty sons and daughters, of the "old man's death," and how since then she had "kinder kep things goin'!" Looking back over her life, she concluded there was more "stir in the West," and she would stay there; the East was "too old-fashioned" for her. She had much to say of the land speculators who had ruined the region about her farm. She had noticed that it took three sets of settlers before the lands were finally held. The first-comers never had money enough to open a paying farm and keep the family meanwhile. "The Indians, poor creatures, they've had a hard time; folks don't think 'em humans, rather kill 'em than not, and cheatin' 'em's all right, 'cause they don't know nothing 'bout money. My old man and me, we've stood by the Indians many a time and helped 'em and I never found 'em ugly. I reckon they've got sense and hearts too!"

As I stood ready to leave, my hostess handed me a pencil and a bit of paper, "I want you to write your name so I shant forget it. One of these days you'll be writing sunthin' and when I see it, I'll say, 'I know her, she stopped at my home!' Our last schoolteacher, she came from Maine. She meant to make a name for herself, so she went west to write for the newspapers and teach. She's gone to Idaho."

Days of sunshine followed the storm and the journey sped forward. As we neared the vicinity of a railroad, actual or prospective, we came upon towns correspondingly stable. The single street was lined with farm wagons grouped before the stores, with their square board fronts. A schoolhouse formed part of the town equipment, and the church, with its "index finger pointing upward," told of the desire for order and morality. We made a halt one day in a town that proved to be a county seat. The court was in session and knots of men were gathered in the street discussing matters. The long shadows of the setting sun fell lengthwise through the little thoroughfare as I entered a store and found myself in the midst of a crowd being addressed by a square-built, red-haired man. He stood with one hand plunged in his pocket and brought the other down on the counter, making the dust fly as he shouted, "Who votes, I'd like to know; white men or Injuns? He'll find out next 'lection, I tell ye, whether it pays to decide in favor of an Injun!"

"That's so!" chimed in a man, his sunburnt face framed in a large straw hat well tipped back. "That's so, Mike; this's the white man's country and it's bound to stay so, too."

"He'd no business deciding on an Injun, nohow. What's Injuns got to do with law? Nothing, I reckon," said a third lounger.

"Just wait till next 'lection. That judge 'll get left, you bet!" iterated the first speaker.

On a barrel sat a tall man whittling out a little spade. Lifting his blue eyes and genial face, he said, "The judge was square. The mare belonged to the Injun, and he'd a right to take his property. He might have taken the colt, too, you know. I'll bet you fellers would not have left the colt!"

"I'd paid for the mare, and had her a year, and the colt was mine anyhow," said the first speaker.

"Stolen property all the same!" replied the whittler.

"I tell ye, the Injun stole the mare too, going into my stable and taking her off. He stole her from me, I tell ye."

"Look here, Mike, you'd have done the same thing and done right too. A man's property is his property wherever it is."

"You talk as if an Injun was a white man. He ain't and never will be. He's a born thief and liar, and we don't want no courts bothering about him, or judges deciding for him; and we won't neither," said a new speaker.

"The judge was square," repeated the whittler, "and Injuns are men, like the rest of us, good and bad!"

"Wait till 'lection, you see who's men and who isn't."

Towns and railroads were soon left behind, and the rolling prairies laid down as "a desert" in old geographies were spread out before us. Here and there in the midst of a breaking stood a queer box-like structure, having a square and an oblong opening. These were the regulation houses, "with a window and door," and were serving to hold for their owners certain tracts of land.[5]

Camping one evening where several houses were within the range of vision, the cackle of hens suggested eggs, so I made my way to a trim cabin, its four-paned window covered by a square of white cotton, ironed in plaits.[6] In the open door stood a tidy little woman, with a tidy little girl who hid her face from me in the folds of her mother's dress. After I had completed my purchase the woman detained me to tell of the late excitement thereabout, how a band of horse thieves had been chased by amateur soldiers, and the men had "hid in that shed just over there" and were fired on, and she and her neighbors had "just shook" as the bullets flew.[7] But the thieves were caught, "least-ways the most of 'em," and she "did hope honest people might be let live in peace."

As I started back to the wagon she walked along with me, the little girl still clinging closely to her mother. "So lonesome indoors, my man's at Randall. Ever been to Randall? I was once. Nigger soldiers there. I saw 'em on parade and they looked just as pretty as a picket fence!"[8]

As we drove westward the houses became more and more scattered and primitive. At intervals along the road stood small, rude boxes raised on poles about five feet high and canted so as to shed the rain. These served as local post offices. The driver of the weekly stage left his mail here or took up any letters dropped in the boxes. It was a wonder where the letters came from, or went to, for not a house was to be seen in any direction, nor did we meet travelers while passing these queer picket guards of news. [Fig. 13]

One day we reined up before a log cabin where some bushy four-o'clocks kept each other company close to the chinked walls of the dwelling. The house boasted two rooms; the front door opened into an apartment, with walls covered by illustrated newspapers; to the left stood a high, plump bed with a white and red coverlet; to the right a low, homemade child's

Fig. 13. "Lone Post Office—No particular where—near Santee Res. Sketched en route while riding. Sept. 24, 1881." Original field sketch (Fletcher, 1881 Notebook 1, 58) enhanced. Smithsonian Institution, National Anthropological Archives (ms. 4558).

bed served as a lounge; two chairs, a chest of drawers, and a well-blackened stove comprised the furniture. The room beyond showed two ample beds and several chests. The kitchen was a shed still further on, where homemade stools and a table served for the family. Everything about the house betokened frugality. The tired-faced mother was neat in her dress and was evidently resting after having cleared away the dinner, enjoying a visit from a neighbor who lived twenty miles away. Six bare-legged children were clustered in the doorway, while the baby sat with wide-open eyes on the rough plank floor poking its chubby fingers in the ample cracks showing the earth below.[9]

The mother bade me take a seat and her visitor hailed my advent with delight. She was a young woman, full of zest and quite willing to ask and answer questions. I had interrupted a conversation about "cleansing the water." I ventured to ask what that meant.

"Ha, Ha!" she shouted in a cordial voice. "Don't you know what that is? I thought everybody knew that! Well, I suppose they don't do such things where you came from. Ma has often told me how awfully green she was when she first came west! Why it's making lye, and putting it in the water so we can wash with it."

Although I was grateful for the information, something about me made her add, "I dare say you'd find lots of inconvenience out here!"

"How do you like this place?" said the elder woman.

"Do you like it better than where you came from?" added the younger, before I had had a chance to reply.

It was a delicate question to answer looking in the faces of the two kindly women. "I miss the trees," I began.

"And the houses," suggested the elder.

"Well, no, I don't care so much for the houses," a little touch of home-sickness coming over me, "but the lack of trees and streams makes it seem desolate."

"So do I!" chimed in both women.

"I was awful lonesome at first," said the elder with a sad cadence in her voice.

"I've been here seven years," the younger interrupted, "and I told Jen yesterday we must have trees. I couldn't stand it any longer."

During the silence which followed I glanced out of the open door over the wide unbroken horizon. "Do you have prairie fires here?"

"Ha Ha!" shouted the younger. "Don't we—every spring and fall; they'd burn us out if we didn't fight 'em."

"Fight them?" I interrogated.

"Of course; don't you know how to make firebreaks? I suppose not," and then she proceeded to enlighten me.

"What wood do you burn?"

"We get it from the river," said the elder.

"How far?"

"Nigh twenty miles."

"Why don't you plant cottonwood trees?"

"We will soon, I hope. It takes so long to get wood."

"Long!" cried the younger woman. "Why one can go in the morning and get back in the afternoon. I don't call that long. Land! Think of what people have to do further west, fifty miles for wood, and burn corncobs and all sorts of stuff besides. Land! It isn't hard here!"

"Sam says he's thinking of going on further," said the elder. "The country is so thickly settled about this place."

In reply to the surprise on my face she added, "The herds run on folks' land and make trouble. Herding takes lots of land."

"Lots more money in it than farmin'," remarked the younger woman. Then turning to me she asked, "Are you going to locate beyond here?"

I shook my head.

"No! Well, what are you going to do then?"

"Study the Injuns!" she exclaimed, repeating my answer. "Land! What's there to study in them, I'd like to know. We want to keep clear of 'em, let alone study 'em. Jen says they're no good, anyhow!"

"I don't think they'd be so bad if they were treated right. Some of 'em's been treated awful, I know that," said the elder, a faint flush coming into her face.

"You're thinkin' of Lem Johnson's affair. You see that out here, near the reservation, lots of cattle get mixed up. Lem, he was rounding up and branding, and several Injuns came along and claimed some of the cattle and Lem got mad, but he dasn't do anything, there was too many of 'em. So he told them they'd better send the agent to see about it, but the Injuns didn't want to. They pointed out some cattle and said they were theirs and wanted them back. Some of Lem's boys came up, and one of the Injuns kept at it, wanting his cattle, talking about his farm and working. Lem, he got so mad with the lies the Injun was telling that he pulled out his revolver and shot him dead and all the boys, they fired too, and killed another Injun and wounded some more, and left 'em to get back as they could. Twasn't right, but you know, Injuns lie so, and no Injun ever works, so it was all a lie about his farm and cattle. Jen says it was."

"When I lived in Michigan, I saw Injuns working," began the elder.

"They're different out here," interrupted the younger woman.

Many miles of unbroken rolling prairie lay between us and the reservation lines. The dwellings of the settlers indicated the shiftiness of the occupants and there was ample opportunity for individual invention. [Figs. 14 and 15] The sod houses when covered with grass and flowers are very

Fig. 14. "Livingston Ranch, Oct. 7, 1881. 1:30 P.M." "Reached there [Livingston Ranch] at 1 P.M. B[uffalo]-c[hip] tried to shoot geese—failed. Women came & visited us. . . . We lost our way & at last were fortunate enough to hit on the only camping place for miles, by our own misfortune" (Fletcher, 1881 Notebook 1, 123). Original field sketch (p. 122) enhanced. Smithsonian Institution, National Anthropological Archives (ms. 4558).

picturesque. In general the family lived in one room. The bed, made by fastening two posts to the floor, fitting cross pieces to the wall, and laying slats across to hold the bedding, occupied one end of the room. The other contained the stove, table, stools, and utensils for cooking. In summer a shed attached to the house served as the kitchen. The dugouts were not so uncomfortable, and they presented advantages during the severe storms which sweep over the country, since they cannot be blown over. [Figs. 16 and 17]

It is difficult to fix any standard by which to judge such houses as lead the vanguard of civilization. Their rudeness and inconvenience are beyond the ken of anyone who has not felt their poverty of comfort, and yet they

Fig. 15. "Ma-choo-e-see-sa [illegible] Oct. 7, 7. P.M. Our prettiest camp. Boundless prairie, brilliant sky, full moon, varied colored grasses." "Went down the gulch to our tent & helped carry wood. When we reached this place the camp fire showed people camped, but the water was nowhere to be seen. Mr. T., B[uffalo]-c[hip] and W[ajapa] started, returned & started again, at last B[uffalo]-c[hip] hallooed & W[ajapa] returned on the gallop. 'Nee, nee, nee', he shouted so we camped. The full moon shone over the prairie. . . . It is the prettiest camp we have had. Miles on miles of prairie, behind a deep gulch, the banks, here & there broken, showing yellow clay. The tall cedars only showed their tops, here & there. An empty log house in the gulch, wood choppers" (Fletcher, 1881 Notebook 1, 123). Original field sketch (p. 124) enhanced. Smithsonian Institution, National Anthropological Archives (ms. 4558).

stand for much of labor, enterprise, and self-denial. Their inmates live mainly in the thought of the future. The present is a makeshift on the way thither; the little cabin glows with unseen proportions in the eyes of the settler, although it glooms in those of the traveler. In either case the cabin is not an ideal, but a necessity, transient in character. It is not so to the Indian. He sees little else. To him the frontier cabin, the frontier life, with

Fig. 16. "'Oo-te-ha-wa-the' Lonesome creek (our worst place full of badness). Oct. 8, 1881 1. P.M." "A hateful place, full of dead horses and cattle skeletons, torn apart by wolves, hides remaining. Big grasshoppers, bugs of all sorts, mosquitoes, vileness generally. Here, last winter some runaway soldiers killed the officers sent after them. Murder haunts the place. Here the Indians used to war, lurking in these gulches peeping over the top of the banks. 'Should have been fighting yet' W[ajapa] says, 'If the white man had not come'. Mrs. T. had a bundle of soldier's clothing in the gulch back of our last camp—rotten—belongs to some of the murdered men. Here women have been killed. We all vote the place 'Pe-az-cha'. Men call it 'Rock Spring'. Lots of cans from meat & potatoes. Wajapa rode off because he heard voices, could find no one. The Indians full of dire stories. The horses even dislike the place" (Fletcher, 1881 Notebook 1, 127). The Omaha name is *Útʰi·ha·waðe* 'Makes Lonesome'. Original field sketch (p. 126) enhanced. Smithsonian Institution, National Anthropological Archives (ms. 4558).

its strange outbursts of energy and lawlessness, is "the white man's way," in which the Indian is urged to tread. [Fig. 18]

It was past noon when the indiscernible but potent line of the reservation was crossed.[10] The road had long since become two ruts that were deep or shallow according to the length of time they had been used and exposed to the action of the wind and storms. Sometimes six or eight pairs

Fig. 17. "Wajapa hi-bé-eía-la. The place where Wajapa threw away his moccasins, October 8, 5:30 P.M." "Up at daybreak. Sketched our pretty camp. Wajapa threw away his old moccasins, he has mended & mended them, linen thread amounts to nothing, only sinew holds. My work basket furnished none. He called us to witness that these moccasins were to be our fore runners. They would tell all the news. Then Buffalo-chip came & stood at the door of the tent & sang a song improvising as he went on of what the moccasins would tell. First they would reach the Poncas & tell how the bad water made us sick, could not eat or sleep, then how the horses got sore, & so on, & so on. Each refrain ending with Hiegh ho, in a queer little shout & turn. My sketch of the place gave great pleasure. Wah-ta-oo-da were said by all. Ga-ha gave me a friendly tap. To name the camp which has no name was next in order & so Buffalo-chip said it should be called the place where Wajapa threw away his moccasins" (Fletcher, 1881 Notebook 1, 130–31). The place-name in Omaha is *Wajé·pʰa hįbé ai-adha* 'Herald Abandoned Shoes'. "Ga-ha" was Buffalo-chip's wife; the name is *Gahé* 'Combed' (as hair). The form "wah-ta-oo-da" is uncertain but ends with *udą* 'good'. Original field sketch (p. 128) enhanced. Smithsonian Institution, National Anthropological Archives (ms. 4558).

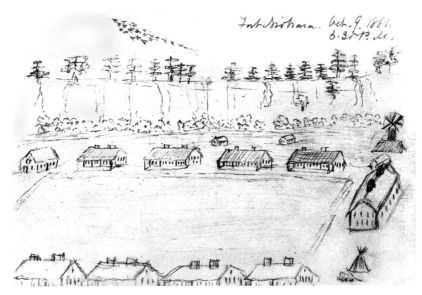

Fig. 18. "Fort Niobrara—Oct. 9, 1881. 5:30 P.M." "When we arrived at his [Waja-pa's] standpoint there lay on the broad plateau the rectangular buildings of the Fort. We descended the sand hill, down, down till we reached the level plain. Far to the left stretched the prairie, the horizon bounded by the rolling elevation; toward the front lay the bluff of the Niobrara, capped with pines; below the yellow clay bare of vegetation, then bushes and trees, these were crowned by the line of plateau which is some 15 or 20 feet or more about the river. At the foot of the hill saw a creek as they are called, this supplies the Post with water—a windmill carrying the water to the houses" (Fletcher, 1881 Notebook 1, 139). Original field sketch, enhanced. Smithsonian Institution, National Anthropological Archives (ms. 4558).

of ruts lay side by side, and woe to the hapless driver who should enter the wrong pair and find his wagon caught on a ridge, the wheels off the ground, and no way apparent to cross or turn out.

Not a vestige of cultivation broke the endless green of the vast horizon. Water was scarce as well as trees; these clung to the few creek bottoms which were below the level of the general surface. Not a thing was in sight, not even a cloud kept company with the shadow of the carriage as we rumbled along. The absence of any sign left the eye without gauge to measure distance or proportion. The intense glare of light untouched by shade added to the silence, made one strangely self-conscious and to realize in a new sense the meaning of the word "alone."

Late in the afternoon, having settled back on the seat and given up trying to see anything, a strange sound caught my ear. It was not like anything I had ever heard, still I knew it was a man's voice. It seemed to tremble through the air, having more penetration than volume, and to rise and fall in as varied cadences as the wind. Looking about I discerned on one of the billowy hills an Indian on horseback, sharply defined against the sky, the head clear-cut and erect, the body at right angles with the horse, the legs hanging straight and free, and the pony with drooping head ambling along, mindful only of his own affairs. The whole outline of the easy figure and the wayward song indicated an absence of any concern with time, or any knowledge of the teeming life I had left behind but which was slowly surging up and destined to engulf these pristine prairies and yonder unconscious rider. As I looked and listened I felt that I was indeed over the border and touching another race where familiar lines were wanting and where old standards would no longer stead me.

TWO

Reporting

"There's the agency!" said the driver.[1]

We were overlooking a valley made up of ravines and knobs—a crumpled, barren-looking region. On the top of one of these elevations stood a cluster of buildings surrounded by a stockade. [Fig. 19] Toward these we made our way. Arriving at the gate I found it locked and an Indian sentry marching up and down inside. He approached in answer to my summons and demanded my business.

"I want to see the agent."

After some delay the lock was turned and I was admitted within the enclosure.

"Where does the agent live?"

The guard pointed toward a dwelling near the center of the line of houses to my right. As I rang the spring bell on the door, a chorus of dogs responded from within, and two large dogs came bounding around the side of the house making straight for me. There was nothing for me to do but stand my ground. The woman who opened the door said: "The agent sees no one except at his office."

"Where is that?"

She pointed to a building near the end of the line. The dogs stood forming an angle and enclosing me; their eyes were fixed on the woman's face as if to say, "Give your order and we'll do it." I could not move, so I asked, "Will you please call off the dogs?"

Fig. 19. Rosebud Agency buildings (identified on La Flesche's list as "Agency Buildings"). Fletcher arrived at Rosebud Agency on October 10, 1881. Original field sketch (Fletcher, 1881 Notebook 1, 178) enhanced. Smithsonian Institution, National Anthropological Archives (ms. 4558).

She looked at me rather contemptuously and made no sound. I was evidently in the atmosphere of petty power so I waited. At length she said, "Go 'long." Whether this was addressed to the dogs or to me I did not care, since the animals parted, permitting me to make my way between them. They accompanied me, however, with barks and jumps to the office door.

On the steps stood a nondescript-looking man, rumpled in dress and dingy in aspect. His low forehead, heavy hair and eyebrows, keen eyes, and large features indicated shrewdness but little breadth of intelligence. He scanned me in a surreptitious manner, as if to see what I represented and wherein I was likely to be of importance. I asked him if the agent was in.

He showed me the door and left me to enter a room having several desks against the wall and men seated at them. No one offered any information, although all looked at me, except one—a tall, slender man, with long black hair falling on his shoulders and a cloud of blue smoke encircling him. He sat with his back toward me, writing before a pile of papers.

"Is the agent here?" I asked of the room in general.

"I am the agent, what do you want?" said the man with his back to me. I advanced toward the desk and waited for him to turn.

"What do you want?" repeated the agent without looking up or moving.

"I have called to report my arrival on the reservation." After several minutes he turned and I caught sight of a nervous, narrow face, sallow in hue.

"Where are you going?"

"To visit ——," naming a certain Indian.

"What are you going to do?"

"Study Indian life."

"Humph."

"Where did you come from?"

"From Cambridge, Mass."

"Who brought you here?"

"No one."

"How did you get here then?"

"In the carriage at the gate."

"How are you going to live while you are 'visiting'?"

"With the Indians."

"With 'em," he repeated, eying me from head to foot. "I don't know about that!"

I smiled as I opened my bag to take out certain papers. I said something about the weather.

"I'll have you understand that I regulate everything on this reservation, but the weather."

Whether this was a joke I did not pause to investigate, as I desired to cut short the interview. So handing him one of several official documents I held in my hand I said, "Here is a letter you may like to look at."

He examined the superscription, turned it over, opened the envelope, took out the sheet, and read a letter from the secretary of the interior authorizing me to pursue my studies and commending me to the courtesy of Indian agents.

The change in his manner was ludicrous. "You are standing," he said, rising and offering a chair.

I declined to sit and said I would rather go on at once to my destination.

He then offered me hospitality and many other things, but having "reported," I did not care to stay longer.

As I stepped out, the same seedy individual stood in the door. He had been watching the proceedings. He made an obsequious bow as I passed.

It had all been so unpleasant and strange that I was glad to escape past the dogs, the guard, and the gate and climb once more into the waiting wagon.

[The kind commandant of the fort to whom I had presented my credentials from the secretary of war had generously provided me with the carriage and given me many friendly words of counsel bred of a long and meritorious experience on the plains and among the Indians.][2] I had been urged to retain the carriage for my sleeping apartment, at least for a time. Perhaps the thought had lingered in the mind of the kind advisor that before many days I would be returning with the vehicle. He had doubted whether a lady could brave the hardships of which he knew and I was ignorant but which would have to be encountered in carrying out the program I had laid down. It was true, too, that no one, no friend, no scientific teacher or worker, would give me encouragement to make this venture among the Indians; but, nevertheless, the desire to see Indian life from the other side, and to try to get at its meaning; to seek for the springs of the Indian's religious thought and ceremonies; to trace out the lines common to the human race; and to do my share toward preserving the record of the people who were native to our country, was too strong to be turned aside. So I persevered and now at last, I was nearing the tent where lived the family that had extended an invitation to me to visit them. This invitation had come about through a young Sioux Indian who was at school in the East, and to whom I had expressed a desire to visit his family.[3]

As the carriage drew up at the encampment, my student-friend, who was home on vacation, came forward as I jumped out and greeted me cordially. Then he presented me to his aunt and her daughter—his own parents were not living. The three younger children, two little girls and a boy, stood near looking steadily at me as they chewed strings and wiggled their toes.

My baggage of all kinds was thrown on the ground, and the vehicle cleared of its motley cargo. The driver lingered, looking at me curiously, as I said: "I shall not sleep in the wagon tonight, but in the tent. My journey is at an end, and as soon as you are ready you can go back."

"I don't like to leave you here alone, Miss," said the faithful man. "You had better let me stay around a few days; you may need me, and want to go back yourself."

"It is true, I may want to go back, and I may need you, but I shall remain here anyhow, and do the best I can. I expect to be here, well, I don't know how long, months perhaps!"

"You can't do it, Miss, and you had better let me stay," pleaded the man.

"You are very kind and I thank you for all you have done, but I think you had better go and get into comfortable quarters as soon as you can."

"If it were done, when 'tis done, then 'twere well it were done quickly," I thought, so, taking a leaf from my notebook, I wrote a note to the gentleman who had started me off, thanking him for his generous and thoughtful provision for my journey, commending the conduct and efficiency of the driver, reporting my safe arrival, and bidding good-bye to the outside world.

Meanwhile the little boy had gotten over his wonder and was busy climbing over the wheels of the wagon at the risk, as it seemed to me, of having his head jerked off by the catching of his scalplock, or his limbs dislocated by the tangling of his dangling breechcloth. As the mother caught sight of his gyrations he was sharply scolded and finally retired, casting reluctant glances at the coach.

"Good night, Miss, I hope you won't be sorry you sent me away!" said the driver as he mounted his box, tipping forward the now empty vehicle. The lash sounded, the carriage drove away, winding over the hills, until even the echo of its familiar rumble was heard no more, and nothing remained to indicate that there was aught in the world but this little valley where I was left standing.[4]

THREE

The Welcome

The mother picked up my bundle of blankets, my bag and other belongings and carried them into the tent. I lingered without, looking at the scene before me, the daughter and two younger children bearing me silent company.[1]

Not far from the tent, the creek slipped rapidly southward between sedgy borders, trees bending over it and often interlacing their branches. A grove hid the northern end of the valley and large trees were scattered throughout its entire length. The bank opposite, as it receded from the creek, became abrupt, and up its steep sides evergreens climbed. The bottom where the camp lay was broad and level, the land gradually rising to the west, toward a smooth hill, over which grazed the hobbled ponies. Cone-shaped tents were dotted along the valley, which narrowed to the south and was lost in a turn of the hills. [Figs. 20 and 21] Here and there an acre of the green sod was broken and corn planted; everywhere men, women, and children were moving about in gay garments, making a picture like a dream, since no reality matched it in memory. As I stood, I became conscious that in some way I was not quite polite according to the ideas of the people, and casting about as to what I ought to do, I concluded I must enter the tent at once. [Fig. 22]

The entrance, which faced the east, was formed by the edges of the tent cloth, pinned together with wooden pins to about three feet from the ground, the lower corners being lapped and fastened by a large wooden

Fig. 20. "View of Spotted Tail Band, Brule No. 1." "Oct. 11, Rose at daybreak after a bitter cold night and determined if possible, to push on. . . . Reached Spotted Tail camp at 3:30. As we drove over the hills the scout went ahead & Buffalo-chip came along side our wagon, & said we were going to the Band of Asanpi" (Fletcher, 1881 Notebook 1, 160). Spotted Tail (the younger) was recognized as the leading chief at Rosebud Reservation; Asanpi (*Asáŋpi* 'Milk') was chief of one of the Brule bands at Rosebud. Original field sketch (Fletcher, 1881 Notebook 2, 24) enhanced. Smithsonian Institution, National Anthropological Archives (ms. 4558).

peg driven well into the ground, thus leaving an oval opening. Over the entrance hung a skin, a corner held by one of the pins which fastened the tent cloth together, and to keep the skin flat, a stick was tied across it horizontally. In order to enter the tent one must lift the stick, turning the skin flap to one side, and, stooping, pass through the low, narrow opening. It looked easy to do, and the Indians were rapid and often graceful in making their entrance or exit, but when I tried to enter, disaster overtook me; I stumbled on the peg which fastened the corners at the bottom, caught my hat on the pin at the top, and the end of the stick on the flap became tangled in the folds of my dress. Trapped at the start, there was nothing to do but laugh at my misfortune, the children joining while I was unhitched and unhooked and set free by the firm hands of the mother. A step for-

Fig. 21. "Spotted Tail House—Oct. 14, 1881." Original field sketch (Fletcher, 1881 Notebook 1, 176). Smithsonian Institution, National Anthropological Archives (ms. 4558).

ward was necessary before I could stand erect within the tent, and then I noticed that my baggage lay at the back part directly opposite the entrance; so passing around the fire in the center to where my articles had been carefully placed on a blanket, I sat down on my bundle of bedding, a little bewildered, wondering what to do next.

The tent was large. [Fig. 23] Fourteen straight, tall pine poles—cut in the Black Hills, as I learned later—were locked together near their tips and expanded at the bottom to form a circle not far from fourteen feet in diameter. The covering was fastened to the back pole, where it was locked in with the other poles, and tied with a low sag to the front, forming a wide aperture for the light and smoke to pass through. The latter was guided by triangular flaps formed by the upper corners of the covering and adjusted like sails by long poles outside the tent. Within the tent, from one of the poles on the south side, hung a cord over the fire to which was fastened a kettle. A crotched stick thrust slantingly into the ground near the fire supported the coffee pot and near the coals stood a large covered bowl. It was

Fig. 22. "View from Spotted Tail Jr.'s Tent, Oct. 16." Original field sketch (Fletcher, 1881 Notebook 2, 24) enhanced. Smithsonian Institution, National Anthropological Archives (ms. 4558).

evident that the evening meal was cooked and ready for serving. Thrust back under the slant of the tent were square packs made of rawhide, ornamented with geometric patterns painted in red, green, and black. Blankets and robes were spread around the circle, on which were placed the bedding and pillows belonging to the inmates. To the left as one entered, I noticed that the cooking utensils and dishes were stowed, and among them, those which I had brought. The south half of the tent had a lining of cloth passed between the covering and poles, making a double thickness around that part which seemed to be the portion occupied by the family.

The elder daughter had sat down not far from me, on my right, and was busy embroidering a pair of moccasins with porcupine quills. The two younger children just beyond her knelt face-to-face; deep in the mazes of cat's cradle, they rapidly shifted the strands from one another's hands, forming combinations of lines unknown to my childhood. As I watched them, the flap over the entrance lifted, and a tall figure bowed itself in and advanced toward me. It was the father; his blanket was wrapped about

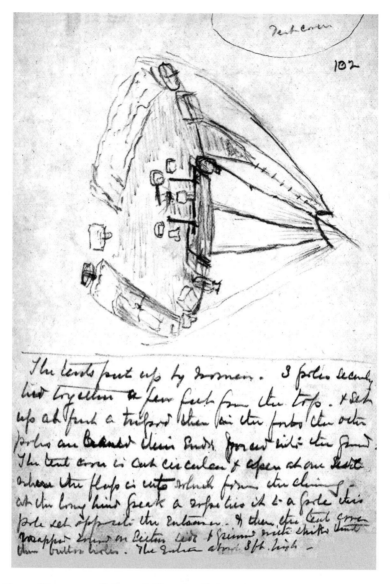

Fig. 23. "Tent cover." Sioux tipi interior. "The tents put up by women. 3 poles securely tied together a few feet from the top, & set up at first a tripod, then in the forks the outer poles are lashed, their ends forced into the ground. The tent cover is cut circular & open at one side where the flap is cut which forms the chimney. At the long hind peak a rope ties it to a pole; this pole [is] set opposite the entrance, & then the tent cover wrapped around on either side & pinned with sticks thrust thru button holes. The entrance about 3 ft. high" (Fletcher, 1881 Notebook 2, 102). Original field sketch, October 3, 1881, enhanced. Smithsonian Institution, National Anthropological Archives (ms. 4558).

him, passing over the left shoulder and held together in front by his left hand, which also grasped his pipe. He held out his right hand, saying "Ah-how" as I rose and took it. Not another word was said. He seated himself just beyond the children, who had not even looked up from their play, and drew his blanket about him, tucking it over so as to form a band circling the body and knees, giving a support as he sat. A slender young man, brilliant with paint and ornaments, soon came in and sat down opposite his father near the door. The youth did not speak to me or even look toward me; the nephew soon entered and sat at my left. In a moment the father bade the son call certain friends to the family meal. The young man arose and, stepping outside the entrance, shouted the message of his father until answer was made from each friend so invited; then he re-entered and took his former position. Meanwhile I sat unnoticed and, not knowing what else to do, I quietly took in the picture around me.

The father's face was strong in outline; his hair, parted in the middle, fell on either side to his waist in two long rolls, bound in strips of beaver skin. The scalplock was divided from the rest of the hair in a small circle on the crown of the head, the hair gathered carefully to the center, and braided in a close, fine braid, and ornamented with one eagle feather. The parting of the hair was painted red. The flat cheeks, absence of eyebrows, and monotony of color made the face appear stolid, and I felt that I must seek for expression in other facial lines than those of my own race.

The father wore no ornaments beside the eagle feather, in marked contrast to the son, whose scalplock was decorated with metal slides and ribbons, his face painted in bands and dots of green and red and yellow, and a shower of necklaces composed of beads and shells covering his neck and breast; his shirt was trimmed with streamers and his arms banded with metal bracelets above the elbow and about the wrist; his leggings were heavily fringed and ornamented, and his moccasins bore testimony to his sister's skill; about his waist he wore a sash and his scarlet breechcloth trailed behind. He presented a heterogeneous mass of color as he reclined and made reply to his father's questions about the horses. He reported upon the sore back of the bald-faced horse and told that he had watered the ponies three times during the day and hobbled them for the night near a certain place where the mosquitoes would not be troublesome. During this family talk the mother had entered and was sorting out the dishes.

About this time the three men who had been invited when the son called out his father's message arrived and were greeted by my host and motioned to their places on the north side of the tent. They leaned over and shook hands with me, and then each one adjusted the ends of his blanket into a little cushion and settled down upon it. All were silent while the mother uncovered the bowl, disclosing a pile of brown cakes, made of flour and water, and with a forked stick began fishing out of the kettle oblong, thin pieces of buffalo meat. Putting some of these and a cake on my plate, and filling my tin cup with coffee, she passed them to her husband, saying as he arranged the dishes before me on the blanket, "The food is poor, but it is the best we have!" The three guests were next served in the same manner, then the children; the nephew and the elder son and daughter had each a dish, but the little ones, who had thrown their string away at the preparation for eating, were given a dish between them. After the children, the father was served and then the mother helped herself.

During the eating, talk began, the three old men leading. Questions were asked me of my journey, of the country I had passed through. Great familiarity was shown concerning all the creeks and trails and I was asked about many I had not noticed. I mentioned one creek where the ambulance had had much difficulty in crossing on account of quicksands. This place was well known and stories were told of ponies sinking in and being drowned and the rescue of persons who had been caught in the dangerous sands. War trails, hunting trails, were inquired about, and tales of the chase recounted. I mentioned a pretty knoll I had passed, noticeable for its clump of trees and sightliness of situation, seeming to form a landmark, I fancied. The old man nearest me said:

"Yes, that is a noted place—there something happened. I will tell you. A Dakota hunting party had there a fight with a Pawnee war party. A Pawnee was killed and cut up. One of his hands was thrust on a stick and set in the ground on that hill which you saw. The night after the fight one of the Dakota young men, crossing the camp circle, entered the tent of his friend and sat down with a groan, saying: 'I can now breathe freer—it was all I could do to get here.'

"Beside his friend there was in the tent another man who was a great boaster, and he cried out, 'Breathe freer! What is the matter?'

"'Since the fight I am in fear, I can hardly go about in the night.'

"'Oh, you are like a woman, afraid in the dark. I am not afraid. I can go anywhere, even to the place where the hand is standing up. I could go and bring the hand here,' said the boasting young man.

"'You could not do that,' replied the first.

"'Oh, I can do that,' was the rejoinder.

"'I dare you to go. I will give you my beaded blanket if you bring that hand here,' said the first.

"The boastful young man started. The hill where the hand was standing was some distance from the camp. The two young men waited for him in the tent. They waited a long time; the man could have gone to the hill and come back again twice; still he did not return. It was late in the night when the two friends started in search of the boaster. Not far from the camp they found him, lying in the grass. He was hardly conscious. He could not walk, so they picked him up and carried him to the lodge. When he revived he had nothing to say.

"Then the first young man said, 'Death is inevitable and yet man fears death!' and he rose and left the lodge.

"In the early light of the dawn the young man returned to the camp singing his death song and carrying the stick on which was thrust the dead Pawnee's hand.

"The young man pitied the boaster and gave him the beaded blanket."

After this cheerful dinner story, it was hard to think what to say. The shadows had deepened and the fire began to cast odd shapes on the wall and one could fancy he saw hands and even heads peering about. Just then a man suddenly thrust his face in the entrance and said, "The young woman is invited to eat!"

"By whom," asked my host.

"My uncle," was the reply.

"She hears," said my host.

As each one finished eating, the dishes were passed back to the mother who piled them up. All were empty; no scraps were left, so that the dog near the door had rather slim fare, until the mother threw him a fresh bit.

My host filled the pipe and passed it to one of his guests, who lit it, holding it for the one next him to smoke; then it passed round, each one of the men taking a few puffs, drawing in the smoke and making a sharp sound as the air passed through the closed teeth. The smoke was sometimes ejected through the nose, sometimes through the mouth. After the smoking, the pipe was cleaned with a stick. The father, rising, said to me, "We will go."

The mother rose and gathered her blanket around her; this meant that I was to make ready to accept the invitation given by the face at the door. I had just eaten and could hardly fancy that another meal must be taken, but the summons of the father was unmistakable so I arose and followed my host. He strode on, his wife, the nephew, and I bringing up the rear. I was wondering what I was to do and how I was to manage not only to get safely inside the tent but to avoid partaking of viands that were not particularly appetizing. There was not much time for speculation, for I noticed the tall form of my host disappear in a tent, and the mother, with a kindly smile, stood lifting the flap to insure at least one less disaster when I should enter. I passed safely through but hesitated where to go. To my left sat my new host, the family in the same order as in the tent I had left—the mother near the door, next the father, and the children beyond. Some old men were on the opposite side and the father who had come with me at the back of the tent with a vacant place beside him. My new host motioned me to that spot. I took the hint and made my way thither and sat down on the ground, for I had no bundle to sit upon, although a clean blanket was spread. The mother and nephew followed and sat beside me.

The food was the same as at my late meal, the manner of serving it the same. I was daunted by the amount placed before me. I could not eat it, and as the plates about me emptied mine remained almost untouched. I was conscious something was wrong but did not know what to do. I determined, however, to throw myself on the mercy of the mother beside me. She listened quietly as I explained my inability to eat, and then helped herself from my dish. It seemed hard to impose such a task on my hostess, but no alternative opened.

As we sat at meal a head peered in at the door, and a voice gave forth the message, "The young woman is invited to eat."

I looked at my host; surely he will decline, I thought, but he asked, "By whom?" and said, "She hears."

The stories of wars and hunts, the food and the smoke came to an end. The father looked towards the host and said: "My uncle, this is all we can do," rose, and once more we started.

As we stepped out into the clear atmosphere of the evening the stars were resplendent and seemed to throw light into the deep heavens where they hung. Below in the valley, the tents were aglow, the fire within throwing a band of yellow light on which were pictured the forms of the inmates, making a shadow world fraught with a beauty that clings to the memory. On the hills echoed the song of a young man, the bells on his legs jingling as he strode off to some dance. There was, however, no time to linger, for my host was in advance following a narrow trail that was scarcely discernible. We were evidently not going home, for soon I found myself at the low entrance of a tent, and the thoughtful mother ready to aid me in passing through.

The same order prevailed within this tent as in the others, and the same ceremonies were observed as before. Despair fell on me as my dish was handed over by the wife to her husband and placed before me by my new host, well filled with meat. It was impossible that I should appeal again to the mother at my side or that she should again eat my portion; such kindness has its physical limitation. I began to fear that my entrance into Indian life was to be barred by these dreadful piles of meat and that ethnological study would be frustrated by my lack of appetite. So perplexed was I that I found it difficult to tell of my journey; I was careful not to again mention the knoll of trees, as I did not wish to encounter the ghastly hand of the Pawnee any more. Altogether I was becoming decidedly depressed when I was startled by noticing the mother produce a pointed stick, and began to thread on it the meat and cakes from my plate. It was difficult to control the relief that came from this unexpected kindness and not to look too happy now that I need not eat. [Fig. 24]

In the midst of my pleasure a head appeared in the door and I heard the fateful words: "The young woman is asked to eat."

Surely I should not be taken to a fourth meal! It was difficult not to rise and enter at once on a mission to preach digestion and physical laws and

Fig. 24. "Oct. 12—Asanpi's house, Reception Teepee, and Son's log home."
"B[uffalo]-c[hip] went ahead and soon we were driven up to the large tent set aside for guests, owned by Asanpi, the chief of Ogallala [*sic*] Indians, one of the bands of the group. A fine comely cordial man, his wife came in & welcomed us and after a little space we were heralded to his house near by, to supper. . . . Our meals served on a piece of canvas spread on the floor between the two beds, our coffee in tin dishes. We sat on the floor. Our host said, 'I am afraid you will find it hard to eat without knives & forks'. B[uffalo]-c[hip]'s wife said, she would get ours & that quite relieved Asanpi. So we ate his viands with our own knives & forks. Ga-ha, B[uffalo]-c[hip]'s wife, saw that I was making but little headway with the pile of meat on my plate & she, without attracting any one's notice, sent word round to me that she would take what I could not eat. Could any one be more thoughtful & courteous! What we did not eat Ga-ha took away with her. When the dishes are emptied they are piled up & placed at the edge of the cloth. Our host ate sitting beside his wife. Later, we were called to supper at Asanpi's son's. Here again we found buffalo meat & bread. . . . When we reached the son's house, the father was there to welcome us, he talked to us [through] a half-breed interpreter. We had had 4 invitations to supper. Buffalo-chip, his wife & Wajapa went to three places & excused us. A plate of pounded buffalo meat mixed with chokecherries was sent to me. Woman's work, I shall take it home" (Fletcher, 1881 Notebook 1, 160–64). Original field sketch (p. 174) enhanced. Smithsonian Institution, National Anthropological Archives (ms. 4558).

then to spring out of the valley and flee to where meals were at least a few hours apart; but a certain purpose, for the accomplishment of which I had come, gave me pause. So when the time arrived I meekly followed the father, hoping the mother would produce a fresh stick and once again come to the rescue. She did so, and I felt that I could never fully repay her for her kindness. I wanted to call her "Mother" at once. I did so soon after.

Stories and questions filled up the time and again the dreadful head appeared at the entrance and said something about "the woman" and "eat." I glanced at my watch. It was after ten. "The woman" had been eating for five hours already. I became resigned and concluded I was doomed to eat for the rest of my Indian life.

A new misfortune now befell me; both my feet were sound asleep. I could not move. The time to rise came; I was motionless. My host had passed out of the tent; the mother, a small, slender woman paused; but I was powerless. I looked at her and pointed to my feet. She laid down her sticks of meat and prepared to lift me. I knew I was too heavy for her. My new hostess, a tall, muscular woman, then sprang up and, stepping toward me, seized me as in a vice and stood me on my feet, but they were useless. I nearly fell, saving myself by clinging to the woman and trying to laugh off my dilemma. All this time the men sat gravely smoking and speaking in low tones. As soon as my tingling, painful feet would bear me, I hobbled out, no one making fun of me, yet surely I presented a ludicrous picture.

Two other invitations pursued me and had to be accepted so that the night was far spent before we turned homeward. As I entered the tent, I noticed that my bedding had been opened out, my blankets spread and pillow arranged for the night. The eldest daughter lay asleep in that part of the tent where she had sat at supper, her feet toward the fire. The little children were sleeping soundly on the side the old men had occupied. The son, who had evidently been guarding the sleeping ones during his parents' absence, now rose and went out and I heard him talking with the nephew. The mother was busy pulling the meat off the sticks; putting the pieces in a bowl and covering them with another, then she carefully laid a knife on the top. This done she turned to the fire, raked it over, covered the coals, and in a few moments was under her blankets. The father had not yet entered the tent. Making all speed I hastened to get beneath the cover of my wraps, glad to lie down and not go to any more feasts. Soon I heard a light stir; it was evidently my host nestling down to sleep and then all was still.

Tired as I was, sleep would not come. The dull glow from the peeping coals cast shadows within the tent; the stars sparkled down through the central opening; the unbarred doorway was free to any hand; the sound of the ponies on the hillside and the distant howling of the wolves, all were so strange and unlike any familiar realities that the sense of isolation deepened within me. Yet as I lay within the lodge, sharing the bosom of mother earth with my Indian friends, the thrill of a common humanity came over me as I recalled the welcome of the stranger and the care bestowed upon her, for thereon were drawn the lines of human kindness in new but living colors.

FOUR

The Chief's Entertainment

The crackling of the fire wakened me, the ruddy blaze warming my face. Glancing around, I noticed that the father was up and out, the mother was stirring about, but the children and daughter still slept. I did not rise at once; I was planning how I should perform my toilet. Privacy was not to be had. I concluded, therefore, that acts such as dressing my hair would have to be performed in public, but I hoped that by and by, when I was better acquainted, I could put up a shawl as a screen and be comparatively retired and comfortable. So, plucking up philosophy, I rose to enter upon a new day and got on fairly well. I took my cup and went outside the tent to use my toothbrush. This strange performance aroused the curiosity of the people who were within sight; they watched me, and perhaps they fancied I was going through a religious preparation, not unlike those preceding some Indian ceremonials.

At breakfast, all the family gathered together and occupied the same places as the evening before. There was no change in the food and it was partaken of in like manner. After the meal was over I went out with the daughter; we strayed down to the creek, up on the hill, and enjoyed the refreshing breezes and clear outlines on every hand. As we returned I noticed several old men entering the tent, and on my arrival I learned that it was proposed that I should go over with them to the chief's tent and meet there a number of the leading men. After the visitors had completed their smoke, the same passing of the pipe being observed as I noticed last evening, they were evidently ready to go to the chief's.[1]

We made our way to a good-sized tent, where a large man, a little past his prime, sat at the south side. He greeted us with an "Ah-how," as we filed around the fire and sat down. There were no women or children present. The tent had been cleared of all family signs except the ever-present kettle hanging over the heap of ashes where the fire had been. Blankets were spread around on which we sat, circling the tent. I was at the back part, the father on my right, the nephew on my left. When all the guests had gathered, a silence fell. The pipe was passed by the chief and smoked with the usual courtesies.

This meeting was not a counsel; that could not have been held without the consent or presence of the agent. It was merely a gathering of leading men to welcome a stranger who had come from the outside world of which they knew so little.

One of the old men said: "We are glad you did not come from the Great Father. When the chiefs go to the Great Father, then our lands grow less. We are given there fair words. I have grown old on the fair words of the Great Father. You see my people. You see us living in this little valley. The buffalo herds are far away; we are forbidden to go after them. We get but few buffalo now. Soon there will be none. We have rations from the government, but they are poor; they are not good as was the game when we were free to hunt and live as our fathers lived. We do not like the white man's food. Some of our women will not eat it. We do not know the white man's ways; we are Indians, we were made differently. We do not want the white men about us; they tell us one thing and they do another. We do not wish our children to be like these forked-tongued men. All the white men desire is our land, they hate the Indian. We must keep our land. What shall we live from if all our land is taken? Whenever we see a white man we know he wants something the Indian has. We are glad you did not come from the Great Father!"

Similar speeches were delivered by several men, treaty stipulations referred to, and statements made that sounded very strange to me and I wondered if they were true.

When all had finished it was clear that something was expected from me, so I said: "I did not come from the Great Father. I do not know him or his counselors. I never saw any of your treaties. I do not know what is in them. I am sorry that white men do not treat you honestly and speak the truth to you. There are many white people, many more than there are Indians; not all white people are good. I suppose there are persons among you who are not good, and I am sorry that some of the bad white people have been out here among you. You have told me very strange things about your treaties and the way your affairs have been managed. I will remember what you have said, and when I go back among my people I will try and find out why such things as you have told me have been done, but I can do nothing about it here. I came here to make a visit among you. I have thought a good deal about your forefathers. I have seen things they have made, and it was because I had thought about your ancestors that I came out here to see you, to talk with you, to become acquainted with you, to be as a sister with you. You have been very kind to welcome me so cordially and my heart is made glad. I shall be happy while I stay with you and when I go back to my people I will tell them about my Indian friends, and the good white men and women shall know you as you really are, and wherein you have been treated wrongfully, they will rise as friends to help you and to secure justice for you. I am glad to be here with you, and I hope you will be glad that I have come."

This speech was met with courtesy, and I was welcomed again.

As we sat talking a child hardly two years old succeeded after many efforts in creeping under the tent flap and poking in her little black head, the hair braided tightly on each side. Spying her father, the chief, she crawled over the lower edge of the entrance and, tumbling and toddling, made her way, shaking off as she passed the helping hands that offered to steady her, until she finally lunged into her father's lap. Here she sat composedly, he holding her securely and now and then stroking her glossy head.

She singled out a friend in an old man nearby and laughed silently at him, showing all her white teeth; he responded with nods and smiles. When we were through our formal talk, this old man softly clapped his hands and the little girl gave a shrill cry and began to bend her body forward and jump. It had been a pretty bit of by-play.

"Can she dance?" I asked.

"Dance," whispered the father to the child, setting her on her feet, and he too began to clap his hands to give the rhythm of the drum.

With one fat fist in her mouth and giving forth shrieks of delight, the baby girl bent her small body and lifted her wee feet, keeping time to the beats. The sound brought to the opening the mother's face, beaming with smiles. This added presence seemed to redouble the joy and vim of the little girl. Everyone was smiling and interested, faces were relaxed, and the burdens of life seemed to have rolled away before the tiny feet of the dancer.

"I wish I could see a dance," I said almost unconsciously, and adding, "You will let me come the next time you have one for I have liked dancing ever since I danced in my father's arms as the baby did just now."

Before very long the men gathered up their blankets and started off, a few remaining to smoke with the chief. After complimenting him on his cunning little girl, and giving her a keepsake, I too passed out.

It was very warm and I was glad to join the mother and daughter as they sat under a shade made of boughs laid upon crosspieces, which were held by four crotched poles, the whole forming a green oblong roof. Here the women sewed and chatted. Spreading out a blanket, I lay down near them, shading my eyes with my hat. All I had heard lingered painfully in my mind. I had never studied the relations of the Indian to the government and hardly knew of the Indian problem, but it was evident that there was one and just what it was I did not know. It was now impossible not to think of the Indians in a new light, as a people struggling with unknown forces, and the question came, "How will it fare with them?" I was looking in the faces before me, the younger one round and homely, the elder one marked with lines and homely too, but neither face was without kindliness and something that was attractive as they chatted and laughed, all unconscious of any life but their own.

My thoughts were interrupted by the nephew coming up and saying, "The chief has sent the crier out to call a dance tonight."[2]

"Where will it be held?" I asked.

"In the large reception tent."

"Can I go?" I hastened to say.

"The dance is given for you."

"Is it? What must I do?" The youth smiled and said nothing. I concluded if anything was expected of me, enlightenment would come if I waited, so I continued: "When will it take place?"

"When you hear the drum sounding over there, then you can go; the dance will begin at that time."

I had heard an old man on the hill shouting out something, but I did not know what he said. He now passed not far from us, paused, leaning on his staff, and called out at the top of his voice the invitation to the dance. For a time serious speculations vanished before the anticipation of the coming festivity, and the hours sped on as I sat alert to catch the sound of the drum and to watch any unusual signs in the camp. I saw and heard nothing; people came and went, and the day wore on without any incident to mark the hours except the slow swing of the shadows as the sun crept toward the west.

It was nearly sundown when I heard the drum, but I did not like to be the one to start, as someone must go to pilot the way at least, if not to remain with me. At last I called the mother's attention to the drum and asked when we should go. She laughed and said nothing. By and by she threw her blanket about her. I was all ready and several of the family started with us. We had a considerable distance to walk; the trail led up and down gullies and over streams. In one of these I noticed a vestige of civilization, a glistening tin can used as a stepping stone. It was a welcome sight and tempted me to linger with friendly gaze, but the party had passed on, unmindful of the vestige, and I must follow. As we drew near the tent the drumbeats grew louder and the peculiar rhythm of Indian drumming caught my ear, a heavy stroke and a light one, like a rebound.

Ascending the bank of a ravine, the tent came in sight. A crowd composed mainly of women and children, although there was quite a sprinkling of men, was gathered in front, forming a wide circle. The mass of bare heads, with shining black hair, red-painted partings, and brilliantly colored faces, made a peculiar picture. As we approached, the crowd opened for us to pass. When we reached the front, I noticed that quite a space lay between the people and the tent. The tent cloth was unfastened, all but a few pins near the top; the lower corners were turned back on either side, leaving the tent poles visible and affording an opportunity for the spectators without to witness the dance within. [Fig. 25] At my right, as I stood looking in, was the drum, fastened by the sides to short stakes driven into the ground. Around it sat six blanketed young men. They were laughing and talking with one another. A fire burned in the center of the tent and a group of kettles stood near it toward the entrance. I was anxious to enter, but as my party held back, I did not like to go forward alone, so I took hold of the mother's hand and moved toward the tent. She laughed, shook me off, and slipped away in the crowd. As I glanced about I noticed that every one of the family had left me and I was entirely alone among strangers. This struck me as queer, but the zest of seeing the dance was so keen that I forgot about it when an old man within the tent arose and beckoned me. I advanced and entered fearlessly, for it required no stooping to pass between the tall tent poles and under the lifted covering. As I made my way around the fire, the young men fell upon the drum with a few rapid beats, accompanying the strokes with short yells. It was rather startling, but I was determined to make no sign of surprise, so I deliberately proceeded to the back part of the tent, where I sat down on the blanket spread there and looked about me.

The tent was very large, thirty-two tent poles making a wide circle. Around the sides men were squatting near together, their blankets held closely about their persons, leaving only their heads visible; not even a hand was to be seen. Their scalplocks were dressed with feathers and their faces elaborately painted.

There were fifty or sixty so seated. [The drummers, just north of the entrance, were also blanketed.] Behind the drummers sat four women, two on each side, their hair neatly braided, the partings painted red, their faces decorated with paint, and their long, slender necks covered with strings of beads and shells. They were clad in green tunics, their blankets were drawn over their shoulders, and they sat very straight and trim. Directly before me, outside the tent, standing framed in the glow of the sunset, was the crowd of people I had left.

Except the single outburst as I entered, the drummers made no sound. Now and then a tall figure, well wrapped in a blanket, walked in, the bells on his legs jingling as he paced forward and took his seat in the silent cir-

Fig. 25. "Omaha dance, Spotted Tail. Oct. 14, 1881." "There are public criers, old men, they often wear a handkerchief about their head tied in front. They called to feasts, dances, announce the giving away of horses, return the thanks of the receiver. When a camp is to move they call the order & time. When I was at Spotted Tail's & he gave the order for a Dance. The crier, an old man got up & went out. When we reached the Feast he went out & cried, & told those who were coming to hurry, as there seemed to be some tardy ones" (Fletcher, 1881 Notebook 1, 173). Original field sketch (Fletcher, 1881 Notebook 2, 24) enhanced. Smithsonian Institution, National Anthropological Archives (ms. 4558).

cle of men. After what seemed to me a very long pause, the drummers began to play, one of them making a few strokes and the others soon falling into the steady and peculiar rhythm already mentioned. In a moment, a single voice among those seated at the drum started the song, beginning on a high, wavering note, swinging around it, on it, and near it, with a gradually falling cadence, much as a butterfly flutters over a flower and alights. At the end of perhaps six beats the other singers chimed in on the same key and strain, the women joining with a high tenor.

This was my first real experience with Indian music, and I was puzzled by it. I could not seem to hear it distinctly or catch the melody and was giving my whole attention to following the sounds when a sudden rustle pervaded the tent, and over a score of men leaped to their feet, dropping their blankets, and in full undress moved forward without pausing, lifting their legs at sharp angles, bending their bodies, turning their heads first to one side and then the other, or moving them up and down while their arms beat the air as they flourished clubs or decorated sticks, all the time keeping time to the deafening drumming and bringing their naked feet down on the hard, bare earth with a heavy thud which jarred me as I sat overwhelmed with terror, my heart out-sounding the drum.

The leaping flames of the fire lent a lurid glare and made their ornaments glisten as they advanced step by step in uncouth attitudes, their bells jingling and ornaments rattling, their feathers moving and the tails of animals snapping, while here and there a dancer imitated the sounds of beasts. In my horror it seemed as though the nether kingdom had arisen and was holding high carnival. All that I had ever read of Indians in my childhood days, all the fearful tales that had ever fallen on my ears, rushed in mad confusion through my mind and mingled with the wild, moving mass of creatures before me. Had it been possible to disappear under or over the earth, to find escape at any hand, I would have fled and never looked back, but I could not move, I could not make a sound; it seemed as if I should die of fright as I sat alone with these distorted, hideous forms that seemed coming down upon me. All at once my senses returned and I said, aloud perhaps, I cannot tell, "You foolish woman, this is what you came for; look at it, study it!" And so ended my first and only fright among the Indians.

This experience has since been of great value, for it has shown how much more easy it is to receive an exaggerated picture than a truthful one, particularly where nearly all the aspects are unlike our own standards of beauty, grace, or even vivacity. The lines which are in common to human feeling are sometimes difficult to discern and are apt to be omitted in portraying Indian life. I have seen many pictures of aboriginal dances and truth bids me say that a large portion of them resemble what I fancied I saw in the midst of my fright rather than what I looked at calmly afterward, when I had learned the meaning, caught the spirit, and was able to find pleasure in the wild freedom of the Indian dance, which is also not without touches of grace. On that memorable evening before an hour was over I was already in the tide of enjoyment as I looked upon the dancers. The supple, lithe forms of the men, the play of the muscles, the sharply defined sinews of the legs brought back thoughts of the old Greek days when the human form untrammeled by conventional garments lent inspiration to the sculptor. The dark color of the Indian skin, the painting, the numberless necklaces, the decorations of feathers and tails of animals, the bells—in fact, the general flutter and rhythmic sounds which enveloped the dancers—made me forget that they wore no garments but the breechcloth.

The dance was not continuous; groups would rise and pass through their figures while the song was being sung. If the singers ended abruptly then the dancers would scatter with a shout to their seats; in a moment the music would be resumed for a few bars and here and there a man would rise and fill out the measure of dancing.[3] After each song there was a pause of ten or fifteen minutes, during which the men sat muffled in their blankets, sometimes silent, sometimes talking with each other as they rested, for it was vigorous work and the perspiration made their bodies glossy.

No one addressed me, and I do not know how long I watched the dancing. No woman besides myself was present except the singers, and I often turned wonderingly toward the assembly outside and scanned the crowd, hoping to see someone of the family I was visiting. At length I spied the mother; I motioned to her to come in, she beckoned me out, and I reluctantly obeyed her call. When I reached her, I was greeted with laughter because I had stayed so long and because I still looked backward at the dancers, for another song had just struck up and the wild, fascinating movements tempted me to stay. But the mother had tight hold of my arm and was pulling me rapidly away, chattering as she went with a female friend who bore her company.

My evident delight with the dance became a favorite story for weeks, the mother gaily acting in pantomime, to her laughing listeners, how she had to force me to leave.

I never told of my fright!

FIVE

The White Man's Shadow

Several of the neighbors came to call upon me; women dropped in and lingered and made it to me a time of searching to find topics of conversation. My dress became an object of interest. The side plaiting on my skirt was carefully examined and the sewing scrutinized. Just how good this was, I did not know; so after a woman had dropped the skirt as though it did not amount to much, I took occasion to look at it myself and discovered that the dressmaker had made her stitches more in reference to the appearance on the right side than to secure evenness and strength. I was asked: "Is that the way white women sew?"

I tried to defend the merits of "milliner's stitch" and exhibited other parts of the garment which I thought presented better specimens of handiwork. The Indian woman listened and looked, then she said: "I don't think that you could sew moccasins."

Evidently I had lost caste through my dressmaker's workmanship. I showed her some lace and tried to explain its manufacture. It was looked at and looked through; then she said, "Did you make it?"

I was obliged to confess, I did not.

Other articles of my dress were examined and it was discovered that I did not make any of my garments.

"You can't sew or make your clothes!" commented my examiner.

"Oh yes I can, but I did not make these I have on. I will show you that I can sew. Let me make a pocket for you and put it in your skirt?"

146

She smiled, but I insisted, and taking a piece of calico, I cut out a pocket. While I was sewing on it several woman gathered about me and watched the process. "There!" I said, when all was complete, "put your hand in. Isn't that convenient?"

The woman put her hand well down to the bottom of the ample pocket, spread her fingers, and lifted the skirt, laughing heartily as she did so. Other women thrust their hands in. The pocket was approved, and soon I found myself in a thriving business, as every person present must have a pocket in her skirt. The fashion raged for days, and I was beset. Then I proposed to show the applicants how to cut and make pockets. Many of the women proved to be deft scholars, but they found the needle more awkward to use than the awl.

One day I was washing some of my garments and this caused a ripple of interest. The women seldom wash their clothing, but wear it until it falls to rags. This habit comes of their former use of skins, out of which they made their garments. These could not be washed and it is difficult for the people to realize that the material of their present dress being different, the garments should be treated differently. Skin garments were cleansed by scraping and then rubbing with white or yellow clay; by this process all the soil would be removed and the tunic or skirt be made as fresh as when new.

After I had been a few weeks in the valley I noticed the mother and daughter washing their tunics and the calico shirts of the men. The lack of facilities and of proper soap made their effort less effective than it otherwise would have been. The substitute for soap among these Indians is the root of a species of yucca.

The first time I received a call from a man with his two wives I hardly knew how to treat them all. I felt confused face to face with polygyny. The women were near relations and the younger showed great regard for the elder wife, who was not very strong and quite handsome for an Indian woman. The two women were harmonious together, and it did not occur to them that there was anything peculiar in a plural marriage. I afterward became well acquainted with the family and was quite attached to the younger wife, who showed considerable mental ability. We used to talk together of many things. She told me of her life, wherein the vicissitudes were those principally connected with hardships, fatigue, hunger, cold, rather than of feeling or stress of thought. She evinced a desire to learn English and to read and to write. When I was leaving the people, she came to me and begged me to ask her husband to let her go with me. She wanted to learn something of the life that I led and to be educated. It was a sore trial to her and to me that I could not effect her release, but she was necessary to the elder woman, who would not consent to the departure.

One day when I was out visiting I was taken to the lodge of a noted man. We found him sitting in state, his oldest wife resting near him, while a younger woman was busy getting the meal ready, and her baby lay kicking and crowing on a spread blanket. On our arrival he sent out for his other wives; he had five. The newest one came bringing her baby on her back. She looked like a startled deer. I have never seen such an untamed pair of eyes as hers; I pitied her and wanted to make friends with the wild creature. She was almost trembling as she stood before me; the baby, however, jumped and crowed in the lightly gathered blanket as I talked to it. This seemed to add to the mother's unrest, and when my head was turned, she suddenly started and ran like the wind to the woods. I expressed my regret at her departure, which was received by the women with indifference and by the man with a sort of pride.

One of the wives had been gathering wild turnips.[1] I noticed her biting off one end, stripping down the thick brown skin with her strong thumbnail, then she handed the prepared turnip to me! I thanked her and wondered how I should eat it. Two others of the wives prepared more turnips for our party, while the father rose and went out. I heard him shouting and the call soon brought together his motley group of a dozen children. He summoned me to behold the dress parade. Such a funny little row, mostly boys, their small scalplocks tightly braided and tassels of beads at the end. They were naked except the breechcloth, which nearly touched the ground behind, making the boys seem, as they stood there, to have three legs. Their faces were dirty from their play. The bright light made them partly close their eyes, so as to leave only a shining line, and whether or not for the same reason, their mouths were open and widespread, showing the jagged outline of teeth in every stage of growth. The little girls had their hair closely braided on each side of their faces and were clad in single tunics in which their hands were clutched. They kept wriggling their bodies and, with one foot slipping over the other, looked very uneasy. As I stood beside the commander I hardly knew how to review the line. I was, however, relieved of my embarrassment, for in a moment they broke and ran, the girls showing their brown soles as they darted off. The boys resumed their game of shinny; when they tussled with each other, their legs and long breechcloths seemed to get in a snapping confusion. The sight made me shout with laughter in spite of all my attempts at control, for they looked like a nightmare of three-legged stools! The father took it all good-naturedly and I hastened to praise his little army as he strode off well pleased with the family display. I returned to the women meaning to talk of their children, but I found the mother in the midst of the story of my dance fascination, to which I listened for the twentieth time.

In the warm weather the cooking was often done outside the tent and the meal eaten in the shade; frequently we had guests and sometimes we went to other families. At the meals the women generally kept together, and often the children, particularly the girls, begged their share and took it to the little tent nearby which either they or their mother had erected. It was what we should call a baby house, only it was big enough for three or four children to huddle into. Many a time I have seen a small, black, shining poll pop up out of the middle opening, both cheeks distended with food, for a feast was going on inside, and when the child caught sight of me, she would suddenly drop and a chorus of suppressed giggles would ripple on the air. The children mimic the life of their elders. Feasts, dances, hunts, wars are carried on by them. Dolls are devised out of grass and bits of rags. These are privately enjoyed by the girls, who like to keep tent, bring wood and water, cook, and mother the dolls, but if a boy comes around, the doll at once becomes a little sister. Both sexes play together if they so desire while the children are small, but as soon as ten or twelve years are reached the social line is drawn separating them. The children are merry, active, seldom denied, never disciplined, but generally obedient. They are greatly beloved and are the open sesame to the Indian's heart.

Trying to behave socially according to Indian etiquette was difficult. At first it was almost impossible for me to see visitors enter and forbear to make haste to greet them and seek to entertain them. But Indian politeness requires that a person, on entering the tent, should be allowed to rest awhile, get his breath, and collect his thoughts.[2] I discovered later in my experience that the important point of interest must not be mentioned early in the interview, nor must the host question upon it, but wait for the newcomer to disclose the matter of his visit, whatever it may be. It never ceased to be trying to me to observe this mode of procedure and it became more irksome as my acquaintance with the Indians ripened into a deep and vital interest in the people. Often I was checked because "I could not wait," always kindly, however, and sometimes I was reminded that haste was one of the failings of my race.

One evening four men, the nephew, and I were sitting around a fire, out-of-doors. Lines of prairie fires were running along the distant horizon and mutterings of thunder were heard. The nephew and I had lingered after the mother and father had returned home, for the end of the valley where we were visiting had a wide outlook that greatly attracted me.

"The white man is always in a hurry, he never waits to hear all about a matter; he goes off like a gun and misses fire," said an old man with a quick imitative gesture. "It is one of his bad ways; it has been hard for the Indian. The white man may not consider the Indian is worth listening to. He may think the Indian is only to be got rid of, and it is of no consequence about him in any way. White men are very cruel, and love to kill," he added reflectingly.

"Some white men are bad, but not all. There are many very good men," I observed.

He looked at me steadily and then said, "Do you know how the white men have killed the game? Did you ever see the great herds of buffalo which God gave to the Indian for his food and clothing? White men came and killed the buffalo, caring only for his hide, leaving the body to rot until the land is white with their bones and the Indian may starve for food. Watch the white man kill the birds; he will wound them and let them die where they fall. He loves to kill with his guns and he loves to kill with his forked tongue."

Near the speaker sat a man about forty years old, vigorous, restless, his face growing darker as he listened. Suddenly he pulled up a handful of grass, exclaiming, "See this! This is the white man's grass. It is marching over the country driving away the buffalo grass, just as the white men are driving away the Indians."³

"The white men killed our game," said a man a little older than the last speaker, his strong face lit by the fire as he fixed his eyes on me. "God made us hunters and gave us the game. We were permitted to kill it that we might live, and our children live after us. Now that which God gave us is gone. What shall we do? The white man loves to kill the game, and the Indian."

"You have certainly suffered from the white men, but not all of them have done you wrong?" I ventured.

"Tell me one who has not?" exclaimed the old man. "Look how the soldiers have hunted us. If they cannot kill us with guns, they do worse, they kill us with whiskey, and they take our women. Look at the blue-eyed Indians around us. Where are their fathers? Do those white men care for their children? Look at the agents, they treat us like dogs, and the traders, they take much from us and give us little in return, making us poor. They all think that we don't know anything, that Indians have no hearts."

"I went to the agent and he called me a dirty, lazy Indian," said the younger man. "If I am dirty and lazy who made me so? Once I was always on the hunt, my children were well fed, I was not 'lazy.' My name was feared among our enemies. I was a man. What am I now? I know not." A pause followed, then he added, "The Indian should never have made friends with the white men, but have killed them all when there were few in number. We had better die fighting now than see our men made old women and our wives taken before our eyes."

"My people have suffered much," said the nephew, "and you must not think hard of them that they speak thus. They have been badly treated."

"Yes, I know they have. Why have they never been taught how to farm, or had schools among them?"

"I do not know; our treaties call for all those things," he replied.

"Are you sure? Surely if the government has promised it will keep its word," I answered.

He smiled[, and I do now as I recall my remark. I was then in ignorance of the government's years of neglect and failure in honor toward these people].

"Perhaps there has not been time," I suggested.

"Our treaty of 1865 and 1868 provided for all these things," he replied.*

"What does she say?" asked the men. The nephew repeated our conversation.

"Umph!" said the old man. "You said you had not seen our treaties. You need not look at them, they are all lies. The white man writes them, he fixes them to suit himself, and then he does not keep them, but he sends soldiers on us if we do not do just as he says. He keeps no word with us. One treaty said all this land should be ours and no white man should come upon this land or trouble us. One day the white man found gold in the Black Hills; then the soldiers came.** Do you know how they hunted us, killing our women and children here, here on our own land, where the white men, soldiers, and all had promised us that we should live forever? They took away the Hills, drove off our ponies; they left us naked with our dead."

It was terrible to sit face-to-face with the sufferers of these misdeeds of my race, and with the uneasy suspicion that all was not right even at the present time between the Indian and the white men.

"My friends," I said, "You make my heart sore. You have been badly treated and I am very sorry. I wish I could help you. I cannot give you back your land, but I wish I could give you some of the good things the white people have. I wish I could teach you to farm, to have herds, to have houses, to read and write, and to speak the English language, and to show you that the white men are not all bad. There are many men and women who love their fellow men and try to help them. Did you never see any such?"

After a pause the old man continued, "I have heard of one or two men who talked well. I was told they had a book which they said was God's words, and that everybody should do as the book said. I don't know anything about it. If the book was God's words given to white men, the book may be very good to teach them how to build railroads and steamboats

* Since this conversation took place I have corroborated all these statements. See *U.S. Stat.* 14:747 and 15:635. [Reprinted in Kappler, *Indian Affairs*, 2:906–8, 998–1007. —Eds.]

** *Eighth Annual Report of the Board of Indian Commissioners for the Year 1876*, 11–23.

and to make guns and whiskey, but I don't think it can talk about being honest and not telling lies, because if it did, and it is God's words, then the white men would believe the words and not lie and steal so much."

"The book does tell men not to lie and steal and says that people must be kind and true to one another. It does not teach about railroads or guns or how to make things but how to live a good life so that one will be helpful to his fellow men while on earth and happy when he dies," I explained.

"I don't know what good it is, if it can't make the white men better," remarked the old man.

"I knew a white man once, whom I never heard tell a lie," said a new speaker. "He was an old man, with glass on his eyes, and he liked to hunt among stones. Maybe he is dead!"

The thunder had crept nearer, and the stars were hid in the heavy rolling clouds; already a few raindrops were falling. The men hastily gathered their blankets and strode off to their tents. I picked up my shawl and followed the nephew with a burning heart as we ran hastily home.

When we were seated about the fire within the tent and the rain was pouring on all sides of our little shelter, I turned to the father and unburdened my thoughts. "I have heard horrible things from the men, of how you have been treated. I did not know it, I can hardly believe it."

"That old woman you saw here this morning could have told you of how her people were driven to the Indian Territory and when they escaped and tried to make their way back, they were shot at by soldiers and then put in a house in the winter and kept without fire or food for four days to force them to return, and when they dug their way out and tried to get north, they were fired into again and nearly all killed. There are many men and women here who can tell you like tales of the white man's cruelty."[4]

"We are called savages," said the nephew with evident excitement. "I do not think we are the only ones. 'You scalp people,' said a lady to me at school, 'don't you know that is very wicked?' I wanted to ask her, why then do your soldiers scalp us?"

"They don't," I exclaimed.

"Ask my uncle, ask any of the old men or women here what the soldiers do to Indians. You will then see who are savages. It makes my blood hot. White men know better than to act as they do out here; the people in the

East don't know what goes on. I found that out when I was East at school. Sometimes I think it were better we all died fighting."

"Oh no. You are being educated, you can help your people," I urged.

"I shall try, but will that make the white man just?"

Here I was, hundreds of miles from civilization, enduring untold hardships, all to search out the man within the savage, [to study the Indian race, only scientifically,] and my task was already doubled, for I found myself confronted with the savagery of my own people. I felt desperate, and the thunder and lightning without seemed fitted to the scene. Turning to the father I said, "Surely you have known some good white people?"

He was silent while peal after peal made the earth tremble beneath us. At length he said, "I remember an army officer who spoke kindly to us, to our women and children, and said he pitied us. He was just. I believe there are a few good white men."

"There are a great many, I assure you," I hastened to say.

He smiled and added compassionately, "You have a kind heart, but you don't know much!"

SIX

An Outline Chapter

It was difficult in the midst of scenes so novel to set aside all preconceived notions and to wait for customs and habits to explain themselves; in a word, to let the Indian paint his own picture, no matter how different it might be from the supposed reality.* The meagerness and aimlessness of the life about me added to the difficulty. The mind became irritated by the baldness everywhere, and hope or dislike sought to invest the scenes with properties that were not intrinsic. There was no escaping the question, how is it that people can live and be content in the midst of such paucity of ideas and activities? The answer could only be found when the vantage point had been gained of putting oneself as nearly as possible in the Indian's place, accepting his conditions, and so haply finding the limitations and range of his thought.

As I became more familiar with the people, I began to see details in their life and customs that at first I did not notice, and through these, new vistas opened to me. I discovered that instead of being in the midst of a community untrammeled by custom, I was living where formalities bound the individual with cramping force and made liberty of thought and action almost impossible. This discovery reversed many popularly accepted

* In order that the reader may better understand the reasons for some of the peculiarities in Indian life, I have in the following pages forestalled my own knowledge on these subjects in point of time during my life among the people.

notions, particularly that one which conceives of the savage as a free man in distinction to the citizen of a civilized community, who is regarded as a bondsman of the law. The truth is that social progress brings freedom to the individual as well as organized liberty to the state, through a coordinated society with its diversified labors, mutual interdependence, and abstract power of law.

The organization of Indian society is based upon kinship. The tribes are divided into gentes or clans and these are composed of persons related to one another by the tie of blood.[1] This tie is binding sometimes upon the father's and sometimes upon the mother's side, according to the law of the tribe. That is, a person is united to the gens by the father, and not by the mother, if the father carries the gens; the descent, therefore, being on the father's side, the child belongs to the gens of its father. This law prevails among the Dakota or Sioux, the Omaha, and other tribes. Some tribes have the descent by the mother. That is, a person is bound to his clan by his mother; she carries the clan and the child belongs to the clan of his mother and not to that of his father. This law prevails among the Iroquois, the Pueblos, and other tribes. Marriage never takes place between members of the same gens or clan. Therefore, the father and mother represent two gentes or clans, two distinct organizations, and the children belong either to the one or the other branch and cannot inherit from both parents.

The gens overrides the family, as we understand the term, and in many respects takes its place. The tribal organization by gentes consequently precludes the idea of the legal family as it exists among civilized nations and holds the people in groups that cannot coalesce.

Each gens or clan bears a distinctive name, has a symbol, and possesses a tradition relating to a common ancestor, generally mythical in character. There is also a list of names belonging to each gens, one of which is bestowed upon each child born within the gens. Although other names are taken by men later in life, their child name is never forgotten. A woman bears but one name from the cradle to the grave. The gens or clan has a fixed place in the tribal circle. If the father carries the gens, then each man must camp with his gens, and his wife, although of a different gens, follows and lives with him. If the mother carries the clan, she lives with her kindred and her husband follows her. In either case, custom requires that the head of the family shall live with his or her group of kinsfolk. Certain gentes, or clans, have certain tribal duties, trusts, and ceremonies committed to them which are hereditary and cannot be evaded. The gens or clan fixes beyond the reach of change the name, symbol, location, and a portion of the duties of the individual member of a tribe.

Honors and property are not accumulated and handed down from father to son, parents to children. Each man must acquire honors and possessions by his own skill and prowess and enjoy them during his life, for at his death his honors die with him, and such of his possessions as are not buried with him are distributed among the kindred in his gens. As a result there is no accumulation of property among the Indians, nor is it possible under a strict tribal organization.

The system of consanguinity prevalent among the Indians includes relationships we do not recognize. In general the following is true of all the tribes. All the father's brothers are called "father"; and, the mother's sisters "mother." The mother's brothers are addressed as "uncle" and the father's sisters as "aunt." All the children of brothers and the children of sisters call each other brother and sister for the reason that the brothers of a man have a claim to marry his wife when she becomes a widow; also, a man marrying a woman has the right to all her sisters to wife. The relationship between the children of a woman and those of her brother varies in different tribes. In some tribes they are cousins, in other tribes they are uncles or mothers, nephews or nieces, sons or daughters to each other, according to the custom in a particular tribe and the sex addressed or addressing. In some tribes, an uncle's daughter is a potential wife of her aunt's husband; consequently she calls him brother-in-law, and all men who are thus addressed by the term of brother-in-law have a right to marry the women who so address them. These potential relationships, although they may never actually exist, affect the position of persons to one another and control many social customs, particularly marriage.

Growing out of this organization of the tribes by kinship is the peculiarity of the Indians addressing each other solely by terms of relationship. These, as we have seen, are extensive, and in a measure unlike our own system. One hears a man address a child as mother, or the child speaks to its mate as son. Until one is aware of the singular laws of relationships, real and potential, it is difficult to make out any meaning to the custom.

There are no family names, consequently there are no surnames among Indians. The personal name belongs to the gens and designates where the man belongs. This name is never mentioned in the owner's presence, therefore, no individual is ever so addressed. There can be no greater breach of etiquette than to ask an Indian man, woman, or child, "What is your name?" To such a question, no reply would be made. The personal name can be mentioned when speaking of the absent, but it is seldom a man will utter the name of his father, mother, or wife, or of his mother-in-law, son-in-law, or daughter-in-law. If for any reason the name is needed, he will appeal to a friend, who will give the desired information. Thus in the social form of address the individual is merged in his kinship.

As each gens has its position in the tribal circle and each head of a family camps with the gens to which he belongs, so within the tent there is a rule fixing the place of each member of the household.[2] The tent is always pitched to face the east. The mother sits near the entrance toward the south, that is, to the left as one enters. This position is convenient, enabling her to slip in and out of the tent without passing before anyone or interrupting any ceremony that may be going on and to easily attend to her various housewifely duties. Here the cooking utensils are kept and a part of the stores. The reserved portion is usually packed away on the opposite side, and no one but the mother would think of helping himself to it. In the middle of the south side is the place of the father. Here he sits when he receives his guests, or entertains his friends, or attends to any of his work when indoors [such as making weapons, implements, regalia, or spoons; the latter are sometimes shaped on the ball of the foot]. At night the father and mother sleep in this space, their heads toward the east. The eldest daughter's place is next; she sits here at meals and at other times when she is not engaged helping the mother or busy with some household task, and here she sleeps at night carefully protected by her parents [with her feet toward the fire]. Beyond her at the rear of the tent is the place always reserved for guests, where they sit and sleep when visiting. To their left, following the circle, the smaller boys and girls are put to sleep; they are not apt to be much in the tent unless the weather prevents outdoor sport, and it must be a severe storm to hold the Indian boy tent-bound. The elder son takes his place near the entrance on the north side, ready day or night to spring up at any call from his parents and to guard the tent in the father's absence. No one sleeps with the head to the west, because the dead are so laid. The above order of place serves Indian society somewhat as our separate rooms do us and it would be as discourteous for a stranger to sit anywhere but at the rear of the tent, unless requested to do so by the host, as for a visitor to enter one of our private apartments and ignore the drawing room. The positions in the tent as above described are so universally observed that one could pass into a lodge at night and not be apt to make a mistake in naming the person he might touch in a given place.

Each gens has one or more chiefs. The man who has the most ability, either as a wise counselor or a ruler of men, is recognized as the principal chief of the gens. All the chiefs of all the gentes form the council of the tribe, and here also the ablest man among them becomes the leader or head chief. The chiefs form a self-perpetuating body; they fill all vacancies in their number caused by death or retirement. Naturally, a chief wishes to have his son or some favorite near relation succeed him in office, so when he gets to be advanced in years he sometimes retires and secures his place to the desired successor. A strictly hereditary chieftainship, one that is dependent solely upon birth, does not exist.

A candidate for the office of chief is generally a man about middle life; he cannot well fulfill the requirements at an earlier age. He must have established a reputation for courage on the battlefield, given proofs of sagacity, and been able to count honors. When a man thinks he has acquired a proper record, then he must begin to electioneer. This is done by feasting the chiefs, making them presents, and seeking in every way to win their favor. There is considerable political maneuvering for office among the Indians. The manner of electing and inaugurating chiefs varies among the different tribes.[3] The duties of the chiefs are mainly connected with the peace and order of the tribe. The office is in part a religious one, and the chief stands as an exemplar. He is regarded as one who has passed through the struggles of life, reached its highest dignity, and is now empowered to restrain the passions of the people, settle quarrels and grievances, assist at the tribal ceremonies, conduct alliances, and have charge of all public affairs. Chiefs do not go on the warpath or lead in battle unless in extraordinary cases, when the entire tribe is in jeopardy. As the chief represents peace and stands in a sacred attitude before the people, so he is prohibited from speaking in a loud voice, walking rapidly, or indulging in any violent action. The failure to observe these rules, in some tribes, involves certain penalties. The office is highly prized and its dignity coveted, and nearly every ambitious young man has the goal of chieftainship before him as an incentive to courageous action. Many chiefs have been made among the tribes by government officials, civil and military. These are called "paper chiefs" by the Indians and have influence only as they are backed by the strong arm of the white man.

The next position below the chief is that of the soldier.[4] All the men of the tribe are trained to war. As young men they go with war parties in the capacity of servants, carrying the moccasins and kettle, preparing the food, and performing other camp duties. When the enemy is reached they are allowed to participate in the fight, and perhaps they may succeed in securing an honor. It is slow work for a young man to get started on the road to preferment and to reach the dignity of being a soldier. When a man has won many honors he becomes entitled to wear certain ornaments[, such as "the crow." This is made of two sticks ornamented with crow feathers and worn so as to stand up against the back, being fastened by a thong about the waist.] From among men of proved valor are chosen leaders and regulators of the hunt; such persons also have charge of the defense of the camps. From their ranks the chiefs are apt to be drawn.

The heralds or criers are generally from one family in a gens: those having the best voices are selected. Every gens has one or more of these old men who proclaim the decrees of the council or any decision of the chiefs. Their position is one of importance and they are always remembered at feasts, and the young hunters supply them with gifts of meat.

The religion of a tribe is so closely interwoven with the governmental duties that it may be said that church and state are one. Each tribe has certain ceremonials which are compulsory, supernatural penalties falling on every member who fails to do his part. These sacred ceremonies are connected with the perpetuity of the tribal organization. Their character and forms vary in different tribes. Beside these tribal festivals there are individual religious duties which are performed in connection with societies. There are many of these societies, each one having its peculiar rites. There is a class of men who possess the rituals and conduct the ceremonies connected with the tribal religious festivals. These form a kind of priesthood, although from our meager knowledge of Indian life these have generally been classed as "medicine-men." The term is a foolish one as it is popularly used, but as designating those who deal with the mysterious, the name fairly well expresses the office of the functionary.

Sickness is frequently regarded as the result of supernatural agencies and treated accordingly by exorcism, but this is not always the case. Many tribes possess quite an extensive knowledge of roots and herbs, and although the name and use of such are guarded by certain societies or persons and the administration of the remedy accompanied by some simple religious observance, the roots and herbs are given solely for medicinal purposes. Amputation is almost never resorted to; the disabled limb is bound up and suffered to unite as best it may. In the treatment of wounds the Indians are quite skillful. [A little boy was accidently shot, the ball passing through the orbit of the eye and out behind the ear. The agency physician said the child must die, but as long as he breathed the Indians kept on with their application of remedies. After four days they declared the child would live, and in a month or six weeks he was about and finally recovered without the loss of his eye.]

There are many societies for dancing and social enjoyment among the men, and also some among the women. There are games that fill up not only the moments, but the day. These are different for men and for women; none are played in common and all are generally for stakes.

The men make their weapons, their regalia, war bonnets, and other feather ornaments. Their dress is more elaborate than that of the women, and the devices on their blankets, robes, leggings, and shirts are often of a symbolic character, sometimes referring to the gens but more frequently to the man's dreams.

The life of an Indian man in the past was one demanding constant vigilance and seasons of prolonged exertion. He had to be always prepared for enemies, and his hunting brought with it double peril—accidents that came of the chase and the chances of a lurking enemy. Hunts among all tribes living in the buffalo country were always held under more or less rigid regulations. All the tribe moved out on the annual summer hunt, which lasted from two to three months. The customs of the hunt varied with the tribes.

The following incident which happened to a Winnebago family illustrates the insecurity of Indian life. The family were out on the hunt and living in one of the little circular huts thrown up of boughs and grass and used as a temporary shelter. It was erected under a large tree. There was an ample opening on the top of the hut to permit the smoke to escape and one day, as the woman was bending over the fire frying out some fat, she saw in her pan the reflection of a face. It was not her own face, so she said quietly to her husband, "Look in my pan." He did so, and she asked, "Do you see the face?"

"Yes," he replied.

"It is the face of a man who is up in the tree, looking down on us," she remarked.

"Keep quiet," said the husband. In a moment he began to tell a story. It was about hunting; as he talked he picked up his bow and arrow. He described the chase, how he gained on the deer. Then, stringing his bow and fitting his arrow, he went on with his story, his animation increasing, while his wife still bent over her cooking, watching the face reflected in the fat. Lifting his bow to make ready to shoot the imaginary deer, he let the arrow fly through the central opening. A heavy fall outside showed that the arrow had pierced the lurking enemy and the husband rushed out and dispatched a wounded Sioux.

SEVEN

The Indian Woman

The tent is the Indian woman's castle. Everything within the little dwelling, and the tent itself, belongs to the wife; the man owns nothing which pertains to the household. Besides these home possessions women generally have one or more ponies and any number of dogs. The wife's property being exclusively her own, she uses it or gives it away without asking the consent of the husband or even notifying him, unless she so chooses. As everything connected with the tent belongs to the woman, so all the work pertaining to the home is her special duty. She tans the skins and shapes and sews them to form the tent cover. She sets up the tent and cares for and manages it. She gathers the wood for the fire, brings the water, and cooks the food. She raises the corn, beans, and pumpkins, preserves the meat, and has charge of all the stores. She fashions and makes the clothing and ornaments; in fact, she is the conserver of life.

Because she does this work, she is not necessarily the slave of the man, and the reason he does not labor in the same manner that she does is not because of contempt for the woman. The Indian man, in common with others of his sex, dislikes to perform duties which custom imposes upon the woman, and hence his opposition to farming and other occupations which in his race are markedly the work of the women. Yet, when sickness incapacitates her, it is not uncommon for the husband to perform the labors of his wife.

The Indian woman considers herself quite independent. She controls her labor, her time, her possessions and follows her own inclinations if she has sufficient determination. Should she choose, she can take down her tent, gather up her belongings, and withdraw to her kindred, leaving her husband to shift for himself, and he would be powerless to coerce her to return to him as his wife. If a husband maltreats a woman without cause, and she so determines, she can appeal to her family, and her husband may be placed in very embarrassing circumstances and find even his life imperiled.

The stability of the family depends entirely on personal inclination and character. There is no bar to the separation of a man and woman; yet I have known husbands and wives who lived long and faithfully together, as staunchly true as if bound by the strongest legal penalties. Indian women possess considerable influence over their husbands, and in some tribes over public affairs. The attachment between parents and children is a marked characteristic, and one of the bright spots in Indian life.

Among all the tribes I have visited I never found a woman over twenty-five who had not been married. A widow generally returns to her relations on the death of her husband, and she is not expected to support her children unaided by their gens. It is expected that the woman will marry again in accordance with her potential relationships; therefore the children, except the youngest, are apt to be dispersed until that event takes place. They may not be all reunited again; this depends, however, very much upon the woman's inclination or strength of character. I have known widows who remained unmarried, held their children together, and maintained a home. No orphans are ever utterly unprovided for. The relations, unless interfered with by white persons, always assume the responsibility of caring for the children. It is difficult for the Indians to understand our orphan asylums. Such institutions are considered as a proof of hardheartedness on the part of the white children's relations.

As all Indians sit upon the ground it seemed strange to learn there were differences to be observed between men and women in the manner of sitting. I had told the mother she must instruct me how to act politely, and she was quite faithful in drilling me how to sit. I was to rest on my right thigh and balance my body so as to leave the lap even and the arms free. It was not the correct thing to rest on the left thigh or to sit cross-legged or draw up the knees as men did. To get up properly was even more difficult to learn, and I was never a very satisfactory pupil. Some women spring from a sitting to an erect position without aid from the hands, but this was a feat beyond my power to accomplish. When very tired, women sometimes sat with the legs extended and feet crossed, but this was an unconventional attitude.[1]

The general costume of Indian women is a tunic or sacque, a scant petticoat reaching nearly to the ankles, and close-fitting leggings, tied in with the moccasins. The cut of these garments varies in the tribes. Formerly the material used for clothing was skins. The deer skin, being soft and pliable, was made into garments; elk skins were used for moccasins; and buffalo for robes, bedding, and tent covers. With the disappearance of the game has come the almost universal substitution of calico and cloth.

The tunic or sacque is generally made of calico or stroud, and the cut varies in different tribes. The Sioux women wear it so as to reach the knees. The sleeves are wide and form a part of the main garment. There is no opening, front or rear; the head is slipped through the ample hole for the neck. The tunic is belted low about the body with a sag to the front, where it is drawn up and over the belt, forming a kind of pouch which serves as a pocket. Articles are put in or taken out through the wide sleeves. [Children are also suckled through the opening of the sleeves.]

Among the Omahas, the sacque is short, the sleeves easy fitting, the neck rounded down in front and trimmed; behind a large square flap or collar falls over the upper part of the shoulders.

The Winnebago sack resembles the Omaha, except the cut of the neck, which is lower in front and "V" shaped, the space being filled with numberless necklaces.

The skin tunics were generally sleeveless, the openings for the arms ample and trimmed with fringing of skin.

The skirt is usually of cloth and is generally ornamented either by the white selvage of the material or beading, or, as among the Omahas, Winnebago, Otoe, and other tribes, by the beautiful ribbon work in which the geometric patterns formerly used for porcupine-quill designs are reproduced in gay-colored ribbons. The skirt is not very wide, and the fullness is put at the hips in broad plaits. This makes it hang rather ungracefully according to our notions, but when one notices that the skirt so arranged does not impede the steps by clinging about the legs and also presents the minimum chance of catching when the woman is descending a bank, its utility becomes a merit. This adjustment of the fullness also proves convenient in horseback riding. The skirt is fastened about the waist by a sash. The sash is woven in a diagonal pattern and is long enough to wind twice about the body; the ends are finished with a deep fringe. To the sash are fastened the match case and the ornamented sheath for the knife, an indispensable article in a woman's dress. With her butcher knife she splits the wood and prepares the food. Sometimes she is obliged to defend herself with her knife, and not always from Indians.

Leggings are ornamented or plain and vary in style in the different tribes. Some are cut like a bag opened at both ends and tied by a garter woven like the sash. Some are bound about the leg. All fit closely to the ankle and meet the moccasin.

The moccasins of the various tribes are different both in form and ornamentation. The finding of a discarded moccasin on a trail will reveal to what tribe the man whose track is being followed belongs. The form and ornamentation of moccasins worn by the women of a tribe differ from those used by the men. Moccasins are much preferred to shoes. They are less expensive, easier to the feet, and safer.

One day I started to make a visit with a young Indian woman; we had some distance to go, and as it was in the spring the ground was very soft and difficult to walk over. I was protected by rubber boots but I experienced much trouble in making my way up and down the steep pitches, being obliged to cling closely to the steady arm of my companion. The cabin we were to visit lay across a creek which ran between steep banks. The bridge was a log. The descent was hard for me; my sure-footed friend laughed at the ridges of black mud piled up on my feet. As I slipped and plunged forward, she held me steadily and I got down in safety, and also over the slimy log. Then she left and with a few vigorous strides was up the bank, and I heard her greeting our friend just beyond. I tried to follow but could make little headway. Halfway up, one foot slipped; in trying to recover that, the other lost its hold and I was thrown on the muddy bank and began to slowly but surely slide down to the creek. As I failed to appear, my two friends returned to look after me, and peering over the bank discovered my wretched plight. A few leaps and they were at my side. Before I could gather my wits I was erect and being steadily walked up the bank. At the top, they cleaned me off with wisps of dried grass and thoroughly laughed at me.

By and by I said, "Show me your feet, and let me see how you walk in the mud." Each woman lifted a trim moccasined foot with the toes well gripped down, so that they could catch in the mud and hold on almost as with claws.

"I can't do that. See!" and I lifted my flat-soled boot, incapable of bending.

"Nobody could walk in those things!" the two women chimed in exultant tones. The younger one strode off, flapping her feet as if they were shingles.

It was pleasant to sit beside the women as they embroidered in porcupine. The gaily colored quills were kept in a small round-bottomed bag, the sides spreading wide open to admit of a free display and choice of colors. The dyes used were principally vegetable dyes prepared by the men, who also colored the quills. When they are about to be used the women flattened the quills by the thumbnail. All the figures embroidered are freehand, designed by the women; some, however, copy favorite patterns. I often watched the women take a short stitch up with the awl, on the surface of the skin, not through it, making a series of holes close together. Through these the quills are passed by the sharp point, making a kind of overhand sewing. The Sioux women are noted for their beautiful work. All the sewing on skins is done with the awl and sinew, the latter being threaded through the holes made by the former.

Making and repairing moccasins forms quite a part of the family sewing and in this the men share, as they must be able to care for themselves when on the hunt or warpath. Strangely enough, sewing was the only occupation which I discovered as common to the sexes, some men being almost as skillful as the women. In all else, in duties, posture, dress—even the robe or blanket being worn differently by men and women—in gestures and in language—for the women use different terminations from the men—the line of sex was sharply drawn, thus presenting a marked contrast to civilized society, where so many of the labors and duties of life are shared in common by men and women.

The ornaments worn by the mother were seldom taken off. On each arm were eighteen bangles made of brass and fitted closely. It looked odd to see her cooking in the ornaments but when she reclined, leaning on her arm, with the firelight playing on the shining bracelets, it added a barbaric charm to her general picturesqueness. Necklaces of beads, of shells, of rows of the dentalium fastened between strips of buckskin, were worn in profusion. Earrings made of the latter, reaching to the waist, were favorite with the Sioux women. Sometimes they wore two in each ear, one tied in the usual place and the other through the upper part of the lobe, the weight often causing the ear to hang over. To see a woman chopping wood with these lengthy ornaments flopping, or to watch her cooking, or blowing the fire, while the earrings touched or lay on the ground, quite cured one of any atavistic tendency to admire these ornaments. The Omaha, Winnebago, and some other tribes prefer silver earrings that dangle in clusters. The women never wear feathers, as these signify honors won in battle.

The hair is parted over the head and braided on each side in long braids, the parting painted bright red. The Omaha women tie the ends together and throw them up on the neck, the braids hanging in loops on each side. The Sioux let the braids hang. The Winnebago gather all the hair into one braid at the back and bind it with beadwork, having a long tassel at the end. It is common among young husbands to braid and dress the wife's hair.

Age determines the fashion of painting the face. The young Sioux women put on a light coating of yellow and red, which over the brown skin gives a rich tint. A scarlet disk, not quite as large as a twenty-five-cent piece, is placed on each cheekbone just back of a line drawn from the outer corner of the eye. The matron paints her face entirely red.

One day I was calling on a noted warrior. His wife, an active and ambitious woman, was not quite in company trim—her paint was dim. While I was talking with her husband she passed out of the room; in a few moments she returned, her face shining in a fresh coat of paint and presenting a blaze of color.

I spoke to her of sewing; she was making a tunic. In answer she turned upon her husband, saying: "I ought not to wear or to make such garments!

The wives of great men among the white people do no work and all their clothes are made for them. My husband is a very great man, even among the white people, and yet I have to sew!"

"I have wanted you to wear white woman's clothes," said the husband meekly.

"Why don't you buy them then!" she retorted.

One day as I reclined beside the pleasant little mother who sat working on the moccasins for her children, I asked, "Tell me what Indian women like best in a man."

She looked at me shyly and laughed, as she said, "White people ask such queer questions."

"Yes, we are all queer, I suppose, but I wonder if Indian women like the same things in men that we do," I went on. She said nothing. "Do they like a tall man?" I ventured. The father was tall. Again she laughed and said nothing. "What do women scold men for, and make fun of them about?" I asked, shifting my point of attack.

"Men should be brave," at last she said.

"Did you ever hear a man scolded for not being brave?" I persisted.

After a silence she went on. "There had been a fight between the Dakotas and the Poncas. A Ponca was killed and cut up. The men talked about it, and a young man heard them. At night he fell asleep and dreamed of the fight that had taken place; he groaned and cried out as he slept. Then an old woman rose up and, seizing a pillow, began to beat him, saying, 'You dare dream of a fight and cry out when you have done nothing! You coward! Wake up.'"

The mother laughed as she imitated the angry old woman flogging the sleeper. After a time she added, "It is not good for a man to dream of what he does not do."

Another day as we sat talking I heard the voice of a woman shouting a message from the reception tent of the chief and asked what she was saying.

"We are called to a dance," said the mother.

"When?" I asked, wondering if I should be brave a second time.

"This afternoon."

"Will there be a feast?" I queried, for I had never gotten over my dread of feasts.

"Yes, a great feast. Many persons will be there. It is a woman's feast and dance!"

"Will there be no men?"

"No, only women."

"Are there feasts at all dances?" I asked.

"Yes, it is good to eat."

I looked at the mother's face. There were no lines there belonging to the glutton, and something in her voice seemed to give a different meaning to the words than mere praise of eating. Following the lead of her tone I went on, "The people must have often been hungry when game was scarce. Did you ever know such a time?"

"Many such times. It is hard to be hungry; when the children cry for food, then it makes one's heart heavy," she said slowly.

"What would you do for them?" I asked.

She looked at me with a dumb pain in her eyes and made me regret the question. I made haste to add, "But that trouble never lasted long."

Again came the look, and then she fell into a silence that I dared not break. I knew not what shadows had been evoked, nor did I know how to dispel them. I was powerless; but I had gained a key to Indian feasting, to the immediate preparation of food as soon as a guest arrives, to the generous helping, and to the custom of carrying the surplus away to serve against want on the home journey. I could also discern why social custom should emphasize by repeated feasts its welcome assurance to the newcomer that he is not in danger from the direst need which can befall a people.

EIGHT

The Woman's Society

Early in the afternoon the mother began to make herself ready for the coming festivity. I watched her paint her face and the parting of her hair. To do this she used a long stick, the end of which she dipped in the paint. I could not help thinking how well the glossy black braids and long white earrings, made of rows of pointed shells, set off her high color as she gave the finishing touch to her toilet by adding a few more necklaces of large white and blue beads. Altogether the picture of the mother as she stood in full dress was not an unpleasant one, although a little barbaric to my educated notion; she seemed quite simple and unconscious of her picturesqueness.

When we were ready to start she gathered up my dishes and took some for herself and then looked at me and smiled as she packed them into a kettle. With this in her hand we passed out of the tent. Many women besides ourselves were wending their way toward the dance, each one carrying her dishes.

"Do all the people take their own cups and spoons?" I asked.

"Always, to a large feast," said the mother, smiling at my ignorance. "No person would have enough dishes for so many people."

I checked a smile as I thought of the requirements of a dinner party and concluded that the Indian plan certainly simplified the work of entertaining.

The daughter did not accompany us, so I asked why.

"She is not a member of the society," replied the mother.[1]

"Do the women here have societies?" I asked, adding, "They have them among my people."

"What do your women do?" was the counter question.

This simple query puzzled me. How could I explain our women's clubs, with their essays and discussions, or the wide-spreading associations that compass all the needs of man and woman? Where could I find a point in common between the world of letters and of action and the untutored woman beside me? In my dilemma I said:

"Sometimes they sew, sometimes they talk," and then stopped, conscious of the flatness of my speech. The mother's face showed she had caught the stupidity of it, so I hastened to add, vaguely, "Do you think you would like that?"

"I never tried it," was the noncommittal reply.

"What do you do in your society?" I continued.

"You will see."

We walked on in silence a few moments and then I began to question her again. "How does a person become a member?"

"It takes many presents. One must give away ponies or blankets and other articles to the members. We do not take in quarrelsome women," said the mother with emphasis.

Evidently I was to see the well-to-do portion of the female part of the community. The costly presents made to members to gain admission corresponded to our initiation fees, while character seemed to be the principal qualification for admittance. Not feeling sure of this latter point I went on to say:

"I suppose you take as members women who have noted husbands, I mean the wives of leading men, no matter if the women are quarrelsome?"

The mother looked puzzled and said: "Men have nothing to do with our society."

"Doesn't it make any difference who the husband is, whether you take in a woman or not?" I persisted.

"White people ask such queer questions! If a woman is bad, what difference does it make who her husband is?"

"I thought perhaps you would not like to refuse a chief's wife even if she should be bad," I replied, feeling I was on the losing side of the question.

"White people are queer," she repeated, laughing quietly to herself.

We walked on, meeting more and more women, some with their babies slung behind in the mother's blanket. A few carried their little ones in beaded cradles shaped like an oblong box, minus one end, the bottom being of stiff rawhide covered with some soft material and the three sides of solid beadwork, and tied together by thongs fastened at the edges, thus securely enclosing the child. [Fig. 26]

Nearing the tent, I noticed that the cover was partly unpinned and the corners turned back, in the same way as at the men's dance. A large number of women and children were grouped in a semicircle before the opening. Occasionally the crowd parted to let two women pass who were bearing between them a pole on which hung one or two kettles filled with broth; sometimes the pole rested on the women's shoulders, sometimes it was grasped by the hand. We entered and took our seat at the back part of the tent. There was no fire, but just beyond the place for it, toward the entrance, stood a group of kettles. I counted thirteen.

The chief's wife gave us a genial smile, showing her small, even white teeth. She was a large, comely woman and on this occasion well decked out. I learned afterward that she was the leader or chief officer of the society.[2] She made an admirable president, as we would say; her very presence seemed to pervade the tent and put everyone in good humor, making them feel welcome.

The members sat about the sides of the lodge, many of them holding babies, either sleeping or awake. For the latter, the mother sometimes made a sort of railing of her arms and within this enclosure the little one leaped up and down, chattering or crowing like any other child. The women were painted and in gala dresses. There was little variety in these except in the pattern of the calico. A few wore a cloth tunic decorated with the much-prized elk teeth. These are rare and difficult to procure, as an elk furnishes but two of the desired kind. A small hole is bored through the root of the tooth, and by this means it is sewed to the garment. Several women had a blue spot about the size of a silver dime tattooed on the center of the forehead. All of the women were rather over medium height and size and some looked vigorous, but there was a general stoop in the shoulders and a hollowness of the chest that told a tale

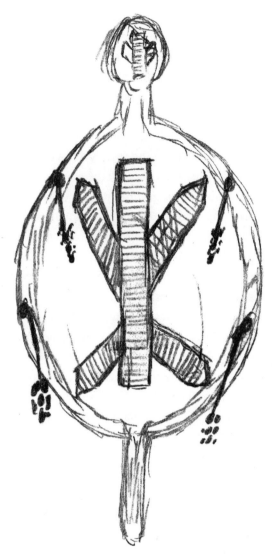

Fig. 26. Beaded case for a baby's navel cord. October 15, 1881. "A part of the navel string of the child preserved. Put in among sweet scented grasses a little case made for it the shape of a turtle—a little head & slender neck, a tail & four legs of long beads—small one at the ends. The body about 3 or 2½ inches long— The case is worked with beads—This is kept [and] as long as kept the child will be well & prospered. The child wears it on state occasions on its back or breast. B[uffalo]-c[hip] [said] if one was asked to take it off and did so the child was given a horse! Poncas do this as well as Sioux" (Fletcher, 1881 Notebook 2, 22). Original field sketch enhanced. Smithsonian Institution, National Anthropological Archives (ms. 4558).

of physical weakness rather than that this form was brought about solely by carrying burdens.

It was quite apparent that the members of the society had made up their minds to forget all trouble; they were telling stories, chatting, laughing, and making fun with a zest that quite took me by surprise. As I glanced around I thought that I had seldom looked upon a merrier set of women, and certainly I had never before seen gathered together so many bangles, earrings, glossy braids, and brilliantly colored faces.

There was one very jolly and large old woman with grayish hair who wore a recklessly flowered tunic and a full contingent of ornaments on her neck, arms, and in her ears. She seemed to be overflowing with fun and as she passed about making her jokes, laughter broke from every part of the tent where she chanced to be. She came and stood in front of the mother and had something to say to the white woman. I could not but admire her robust, erect figure that seemed to defy age and hardship. Sometimes she would dash out-of-doors and call the invitation to the dance in a loud voice, warning the latecomers that they would be obliged to eat out of the big dish! At this everyone shouted with laughter, both within and without the tent.

"What does she mean?" I asked of the mother.

"The last to come is made to eat out of a big dish and they must eat all that is set before them, no matter how much," she replied laughing.

"Is the old woman an officer of the society?" I questioned.

"She is the one who calls out the invitation."

"Who told her to be the crier?"

"The leader," said the mother.

"Who chooses the leader?"

"The society agree together who shall be leader."

"What other officers are there?"

The mother began telling them off on her fingers, turning down the little finger of the left hand with the right forefinger. "There's the leader, and the keeper of the drum, and the mistress of ceremonies, and the crier; there are four of them," she said, holding up the left hand with the four fingers doubled down and then letting them straighten and stand erect. "The society chooses the leader," once more touching the little finger as before and then rapidly along the other three, adding, "she selects the others."

"How long do they stay in office?"

She turned and looked at me, making no answer.

I had forgotten when I asked the question that I was with those who kept no count of time.

The drum was placed nearly opposite the middle of the south side of the tent. It was a large drum of white man's make [the outside covered with a broad belt of red cloth beautifully embroidered with porcupine quills]. Four stakes were thrust into the ground and to these the drum was tied so as to raise it a few inches from the floor. The upper end of each stake was shaped as a face, and the length of the stick decorated with ribbons and brass ornaments, presenting quite a festive appearance. Six women sat about the drum.

"Are the drummers selected by the leader?" I asked.

"They are good singers, and good singers can sit at the drum," answered the mother.

"Can anybody sit anywhere?" I continued, bent on information.

"Every woman sits in her place," she replied.

"Can't a member change her seat?"

She made no answer but laughed in such a way that I knew I was again on the track of the "queer questions."

Just then the leader signaled the music to begin. The women beat the drum in seemingly the same rhythm as the men and sang in a high chest voice and nasal tone. Some voices, however, were clear and bell-like. As the song progressed no one rose to dance, and in my wonder I exclaimed: "Are not the women going to dance?"

"That is not a dance song," said the mother, her face broadening in a laugh as she spoke. It was clear that I was quite verdant in Indian matters, and this last question was too good a joke for the mother to keep. She told it to her neighbor on her right, who bent over and looked at me and laughed, and then she passed the joke on to her neighbor. The mother leaned over and told it to the woman on the other side of me, and soon the story traveled around the tent and all the members were looking and laughing at the white woman who did not know a—what shall I call it— cavatina from a polka!

After a pause, a rapid air was started and the mother gave me a vigorous nudge with her arm. Just then I caught sight of the jolly old woman, the crier, dancing around the circle, throwing out her right foot now and then to poke a woman and bid her get up and dance! These invitations were greeted by merry retorts as the women rose to comply. While the dance was going on the mother said, "You, get up and dance."

I was surprised into a hearty laugh at the bare idea.

"Get up and dance," she insisted, her face brimming with fun.

"I don't know how," I protested, as she urged. At last I said, "You must first teach me."

For a moment, I feared that the muscular old crier, who chanced to be near me, might take me in hand, but she passed on and I felt safe. She was always the first to rise at every dance and the last to sit. She always looked triumphant as she rested, wiping off the perspiration from her good-humored face.

During the dancing songs two women having rattles of gourds, filled with small stones, rose and danced behind the drummers. They held the rattle erect in the hand and kept time with the drum by lifting the forearm. The rattles sounded a little like castanets and added to the spirit of the music.

The women kept their feet closely together as they danced, rising on the toes and giving a kind of jump which shook every part of the body, making the earrings and braids fly when the dancer was fairly underway. Sometimes the women remained dancing in one spot and again they would move sideways, around the fireplace, still keeping the feet together and giving the jumps already described. At the close of every dance they gave a loud, vibrating cry, made by tapping the mouth rapidly with the fingers.[3]

The afternoon wore on and the mood of enjoyment seemed to gather force. Everyone took turns at dancing. When a mother was seized with a desire to dance she would hand her baby to a neighbor who was resting and then join the bobbing throng. One woman sitting near me had three children in her lap at once and she gaily accepted the charge.

The mother called my attention to a young girl who was evidently the youngest person present. "A new member," she said confidentially. The girl was dressed in a tunic of dark blue cloth, the waist ornamented with young elk teeth. She was slender and very prim. She danced near the drummers, keeping in one spot. She never smiled but rose promptly with the song and jumped dutifully throughout its continuance. She called to mind a model little schoolmate of mine who never mussed her dress or obliterated the creases of the iron on her apron; those straight lines were a continual reproach, and I used to wish some common calamity might cause a wrinkle somewhere. I caught myself wishing that the precise Indian novice might lapse into a touch of mirth, but she remained erect in the midst of the undulating fun that surrounded her.

One of the songs was unlike the others in that the accompaniment was played by lightly tapping the sticks on the frame of the drum and the quaint, plaintive melody was sung very softly. I turned to the mother and said: "Will they not sing that again; can't I ask them to repeat it?" She smiled but shook her head, negatively. I wanted to catch it and write it down, for it was the most pleasant music I had yet heard or that I have ever listened to among the Sioux Indians.

The dance just before the feast was peculiar. At a certain part of the song all the women bent their bodies forward at the hips, rising and falling at certain cadences. At its close, the tall mistress of ceremonies arose and walked slowly to the left of the entrance, carrying a wand about two feet long; the handle end was ornamented with quillwork, the other part was slender and pointed. She paused before the woman seated at that end of the circle, then laid the wand upon her head and passed it down over the forehead and ridge of the nose, the mistress saying as she did so, "One." Stepping to the next woman she repeated the action and so on around the circle. After the enumeration was completed she took her appointed seat on the north side of the tent, to the right of the entrance.

The woman who had been first touched by the wand began to offer her thanks; first, she thanked the giver of this feast, calling her by the term of relationship she bore to the speaker; then the woman thanked the society. The person addressed and the society made response. When she had finished, the member to her left repeated the same formula, only changing the term of relationship to suit her position toward the feast giver. So the thanks passed around the entire company. If a woman failed to speak up clearly she was bantered by the elder women. Everyone, however, seemed to enjoy paying this tribute of gratitude and courtesy.

After a moment of quiet the mistress of ceremonies arose and called on several women to help her with the kettles. These were now uncovered and sorted. The members placed before them their dishes. The mother set out mine ready for my use; the kettle she had brought she put behind me, well under the slant of the tent. Two of the women selected started, each one with a kettle; one began at the left of the entrance, the other at the middle of the back part, and each one passed around one half of the tent circle and filled the dishes from the kettles carried. After all were helped no one offered to touch her portion but sat in silence while the mistress of ceremonies advanced to the fireplace, dipped a spoon into one of the kettles, and taking out some of the food, lifted it toward the heavens, turned it about to the four quarters, and then dropped it in the ashes. This done, she advanced to the south side of the entrance and stopped before the first member; taking up with the member's spoon a little food from her dish, the mistress put the morsel in the member's mouth. Passing to the next woman, the same action was repeated and so around the circle. During all these ceremonies everyone remained gravely silent; even the children seemed to catch the solemnity of thus acknowledging the gift of food and the bond of sisterhood.

The menu consisted of four courses:

Meat cut in small pieces, boiled in thickened broth
Plum broth, thickened
Chokecherries, stewed
Soup, indescribable

The soup is always served last at an Indian meal.

It seemed as though I could not partake of the viands, although I tried to do my duty. In the midst of the struggle, the mother, without warning, seized my dish and I heard her empty it into the kettle behind me. At the proper time she disposed of my portion of the other courses in the same manner. Then I recalled her smile and glance at me when she provided herself with the kettle before we started. She had suspected my lack of appetite!

After the feast was eaten and each person had put her dishes behind her several gifts were made to different members. A woman who received a new tunic put it on over the one she was wearing, chanting her thanks. Not long after a second garment was given her; she tied this in a roll about her neck, singing her thanks. A third garment she spread in her lap, as she gave her thanks. The mother told me this was the first time the member had attended the society since the death of a relation and the gifts were in recognition of the fact.

The leader stepped out and returned, bringing in her husband. She bade him call off his brave deeds. He stood near the drum; at each tale of prowess the drum was struck and all the women shouted. When he had completed his list he walked out and the leader rose and threw a small stick in the lap of the mother beside me. This signified the gift of a horse. The mother returned her thanks, and the old crier sang outside the tent the praises of the generous deed.

Suddenly, in the midst of the merrymaking, everyone became silent; the crowd outside fell back, the women drawing away their wondering children, as a naked man with his hair cut short came in sight. In an instant, every woman had thrown her blanket over her bowed head and became motionless. The man slowly entered the tent. A woman near the door rose and threw a blanket over his shoulders; with this hanging upon him, he passed around the circle, laying his hand on each muffled head, repeating in low tones the tidings of a sudden death. It was pitiful to feel his cold hand on my head. A few suppressed sobs from the women told their responsive sympathy. He passed out of the tent, wailing as he went, and spreading the sorrow throughout the valley.[4]

All signs of mirth had disappeared, everyone sat hushed, for the deceased had been a member of the society. After a time the now-saddened women stole away. The mother rose, gathered up our dishes and the well-filled kettle. There was no smile on her kind face; the tears on her cheeks and the faraway look in her eyes showed that memories were stirring, that she had felt the heavy shadow of death fall across her simple life. The stars were coming out one by one in the east while the west was still aglow as we turned homeward, each of us silently thinking of those who shall walk the earth no more.

NINE

Acting out a Vision

In tent life the small boy was a factor of trouble; when the meal was cooked and ready for serving, he was seldom to be found. The mother generally rose and went in search of him and more than once he was thrust with emphasis through the opening of the tent and presented a rueful countenance as he plunged among us. Shinny or some game was to him far more important than eating. The little girls were always near at hand; they were apt to beg their share of the food and carry it away in order to have a feast in the play tent.

"Boys are troublesome," said the mother after one of these family perturbations, "but on the whole they are not so difficult to bring up as girls."

"I should think the girls were easier. You never have to run off to find them," I remarked.

"That isn't much to do. See the trouble I have to teach the girls how to sit. I must watch that they do not act like boys; and then their hair," and she cast a worried glance toward the two black heads that were busy over a couple of dolls.

"Is it much more difficult to braid their hair than the boy's scalplock?" I asked.

"His hair is cut close, I don't have to brush it and watch it to keep it clean and in order. Then see their clothes!"

To be sure the boy made a strong case on that point, as he was guiltless of any garment but his dangling breechcloth, while the girls each had on a single smock. "So much sewing for the girls," she continued, "and one must be careful of daughters."

"I have heard a good many white mothers say the same thing."

"If the boys have enough to eat, it is no matter how they sit, or where they go, or what they wear," continued the mother.

"Daughters, however, help you a great deal," I suggested.

"Yes, they help after they are taught. There are many things to teach a girl, but now that we have so little game there is not much for a woman to do."

"Your daughters can go to school and learn to do new things, since the old duties are passing away," I replied.

The mother laughed, then rose and passed into the tent.

"Your aunt hardly favors education for girls," I remarked to the nephew.

"I don't know," he replied.

"What shall you do when you return from school?" I asked.

He was silent for a time, then he said, "What would you do?"

I looked at him and felt the embarrassment of the question. The valley afforded but little opportunity for farming; the soil on the hills was light and seemingly without depth. The more I contemplated the situation, as if it were my own, the more I felt that I should decline to cast my lot in this region. At last I said, "I'll tell you honestly what I should do. I should leave this place and find a spot better adapted to farming."

"There is little better land anywhere on our reservation," he replied.

"Then I'd go elsewhere," I declared.

"You are not an Indian, you can go anywhere," he answered.

"So can you," I rejoined.

He shook his head. "White people don't want Indians among them."

"An educated Indian is different," I remarked.

"Educated or uneducated, they are all Indians to the white people. They see no difference."

"You take too desponding a view. You know of many Indian pupils who live with white people in the East—why not here?"

"It is different. I can't tell why. We Indians suffer a great deal from the contempt put upon us. You should hear the questions asked us, see the looks cast upon us. I often think we are regarded as curious animals only. You know the government expects us who are educated to return to our people, so I must stay here and do the best I can!"

The outlook was gloomy and not an element of prosperity was discernible. If the young man were of the stock that made New England blossom in spite of rocks and an inclement climate, he would be able to invent some way to overcome disabilities and to find a livelihood here; but he had no such heredity and there was no constituency to help him, either among his own or the triumphing white race. The old trails familiar to his forefathers were useless and he must build a new road at great cost.

In the face of the difficulties that beset the progressive Indian, I did not wonder at their persistent clinging to a past that had, after its fashion, sustained the people in the days gone by. Nor was I surprised at the zest shown by a large portion of the people in their native religious ceremonies. Their modes of expression and appeals for help borrowed a pathos from their environment; behind them lay their fading past, before them a heavily clouded future.

From many of the tents throughout the valley, poles with streamers attached were thrust through the smoke flaps or stuck in the ground beside the lodge. These were the symbols of prayer. If anyone was sick or in distress, poles were at once raised. Similar emblems were always about the graves or attached to the scaffolds on which the body was placed. A general belief prevailed that spirits, or the unseen powers, were sensitive to any artificial disturbance of the air causing a breeze; the fluttering of the calico tied to the pole, therefore, bore forward the petition of the supplicant to the invoked deity.

There were families that kept sacred stones which they used to paint either entirely red or one side red and the other side blue. The putting on of paint on a stone or any object and also upon the person was always a part of a religious or social ceremonial. It formed a part of the formal approach so essential to the Indian mind. The dead were painted that they might meet the spirits in a guise befitting so solemn an occasion.

The vision which appears to a man where he fasts during his early religious experiences is perhaps the most sacred possession of his life. Frequently he hears a song in his vision; this he never forgets, and this he sings in the day of trouble. The animal he has seen in his dream is supposed to lend its peculiar powers to the dreamer.[1]

After the fast in a lonely spot where the vision has been vouchsafed, the youth returns to his father's lodge and makes no mention of what has occurred, nor must he speak much for four days. At the end of that time he is permitted to seek out an old man who has had a vision of the same animal. After smoking together, the young man may tell the elder that a vision has been secured. Should the young man speak of his vision before the four days had expired, and then to anyone but the proper person, he would lose all benefit of the dream.

Next he must travel until he meets the animal he has seen and secured it for himself. This trophy becomes the visible sign of his vision. He wears it upon his person when he goes to war or on other solemn occasions.

In every tribe there are many societies, religious in character, which are composed of persons dreaming of particular animals, such as elk, deer, and buffalo. A man's vision determines to which of these societies he may belong. To join, it is needful to provide a feast and many gifts to be distributed among the members. It takes time to accumulate a sufficient number of these needed articles, and the female members of his family help him by making ornamented robes, moccasins, etc.

I had heard that a young man, a relative of the family, was about to join the Elk Society.[2] He had fasted and had a glowing vision. There are said to be four colors which pervade visions: the white cloud, red cloud, blue cloud, and yellow cloud. [This man's vision had the yellow cloud.] His mother and sister contributed of their handiwork, and now the time for his acting out of the vision drew near and I was on the alert to see the festival.

The day dawned bright and balmy with patches of light clouds to break the deep blue of the sky. Early in the morning the members of the Elk Society gathered at the invitation of the neophyte. A new tent had been expressly prepared and was set up west of the camp; this duty belonged to the women members of the society. Around the top of the tent were painted four blue bands; across the entrance an elk was drawn in red, so that whoever entered the lodge passed through the body of the animal.

A pole had been cut by a relative of the young man and upon it were hung offerings of calico and bunches of reeds, each one having fastened to it small quantities of tobacco tied in cloth.[3] This decorated pole was set up in the tent a few feet from the entrance. Back of the pole was a sacred dish containing water, on which floated a few leaves. I was told by an old man, "We must have water for our health, so we put water there as a prayer, and the leaves are medicine to cure disease." The fireplace just behind the dish was covered by sprays of artemisia, on which lay an oblong looking glass with lines of fine, dark-colored earth extending from corner to corner, forming a cross. The same man explained this symbol: "The looking glass reflects the light and the sign of the four quarters or four winds, made of fine earth, shows that the light is everywhere over the land. Therefore none of these Elk members shall walk in darkness!"

Beyond the looking glass the sods were cut out in the shape of a large oval and the earth beneath them made fine. In the middle of the oval the symbol of the earth and four winds, a square with a line projecting from each corner, was hollowed out. A coal was dropped in the center of this figure and sweetgrass laid over it to smoulder. Two pipes were passed through this smoke, then lit and ceremoniously used and laid one on each side of the mellowed earth. The stems were put toward the east and offerings of food placed near the bowls. Four young women dressed in green were seated on the right of the entrance. They were to assist in singing and in the long outdoor dance.

The young man who was to act out his vision had seen it in the yellow cloud, so his body was painted yellow. He and all the other men of the Elk Society sat at the back part of the tent and were painted in accordance with their respective visions. They all wore masks to resemble the elk. The antlers were ingeniously formed of boughs rolled with cloth. One of the masks had a small round looking glass, like a single eye, fastened on the forehead. Others had them in place of eyes.

When the members were masked and painted they presented a grotesque appearance but everything, as I afterward learned, had its symbolic meaning. On the back of one man a blue circle was drawn; in the center a splinter of wood was passed through the cuticle and an eagle feather dangled from the wood. The splinter represented a wound, the eagle feather showed it to be honorable, the blue circle was the four winds which blow away disease and baneful influences. All of this was a prayer that any wounds he might receive should not bring death.

The entire morning was consumed in these elaborate preparations. Early in the afternoon the young women passed out of the tent and moved slowly up the valley. They had not gone far when the men followed, one by one, emerging from the tent, each taking attitudes indicating caution, as an elk might step forth from cover and look about him. The girls kept on in advance. Sometimes the Elk men would leap, crouch, trample the dirt, or move noiselessly along. Several of the dancers carried hoops in their hands containing mirrors, from which they cast reflections of the sun upon the ground.

This singular company followed the prettily wooded stream, although they frequently doubled on their tracks. The girls did not once turn to look at the dancers, who came after with wild but not unseemly antics. In all Indian ceremonials a ritual of steps is observed, differing from the ordinary dances. The whole movement of this long dance with its queer posturing and actions was not without untrammeled grace and spirited movements.

Men, women, and children flocked after the Elk men but never came very near them. The silence and intentness of the spectators bore testimony to the serious character of the festival in spite of its seemingly incongruous elements. Four hours were consumed in the slow progression up and down the valley.

As the dancers neared the tent from which they had started, an old man drew my attention to the east, and then I saw penciled against the sky the fragment of a rainbow. Everyone was soon looking at the favoring sign and all faces were bright with the promised blessing. I could not help glancing about for indications of rain; there had been some all day and now the buttes were golden in the setting sun and the few fleecy clouds were pearly and light. It would have been easy to share the popular feeling in a miraculous indication. An Indian friend turned and said to me: "That rainbow has come directly from the God to show that the young man has faithfully acted his vision, that his vision was true and his prayers accepted. He has done right. The God has seen it and told us so!"

Hundreds of persons watched the dancers. Young men stood in groups, their white cotton blankets drawn over their heads and faces, leaving but one eye exposed. Older men were bareheaded and looked on with gravity. Old men and women came out of their lodges and lifted up their wrinkled arms in sign of thanks as the dancers passed. Occasionally a man darted out of the throng, came abreast with the dancers, squatted on the ground, and made symbols on the loose soil. They were working a mystery to bring back the elk and the game that had disappeared from the country and thus to restore the past condition of the people. The festival and the appearance of the rainbow seemed to awaken in the people a religious fervor.

At last the dance was over. The young man was the last to enter the tent and acted like an elk retiring to a place of quiet safety. The men unmasked and in due time passed out to the well-earned feast. The tent was soon lowered and the consecrated articles left for the elements to disperse. No one cleans up after an Indian festival; the ubiquitous small boy generally avails himself of any handy articles, for he is not yet within the pale of observances.

As I lay on my robes that night looking up at the stars it seemed as though a rift had been made by the strange and almost incomprehensible ceremony of the day, permitting me to look into a different world of thought and belief. The pathos of the scene dwelt with me, the men seeking by signs and symbols to recall the lost game, blended with the talk of the Indians around the fire of the student's outlook for the future, and I fell asleep wondering how the great gulf between the two races was to be bridged.

TEN

Journeying with the Indians

A visit to some friends of the family was decided upon. We were to travel hundreds of miles to the Missouri River, where the people lived. A dozen or more families made up the party. On the day designated for the journey everyone was astir while the stars were still shining. The shadowy forms moving about the entrance to the tent and the boiling kettle warned me that I had better get up and be ready for breakfast. The cool morning air gave a zest to appetites and to anticipations.

As soon as the meal was over the mother went out and with rapid steps and bent form passed around the outside of the tent, pulling up the tent pins used to hold the tent cloth taut and throwing down the poles which supported the smoke flaps.[1] The daughter took out the round, slender sticks which fastened the tent cloth together in front. [Then the women stood for a moment looking toward the chief's tent, and I noticed as I looked around that the women at the other tents were also pausing and glancing in the same direction. In a moment the chief's tent cloth was loose and fell to the ground.] Then the mother and daughter each took a side of the tent cloth and folded it in plaits until they met at the back pole; this was tipped backward and allowed to fall to the ground. The cloth was loosened where it was tied at the upper part of the pole and rapidly doubled up into a compact bundle.

It seemed strange to look through the open framework of the lodge that had been my home for so long a time and to realize its simple structure and to see the shadows of the poles fall in lines across my bedding and meager baggage, now tied up and ready for the journey. But there was no time to indulge in reveries, for the mother was already lifting the tent poles out of their earth sockets and throwing them down, leaving the circle free of access.

Meanwhile, the boys were off with many a whoop and snatch of song to gather the ponies. The men were busy looking after the wagons, or else were sitting in groups discussing the journey and the routine of the intended visit or attending to the packing of the gifts to be bestowed, for all visitors are expected to bring presents. The younger children ran here and there, undisturbed in their play by the commotion. Soon the boys came riding along, swinging the ends of their lariats in wide circles and driving before them a motley herd of ponies, some frisking and galloping and others in a dogged trot. None followed a path or kept in a straight line but spread out on each side in the onward movement. The mother and daughter made a dash as the ponies came abreast and secured their animals. Some submitted to be caught, others rebelled. [Then the young men mounted and galloped off to head about the refractory ponies, finally bringing them in quite tamed.]

Those families who had no wagons took the packs containing gala dresses and the bags filled with meat and corn and adjusted them on the ponies like panniers. Tent poles, which trailed behind, were fastened to each side of the horse and a skin or blanket fastened between. Here the young children and the puppy had a comfortable time together as they journeyed. It took from four to six ponies to carry the belongings of a tent. There were enough animals for all the men, women, and older children to ride, and colts running free.

Two other families beside ours had wagons. The mother tied some of our tent poles on each side of the wagon box; the rest were packed upon ponies. She dragged along the harness and slung the mass of straps and buckles on the ponies' backs. They gave a slight start as the load dropped on them. The buckling was quickly done by the two women, and a portion of the stores placed in the bottom of the wagon. Finally, the kettle and coffeepot were picked up and the cavalcade moved. The three vehicles rumbled along with squeaking wheels, for someone had forgotten to use the wagon grease before starting.

The delight of being "off" affected everyone. The elder people enjoyed it sedately. The young men dashed about on the hills, where they stood like silhouettes against the cloudless sky. Now and then the men dropped from their ponies and lay flat on the ground while the animals nibbled unconcernedly.

The father sat on the high spring seat of the wagon. Driving having been accepted as a manly occupation, the woman seldom took the reins if a man was along. According to custom, I was forced to sit in the bottom of the vehicle, with the stores. This tempered my delight, for it is hard, teeth-chattering work to ride on the bottom of a springless wagon. Sometimes it seemed as though my head would be jerked off and I envied the people on ponies. Each hour made it more difficult to endure this new hardship. As I looked to see how the women in the other wagons were getting along it seemed almost incredible, but a woman had curled up in the bottom of one of them and had gone to sleep!

It was needful to drive slowly, not only on account of the smallness and weakness of the grass-fed ponies but that the party should not get too scattered or the wagons too far in advance of the animals with packs. Now and then a man on a pony ambled along by our side and conversed with the father. The women generally kept together; the girls were not allowed to leave their relatives, so the gallants had no chance for a flirtation.

All day we rode over the prairie, starting up the birds, seeing the flash of the antelopes, or catching sight of the retreating wolf. My great fatigue made the day seem long and my watch pointed at three when I noticed far in the horizon something that looked like bushes and a bluish tint in the atmosphere. I recalled that the Indians had mentioned the latter as a sign of water, and I secretly hoped that it was the indication of the presence of the creek where we were to camp. The jolting had made every square inch of my body ache. Soon the welcome sight disappeared and again all was sky and grass. By and by, as we rose on a slight elevation, there lay a valley through which ran an ample stream. The tint I had seen was caused by the water and the bushes were the tops of the trees [which bordered it]. Men, women, and children were glad at the prospect of camping. The places to pitch the tents were selected by the women. The father followed with the wagon to where the mother had driven the ponies. She had chosen the spot where the bottom was widest, and well back from the stream. As for me, I was glad to climb out of the instrument of torture and throw myself on something practically immovable.

As I lay I watched the mother set up the tent. First she picked out four poles and laid them two by two so as to cross at an acute angle about three or four feet from their tops, when they were firmly bound together with a thong; then she raised and spread them, and the four poles stood as the skeleton of the lodge. There is a prescribed order in placing every pole and resting it in the crotch made by the tied poles, that all may be well locked together and the tent rendered secure. The back pole is then laid down at a right line to where it is to be raised, and along its length the tent cloth is unfolded and tied at the upper end; the pole and its cloth are then slowly raised and allowed to fall in the place left for it in the crotch. The mother and daughter each took hold of a side of the tent cloth and carried it around the frame until they met in the front. The pins were next put in to hold the cloth together, and then the mother walked about the tent pulling forward a pole here or shifting one sideways there until the cloth was straight.

With the large wooden peg for the front corners, she dug a hole on the spot where the end of a tent pole rested, putting it to one side so as to get at the place; when the hole was about six or eight inches deep, the pole was dropped in the socket. The large peg was driven through the two corners and the entrance formed. Other pegs were thrust through loops fastened to the lower edge of the tent cloth and soon it was taut and without a wrinkle. The smoke flaps were next adjusted according to the wind and the tent was ready for occupation.

The little girls who had run off on our arrival were now seen coming with their arms full of dry twigs. The mother seized her axe and went with the other women to gather wood. Meanwhile the father, sons, and nephew were attending to the horses, leading them to water and taking them off where there was good grazing. The daughter and little girls were busy carrying in the bundles, I mildly protesting that I would bring in my baggage, but I was too tired to rise, so they carried my belongings. The mother returned with her burden strap across her head and breast and a load of wood on her back, while the daughter and a girlfriend from the tent nearest ours took their kettles and strode away toward the creek. In less than an hour the thin blue smoke was curling through the tent flaps and the kettle giving forth savory odors to the hungry.

In the midst of the bustle of settling, the old men sat in groups, some of them smoking together. They seemed to have no part in the stir about them. The young men, after the ponies were cared for, lay at full length resting on their elbows, their ornaments glistening in the sunlight as they kept watch through the swaying grass of tents where coy maidens were on household cares intent. The small boys were already busy shooting arrows of grass, and the little girls were lugging the babies about. By and by came the welcome call to supper and in a moment no one was to be seen outside and the hum of voices and clatter of spoons was heard within each conical lodge.

The meal over, we all went out and lay down in the shade watching the long slanting shadows until the sun sank in a heavy cloud. Something in the air and the sounds of the birds seemed to portend a storm, but no one spoke of it or seemed disturbed at the prospect. The clouds rolled up and an ugly, sickish-green hue pervaded the heavens, which darkened rapidly. The wind gathered force, the long prairie grass lashed about, and the trees by the stream creaked as they bent and shivered. The women were busy pounding the tent pegs more firmly into the ground and laying the tent flaps over closely so as to make all secure against the wind.

There was a wild beauty in the gathering tempest—the lightning was darting in every direction, the thunder rolling, and a dense line, almost black, was advancing directly toward us. A storm at sea is grand, for the ship companions one in the fight with the elements, but a storm on the plains meets one single-handed. There is no chance to offer battle, no refuge in flight. Man seems impotent as the elements march upon him. The storm held me spellbound before its majesty. I was suddenly brought to my senses by the mother catching me by the arm and drawing me rapidly to the tent. We were hardly in when the crashing of the trees and the swaying of the tent told us that the tempest was on us; the wind roared and the rain fell in torrents. We were all of us standing by the tent poles, holding and bracing them, hoping they would withstand the pressure of the wind. There was no time to let go long enough to pass the finger along the pole from the highest drop of rain to the ground, in order to form a channel for the water to run off without dropping: all hands were too busy striving to prevent disaster. After one terrible blast screams were heard, and we knew someone was tentless. The rain and hail beat about us and it seemed as though the tent cloth must be torn to shreds. After a long time, so it seemed to my weary body, the wind lulled, but the rain kept on. It grew dark, the fire was out, and except when the flashes came we sat in inky darkness; there was not sufficient wood gathered to make a fire, and it grew chilly. Gathering more wraps about me, I sat on my bed, watching. As the evening sped, I noticed by the aid of the lightning that the members of the family were lying down and falling asleep. They were like nature's children and took her moods simply.

I determined to try and sleep too. I lay down, but the vivid glare which at times made it almost possible to see through the tent cloth, the trembling earth as the thunder swelled and roared, the pouring rain, and the now wildly rushing creek made sleep impossible. As I lay, almost breathless at times, the storm gathered new force and the tent swayed horribly. I sprang to my feet with a shout that roused the sleepers, none too soon, for three of the poles were drawn from their sockets and the rain was pouring in. Again in the glare and darkness we stood bracing the poles.

"Is there danger from the stream?" I asked of the nephew, who stood holding the poles next to those I was grasping.

"That is what my uncle was saying."

"What does he fear?"

"It may rise and carry us off. It has an ugly bottom full of quicksand."

"We are some distance back from it."

"My aunt says she thinks the water will not rise high enough to bring danger here, but she fears other tents may go."

We stood listening to the increasing rush of waters, wondering where the line of safety might be. Again came a lull; the rain abated, the lightning ceased, and the thunder rolled further and further away. By and by, only the angry stream remained of the former din. The mother stepped out and was gone a short time; then she returned, putting her head in the tent, uttered a few hurried words which made the father and nephew hastily follow her. I was left alone with the daughter and little children.

I could hear shouts, but the raging water deadened all other sounds. I felt my way to the entrance and looked out. The clouds were breaking and in the rifts stars were shining. The stream seemed perilously near. In the distance I saw men moving about with lighted fagots of wood. As I watched, suddenly a figure was near me. "Who is it?" I asked that I might not be run over.

"I've come for you," said the nephew, "to see if you can help a woman. We have saved her child, it is not drowned, but she lies like one dead."

Finding my little haversack containing my small store of medicines and throwing it over my shoulder, I was off. "You must let me hold on to you for I can't see and know I shall fall," I cried to the nephew, who was somewhere near.

He returned and, taking me by the arm, bore me over the beaten grass to a tent wherein was a light. The people were in great alarm and said as we entered: "She is dead."

I glanced at the woman; she was rigid and the blood was oozing from her nose. "She is not dead," I replied, feeling the pulse. "Let someone make a fire quick and heat me water."

I administered a few drops of brandy, wiped away the blood, and applied restoratives.

"Rub her feet and hands," I said to the bewildered lookers-on.

It was pitiful to see them try.

"Do it this way," I said, seizing one of the cold feet and rubbing it vigorously. When I had four persons at work, the nephew came and said, "What do you want to do with the water?"

"To put at her feet," and then I stopped. What should we put it in? There were no bottles or vessels to be had. "What can we put it in?" I said, repeating my thought aloud.

"We have it in the coffeepot," he replied.

"Bring it here then, if it is hot."

It was dire necessity, but the coffeepot must serve as a hot-water bottle. As the nephew entered, two men came in with him and walked directly to the woman. Everyone stopped rubbing.

"Go on!" I said, but no one obeyed, and one of the men took the woman's head and began to force open her mouth and pull up her eyelids. "Who is he?" I asked of the nephew.

"A medicine man," he replied.

"Tell him I will take care of the woman. Let him stay and see how I will do it." I felt sure I should succeed and so ventured to assume the case.

"He says," repeated the nephew after he had interpreted my remark, "that her eyes must be opened."

"Tell him to wait, she will open them herself when I get through."

Meanwhile, I had adjusted the coffeepot, secured more friction for the legs and arms, and again administered restoratives, taking care to keep between the woman and the medicine man. I never worked harder, and before long I noticed a relaxing of the muscles and a few gentle breaths. In a few moments she opened her eyes. The men silently watched her and then rose and left the tent without a word. When the woman was quite restored, I left her snugly tucked up, with her rescued baby sleeping in her arms.

The morning broke clear, and the camp was late in getting started. We had an ugly stream before us; fortunately it was not very deep. I watched the men take some poles and securely fasten them across the top of the wagon box. That done, I was told I was to ride there and to be sure and hold fast! During my passage I was too much occupied trying to keep on my perch and to protect my medicine and notebooks from the surging water all about me to observe much that was going on elsewhere. The ponies pitched and plunged in the stream, the wagon dipped and tilted. Indians, breast-high in the water, manned all of the wheels and walked at the ponies' heads. Every precaution was taken to prevent disaster. The men were obliged to keep stepping rapidly to prevent their sinking in the treacherous sands. Once I thought we were going over, but the wagon was saved by a vigorous effort. I was glad to get to land. As I wrung out my clothing, for the wagon box was filled with water, I watched the men and women and ponies cross the stream. The children and puppies were carried high on the shoulders. The clothing was rolled up and transported in the same way. The comparative ease with which men and ponies waded and swam across made me realize how closely related wagons and bridges are to each other. It took considerable time before all were over, as families had to assist each other. I noticed my patient of last night moving about much as usual. She gave me a shy smile as I caught her eye during the drying operations on the sunny bank.

The day's ride proved even more fatiguing than that of yesterday and I made many plans to get out of the bottom of the wagon, none of which seemed feasible when I came to the point of putting them in execution. The only comfortable place to travel was on the spring seat beside the father, but that would upset all notions of etiquette, so I determined to endure the bottom, for there must be such a thing as getting used to it, even as there had been to sleeping on the ground.

We struck a camping ground earlier than yesterday. The heavens were clear and I hoped for a quiet night. Happily it proved such. Day after day we journeyed. Sometimes we were obliged to halt on account of a storm; sometimes we were overtaken by one; then we would crawl under the wagons for shelter. As we neared the Missouri the outlines changed and the country appeared more broken. At last as I looked toward the east I saw the unmistakable blue tint and asked if the Missouri did not lie off among the hills and learned that it did; we were nearing the end of our journey.

Not long after we stopped at a place where it seemed queer to make a halt; the tents were not put up, but everybody became very busy opening packs. The brother, I noticed, opened a pack and began to take out his gala dress and array himself; two other young men were also making themselves gorgeous with paint, necklaces, and all manner of finery. Some of the leading men were gathered together in consultation.

"What are we all stopping for?" I asked of the nephew.

"The young men are going to be sent forward with the gift of tobacco— the little bunches are being tied up. These are our visiting cards! We shall follow on slowly, after the young men are started and the people are dressed."

I watched the gallants receive the "cards," then go off at a rapid gait and disappear over the hill. Meanwhile men and women were busy with their paint sticks, and packs were lying open in every direction. I felt rather dingy in the midst of all this profusion of color and ornament, but I had nothing else but the garments I wore and a simple black silk, stowed away in case I ran suddenly against civilization. So I waited for my friends to complete their toilets. It was an odd sight to see so many persons intent on looking fine, the vast prairie their dressing room, their only mirror each other's eyes or the small looking glasses of the dandies. By and by all were ready, even the children having received fresh daubs of paint, and we moved slowly forward once more.

After a few miles a cluster of white tents came in view, but before we reached them we again halted. In the distance were seen a dozen or more Indians with their robes wrapped about them, walking toward us with a stately tread. Each man carried his pipe. As they came near they greeted us, but there was no hand shaking except with me.

Each one of the newcomers took a family in charge. We followed our host to his ample tent, where we found the kettle already filled and the welcoming feast in preparation. The tent we had used in the journey was not set up; we were to be entertained in the tent of our host. His family, all but himself and wife, had been scattered among relatives to make room for our large party—we were nine. Eleven of us were, therefore, to dwell in one tent. Already the calls to feasts had begun, and the night bid fair to be spent in driving away all thoughts of need and in renewing the bonds of friendship by giving and receiving gifts, all of which was done with dignity and good cheer.

ELEVEN

Natives and Visitors

The camp was astir with the spirit of hospitality; everyone was in gala dress and care seemed banished. The women amused themselves and me by trying to initiate me into some of their games. One game was very pretty and the women were exceedingly deft in playing it. The game, which is of the same order as our "cup and ball," consists of catching upon a slender needle of bone the small bones of the foot of the deer, which are strung on a thong attached to the needle. The women twirled the dependent thong and caught the bones, making many counts, while I was able to score but few. I was encouraged, however, to persevere, and promised success if I did!

As we were playing I noticed a little girl busy throwing something around her head, saying some words. At length I asked what game the child was playing. The women looked toward her and began to laugh and the child joined, in an embarrassed way, her open mouth showing where a tooth had been newly lost.

"She is asking to have her tooth grow again. She must say it four times and bury the tooth in the ground," said the mother.

Here as elsewhere I observed that when a dish was covered, a knife was carefully laid on top. A child toddled up and took off the knife; its mother suddenly rose, caught the child, and replaced the knife, drawing in her breath, making one of the exclamations of pain, followed by a sharp sound caused by pressing the tongue hard against the teeth and then withdrawing it. I stepped out of the tent and confronted the nephew. I asked him what harm would come if the knife was removed.

"That keeps the ghosts away!" he replied.

"Tell me about it," I asked.

"Ghosts will meddle with food, and if anyone should by chance eat food that a ghost had tasted, harm would come to him, but ghosts will not touch a knife; that will keep them away!"

"Are ghosts around all the time?" I asked.

"So it is said," he replied.

As we were talking I happened to glance toward the agency where several strangers were loitering about, talking together. The trader also seemed busy, and Indian regalia was being shown and purchased. It was long since I had seen so many of my own race.

"Who are those men?" I asked.

"I don't know," said the nephew.

Our host came along and I made the inquiry of him.

"Men from Washington," he answered.

"What have they come for?" I asked.

"To talk about that cow I suppose."

"What cow?"

"The white men have been buying land of us with the promise of cows; they get the land, we don't get the cattle. We are tired of the white man's cow."

"Why don't you go and tell these men from Washington that you have not received your payment?" I asked.

"It would do no good. These are like all the rest. They take our land and buy our ornaments from the trader, or some Indians who care little to whom they speak. White men all despise the Indian because they can cheat them. Look at them now," he said with contempt in his voice and face.

Turning that way I saw one of the men trying on moccasins, another girding himself with a sash, and a third had fitted a war bonnet on his head and was strutting about playing big chief, while all the others laughed with unmixed jollity. It was funny, looked at from any standpoint but that of the Indian.

Just then a young man of the party sauntered by clad in all the Indian toggery he had been able to purchase: leggings, sash, moccasins, knife case, match-box ornaments; he carried a pipe; only his shirt and hat, which was decorated, belonged to his eastern suit.

"Speak English?" he asked of the nephew.

"A little," was the reply.

"Been to school somewhere?"

"Yes."

"That girl your sister?" meaning me; my large hat shaded my sunburnt face.

"No."

"Half-breed, ain't she?"

No answer.

"Umph! Well you and she and all you Indians ought to be at work. It's work makes a man! Look here, what do you think of that pipe? I bought it of a man over there. He wouldn't sell it under four dollars. Did I give too much?"

No answer.

"Is four dollars too much money for the pipe?" he repeated.

"I don't know," the nephew replied.

"Well I don't care. It will do for my collection. Has the old fellow there," indicating my host, "anything nice to sell?"

No answer.

"Does the girl speak English?" meaning me.

No answer.

"Umph! You're a stolid lot!" and he marched off whistling "Pinafore."

"Well, that's extraordinary," I exclaimed, when the young secretary was out of earshot.

"Maybe it is to you, but we are used to it; as used as we ever shall be!" replied the nephew.

"A white man who puts Indian clothes on has no self-respect," said my host, who had understood nothing of this talk. He stood like an old Roman wrapped in his blanket. "Our dress was that of the hunter. It means something to us. It means nothing to the white man."

We were joined by an Indian who was anxious to farm but lacked implements. He spoke of his need, looking wistfully toward the group of men from the capital.

"Would it not be well to tell them what you want and why you want it? Those men were probably sent here to look into your necessities; they are making fun just now, but they would listen to you," I suggested.

"You do not know how those men do out here. They talk to a few whom the agent sends for, and if the tribe is gathered, then only the white men talk. They have never any time to listen to us. I have been told too that the interpreters do not always carry our words straight. The agent appoints the interpreter; if he does not please the agent, the place is taken from the man. He pleases the agent, and it is hard to get our wants known. We are called troublesome Indians if we find fault," said my host.

"But this man wants farming implements. He can ask for them and that would surely be told straight," I responded.

"He can ask," said my host in a tone that implied he will get nothing.

"The missionary gave me seed last year, but I could not reap my crops, only with my knife. We could get no implements," said the man, still looking toward the laughing group of white men, who seemed to be greatly enjoying their outing.

By and by wagons drove up. Valises were brought out and the men from Washington drove off without a word or even a reconnaissance among the people, leaving the reservation utterly unmindful of the human beings who by the strange fortune of events were stranded upon conditions brought about by naught of theirs. I watched the delegation drive away, laughing and bowing, while the agency groups of officials seemed equally well pleased that everything had gone off so felicitously. The contrast between the white folk and my Indian companions was startling; over these latter men settle a gloom that looked as though it must deepen into night.

The following day news came that one of the prominent men was dying.[1] He had fallen and his injuries were internal and beyond the reach of cure. [Figs. 27 and 28] We all hastened in the direction of the tent. Over the hill I saw a file of men making their way; they were elaborately painted and dressed, and all carried guns. Many people were going toward the tent by twos and threes. When we arrived the man had just ceased to breathe.

Fig. 27. "Haw ha-ka-nagga. Standing Elk's house." "Rode over to Standing Elk's [Sioux] camp [Tuesday, Oct. 18, 1881]. As we drove down the barren hills saw on end of the plateau, several teepees & log houses. About one of the tepees crowds were gathered. Buffalo-chip who was in advance with Standing Elk, rode back & said, some one was dying or about to die in the tepee" (Fletcher, 1881 Notebook 2, 25). Standing Elk (*Heȟáka Nážiŋ*) was a Brule Sioux. Original field sketch (before p. 28) enhanced. Smithsonian Institution, National Anthropological Archives (ms. 4558).

The lower corners of the tent cloth were pinned back and he lay dressed in his best, his face painted red and turned toward the east. Upon the rack outside, strips of gay-colored calico were being spread. The packs belonging to the household were emptied of their treasures; embroidered garments and regalia of all kinds were being displayed prior to giving them away. Within the tent the women were wailing. The wife cut her hair and threw it upon the ground. A near relative stepped to the opening of the tent and called to the spirits to come and join the relative who was just starting on the unknown road. The favorite horse was brought and strangled before the tent, where he lay limp after the struggle. The men I had seen filing over the hill now sat in a row some forty feet from the tent, facing it, and singing in low tones the song of death. After a time the wife and

Fig. 28. "Soldier Creek. An Indian death scene Oct. 17, 1881." "This man, Kick, [from Standing Elk's camp at Rosebud Agency] was at the beef issue. He went home and worked hauling some logs, felt a sort of click in his chest, and became weak lay down & grew weaker and weaker and died at daybreak. The nearest of kin goes out of the tent door and calls—A forerunner has gone to the spirit land, come and meet him. His horse, the best one, is shot as soon as possible. The wives open their packs and empty their store—calico, beadwork, &c.. These are thrown on the railing beside the tent. . . . His horse lay dead as in the sketch. The row of heads were the Omaha Club. These chanted long and low the death song. His dog came out—these men shot it. It turned and cried piteously was shot three times and then fled on up the hill at the rear of the tent and there lay down and died. By and by one of the women went up to where it lay and with wailing dragged it down & it lay as in the sketch. The tent was open as in the sketch— people went about it, women wailing. There was some sort of feather ornament hanging over his head—sketch—This was his war bonnet. The women wailed—the gay colored calico fluttered, and the bright beadwork, contrasting strangely. By & by, a man came & called this was the giving away of the dead man's horses. Then the wife and mother came out wailing. The dog was dragged toward the Omaha Club. This was a gift for a dog feast. They carried two bunches of the calico and threw them before the Club. Then they passed down the line laying their hands on the head of each man, wailing as they passed. Beadwork and calico were given to the women" (Fletcher, 1881 Notebook 2, 29–31). Original field sketch (before p. 29) enhanced. Smithsonian Institution, National Anthropological Archives (ms. 4558).

Fig. 29. "Old block house Ft. Randall." October 25, 1881. "Two of the block houses remain (see sketch). In these houses the women and children were sent for safety, and sometimes kept for weeks" (Fletcher, 1881 Notebook 2, 142–43). Original field sketch (between pp. 145 and 146) enhanced. Smithsonian Institution, National Anthropological Archives (ms. 4558).

man's mother came out from the tent and passed along the line of men, sobbing. They paused before each man and laid a hand on his head. The dog chanced to run along and a gun was leveled at it and fired. The poor beast turned with a piteous look and ran bleeding up the hill behind the tent. I saw it fall. A woman followed and dragged it back by the tail and left it near the horse. To the left of the tent, outside, stood the relatives wailing their sympathy. The gifts were distributed, the body wrapped up and carried to the hill, the tent taken down, everything given away, and nothing but a trampled circle remained of a home that twenty-four hours before had been filled with the cheer of affection.

The widow, bereft of all her belongings but the ragged garment she had put on in her grief, sought shelter with her kindred, but she soon left them to go and weep beside her husband's remains that lay on the scaffold.

It was a haunting scene to me. The next day the rain fell and the wind blew. In the lull of the storm the wails of the widow were borne to my ears. I wondered, as I sat by the fire surrounded by my host's family and the little mother's unbroken gossip, if my companions heard the cries. They said nothing about it.

"Where do the dead go?" I asked.

"You have seen the path their feet have made," said my host. "It is that band across the heavens," meaning the Milky Way. [Fig. 29]

TWELVE

A Religious Festival

Having made friends with some of the leading men [fig. 30], it was agreed to describe to me a sacred festival, not often enjoyed, relating to the white buffalo.[1] The white buffalo is rare and generally remains near the center of the herd, which makes it difficult to approach. It is therefore considered as the chief or sacred one of the herd, and it is consequently greatly prized by the Indians. Owing to the scarcity of these animals an interval of many years usually passes before one is captured.

In order to keep the hide, the hunter must have four sons. If the man who kills the white buffalo has four sons and yet is not able himself, or with the assistance of his relatives, to provide the feasts and presents necessary for the full enjoyment of the privileges the ownership of the buffalo entitles him to, or, if for any reason he desires to forego the honor, he may barter the hide, which is highly valued. One was recently exchanged for three horses and a mule (equal to between one and two hundred dollars). The news of the capture of a white buffalo soon spreads beyond the limits of a tribe and proposals for its purchase are often received from remote points.

The ceremonies pertaining to the white buffalo are very elaborate and detailing them occupied three days, a part of the ceremony being acted out. During all the time we were talking of it, great care was taken to close the tent tightly; no one was allowed to be present but a few chosen men, and guards were placed outside to prevent eavesdropping. The weather fortunately continued to be fine; a storm would have broken the narra-

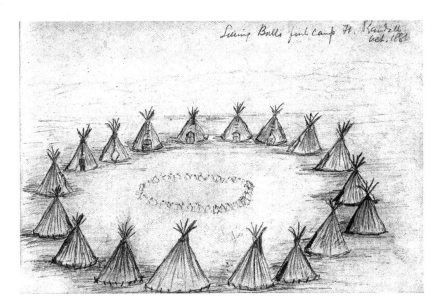

Fig. 30. "Sitting Bull's first camp Ft. Randall. Oct. 1881." "The camp of Sitting Bull when we first came was on a terrace or plateau back or west of the Post—tents in a circle. There are 168 persons—men, women and children. These are counted every morning by the officer of the day and once a month by the Col. at the close of month" (Fletcher, 1881 Notebook 2, 146). Sitting Bull was the leader of a band of Hunkpapa Sioux who were held as prisoners of war at Fort Randall. The sketch dates to October 27–29, 1881. Original field sketch (before p. 150) enhanced. Smithsonian Institution, National Anthropological Archives (ms. 4558).

tive, probably irrevocably. It became known that sacred things were being revealed to me, and a superstitious dread prevailed, lest punishment should follow what to some was considered a sacrilege.

When that point of the description was reached which referred to the black earth, the old priest who was talking was interrupted by one of the younger men, a person of unusual intelligence and vigor. He rose and with eyes fixed on mine advanced directly toward me and, halting, regarded me with closest scrutiny. After an awe-inspiring silence he extended his hand in greeting. Then he said, "We pray by these things and they are great. We never talk about the white buffalo skin except when we drink water at council feasts. You have tried to help us and you are the first and only person to hear of these things."

I replied that from my heart I thanked them for what they told me, that the white people knew little of the Indians' religion and only the Indians could explain it. The more they told me the more I could help them.

The chief then instructed the men who were describing the ceremonial to be very careful not to make a mistake or miss a word lest evil befall them.

As I entered the chief's tent one of those three days a man came rapidly toward me. He was naked and he looked angry. Other Indians followed him into the tent. The priest said, "Evil has come to us!"

An Indian repeated angrily, "Yes, evil has come to us of your talking."

"My friends, what has happened?" I asked.

"A woman was nearly drowned; this man," pointing to the naked person, "hardly saved her."

Another man added, "A child nearly choked to death coughing."

The men who had talked with me seemed troubled and embarrassed. The chief sat with bowed head, drawing figures on the earth with a stick. The other men were very angry. It was a critical moment. Rising and crossing the tent, I extended my hand to the naked man, saying, "Friend it is good fortune. The woman did not drown, you saved her," and turning to the other man I added, "and the child got well."

This new aspect of the case, being borne out by the facts, met with approbation, for the naked man accepted my hand and then resumed his clothing. The others all proffered me their friendship.

On account of this episode only two men, who were, however, the most important ones, were willing to talk, and they thought it best to adjourn to some distance from the tent where we might be quite unobserved. They painted themselves for the occasion, with red on their faces and blue stripes on their hair. Their pipe was also freshly painted red.

Before resuming the narrative the two men seated themselves toward the sunrise, lit the pipe, bowed to the earth, and passed it, uttering a prayer. They were very serious and anxious that no mistake should occur. They would not draw any diagrams but allowed me to draw some and corrected my mistakes.

The better part of two hours was consumed in making the diagram showing the transfer of the down of the eagle from the consecrated board to the black earth. Every detail was acted out, not one omitted.

At a certain part of the ceremony the four sons of the owner enter and sit at the left of the priest. When all is ready the priest again consecrates his hand in the formal manner and takes up the pinch of meat at the eastern side of the dish and, holding it up, says, "Son, when men come to your tribe, give to them gifts, moccasins, horses, and other things, as I now give you this meat; it will go into your body and make you to live long, so you will help those who come to your people." The meat is then put into the child's mouth, who eats it.

Again consecrating his hand, he takes the pinch of meat on the south side and, holding it, says to the second child, "Son, if you are visiting a tribe, or are camping anywhere, and see an orphan child, give him half of what you possess if it be ever so little; as I now give you this meat, it will go into your body and make you to live long; so by your acts to the child you will raise it up."

Repeating the consecration of his hand and taking the pinch of meat from the western side, raising it, he says to the third son, "Son, if you are living in a good lodge and prospering you must treat well (i.e., entertain and give presents) all that come to your lodge, and children will be born to you; as I now give you this meat, it will go into your body and make you to live long, so children will be raised up to you, and they shall follow in the path of your father."

Passing his hand through the smoke in the ceremonial manner and taking the pinch of meat from the north side of the plate, raising it, he says to the fourth son, "Grandchild, if any of your relatives be wounded, make the smoke of sweetgrass, so will you become head of the chiefs; as I give you this meat, it will go into your body and cause you to live long, for in this way all my sons have been fed."

At the end of this ceremony kettles of food are brought in; the chiefs eat of the pounded meat. All the tribe are called to a feast outside the enclosure; each one partaking must paint his face red. After these ceremonies have been performed, the gifts are all laid at the feet of the hide. The pipes are given to the poor of the tribe, presents of horses are made to the priests, and the owner of the hide parts with his garments and steps forth from these initiatory ceremonies, naked. The people at once contribute clothing to him, present him with a tent, and he begins life anew.*

The old priest said toward the close of his description of the festival, "Thus my grandfather did, thus he was made a holy chief, and his son after him, and I too, who am now an old man, have followed in his steps. I must do thus to do right, and I try to do right and teach my children so that they may follow in the right way and live long."

At the close of the narrative the younger priest said, "Look at me. I look at you and I shall never forget you. Look at me, you are never to forget me."

As he paused for my reply, I said, "I am glad you will never forget me, and I shall not forget you."

Rising, he approached me and with great earnestness fastened his eyes upon me, saying, "Promise me that no harm shall come to me or my people because of what we have told you."

"I do not think any harm will come to you because you have talked to me," I answered.

A second time he asked my promise and I made the same answer. Meanwhile the old priest sat bowed to the earth and evidently reciting some

---

* Nakedness is the sign of sore trouble, bereavement, or great humility. In many ceremonies the laying aside of clothes is the symbol of a kind of self-abnegation. When the ceremony of piercing the ears of children takes place, the gaily dressed child is stripped of its clothing and this is then given away. The religious teaching and formulas of the Indian demand much giving away. In the absence of genuine commerce this becomes of great importance to the people as a legitimate mode of exchange. When the Indians come in contact with our civilization, it leads to misunderstanding and misfortune. Accumulation with the Indian is always for the purpose of disposing of his goods to secure honors, which, although they may be social, are all closely connected with religious forms, church and state being completely at one in the primitive forms of society. This long habit, bred of religious custom, tends to what we denominate improvidence and shiftlessness when practiced in the midst of white environment, and this heredity of training is a factor to be considered by those who labor to civilize the Indians.

formula. A third time, with increased earnestness, the same assurance was asked, and I made the same reply. Then coming still nearer and looking at me with an expression I shall always recall vividly for it showed me how profoundly sacred had been their disclosures, he said, "Promise me by your God that no harm shall come to me or to my people because I have spoken to you of these sacred things."

"My friend," I answered, "you ask me to promise you that which only God himself could promise. I will pray my God that no harm shall come to you or to your people because you have talked with me." Then, extending my hand, which he took, this strange scene came to a close.

THIRTEEN

The Ghost Lodge

A half-dozen poles had been raised about the lodge of a man of some prominence. He was in sore trouble. His son, a youth of promise, lay ill, and the father had called in the medicine men to practice their arts of exorcism. I had heard the peculiar rapid beat of the medicine drum night after night. That alone seemed to me to be enough to shorten the days of the patient. The lad was dying of rapid consumption, and there was no help for him. The father was still young, not yet forty, and ambitious of tribal honors. He had been a warrior and also sedulous in observing all the rites peculiar to his people.

At last, in spite of all his efforts to avert the dreaded blow, the son lay dead.

"He will keep a ghost lodge; the holy man has been sent for," said the grandmother.

"What is a ghost lodge?" I asked.[1]

My host replied: "In old times it used to take two years to perform this ceremony; now a man goes through it in one winter. I have kept a ghost lodge. A man wins honors who does so." After a reflective pause he added, "It was hard to do it, as we used to observe the custom, but everything is changed. We are losing all our customs; the Indian will soon be gone," and the old man settled back into silence.

I wandered out near the tent where the youth lay dead and heard the wailing of the relatives, and through their cries I caught the chanting of the holy man. Then I saw a person go out and by and by he returned with the crier. Keeping watch a while longer, I saw the crier emerge carrying a pipe and pass on into the tent of an old man some distance off. The breeze played soft music in the tree under which I lay, and the soft clouds gathered and melted in the bright blue sky. Everything seemed to breathe of new life and joy—the wailing yonder seemed like some memory of winter gusts and storms that cut across the genial air. How long I lay watching the lodge that I did not like to enter I cannot tell, but at length I saw the old man to whom the crier had gone leave his tent and slowly make his way toward the house of mourning and enter it. Again I waited, and after a time the old man appeared with the holy man; they were carrying a long piece of red cloth. They walked toward a hill some distance from the camp, and there they seemed to be busy for a time.

Meanwhile, the tent was being prepared for the funeral; the front was partly unfastened and looped back; this left the interior exposed. The lad lay facing the east dressed in his best, his face painted red. His father sat beside him, wailing, and the mother unbraided her hair and cut off portions of it. After a time, men arrived bringing gifts, which were laid aside. Late in the afternoon the body was well wrapped up and carried up on the hill, where it was placed at rest amid the wails of those to whom the lad was dear.

I turned back to the tent where I was visiting, filled with sympathy for the mourning ones and turning over in my mind as to what could be the meaning of the ceremonies I had seen at a distance. That they had something to do with the religious thought and consolation of the people I had no doubt, but to get at them was a difficult task.

As we sat about the fire I told my host what I had observed in the morning and asked him to explain it to me. Before he had time to answer, two friends came in, and the pipe was lit and passed. As we were all well acquainted I repeated my question. The oldest man said: "The spirit of a man is like a shadow, always with him, but when the man dies, then the shadow gradually fades away. As long as any part of the body is preserved the spirit will linger near it."

"A man's spirit knows the clothes he wore, so we never keep back anything a man wore in life," added the second friend.

"A man who keeps a ghost or shadow lodge keeps about him the spirit of his child all that time, and a man who does that must be very careful. It is hard to keep a lodge and have no harm come of it. These two men have both kept ghost lodges successfully," said the oldest man.

"He," said the second friend, referring to the previous speaker, "has kept three ghost lodges."

"Yes. I know all about it. I will tell you, these men shall hear me."

From the conversation that followed and lasted well into the night I learned the following facts and they were afterward confirmed by several persons.

If, on the death of a child, the father desires a ghost lodge, he speedily sends for a holy man, who on his arrival at the father's tent takes a pipe which is handed him and fills it, chanting a ritual suitable to the occasion. One of the criers of the camp is called and he receives the pipe and starts for the tent of a man who has successfully kept a ghost lodge. As the crier enters the tent he says in an intoning voice: "The one who sends me wishes to keep a ghost lodge," and offers the pipe. The man addressed accepts the pipe, lights it, and smokes in silence. When it is finished he goes to the father's tent where the child lies dead.

After entering the tent and observing a brief silence, he walks over to where the child lies dressed in its best clothing, its face painted red, and taking a knife cuts off a lock of hair just above the forehead. He then hands the hair to the mother, who takes it, wraps it in a piece of new cloth or skin, and lays it away, where it remains undisturbed for four days. Four yards of red cloth or a deerskin painted red are divided into two parts. One part is carried out beyond the camp, to an elevation, and buried. This is an offering to the earth, and the chanted prayer asks that the life, or power, in the earth will help the father in keeping successfully all the requirements of the ghost lodge. The other part of the red cloth is lifted and offered to the buffalo with a prayer that food may be granted to the father during the period of the lodge keeping. After this ceremony, the cloth is cut into eight strips and given to eight men who have successfully kept a ghost lodge. This is a request for their goodwill and help. [These ceremonies are performed by the wakan (holy) man and the man who cut the child's hair.]

The society to which the father belongs presents him with horses and friends make gifts; these are all treasured against the day of final ceremonies. After these preliminaries, the body of the child is buried with the usual rites.

The duties of the father begin at the time the hair is cut and continue until the closing ceremonies, six months or a year afterward. During this interval he cannot eat dog meat or any flesh scraped from the skin or hide of an animal. He cannot cut open the head of any animal to get the brains, or strike or break any ribs, or do any butchering. He cannot take a gun, pistol, arrows, or any weapon in his hand. He cannot run, go in swimming, make any violent movement, shake a blanket or his clothing, or in any way disturb the air. No one must pass before him or touch him, and to prevent this disaster, a coal of fire is always kept about two feet in front of him as he sits in the tent. Although he remains with his family he must live apart from his wife and on no account take a child in his arms, for if he should so forget himself the child would surely die.

During the four days the hair is laid away the mother and sisters, or the near female relatives, make a small buckskin bag in which the hair is placed. A pack of the same material or of cloth is prepared, having buckskin thongs with which to tie it. A new tent is pitched not far from the father's tent, the opening toward the east. [Formerly this tent for the ghost lodge was set a little within the tribal circle or open space, out from the line of living tents.]

On the fourth day the holy man and the man who had cut the hair from the child repair to the tent set apart for the lodge and make up the pack into a roll about six inches in diameter and two feet long, enclosing the buckskin bag containing the lock of hair cut from the child and the pipe which had been filled by the holy man and sent out by the father. To these are added any other articles which the parents may choose to contribute. Three crotched sticks are cut by a male relative, and for the honor of doing this he gives away the value of a horse. On these sticks the pack is tied. A fire is made in the center of the tent, back of which an oval is drawn upon the ground about three feet in diameter, having an elongated opening at the east. The sod is then removed from within the figure and the earth thus exposed is mellowed and made fine. Down from the wild goose, colored with red ochre, is placed along the outline of the figure. Behind the oval figure the three crotched sticks are set up, having the pack fastened to them where they come together. A bowl and a wooden spoon are fastened to the outside of the pack.

No woman but the mother of the child is allowed to enter this tent. She has charge of the pack but can only pass into the tent when performing some duty incident to the lodge keeping. When entering the tent she turns to the left and makes the entire circle, always going behind the pack and passing out by the right. All who enter the tent must observe this same direction and no one may pass between the pack and the symbol drawn on the ground or between that and the fire. Nor can anyone turn back on his passage around the tent, for one must always move in a continuous circle from left to right.

On clear sunny days when the wind does not blow the mother carries the crotched sticks, with the pack tied to them, outside the tent, setting them up in front of the entrance. As the sun declines she returns the pack to its place in the tent. When it thunders, or if a gun be fired, or any unwonted noise heard, she must hasten to cover the pack. If, when the pack is out-of-doors, a sudden wind should rise, the mother must instantly take the pack into the tent. Thus her constant care is necessary.

Every day the father of the child enters the ghost lodge tent and the mother, soon after, sets kettles of food inside. The father loosens the dish from the pack, a small quantity of the food is placed in it, and the dish set down near the pack. The father takes a bit of the food from the dish with his fingers and, lifting it, says: "We offer this food that you may help us, that we may escape ill fortune. We ask you to help us to avoid any sickness or misfortune that may lie in our path." [This is the usual form of asking a blessing. This ceremony takes place at every feast, dance, or ritual observance where food is eaten. The father does not address the ghost pack but the deity or life of the animal food.]

The offering is then dropped upon the mellowed earth and buried in it. During this ceremony, persons of the male sex may be present and sit on the north and south side of the lodge. It is usual for orphans, the aged, or anyone in need of food to repair to the ghost lodge to share in this daily feast given by the father as a religious hospitality.

In the tent, certain rules must be observed: the mode of entering, moving about, and leaving have been already mentioned. No one may blow the fire with his mouth. When it needs to be enlivened one may gently fan it with the wing of a bird. No one may spit toward the center of the tent, but if he needs to cast anything from his mouth, he must turn his head and throw the saliva behind him. No tales of fighting, nor any quarrelsome words, nor any subject which is "bad" must be spoken of in a ghost lodge. Quietness and friendliness must pervade the tent.

If at any time during the period of keeping the lodge the father should by accident hear of any violent words or deeds he must at once perform certain rites which will avert the evil consequences to him and his family. He must take a few coals of fire and lay on them a bunch of sweetgrass or sprays of cedar. As the smoke rises he must crouch over the coals, bringing his blanket close about his body, drawing it over his head and face so as completely to shut him in with the smoke; sitting thus while the aromatic fumes circle his entire person, he thinks of the duty of carefully fulfilling the ritual of the religious ceremony and by his faithfulness arresting disaster and securing good fortune for his kin.

During the months occupied with these duties, the man can do little more than fulfill them. As he is debarred from hunting and providing food and raiment, his needs are supplied by his kindred. It is not enough that his avocations should be peaceful, but it is his duty to relinquish any hard feeling he has had and forget old injuries. The keeping of a ghost lodge is a signal of peace and cancels all grudges between parties. The father may not smoke with anyone lest he should consort with a man who was at enmity with some other person. The Indians in explanation pointed out that it was for the purpose of enforcing peace in a man's actions and thoughts that he was forbidden to take weapons in his hand and the coal of fire placed before him while sitting in his tent was indicative of his setting himself apart for this religious duty, "the coal being like a partition between the father and all the world."

During these intermediate months, the family is busily employed making eagle war bonnets; embroidering moccasins, tobacco pouches, tobacco boards; fashioning pipes and ornamenting clothing; and gathering together a large amount of possessions to be given away at the closing ceremonies. After a ghost lodge a family is often left in poverty, but with the Indians it is not accumulation but the record of that which a man has given away which entitles him to respect.

Anyone of the same gens[2] as the father who lost a child after the ghost lodge had been inaugurated and who desired to join in the ceremony could prepare a similar pack and tie it to the one in the ghost lodge. Each family thus represented must contribute its quota of gifts at the final day.

An incident occurred to an Indian whom I knew who was keeping a ghost lodge. He, in common with all his band, had attended the tribal sun dance. One day while there he forgot the duties of the ghost lodge and suffered his six-year-old daughter to approach him and he took her in his arms. Too late he recalled the penalty he had incurred. A fortnight later when I entered his tent, where he was sitting with the coal of fire before him, I saw the girl lying sick unto death on the opposite side of the lodge. Bending over the child it was evident that she was beyond any medical aid. Her father accepted her fate as a punishment he had merited. Her mother was hopeless and sat without, working on moccasins to be given away on the approaching final ceremonies, while the brothers and sisters were racing over the hills, pictures of careless health. It was a striking scene. To every inquiry I made as to the cause of the child's illness—cold, fever, or the like—the invariable answer given by relative or acquaintance was: "Her father forgot and took her in his arms." It was impossible to present to the people any natural cause for the child's illness. Her mortal sickness was accepted implicitly as another evidence, supernaturally given, of the sanctity and power of their religious ceremonies. Next day the child died, leaving her parents full sore at heart.[3]

Later, while visiting among a band of Indians, I was so fortunate to receive an invitation to attend the final ceremonies of the ghost lodge. Sometimes people from other tribes are invited and travel hundreds of miles to be present. On this occasion several tribes were represented.

For four days preceding the ceremonies the crier proclaimed that the packs were to be opened and the gifts distributed. During these days, the families having a part in the ghost lodge were busy preparing for the coming feast. A man who has successfully kept a ghost lodge is invited to be the master of ceremonies and for this service he receives large presents from the parents represented in the lodge.

At last the final day arrived clear and cloudless. From early morning to well on toward noon the women were engaged carrying from their tents the gifts, singly or in packs made of rawhide or in wooden trunks, and placing these at the door of a new tent set up to receive them. On this final day all signs of mourning are put away. For the first time since the death occurred the immediate relatives braid their hair and everyone appears in gala dress.

Forty-two great kettles hung from crotched sticks over the fires, and the beef soup and dog stew flavored with dried cherries or turnips sent up fumes of steam. The sticks used to stir these viands were forked, having the end ornamented with beads and ribbons. Young girls were bringing water from the creek, the older ones grinding coffee, and all were busy preparing food for the great crowd of guests. Over eight hundred people had gathered to this feast and were scattered over the grass. The abrupt outline of the buttes; dark evergreens marking the gullies; the narrow valley through which flowed the clear, rapid creek with its border of shrubs and large, graceful trees; the green bottomlands dotted with white tents, while a few were scattered over the hills that rose in terraces to the east; together with the vast throngs of gaily dressed Indians, combined to make a picture full of color, spirit, and a wild beauty all its own.

The new tent set up for the reception of the gifts is placed near the ghost lodge tent, the door facing the east. Near the center a fire is kindled and a figure drawn on the ground and prepared similarly to that on the floor of the ghost lodge. Four live coals are laid on the mellowed earth within the figure and sweetgrass dropped on them. Outside the figure eight coals are placed, four on each side, and sweetgrass laid on to smoulder. On the north and south side a buffalo chip is set. Back of the figure the sod is removed so as to leave a narrow, oblong figure in the earth on which sprays of artemisia are spread like a mat; behind this the presents are arranged in piles, one pile for each ghost represented in the lodge.

After this arrangement is completed a feast is given, and while that is in progress the women set a row of crotched sticks in front of the tent, laying on poles to form a framework on which they spread for exhibition the gifts they had previously made into piles at the back of the tent. When the feast is concluded the master of ceremonies distributes these gifts, reserving those which are to be given away in the ghost lodge tent. Visitors and the poor are remembered in the lavish bestowal.

The interior of the ghost lodge is now rearranged in the following manner. The space occupied by the packs is marked off in an oblong, the sod removed, and the ground spread with artemisia. The figure having the mellowed earth in which the offerings of food have been buried each day is covered with a red cloth. On the center is laid a disk of shell; eight live coals, four on each side, are arranged outside the figure and sweetgrass laid on them. Four buffalo chips are outside of these at the four corners. The different packs are loosened from the initial pack and each one fastened to sticks about four feet long, bound with hide, and an ornamented oblong piece of hide having a face rudely outlined in paint is hung in front of each pack.

There were nine packs on this occasion, three belonging to young men, three to boys, two to girls, and one to a woman. Upon the packs belonging to the young men were fastened eagle feather war bonnets. These effigies were arranged in a semicircle on the south side of the tent, the sticks being thrust in the ground and the gifts contributed by the relations of the dead person piled about his effigy.

Only men who have kept a ghost lodge are entitled to sit in this tent and join in smoking the pipe, which had been filled with the appropriate ritual. The man in charge of the ceremonies distributes the gifts which rest about the effigies to the men present. In so doing he is particular so to dispose of the articles as, for instance, to avoid giving an eagle war bonnet to a man who had received one on a previous and similar occasion. Such items are well remembered in an Indian camp, for it is in this way that possessions change hands. The men who receive at this time will save up their treasures and give them away at some future religious or secular festival.

To give an idea of the value placed upon the services of the master of ceremonies, the following articles were given to him alone: four garnished buffalo robes embroidered with porcupine quills, four woven sashes, four calico shirts, four pipes, four plugs of tobacco, four hatchets, six pairs of moccasins, six dishes, six tin pans, seven yards of calico (a dress pattern), ten butcher knives, two pairs of leggings, two strings of bells, two curtains (strips of tent cloth used to protect the sleeping place), two comforters (bed quilts), one lariat, one hoe, one bed made of reeds,[4] one steer, and two ponies.

Among the articles given away on this occasion the following were counted: thirty-two ponies, one hundred pairs of moccasins, ten shawls, seven buffalo robes, three war bonnets (of eagle feathers), eight calico dresses (made up), besides numerous tin pails and cups, knives, coffee-pots, tin pans, looking glasses such as the young men wear, embroidered beaded dresses, knife cases, match cases, bows and arrows, wooden bowls, balls, shinny sticks embroidered with beads, a quantity of dried cherries, squash, pounded meat, and other things.

When all the gifts were distributed the packs were opened, the pipes were given to poor men, and the hair was once more handed back to the mother, who either keeps it or buries it. After this is done the soul of the child, which has been supposed to linger about the pack, is free to depart.

The shadows were gathering in the valley and the last glow fading from the buttes as the tents fell and the poles were gathered and carried off by their possessors, for not an article used in this strange ceremonial remained in the possession of the parents, who had thus paid to the full their tribute of affection for the dead and proved themselves faithful to the custom of their ancestors. The stars came out and shone over the silent plains, for the men, women, and children had vanished with the day.

FOURTEEN

Beef versus Men

Once more we were journeying over the prairies.[1] The grass was dry and yellow. The winds blew and the nights were getting cold. By taking a shorter path to our destination we had lessened our chances of fuel, for but little wood was to be found along the present route. One cold stormy day we were forced to camp early where there was water but not a stick of wood; not even a bit of brush was to be found. I had been ailing and on this day I fell ill; in spite of all my efforts at concealment, my suffering was discovered.

As I lay on my robes I noticed the mother readjust the tent poles so as to spare one. Soon I heard her chopping. She came in and made a fire with a part of the pole and drew me near the genial blaze, while she cooked for me. It was distressing to think of the sacrifice she had made to procure me warmth and prepare food that I could hardly swallow. I feared for the result of my sickness and while I was able, I wrote a note stating my illness and exonerating my Indian friends of any carelessness in case of my death, and indicated the disposal of my notebooks and my body. This I enclosed in an envelope and addressed it to the Indian agent and gave it to the nephew to present in case of necessity, taking care, however, not to alarm him.

How hard the ground felt to my aching body. The pain that came with every breath seemed to sap my vitality. The storm had cleared and it had turned very cold. In the night the covering to the entrance blew off and I could not keep my eyes from the black spot and wondered if I should see there the glare of wolf's eyes, for I heard animals prowling around the tent. At last dawn came. The mother used up the remaining portion of the pole to cook breakfast and insisted on my taking something hot. All the day as we traveled I became unconscious at times because of suffering, but no one knew it. After a few days I was better again.

In our forward track the heavens were dark, the air filled with smoke, and charred grass dropped upon us. A prairie fire was raging in front and moving our way. From an elevation we caught sight of the great wall of flame stretching clear across our path. We halted. Men went back and set fire to the grass behind us. The flames leaped and roared, spreading in every direction; the birds flew in fright and we stood encircled with fire. As rapidly as possible the people retreated to the blackened ground in our rear. There was no time to lose; the oncoming column was getting perilously near. The ponies were restive; the dogs were afraid; and the children cried, clinging to their mothers. Our wagon was not far over the blackened line. When the advancing flames scorched our faces they seemed mountain-high as they shot up and snapped off their edges into bits of fire. The roar and crackling was fearful. I was lifted out of the wagon; the terror of the animals rendered it unsafe. But there was no escape; before, behind, on both sides of us danced the lurid messengers of death. In a few moments the flames in front fell and the earth lay a smoking mass. We rode all that day over the black trail of the fire and saw the little animals lying scorched and dead.

A portion of our journey was along the path taken by a tribe during one of the removals ordered by the government.[2] This removal took place in winter. The creeks were frozen and men, women, and children waded the icy streams, leaving tracks of their cut and injured feet on the dead grass. The suffering was great and many died. We passed the graves of those who dropped by the way. The Christian Indian's resting place was marked by a rude cross; by its side floated the faded strips of calico, torn with storms but clinging to the poles, that indicated where lay the heathen brothers. The bones of the ponies that starved to death on that winter march lay bleaching on the plains. It was heartrending to listen to the tales of the people who recalled that journey. The missionaries, some of them women, accompanied the people and for their faithfulness more than one paid the debt by life-long suffering from the exposure encountered. The chapels that had been erected by contributions from Christian men and women, after being stripped of all movable articles, had to be abandoned as the agencies were deserted. They stood like monuments of desolation with their gaping windows and wind-rent roofs. The air as we rode seemed full of wailing. The prairie fire swept by the trail but left untouched the cruel record of "man's inhumanity to man."

When we arrived at the agency not all the feasts of welcoming friends, the stir of ration day, nor the tolling of the mission bell calling to prayer could divert me from the memory of those miles of travel along the line of the removal. I realized as never before the treatment the Indians had received at the hands of the government. I also know that the one I had seen was not the only trail left by this same tribe of Indians, for they had been removed eight times in ten years. I knew, too, that hundreds of such trails lay crossing our country, from the Atlantic to beyond the Mississippi, trails red with blood and hateful with treachery born of the greed and power of the white race. As I thought of these things I wondered at my own welcome among the Indians and why they ever spared any of my kind. More than all I wondered that any ever listened to the teachers of the religion professed by the people who had seldom shown the Indians anything but wickedness.

I followed the sound of the mission bell and entered the chapel and sat down near the door. Before me were gathered the women, their blankets about their shoulders, their heads covered only by their glossy hair. Opposite were the men, some in cheap "citizens" clothing, some in a mongrel costume, others in undisguised Indian dress. Within the altar rails moved the clergyman clad in his white vestments. At the reed organ sat a young Indian. The words of the service were in the sonorous Dakota tongue and the music rose and fell in the familiar cadences that echoed long before these prairies were known to us.[3]

When the benediction was over I walked silently through the gloaming to the tent of my new host. He was a tall, serious man. He deplored the conditions of the people, huddled near the agency as they were practically required to be in order to receive their dole of rations. It was not a pleasant sight to look upon strong men and women forced into idleness and pauperism by the "feeding system." It was explained to me by a government official as far cheaper than fighting Indians. "Feed 'em enough and they become like any animal, too lazy to give trouble!"

I watched the distribution of tickets, saw the women bring their long bags in which the flour was dumped, so many pounds to a family, and a small cutting of pork dropped on the top. There was plenty of jostling and chattering and scraping up of fallen bits.

"I'll show you a scramble," said a good-natured official, and he threw out a few handfuls of hardtack, shouting with laughter as the poor creatures clawed and tumbled over each other to get at the food. It was like scenes I had witnessed in zoological gardens, and the keeper of the animals and the keeper of these human beings seemed to regard their office and the actions of their charges in the same light. I turned away sickened, not at the Indians but at the devices of my own race to rob another race of its manhood.

Seated about the fire in the tent the talk turned to the future of the Indians.

"I want to farm," said my host, "but there is no land here. I found a little place and broke a few acres, but I have no implements. I have no money and it is difficult to earn any so I can buy tools. I don't know how to work very well. I want to learn. The money we received for our land is spent for us in rations. We have to be here to get our food, so I can't go away."

"What have you raised on the acres you tell me of?" I asked.

"Those who asked obtained some seed. I received corn; it made a row about ten feet long. I think about one grain in twenty came up."

"Is that all you planted?"

"Twenty potatoes were given to each head of a family. I planted all those. Many Indians broke land but they could get nothing to plant," answered my host.

"It is hard to try to farm when you have nothing to plant and nothing to work with," said a friend who was spending the evening.

"Our treaties call for implements," said my host. "I do not know why we are not given them."

"Why don't you ask the agent about it?" I inquired.

"I never go to the agent," he replied.

"Why not?"

"He does not treat me as if I were a man. I would rather suffer than speak to him. I can die!" he replied.

"We have no schools here," said the friend. "The missionaries tried, but they gave it up. I have sent my daughter away to school. When she comes back I hope I shall have some land broken where I can farm. I mean to build a house. She shall have a better place to live in than I have now."

"I have a son at school," said my host, rising and opening a pack. He took out a picture and held it before me. It was a tintype of a lad clad in uniform. "My son writes to me," he continued, handing me two well-worn letters written in struggling English.

"That is very pleasant. Your son seems to be doing well," I remarked, as I handed back the treasures.

The father smiled but said nothing. His little grandson came along, stepping with the consciousness of budding manhood. He was not quite five years old, well coated with prairie, and clad in a breechcloth. My host caught him and held him quietly for a time, then he said, "I would like you to take my grandson back with you. I want him educated. I will give him to you!"

I looked at the little fellow. His scalplock was tightly braided and decked with brass beads. His hands grasped a bow and arrows. His two shining black eyes were fixed upon me. What could I do with the child stranded as I was, and yet I felt I could not wholly refuse the boy, so I said, "He is very young yet. Keep him until he is larger, and then I will remember what you have said. Do you think you would like to go away with me?" I asked of the child.

He shook his head with vehemence, making his scalplock fly.

"Are you always going to stay with grandfather?"

He changed the motion of his head, with equal emphasis.

"Shall I take little sister with me?"

That question called a halt. He looked at me steadily, then suddenly opened his mouth wide, and a yell came forth that bore testimony to the strength of his lungs.

"I will not take her!" I cried, hastening to search for something with which to pacify the child. For several days he kept close watch of the little girl.

Not far from my host's tent stood a log house built by his eldest son, a neat piece of work considering the lack of training and facilities. Further on was a cabin in process of erection. An old man was building it. He had but one tool, an axe. He had chopped down the trees and hewed the logs with one end of the axe and with the other end drove the nails to hold the house together.

It was pitiful to see these and many other evidences of a desire on the part of individuals to do something. Many of these efforts were futile or ill-directed: the people had no way of learning anything. They were hundreds of miles from any sign of civilization, although the wave was slowly creeping toward them. There was nothing at the agency to stimulate enterprise. The agent and employees had all they could do to keep themselves straight with the requirements of their office. Little time, if there should chance to be inclination, remains for the philanthropic and difficult work of helping the Indian toward civilization and self-support.

It was clear that the agency system, with its [tear in manuscript] foundation, rotation in office, and ignoring of the Indian as a responsible being, had little in itself to recommend it for the task of civilizing the Indians. If the agent happened to be an energetic, humane, businesslike man, he could infuse some of his own life into the dry bones of the system, but the labor was Herculean and the man must work for virtue's sake and receive thence his reward. I have seen such men among the Indians, battling nobly against odds and conscious, as the fateful fourth year rolled round, that they were liable to move on and leave their fields for weeds or the experiments of a new hand.

The day for issuing beef was always an occasion of curiosity [fig. 31] and young officers from the forts not infrequently rode over to witness the scene.[4] As all the Indians were present, every one dressed in his gala costume. The different bands gathered on the hills surrounding the corral into which the number of beeves to be issued had been rounded up and driven, ready for the day. The interpreter sat on the fence and outside stood a crier, who called out the name of the head of each family as the steer for him passed out the gate.

Fig. 31. "Where the ration of meat was issued, Oct. 17," at Spotted Tail's camp, Rosebud Agency. "The cattle were rounded up by the cowboys & let out one by one—the interpreter marking off on a book as he sat on a fence—A crier called the Indian & as the steer issued the Indian either chased or shot" (Fletcher, 1881 Notebook 2, 24). Original field sketch (between pp. 23 and 24) enhanced. Smithsonian Institution, National Anthropological Archives (ms. 4558).

As the animal emerged, the men to whom it belonged began the chase, driving the creature up and down steep ravines, firing at it, the steer plunging about and sometimes rolling over and over into gullies, weltering in blood. The herders joined in the sport and fired shots that seemed calculated to wound and aggravate the animal; boys were encouraged to shoot little arrows into the steer to make it run. It was a brutish scene and one for which white men were entirely accountable. [Issuing cattle in this manner is a disgrace to the government service.] The Indians butcher the animal for themselves, men and women taking part in cutting up and preparing the meat. This work could be done without the preliminary mock hunt, the influence of which is not good on the white people or the Indians, and life is also endangered, for bullets fly in every direction, as the cattle are often chased for a considerable distance.

I was told it would take too long to issue differently, but that difficulty is overcome at some agencies, and it is not insurmountable at any one of them. I was also told that the Indians preferred this method of receiving their beef and it would be dangerous to thwart them. Several of their leading men and other respectable Indians told me they did not approve of it. They said they tried to kill their steers quickly[, but they were often in danger from the shots of other men]. I know these statements to be true, for I have seen them at issues so manage to dispatch their steers at once. There is a rabble element in every tribe as in every community. Unfortunately, this class is often given undue prominence, to the discredit of the better class of Indians, who frequently fail of a hearing. Politicians excel in tribes and these men are not always of the best class. They find ways to make places for themselves and their friends and to substitute their own selfish views for those things which would be for the good of the people whom they often greatly misrepresent.*

One day a child in a lodge where I was staying was taken very sick. I begged the parents to go for the agency physician, but they were unwilling. "He will not come," said the father, as he sat by the little sufferer.

"I will go!" I said, and in an instant I was speeding with all haste to the agency, for moments counted in the life of the child. Arriving at the physician's home I told of the case and asked him to come.

"I do not go out of the office. Let them bring the child here," he replied.

"It is too sick to be moved," I said.

"I cannot break my rule," answered the doctor.

"It is only a short distance and the child may die," I argued.

---

*The custom of issuing cattle on the hoof and permitting the Indian to shoot steers in the manner described has been frequently prohibited by the commissioner of Indian affairs, who has characterized it as "no better than a bull fight," but many white people living in towns near certain agencies make picnics to witness the scene and uphold this activity as a means of obtaining an exciting spectacle. [In 1890 this practice was finally prohibited and replaced with the issuing of butchered meat, thereby depriving the Indians of the intestines and hides. See *Annual Report of the Commissioner of Indian Affairs*, 1890, p. clxvi; Prucha, *The Great Father*, 2:644. —Eds.]

"I never break my rule," he said, rising.

Another time I chanced on an agency physician, a young man, full of jokes and good humor. "Awfully slow place for a young doctor," he said, "but it's good for practice. One can make lots of experiments; it's no matter how many Injuns die!"

There are men of different mold. I have seen them, caring for the people, riding miles in sleet and snow, sitting up night after night to try and conquer disease. Men poorly paid, as are all Indian officials, but men who worked not for mere pay but for the good of others.

Living with the people I looked across the race line and faced specters that would not be laid to rest. The Indian reservation is an anomaly in a civilized land. It is exempt from law and from all the guards that public opinion imposes on a man; the light of intelligent scrutiny of economic conditions hardly glimmers, then, and whoever is present in an official capacity shows forth his inherent character, whether it be selfish or noble, for he governs a people but is not permitted any control or practical knowledge of their affairs. Such places are not safe or helpful toward manly progress.

PART TWO

The Omahas at Home

FIFTEEN

Among the Omahas

The September sun had spread a golden hew upon the wide rolling prairie and the wooded bluffs of the Missouri as I entered the Omaha reservation.[1] The outlines everywhere were broad and gracious; the bottoms were rich and loamy; the uplands clothed with verdure; a fairer land it would be hard to find in all the borders of Nebraska. "Ah!" I thought, "now I may study the Indian in quiet; surely happy aboriginal life is here, unblotted by the faithless touch of the lawless white man."

As I drove over the trail, log cabins were seen nestled amid patches of ploughed land; here and there a tent gleamed among the trees. Suddenly my eye caught sight of a singular object, like a verdant dome, with smoke ascending from it. "It must be an earth lodge!" I exclaimed, leaning out of the wagon to keep the dwelling in sight. How unobtrusive it looked! It seemed as though mother earth had lifted a little of her covering to let her children creep in, that all might live together undisturbed. The asters climbed up over it; the grass clung around it; and only a black circle at the top, where the smoke had scorched the green, gave sign of man's presence. The door of the long entrance, protected by a hanging skin or blanket, looked strangely inviting. Men were riding on the tops of the hills, snatches of their song floating down to us; women passed by in twos and threes, striding along at a swinging gait; while, near the lodges, groups of children were at play. Up and down hill we rode, splashing through creeks or crossing them on rickety bridges; on, following the old military road, past the large building put up as an infirmary by some well-meaning official, but the people refused to part with their sick, and now the government has just opened a boarding school; the children in cheap and not over-tidy clothing stood gaping at the wagon as it drove by: on we go, passing a few little houses, guiltless of paint, that had been erected for employees and the trader, and the old day school on the hill, now used as a recitation room; still on, leaving behind the agent's house, white and pleasant-looking amid the tall trees and ample dooryard; out we rode, beyond this cluster at the agency, which formed a standard of civilization to where the green bluffs rose and fell with streams threading through the bosky bottoms.

As the vehicle rattled along on a high ridge, from whence the land sloped away on each side, to the right, down in the midst of trees, ploughed fields, and haystacks, nestled an unpainted house with a porch in front; the blue smoke curling from the chimney suggested supper time. A restful, home-like look pervaded the picture. A tall woman stepped out of the house with a red shawl hanging over her shoulders, and, shading her eyes with her hand, looked toward us.[2]

"There's mother!" exclaimed my companion, her face glowing with happiness and affection. Seizing the first article she could reach, she waved it with ardor, and the tall figure in the valley responded and then turned and rapidly entered the house. On we went for a few hundred yards farther, then turned off on a side trail, and in a moment a frame house, newly built, came to view in the midst of a grove of tall oak trees. A young woman with a baby in her arms stood at the door.

"My sister!" said the girl at my side, as she caught sight of the group, "and the baby—I've never seen him!"

A moment more and the sisters were in each other's arms, kissing and crying for very joy. Before long I was made welcome. I had come at the invitation of the elder sister, my companion, whom I had known in the East, where she had nobly pled for the rights of her Indian relations who had been driven from their homes to the Indian Territory. To her, and to her singularly gifted family, the Indians are much in the past, and the future promises to increase the debt.

Everywhere was the bustle of arrival, unloading the wagon and greeting friends who hastened to welcome the returning sister. Out through the trees came the tall figure wearing the red shawl, and with a run and jump, the daughter was in her mother's arms. The father was but a step behind and received as fervent an embrace; then, taking her father and mother each by a hand, the three advanced abreast and the daughter presented me.

The mother's face was comely and replete with kindness, her eyes full and expressive, her features regular, and a ready, winning smile on her lips. It was no wonder her daughter loved her so much, she was so full of energy and unfailing unselfishness. Years of friendship have only added to my own high estimation of her remarkably lovely character. I could not feel strange as she took me by the hand and gave me a cordial grasp, with a smile that rippled over her face and melted in her eyes.

The father was equally noteworthy. He was but little above medium stature; a fine muscular form, showing great vigor and power; his well-formed head, high forehead, finely cut features, and remarkably brilliant eyes made his face marked among men; his manner was dignified, courteous, and cordial.

I found myself sitting apart, watching the group that gathered that evening; they were so full of life, vivacity, and individuality: the father and mother and the three daughters, the elder—my companion—vivacious and brilliant. The next sister—my hostess—so like her mother in feature, her expression indicating a rare mind and strong character, without a touch of guile. Her husband, brimming with hospitality and a ceaseless activity in behalf of his house, his wife and baby, his guests, and all his affairs. The next younger sister, quieter than either of the others, having a plump figure and kind face, was very bashful and kept in the background with her young, handsome husband, who was equally quiet and shy.[3] All the daughters spoke English fluently and used it as they talked together. The grandmother, who moved about sharing the baby with its mother, bore marks of early attractiveness, and it was clear from whom the daughter had inherited her ready smile. The grandmother's sprightliness of manner was remarkable and recalled the drawing room rather than the camp. Her old half-sister, always spoken of as the "oldest grandmother," leaned on her staff, bent with age, her face and hands shriveled, but she was full of good cheer and had a nod and a smile and cordial welcome that extended even to the stranger.[4]

Friends had ambled over on their ponies; these stood hobbled, nibbling the grass nearby. Their riders were tall, broad-shouldered, well-developed men; they were addressed as uncles and grandfathers, although they were all in their prime.

The house was overflowingly full. The husband looked in, rubbing his hands, saying, "I've made a fire out under the trees; you'll be so comfortable there, plenty of room for everybody."

"Our house is small," said the wife, turning to me, "but not our hearts."

We were gathered about the cheerful blaze, the husband spreading a buffalo robe for me, saying as he did so, "You might take cold, you aren't as used to being out-of-doors on the ground as we all are."

I threw myself down on the comfortable robe as I thanked my host and scanned the group. One tall man, with his strongly hewn features, looked like the twin brother of the "old man of the mountain," in the faraway notch of the white hills; I used to call him that to myself.[5] He sat with his blanket tucked about his knees, splitting blades of grass with his nail and slowly nibbling as he talked, breaking now and again into a hearty laugh. Beside him lay a man as tall and even larger, resting on his elbows. His face was heavy, and his thick hair hung loose to his shoulders. His features looked as though they were merely blocked out, not finished; he was placing bits of twigs in forms on the ground, now and again lifting his great head to look at a speaker and joining in the laugh with a deep musical voice, then tossing a twig in the fire for emphasis. Beside him squatted a smaller man, full of nerve and sprig. His face was strongly cut, but the lines were also delicate about the nostril and mouth. His eyes flashed and he talked rapidly. He had a knife and was busy with a bit of wood. He shifted his position frequently and bantered the other men at times. Near me sat a tall slender man, very dignified and sedate. He was evidently one much respected. He said little, but when he spoke, in a quiet voice, he was listened to with marked deference. On the other side of me was a smaller man sitting crossed-legged; his face bore lines of suffering. His clothing looked worn, and his hands indicated constant toil. He was evidently a favorite, although backward from a sort of native modesty. The father and eldest daughter sat near together; the other members of the family were grouped nearby. My companion was giving a racy account of the doings in Washington, and her sallies at the way Indian affairs were progressing brought about laughter or earnest discussion.

The Poncas were talked of and the "old man of the mountain" delivered in mock heroics, to the great amusement of the company, a part of the speech he had recently heard in Washington, given by Red Cloud when he offered land to the Poncas.[6]

"The land was not his to give, it was always the Poncas' land," said the nervous man. "That is the way with the Sioux, they like to talk big."

"If white men were not always in such a hurry, they would not have made the mistake of putting the Ponca land in with the Sioux land," said the first speaker.

"White people are afraid of the Sioux and will give them anything," said the other.

A pause followed. The husband threw a fresh stick on the fire, and all eyes were turned to watch the flames catch at the little twigs and snap and sparkle along the log.

"You have been to Washington several times, have you not?" I inquired of the father.

"Tell us about your first journey," asked one of the daughters. The sister hostess had taken her seat near me and interpreted the talk as it passed around the fire.

"When I went to Washington first it was many years ago. The agent made all the men dress in citizens' clothing. Some did not know how to wear all the articles and found the straps and buckles very troublesome. The shoes hurt their feet, and it required someone to see that they did not lose their things. We were to meet the stage in Iowa, and we had to walk to the starting point; when we got there, the stage would not hold us all, so some rode and others walked, taking turns at both kinds of traveling. On the Mississippi we took a steamboat and went up the Ohio until we met the cars and so reached Washington. It was a small city to what it is now; there were few large buildings, one quickly got into the country, and when it rained it was mud everywhere! The government used to take Indians to Washington to let them see how great and powerful the white man was, and I think it was a good plan. Indians see so little of civilization that it is hard for them to understand what it means. If they could see more of the educated white people, see their farms and their houses, their factories and workshops, their schools and churches, the Indian would appreciate more the value of education and of learning to live like the white people."

Checking himself, he added a moment later, turning to me, "You know all this, and these men must be tired hearing me talk about education and civilization, for I have never stopped for many years back."

"One can't say too much about such things," I observed politely. I was much interested, watching the speaker's face and the anxious glance toward the group present, much as a father looks toward his children who are slow to accept instruction.

"All these men are workers," continued the father, "all belong to the young men's party."[7]

"What party is that?" I asked.

"Those who opposed the old chiefs and wanted to farm and own their lands; sometimes it is called the citizens' party. We are growing stronger every day," said the father.

"Did you want to have new chiefs in place of the old?"

Everyone laughed as my question was interpreted.

"No, we have put all the chiefs out and have now a council, but a great many would like to be chiefs yet!" said the father with a constrained laugh, while a conscious look stole over some faces in the group.

"What was the matter with the chiefs?" I questioned.

"In old times," the father replied, "the office was honorable, but when the traders came—they used to be Frenchmen before the Americans held the country—the traders bought up the chiefs and introduced whiskey; and when the agents were put over us, they soon became mixed up with the traders, and it seemed as though the Indian was doomed to every degradation. After we sold our land[8] and had large annuities, the money used to be shipped in boxes, a thousand dollars in a box. These would be portioned out to the chiefs and they were to distribute the money. This was not always done justly; there was a chance for favoritism and for keeping many Indians in debt to the traders, and if he had contrived to control the leaders, very little money reached the Indians. The chiefs opposed progress and were more anxious about their positions than about helping the people.

"Something happened several years ago, which I will tell you, that made the people see the danger they were in from the chiefs. The agency clerk, who was an honest man, came to me one day and said, 'The agent has bought cattle for the Omahas and I have seen them. They are old, worn-out oxen which have been gathered by a man who is a friend of the agent and to whom the agent has paid more than double the worth of the cattle. You must get the chiefs together and tell them not to sign the receipts for the cattle. You know the people have not hay enough to keep the stock, even if they were strong. Should the agent try to force the chiefs to sign the receipts, bid the men insist on seeing the stock first and then they will know for themselves whether the cattle are worth purchasing.' I called the chiefs together and repeated what the clerk had told me.

"In a few days the agent summoned the chiefs and told them he had purchased cattle and that they must sign receipts for them. The chiefs asked to see the animals. The agent said, 'I have seen them, and it is just the same as if you had seen them. I am your father and wish to treat you just as my children.[9] I know what is good for you, and these cattle are what you need.' Still the chiefs insisted on seeing the purchase. 'I am in a hurry,' said the agent. 'I must send these papers on to Washington at once.' The men kept on in their demand to see the cattle. The agent said, 'If you will not sign the receipts, I will depose you and put other men in who will sign these papers!' In the face of these threats, the men signed. The cattle were brought on; they were old and decrepit, every one of them died on the bottom that winter, not one lived until spring. It was in the fall that the chiefs receipted for the stock. When the people saw what the chiefs had done, everyone felt uneasy, not knowing what would be signed away and fearing that someday they might even lose the land in this manner and be left powerless. The office of chieftainship had become corrupt, and it was best that the people should have a voice in their affairs since the chiefs were demoralized and no longer listened to the wishes of the tribes."

"He," said the nervous man, indicating the father, "was deposed and banished from the reservation, because he would not sign false receipts at the request of the agent."[10]

The huge man, who was reclining on his elbows, looked up, saying: "I will tell you something that happened when I belonged to the soldiers.[11] All the people were summoned to have the census taken before a payment was made. Everyone came. All the chiefs, soldiers, and men were present in a large earth lodge. Some of the chiefs had complained that they did not receive all the money which was due the tribe. The agent had heard that there was dissatisfaction. When he came, he brought a table and chair and all the money in a bag. He emptied the money on the table, it was all in gold pieces; then he laid a revolver on one side of the pile and a sharp knife on the other. One of the chiefs walked up to the agent and asked, 'How much money is there in the pile?' The agent threw himself on it and said, 'The money shall not be counted!' and, hustling it into the bag, he added, 'You shall not have any of it.' The chief replied: 'The government must have sent it to you, for you act as if it was yours.' The official went off with the bag, the Indians ridiculing him. In a few days the agent sent word he was going to give out the money. He did give out some of it, but how much was in the bag, the Indians never knew."

"That agent stole forty thousand dollars," exclaimed the nervous man.

"The government paid us about thirteen thousand dollars of the money this man stole. It was the best settlement we could make," said the quiet man at my side.

"I think the agents consider Indians to be fools," said the "old man of the mountain."

"Some of them are fools," interrupted the nervous man, whereupon there was a general laugh at the Indians' expense.

"You remember," continued the first speaker, "the old fellow who called us all up on the hill yonder under the big oak tree, and when we got there, how he told us that he was sent to be our father (laughter), by the great father (laughter), and he was going to take care of us, give us horses, cattle, sheep, pigs, wagons, and build us homes (more laughter); we were to have farms and not to be sick or die any more, for he had studied medicine expressly so that we might live long and be fat (loud laughter)! After he had talked, he bade us all shout for joy, and then all the people shouted themselves hoarse!"

"I told you the Indians were fools!" exclaimed the nervous man. This speech started the laughter afresh.

"Did you get all these things?" I asked.

"We got some old army harness and a few wagons so wide-gauged that they would not travel in the trails the white people had made; always one wheel up on the bank and one down," his gestures expressing the uneasy motion of the vehicle.

"The people cut a forest of trees into logs to build their houses. You can see some of the logs rotting now, where the old sawmill stood," said the man with the hard-working hands.

"When the commissioners came out," said the huge man, "an old man came into the council carrying his wife's burden strap. He walked up to the agent, saying, 'Look! you can see the mark of the strap on my forehead from carrying wood, and you promised me a wagon and horses to haul and work.' Then he turned to the commissioners, pointed to the agent, and said, 'Take him home with you, we don't want him!'" and everyone laughed again.

"That agent did a good thing, he got back some of our stolen ponies," said the father.

"How did you like our fifteen-hundred-dollar bridge?" asked the nervous man of me.

"I don't know what he means, I crossed no good bridge, of that I am sure," I said to the hostess sister.

"Yes, you did cross it," said the eldest sister, laughing.

"Where?" I asked.

"When you went through the slough this side of the agency."

"There was no bridge there!" I replied.

As soon as the laugh occasioned by my remark permitted, the "old man of the mountain" explained: "To reach the saw and grist mill the people had to cross that place and going to and fro was difficult. We wanted a bridge there and we petitioned for it. The agent estimated that it would cost twelve hundred dollars and, as we heard, he was allowed the money. About that time he had some of the Indians cut willows and spread them over the slough; the next rain washed them away, but the bridge never got out of the agent's pocket."

"Do you remember one day," said the huge man, "when we were talking about that bridge, the agent came along and sat down near us, and how a young man went up and took off the agent's hat and tapped his head and then turned to us and said, 'That accounts for it; listen!' and he tapped the agent's head again, 'It's hollow!' and when we all shouted, the agent looked bewildered; he couldn't make out what we were at!" and everybody laughed again.

"I am going home," said the nervous man. "You will all be in bed tomorrow, and I shall be the only one working."

"You think nobody but yourself works," said the huge man, slowly getting to his feet.

The company had risen; the fire had fallen to coals; the stars looked steadily down through the restless leaves; I heard the ponies trotting off, the men talking as they rode; the father and mother and the family had already reached the woods on their homeward way; I stood alone, wondering why I could not escape the ill conduct of my race, and I caught myself saying aloud:

Oh, wad some pow'r the giftie gie us,
To see ourselves as others see us![12]

"You can't see!" exclaimed the sister hostess, hastening forward and taking me by the hand, leading me to the house, where I found my hammock hanging from the rafters, my belongings adjusted by themselves in one corner, and all care possible bestowed on the stranger guest. I could see, that was the trouble!

SIXTEEN

The Young Mother

During the bright autumn days the corn was ripening and the hay ready for mowing and stacking. Almost everyone near where I was staying was busy with the crops, men, women, and children working in the fields. Now and then women, old and young, dropped in for a little chat; the men gathered in the cool evenings. Almost every night the husband lit a fire beneath the oak trees and we held a reception under the stars. It was picturesque and I never became tired of it. My hammock was hung from the boughs, and I used to lie in it, rolled up in a soft robe, and from my vantage point watch the faces, expression, and gestures of the men and women as they talked. Sometimes during the daytime I lay in my hammock as the sister-hostess rocked her baby or sewed on its little garments. We talked much of people and things during those hours.

"Where did you learn such good English?" I asked one day.

"At the Mission.[1] Father sent us all to school when we were little. We did not like to go very well, we would rather play, but when we ran off home, as the other children did, we were whipped and taken back at once. We concluded, after while, we would rather take our lessons than the whipping. I believe father was almost the only Indian who used to whip his children. It did us good, though."

"Your father does not speak English?"

"No, he speaks French. I believe it is the kind spoken in Canada that is different from the French spoken in France, is it not? I think I have read somewhere that it was."

"It is different somewhat."

"Was it education that made the difference?"

"Yes, the emigrants who came to Canada were not all educated men and women, nor were they provided with schools; that is one of the reasons why their descendants speak a patois."[2]

"It is wonderful what education will do," she went on reflectively. "We children can't be too thankful to father for keeping us at school and to the Mission people for teaching us. We don't know much, but it is better than nothing; we have now got the chance to learn. I love to read, but dear little baby takes up so much of my time, and needs so many stitches, that I am afraid I shall be an old woman before I can study again."

I smiled as I looked at the young face; it seemed as if it could not grow old and wrinkled, like the "oldest grandmother."

"Education is wonderful," she went on, "but it is not everything; it will not make a good man or woman. There are some Indians that are real good; they are honest, truthful, hardworking; they never tell unkind stories; they do just as well as they know how; but they have no education—I wish they had. Then there are men I have seen, white men and mixed-bloods, who are educated, and they are wicked and selfish and make other people miserable. I think God means we shall take care of our hearts first and have them right; that will help us to do the best we can with what we have in our minds, whether they be educated or not. I mean to have my baby a good boy, as well as a knowing one," and she kissed the sleeping child.

I wondered if I were dreaming or really listening to an Indian mother. Her low, gentle voice, pure English, saying such wise words, made her like one of my own race.

"Where have you traveled?" I asked, more in answer to my own thoughts than to what she had been saying.

She looked up at me a moment before she answered, "I have been up to Sioux City." She paused and then continued shyly, "That was when I was buying my wedding dress. I have never been so far away but that once."

"Have you never been East, or to any of the larger cities?"

"No, I've never traveled except in books. I want to, though. I want to see the ocean. You have seen it; tell me about it."

I tried to picture to her the scenes that lay lovingly in my memory.

"Wait a moment," she exclaimed, rising and dropping her sewing as she passed rapidly into the house with the baby in her arms. In a moment she returned, bringing a medium-sized shell. "Listen," she said, putting it to my ear, "does it sound like that? I have been told that no ocean shell ever loses the sound of the sea. It is pitiful, isn't it? It is like homesickness. Sometimes I think it is wrong to take them away from the place they love so much!"

It was not needful to break across her sweet fancy with any prosaic definition of different sounds produced by varied forms. Already in my mind, as I looked at this woman, were echoing the lines:

> Though inland far we be,
> Our souls have sight of that immortal sea
> Which brought us hither,
> Can in a moment travel thither,
> And see the children sport upon the shore,
> And hear the mighty waters rolling evermore.[3]

She sat stroking the shell. "How pretty it is!" she said. "I like the colors so much, and I like colored stones too. My eldest sister has a good many."

"Did you ever study how the earth was made; the rocks, the soil, the hills and valleys?" I asked.

"I have read a little about it, but I don't understand it. I can't conceive of the earth different from what it is, and yet I know it must have been made."

I tried to explain about the formation of the region around us and the work done by the Missouri.

"How wonderful it all is," she exclaimed, "and the stars too; to think that they are worlds and perhaps there are people on them who may be talking about us, our world, I mean. Sometimes I think these things are more marvelous to me than to a white person. You know, the white people have known all these things for so long a time that it is born into their children. I don't mean their children know it, but their minds are all ready for it, sort of shaped so as to receive this knowledge. I am an Indian. My forefathers knew nothing of all these wonderful things, and I wake up to it, like the first woman. I often wonder, when I am holding baby, how that first woman felt, if she was afraid and strange, and what she thought when night came on! Of course, she could not know how long the darkness would last."

"Did you ever read a sonnet on night written by Blanco White?" I asked.

"No," she replied, "can you repeat it?"

I began:

Mysterious Night! when our first parent knew
Thee from report divine, and heard thy name,
Did he not tremble for this lovely frame,
This glorious canopy of light and blue?
Yet 'neath a curtain of translucent dew,
Bathed in the rays of the great setting flame,
Hesperus with the host of heaven came,
And lo! Creation widened in man's view.

Who could have thought such darkness lay concealed,
Within thy beams, O sun! or who could find,
Whilst fly and leaf and insect stood revealed,
That to such countless orbs, thou mad'st us blind!
Why do we, then, shun death with anxious strife?
If Light can thus deceive, wherefore not Life?[4]

"That is beautiful," she said, "and it is true too. How delightful it must be to be able to think and to say such beautiful things and in such a way as to make everyone happy who hears them. How lonely the world would be without books!"

"And babies," I suggested.

She laughed, and kissed the child.

"He is as pretty as the shell, don't you think so?" I questioned.

"He is funnier, and so much dearer!" she answered.

Suddenly the baby squirmed and kicked and twisted out a shrill cry. In an instant the shell and everything else were forgotten, and all manner of arts were practiced to soothe the little fellow. The cry had reached the grandmother in the house and brought her at once to the child. Taking him out of the mother's lap she threw him up on her back, the little arms clasping her tightly around the neck; then she drew up her shawl over him, and the baby fell into a pouch-like arrangement, looking the picture of comfort. The grandmother moved off under the trees, lifting her shoulders gently and swaying her body as she crooned, making a sound like the wind in the pines.

"What is that song your grandmother is singing to the baby?"

"It isn't a song, but it's the way all Indians sing to the children. It is astonishing how they like it, and how it soothes them. Baby likes it much better than when I sing English songs to him. I wonder what makes him?"

"It is a queer, faraway, out-of-doors sound," I said. "Maybe it awakens echoes of the forests your ancestors lived in and loved, like the sound in the shell."

She laughed, saying, "I never thought of that; we Indians all love the forests and to hear the wind in the trees and to feel it blow through our hair."

We were still for a time, then she suddenly rose and said: "You know I am learning to make butter, and I must run in and look at my milk while grandmother has the baby. I shall churn today, and I do hope I shall succeed."

Away she skipped, leaving me comported with a picture that filled in with no preconceived ideas. No one will believe me if I tell of this young mother and her talk, but it is nevertheless true, I said to myself; and down the talk went in my notebook, as testimony taken on the spot. When I had nearly completed writing, she came back, warm and a little breathless, bearing a yellow pat on a dish.

"I don't think it is quite right," she said perplexedly, "ought it to be so milky?"

I tried to look wise and examined it critically. "Perhaps you have not worked it enough," I suggested.

"I did just as Mrs. Smith told me. I suppose I am stupid, and I am *so* tired," she said, the tears coming into her dark eyes.

Taking a bit of the butter on a little stick, I tasted it. "It is very good; I wouldn't touch it if I were you."

"Wouldn't you?" she said, brightening.

"No, I wouldn't. As you make more butter, you will learn by experimenting—go put it away and come back to me."

She returned to the house and was soon seen coming toward me. I rose from my hammock, saying, "I want to put you in and swing you so that you can see how pleasant it is as you rest."

With merry words and laughter she was at last safely in and I began to gently swing her. She was very sober; in a moment she cried, "Don't, don't! I shall be very sick, please let me out."

I hastened to get her on her feet. "That is too bad!" I exclaimed. "I shall fix up a place for you to lie down beside me; you are very tired from churning, even dogs can't stand that."

"Can't stand what?" she asked.

"Churning. Didn't you know some people make the dogs churn, and the poor beasts when they get through throw themselves down as if life had no further charm for them."

"Well, I am very tired," she said, laughing, "but not quite as bad as that."

As we rested, she on the grass, I in my hammock, I questioned, "Do the Omaha women paint much? I've not yet seen a single one painted."

"No, the women seldom paint, only for certain dances; then they paint the parting of the hair red, and back on the cheek, at that little stiff point that forms the entrance to the ear; I don't know what you call it!"

"Do the men paint?"

"Only the young men, when going to dances, and the men who are members of some sacred societies. The Omahas are said to be very plain in their dress and ornaments. They are, I think, judging from the other Indians I have seen."

"Nearly all the people work," I remarked.

"A great many do. Every family more or less. Some have very little land broken, and some large farms. Our tribe always cultivated the soil and raised corn, and that helped a great deal. The tribe used to go out on the hunt and get enough meat to last often all winter, but sometimes the suffering for food was very great; the meat would give out, and we Indians find it hard to live without meat. I believe we could do without anything else better. That is one thing that makes the present condition trying. The people are poor and can't afford to buy much meat, and sometimes I wonder how they do live. They are not fed by the government, that is one good thing; I think that is degrading, and so do all the better class of Indians."

Her gentle voice was vibrating with emotion, and I dreaded any further disclosures of the white man's wrongdoing.

"Let me ask you something," I said. "Do you think you can make me understand why you called that young man who was here last evening 'grandfather,' and the little girl who ran in this morning 'mother'?"[5]

She laughed merrily. "I never thought about it, but it must sound queerly to you. The young man was father's uncle, and so he is my grandfather."

"I don't see why," I interrupted. "Try and begin at the beginning."

"Where is the beginning?" she inquired.

"Well now," said I, taking out my notebook, "you call your father and mother as we do, and their brother and sister you call 'uncle' and 'aunt.'"

"No I don't," she interrupted. "I call all my father's brothers 'father' and all my mother's brothers 'uncle,' and my father's sisters 'aunt' and my mother's sisters 'mother.'"

"Wait until I write that down and can look at it!" After writing and studying it, I said: "Then you have no uncles on your father's side or aunts on your mother's?"

"No."

"Go on, now, what do you call your cousins?"

"I haven't any," she said.

"Oh dear! This is dreadfully puzzling; tell me what you have."

She good-humoredly went on: "I call all those whom you call cousins 'brothers' and 'sisters,' except the children of my uncles and aunts; of these I call the girls 'mother,' the boys, 'uncle.'"

"What is the reason of that?"

"I don't know as I ever thought about it, but of course there is a reason. Maybe this is it. You see, a man has a right to marry his wife's niece, his wife's brother's daughters, and we always speak of relations which might take place just as if they actually existed. So the daughter of my uncle might be my father's wife and I would then call her 'mother.'"

"Let me write that down. Yes, I see, the girl would be called 'mother' because your father could marry her, and the boy 'uncle' because he is 'brother' to a 'mother,'" I said slowly.

The Young Mother   249

"That's it! You have it, it is very easy, you see," she said triumphantly.

"I wonder now if I can figure out why you call your father's uncle 'grandfather.' Oh yes, I see. The uncle's daughter might be called by your father 'mother,' and you would call the father of the person your father called 'mother,' 'grandfather,'" said I, with a sigh over my mental effort.

"That's it, you see how very simple it is; I never thought it all out before. It is very simple!"

"I am glad it seems so, but I am sure I should have to work out all my relations like algebraic problems and never feel sure I had got in all my might, could, would, or should-be mothers, uncles, and grandfathers."

She laughed and said, "It does make trouble, but not that way; it is about getting married. You see, every girl has ever so many men who have a right to marry her. Every man whom she calls 'brother-in-law' has that right."

"Wait a minute, let me get that down. Whom would you call 'brother-in-law'?"

"All the husbands of my sisters, and their husbands' brothers, and the husbands of my aunts."

"I can understand calling your sisters' husbands 'brother-in-law,' but their brothers, I don't see why."

"According to Indian custom a man has a right to marry all the sisters of his wife. You know polygyny used to be the custom," she said, her voice dropping.

"Oh, I understand; these brothers are potential relations, and you say this sort of relationship makes trouble in getting married. Tell me about that. Have I seen anyone to whom this makes trouble?"

"Do you remember the girl who was here yesterday with her mother, who you said was so handsome?" she asked.

"Yes, she was handsome, about twenty, I should think."

"She is the oldest unmarried girl on the reservation. She is as old as I am! Her sister is married to a man—you know him, he is a very influential man—and just because of his claim to the girl, the young men are afraid. Of course her brother-in-law wouldn't take two wives, but the old custom keeps her single. The young man who marries her will have to give ever so much to get rid of the claim on her."

"Is that the meaning of presents given for a girl?" I asked.

"Yes, that is in part the reason. You see, there are many persons to be recognized, and Indians always recognize a claim by a gift; and, too, the young man must show that he cares enough for the girl to part with something valuable for his wife. Of course I don't know, but when I read the hard things that are said about Indian marriages and Indian women being bought and sold it seems to me it is unjust. The white people often marry for money, for honor and position, and I am sure, if the novels I have read are true, there is a great deal of matchmaking among them, and it doesn't seem as decent to me as the Indian way, after all. I do not mean to be hard on the white people," she said, with an apology in her tone. "There are ambitious fathers and mothers among the Indians, but the presents made are a necessity, you see."

The grandmother came near, and the mother held out her arms for her baby; he was awake and crowed as he caught sight of her. Several moments were given up to mutual admiration, the old and young mothers seeming of one age before the baby king. The mother talked baby talk in English and the grandmother kept up an equally vigorous conversation in Omaha. When a lull occurred, I asked, "Does the grandmother talk baby talk, too?"

"Yes, Indian women indulge in that luxury," she said, gaily tossing up the happy child. "Don't they, little boy? They are all just as silly as your mother."

The grandmother left us, and the mother sat twining the baby fingers over her own. At last she said softly, "There is a notion among the Indians—of course it is only a notion—that there are certain persons who can understand the talking of babies. So when the little ones are in distress the parents send for one of these persons to listen to the child and find out its trouble. Sometimes as I listen to baby it seems very natural that the Indians should believe that thing; I can't laugh at it."[6]

SEVENTEEN

An Indian's Story

The Omaha tribe lives in the state of Nebraska, about eighty miles north of the city of Omaha, which takes its name from these Indians. When they sold their hunting lands to the government in 1855 they reserved a tract and intended to include in it their old village site, but by some mistake this was left out to the north. Their reservation, however, was ample, fronting on the Missouri River and extending west so as to embrace a part of the fertile valley of the Logan Creek. The region selected had been their home for several generations.

Their traditions carry them back to the Ohio Valley, where they lived with other cognate tribes. Driven by wars, they moved westward and crossed the Mississippi. During this migration the tribes became separated, the Omahas moving to the north; hence their name, meaning "upstream," the Quapaws going downstream. It is probable that the date of this parting can never be fixed definitely. We know that it took place sometime previous to the journey of De Soto about 1540, as he found a tribe called Quapaw living on the Arkansas in the vicinity where they made their first cessions to the government, early in the present century, thus showing that they had not migrated in the three hundred years during which they have been known to us. Their name, Quapaw, means "downstream" and is the complement to the Omaha, or "upstream," name. The traditions of both tribes tell that they were once one and parted while hunting. The languages of the two are almost alike; the people can understand each other in part. There are other tribes closely related to the Omahas and which probably shared in the early western migration—the Poncas, Osages, and Kansas. These three names appear in the gentes of the tribes, but not the two geographical names, Omaha and Quapaw. The Osage and Kansas did not accompany the Omahas to the north but found their way to the rivers which now bear their names. The Poncas and Omahas kept together and passed up the Des Moines, building villages at different points until they reached the headwaters, near the red pipestone quarry.[1] After a time, being still pressed by wars, they turned west to the Missouri, crossed it at the mouth of the White River, and slowly descended on the west bank of the former. At the Niobrara the Poncas remained and the Omahas moved southward to a creek now bearing their name and which rises in the hills on their present reservation; upon its banks they built their village and have dwelt in that vicinity to the present day. They have occasionally been driven by wars to a temporary exile or induced by the government to move nearer an agency, but they have always gravitated towards the village site chosen by their ancestors.[2]

Of the various tribes living in Nebraska when the white settlers first entered the territory, the Omahas are the only Indians remaining on their ancient homelands. Their attachment to the locality is remarkable and made me feel, while among them, that I was but an emigrant on this continent; no part of the country had in the 250 years of my ancestral hold on it built itself into my thought and life as was this region interwoven with the customs, ceremonials, and myths of these Indians. They possessed the land in their thought, in their love; they had companioned it, but they had not conquered and utilized it, or mastered it, after the manner of the white race. The Indian lives on and passes over the land but leaves no felled forests, leveled hills, or dammed-up streams to mark his presence or ownership. His mounded graves seem to form a part of the landscape; his villages melt away, and only a sunken circle of an enhanced verdure marks the site of his ancient dwellings.

Having explored the remains of the primitive habitations of the Ohio and Mississippi Valley,[3] it was with the zest of a student that I took my way over the hills to visit an earth lodge, to enter a probable counterpart of the ancient dwellings that had excited my archeological ardor. The lodge lay in a charming valley surrounded by wooded hills folding in on one another. A stream rippled between grassy borders and divided the meadows north and south. Acres of corn stood ripening in the mellow sunlight, and fields from which the wheat had been cut looked shorn and ragged. A primitive stable of saplings and hay, a wagon under a shed, and several farming machines gave signs of thrift and industry. The outside of the dome-shaped lodge was covered with flowers and grass, and also the long entrance stretching out toward the east, like a handle—that, by the way, is the meaning of the name given to it by the Indians. The hanging over the outer door was lifted and fastened to the ceiling; as I passed through the passageway, some eight or ten feet long, I noticed on each side the tall yellow grass, bound closely in place, between the framework.

Lifting the skin over the door at the farther end, I entered the lodge. I found myself in a large circular room; the ample opening in the rounded roof let in a flood of light upon the central fire and the area about it. Eight large posts formed a circle halfway between the fire and the wall; from half of these hung blankets and robes, forming a kind of arras, shutting off part of the lodge. Along the wall, which was about five and one-half feet high, were arranged at intervals divans made of willow saplings, whereon robes and blankets were laid. These beds served as a lounge or seat by day. Packs, trunks, and boxes were stowed away, much as in a tent; on the posts and walls were hung gay-colored articles of apparel and ornament. The tempered light gave tone to the picture and fascinated the fancy. There were so many artistic possibilities in the scene. Near the entrance stood a large wooden mortar, made from the trunk of a tree, the bottom pointed so as to be thrust well into the ground. The grandmother was pounding corn with a tall pestle. Near the fire was a dark-browed woman, statuesque in figure and feature; in her lap lay her brilliant-hued quills and the moccasin in the process of decoration. Opposite her the husband, a large-framed man, lay at full length on a robe, laughing and singing, while his little boy was doing his best at a vigorous dance just beyond the stretch of his father's arms. The kettle was bubbling over the fire and the coffeepot sending out an appetizing odor. The day's work was over, and I had caught the family at their relaxation.

Greeting my friends, I sat down and begged the child might go on; but the little fellow had caught sight of the bright knob of my umbrella and was meditating thereon with such fixed attention that it had taken the dance out of his heels and sent it up to his eyes. The boy was greatly cherished. He was the only living child; many little brothers and sisters had been laid away when only a few days or months old. He seemed as sturdy as the oaks on the circling hills. The father had risen, drawn his blanket about him, and seated himself; the women kept on with their occupation.

We had all met many times before, so that I felt free to speak my mind upon the topic which just then was so much interesting me, the earth lodge. After a few moments I expressed my pleasure at being in one of these buildings, told tales of my adventures with the earth circles in the Ohio Valley, and mentioned that I had seen some circles in parts of the reservation and wondered if they could have been old Omaha lodges.

"No, they were here when we came. There are places where there are groups of these circles; sometimes you can pick up arrowheads and pieces of broken pottery."

The grandmother rose during this talk and in a moment came toward me bringing a shard, telling me where she found it.

"Not far from here. Would you like to walk over?" asked my host.

In a moment we were off, and making our way to the top of one of the hills, I found myself on a level plateau overlooking a bottom on the opposite side of the Missouri. The river on this side hugged closely to the steep wooded bluff. Almost at my feet lay one of the familiar sunken circles.

"I'll burn off the grass and we will see if we can find anything," said my host.

Striking a match, he touched the dry yellow grass here and there, and in an instant I was surrounded by a wall of flame that rose and fell, leaving a blackened circle. My host beat out the fire when it had done its work, and we were soon walking slowly around, searching for signs of the olden time. I had hardly moved two steps when an edge caught my eye, and in a moment I had a perfectly formed arrowhead with a double flange. It was a beautiful specimen, and the only one we found that afternoon.

The shadows were deepening as we sped down the hill. Nearing the lodge, I recalled the odor of the evening meal and wondered if there might not be reproachful looks, if not words, in store for us; but no, when we were comfortably seated, the meal was served. As we ate we talked of the find and the groups of circles.

"There is one place," said my host, "where I think there must have been a village, and the people who lived there did not raise corn for I never could find a sign of a cache. Those Indians must have lived entirely on game."

"You build the cache near the lodge, don't you?"

"Yes, near the entrance."

"I'll show you," said grandmother, "the women build them. We dig them out and the young men take off the dirt in robes, the ends are tied so as to make the robe like a basket. We line the caches and make them tight, and everything keeps well in them. When we used to go off on a hunt, we concealed the openings of the caches, for fear that enemies might break them open and destroy our stores."

The mother, in gathering up her articles, missed her knife and until it was found all was commotion. At last she spied the boy, intently busy with a piece of wood, and the sought-for knife in his hand! She was at his side in a moment and, wresting the knife from him, gave the child sharp words and a thump on his back; he responded with lusty screams and ran to his father for solace.

"Don't cry for a little thing as that," said the man. "You may live to have your face cut for flirting with another man's wife."

As the sobs subsided, I turned to the father and said, "That is a queer thing to say to a child, what does it mean?"

"We say that to our boys, that they may learn it is bad to do such things; that they will suffer if they do them," replied the father.

"Is that how a man is punished for such misconduct?" I inquired.

"The husband may cut the face of the offender, or bruise him, or burn up his property, and the man is never permitted to defend himself; nor will he be sustained by his relations. It is a bad thing."

The wife threw more wood on the fire; the blaze leaped up, lighting all parts of the lodge, bringing out new aspects and arousing my interest afresh. Looking about, I remarked: "It must be quite a labor to build such a lodge."

As I was speaking two men came in. One, a tall sedate man whom I had found to be a good deal of a philosopher; the other, a smaller man full of fire and élan, although past his prime. Both men were acquainted with me.

"What have you found now?" asked my friend the smaller man. "You are always seeing something."

I showed my treasure.

"That is a good one!" he exclaimed. "You had better give it to me; I'll wear it as an ornament."

"No, I am going to keep it myself. I dare say you could make one. I couldn't, so I'll not part with this."

"I used to see my grandfather make them when I was a little boy. I don't think I could make one as good as that."

"Could you make a lodge like this?" I asked.

"Men don't make lodges," chimed in the grandmother.

"When the women are lazy a man can't have a lodge," said my friend, with a merry twinkle.

"I'm afraid I should be lazy if I was an Indian woman."

"You are always doing something when I see you, generally with a book and pencil, but I don't know as that amounts to much," he rejoined, and all the company laughed.

"You wait and see, maybe you'll believe in my pencil yet."

"We all believe in you," said my host, gallantly.

"That is good," I replied, "because I believe in all of you. Now tell me about building a lodge, and begin at the beginning and fancy we are standing out in the valley; what would you do first?"

"Take a smoke," put in my friend, who was already puffing at a pipe.

"You would," I said laughing, "but you," turning to my host, "what would you do?"

"I think I'd smoke with my uncle, here," he answered, carrying on the joke.

"Grandmother will tell me. What is the matter?" I cried, for my friend was now violently struggling to get his finger out of the heated bowl, where he had put it to press down the kinnikinnick. "Can't you get it out? Let me help you!" But before I could do anything, he had lifted the hand with the pipe hanging to it, and with a snap flung the bowl off. The fragments barely escaped hitting three young men who were just entering the lodge, and they joined with the others in laughing at my vigorous friend, who, however, was not seriously burned.

The sedate man supplied a pipe and my host took up the conversation. "Well! As I couldn't smoke, I may as well put down a stake and with a strip of rawhide begin to mark off the circle of the lodge. Then the sods are cut off and the earth taken out for nearly a foot deep and the soil tramped."

"And fires built over it to dry it out," interpolated the grandmother.

"We calculate how many posts we want, and how many crotched sticks, and these are cut and stripped of their bark and made the right length."

"The men help in that," added the grandmother with a nod.

"Then we set up the posts," my host went on, never heeding the interruption of the old woman, who kept up a sort of running accompaniment to her son's narrative.

"We," said she, "the women do that."

"Against the posts we place willows and bind in tall grass. You see how the roof is held by the inner row of posts. The men—listen, Mother, I said 'men'!"

"That's right, the men do it," she replied.

"The men adjust the opening when the framework and interlining are completed, then we put on the sods and the lodge is done."

"After the lodge is finished," said my friend, "the family makes a feast and before they eat, they take some of the fat of the buffalo and anoint the posts; that is our way of consecrating the house. We used to do the same thing whenever we returned from the hunt. We were taught never to forget to give thanks. We lifted the pipe when we smoked. We lifted the food when we ate." Looking around, my eye caught sight of a dog's head over the edge of the opening.

"Isn't that funny?" I exclaimed, pointing to the eavesdropper.

Instead of laughing, my host was thrown into great agitation. "Go beat that dog!" he cried to the young men, who instantly started out and in a moment the yells of the beast showed he was caught and punished.

"He was doing no harm," I remonstrated.

"Don't you know that is a sign of bad luck?" said the philosopher.

"No, I didn't; what kind of bad luck does it bring?"

"Some say death, but I say more likely dirt, knocked off the roof into the food cooking over the fire. Indians have many superstitions," he said, as he quietly drew a puff of smoke.

"So have the white people. I don't quite like to see the moon over my left shoulder; that is supposed to keep away good luck all that moon."

"Indians don't care over which shoulder they see the moon, but a circle around the moon brings a war party," said the sedate man.

"I wonder what kind of a circle I cast when I went all alone on the war-path to the Pawnees," queried my friend.

"You made a lively circle just now when you threw the pipe off your finger," I ventured, and all laughed at the memory of the gyration. "Tell me about your going on the warpath."

Everyone settled himself, my host calling to him his little boy and holding him tightly in the fatherly arms.

"We had been at peace with the Pawnees, but trouble broke out between us again and I determined to go on the warpath and to go alone. I had lived for a time with the Pawnees when I was young and could speak their language. So when I reached their village in the dusk of the evening I mixed among the people and answered their salutations without being detected. I waited about for the village to get quiet. I had watched the ponies brought in and put in the enclosures near the lodges; the Pawnees live in earth lodges like this. By and by all was still, except two young men who walked about singing. It seemed as though they would never stop, but after a time they went in a lodge and brought out a skin and lay down on the handle of the lodge and sung themselves to sleep. I went up and looked at them as they lay side by side. As I gazed on them I thought, 'Now I can win honors. I can strike this man and kill him, and strike the other one before he has time to rouse the people, and make off with two scalps.' It was a great temptation, and once I had my club lifted. Then I remembered that our family were without ponies. I had come for ponies; so I turned and left the young men and went into the stable. I picked out a young horse with a buffalo tail tied about his neck, showing he was a running horse. He led easily and I drove the others out; just as they were passing the stable door, an old man came to the entrance and said, 'Who are you?' 'Who are you?' I replied, striking him down with my club. The voice had roused the young men; they shouted and awaked the others and before I could get out of the village everyone was in alarm and giving chase. I ran with all my might, leading the horse and driving the others. The people were in pursuit; men and women and children were shouting and bullets were flying. Still I kept on. I slipped the rope over the nose of the horse and mounted him; he rose on his hind legs, then kicked up, and I lay on the ground. I kept hold of the rope, however, and ran on, he following. I lost the other horses during my attempts to ride, for I tried five times to mount that colt and was as many times thrown. After a long while the firing grew less; the darkness favored me, and at last only here and there a shout was heard. When I knew I was safe, I tied the mouth of the colt, mounted him, and let him jump and kick until he was tired. I stayed on. After some days, I returned to the village bringing my Pawnee colt."

The young men had listened with avidity to the story, which was told with graphic words and gestures. My friend caught their eyes as he went on. "I thought that was noble action; I thought that was a good thing to do. Look here, young men," and he stripped down a legging and showed a wound in his leg. "That, too, I thought honorable. Now look here, young men," and he spread open his two hands, calloused with work. "Look at those scars; those are the scars of labor, those are where my honors lie; those are the fitting signs of manhood! Try to win such as these, and when you look at them they will not stand for killing or stealing but for honest work, for that which will bring food to your family and make your home happy."

Turning to me, he said, "Years ago I looked about me; the game was gone, the white people were gathering around us. I saw that if the Indian was to live he must go to work as the white man. I had nothing to work with. When the harnesses you have heard of came there were not enough to go around. I had none. A white man loaned me a pair of collars. I made my double trees and fixed up a sort of harness as best I could and put my ponies to the plow. I did not know how to work, but I took hold of the plow and my wife held the reins. I raised corn and sold it. I went to Sioux City and bought a harness and a plow of my own. I cut the wood to build me a house that should have three rooms in it. I had a stable. I sold my six ponies for two American mares; one had a colt. I had pigs, too. One night a prairie fire swept down upon me and burned all I had: horses, harness, pigs, and the materials for my house. I was left with only my blanket. The citizens' party helped me. Two men alone gave me eighteen dollars in money, one gave me a set of harness, another a plow, and I received many other things besides. The agency people helped me; they gave me eleven dollars and three pigs. Some white people raised twenty-two dollars and I started again. You know my little house. You have seen my farm. I am growing old. I have not many years to live. There is one thing I am always thinking of—a title to my land. I may never know the good it will bring, but my children will know, and for them I think and desire this thing. The reason I have worked so hard is that I have wanted to set an example to others and show them how an old man could work, simply because he wished to do so."

As I looked at my friend and thought of his life, his manly grappling with new ideas, his working faith in them, I wished the earth lodge might expand into a great auditorium and that thousands might hear what I had listened to and might see and touch those horny hands and say, "My brother!"

EIGHTEEN

Child Life

Indians greatly desire and love children, nor does it seem as though either sex is an especial favorite. I never chanced to hear anyone say, "I have only daughters," in the sense of a misfortune; girls or boys, they are all dear little children. Unfortunately, the hard life of exposure to which the people are subject makes it difficult to raise any but the strongest children, and the mortality among those under five years casts a shadow over almost every home.

The Indians believe strongly in parental influences and the child is supposed to imitate all its mother does; therefore, certain occupations are avoided by her as dangerous to the offspring. Among these is sewing with the awl. There is a pretty conceit, which implies that children have a subtle knowledge of each other. A mother who desires to know of what sex her child will be takes the opportunity during the visit of a friend who has a little baby with her to hold out to the child in one hand a bow and in the other hand a burden strap. If the baby takes the bow, the mother's little one will be a boy, if the strap is seized it will be a daughter.

When the child is about five days old, the father gives a feast and invites the principal men of the gens into which the child is born.[1] Those men who belong to the subdivision of the father cannot partake of the food because they rank as hosts, the same as the father, and no one giving a feast ever eats of it. An old man of this subdivision of the gens, who is chosen for the duty by the father, bestows a name on the child. This name belongs to those which are peculiar to the gens, each gens having a series of its own. Sometimes during this ceremony of bestowing a name the child is painted to represent the mythical ancestors of the gens, and the articles, which no member of this particular tribal division must ever touch, are laid beside the infant, who is told he must ever hold these objects as sacred. These taboos vary in the different gentes; in one, it is the red ear corn; in another, it is the green paint; other taboos are elk, parts of the buffalo, the deer, birds, or reptiles. Penalties are attached to any infringements of this rule: white spots will come upon the body of the offender; he will have sore eyes, blindness, or other physical calamities.

One day, speaking with a leading man in the tribe upon the subject of these taboos, he said to me, "Did you ever notice my hands? Look how spotted they are." They were strangely mottled. "I am forbidden to touch the male elk," he continued. "At one time a pair of moccasins was made for me out of the skin of that animal; I wore them, and this is the result. I cannot account for such things. I know of many instances where persons have been punished for like carelessness or disobedience."

The baby is the constant companion of its mother.[2] Soon after birth it is laid in its bed. This is a board a foot or more wide and about three feet long; on it is put a thin pillow of feathers or several layers of some soft material and covered with a cloth. The baby is bathed daily unless the weather is too cold. Clad in a single smock, it is laid on its back and swathed to the board with broad bands of skin, calico, or flannel. Boys are swathed differently from girls. When the baby is sleeping its arms are bound in and so kept covered. This custom of binding the child on the board has certain indisputable advantages. While the child is young its neck is supported; it is not lifted by the arms or liable to twists and jerks; it is not uncomfortable and is secure against accidents. The board is only used during sleep, while being carried about, or if the mother is busy. At other times the baby is allowed to lie on a blanket and kick to its heart's content. The board is not often used after the child is six or eight months old, but the practice is long enough to produce the flattening of the occiput, noticeable among nearly all the Indians, caused by the child always resting on the back of its head.

Children are never allowed to cry if it can be prevented; any man or woman will soothe a child rather than let it fret, and in case of sickness the father shares in the care of the little ones. It is a common sight among all the tribes I have studied to see a man swinging his child in a sort of hammock, made by lapping a skin over two loops of cord, while he is busy making some implement or ornament.

In old times the Omaha boys and girls went barefoot and their hair was never cut until they could walk steadily, when they were about three years old. At that time the following ceremony took place.[3] When the grass was well up and the corn planted the parents took the child to the tent of a certain old man, whose hereditary duty it was to cut the hair of the children for the first time. In preparation for this event the mother made a pair of moccasins for the child, and gifts of robes, moccasins, and arrows were provided for the old man.

On entering the tent the mother addressed him, saying, "Venerable man, I desire my child to wear moccasins." The little one was led to where the man sat. He then gathered up in his left hand the hair growing on the top of the child's head, tied it, and cut off the tuft and laid it away in a sacred pack. He next lifted the little feet and clothed them in moccasins; then, grasping the child by the arms near the shoulders, lifted it, turning it slowly to the left and, setting its feet down at the points of the compass, turning it completely around once. This action he repeated four times. When the feet touched the ground for the last time he gently urged the child forward a few steps, repeating this invocation: "May God have compassion on you. May your feet rest long upon the earth. Walk forth now in the path of life." Children who passed through this ceremony were said to be less wild and better behaved than others whose parents had neglected it.

When the child reached his father's tent, his hair was cut after the fashion of his gens. It was an odd sight to see the heads trimmed to represent the animals sacred to the gentes. Those belonging to the turtle group have all the hair shaved off but a fringe around the line of growth; four locks are left, one over the forehead, two on each side, and one at the nape of the neck. The bare head represents the turtle's shell; the locks symbolize his head, tail, and four feet. There is a style for every gens; these represent the buffalo, elk, deer, bear, birds, etc. Every spring the parents cut their children's hair in this manner until they are about seven or eight years old, although they are never again taken to the old man. By this and other customs the children are taught during their most impressionable years in a manner they can never forget the mythology of their particular gens and also that of the tribe.

The affection borne children by their parents is manifested in many ways. Among them is the following custom connected with the warpath. A man who has a son for whom he is ambitious to secure a valorous career will join a war party or even go forth alone, carrying with him the moccasin of his child. When the farthest limit of the journey is reached, he lays the moccasin upon the prairie, saying, "So shall my child walk far and bravely over the land."

It not infrequently happens that grief leads a man to risk the dangers and accept the activities of the warpath, that in the midst of unfamiliar scenes he may assuage his grief. If a child's death is the cause of the man starting out, he takes the child's moccasins in his belt. Should he slay anyone, the moccasins are laid beside the dead man in the belief that the child will thenceforth have a brave companion in the other world.

The days are full of sport to the little ones. They manufacture their own playthings, modeling them out of clay or devising regalia from corn husks or dried grass. Corn-husk war bonnets are made by the boys, and as these cost much labor they are sometimes carefully preserved. The children are fond of playing "going on the hunt," in which girls and boys join. The girls take down the tents and pack the poles, made of sunflower stalks, to the sides of the boy ponies. Some ponies are very troublesome, and boys are often remembered by the girls as good or bad pony-boys. It was amusing to watch the mimic life of the children; the camp would be attacked by war parties, then corn-husk war bonnets came in use, and sometimes captives were taken. It was droll to see the tents made of a couple of shawls and the difficulty of the players when crowding in; feet and legs were apt to protrude when "play it is night" was in order. Boys were not the only ponies. Sunflower stalks, with one flower left on at the tip to represent the ornament on the running horse's neck, were used in races. Generally the boy trailed one or two stalks by his side; these not only served as reserve horses, but they helped to increase the dust and thus add to the impressiveness of the occasion. The plays were unusually free from fighting, but some of the sports of boys were quite rough, such as the kicking matches. It was astonishing how their legs could fly.

The boys, while the tribe was on the hunt, indulged in a favorite pastime called "To strike the little birds." A party of fifteen or twenty boys cut willow branches about three feet long and leave four twigs like barbs at the end. All are thus armed but one boy who is called "the carrier"; he is provided with a small blanket in which to gather up the game. The boys range themselves in line on the top of a hill, and at a signal, start down at a run, each one circling wide his stick and making a prolonged whirring sound. The startled birds rise out of the tall grass and soon drop to the ground through fright as the sticks are hurled at them. The fastest runner secures the first bird and immediately scalps it; meanwhile the carrier runs on ahead, stops, turns, and faces the boy, who gently tosses the scalped bird to the carrier, who must tremble violently as the bird is thrown to him. This pantomime means that the carrier when he darts ahead represents the bird, and the scalped bird, the stick thrown. The boys say, "If the carrier did not tremble, bad luck would attend the sport." One of the older boys counts the birds and the hunters, then portions out the game accordingly. As many as fifty birds are often caught; some are worth more than others on account of their size; for instance, a prairie chicken is equal to four or five little birds. These values enter into the division of the game. The birds are dressed, three or four spitted on a stick, and roasted before the fire; a feast follows.

The girls thread the wildflowers upon grass or string and make necklaces. I often had a half dozen given me in a day, and I always wore them all. The children soon found out my love of flowers and I was never without them during all the summer days. One cold, blustering afternoon, when the trees were bare and the leaden sky bent over the naked, stripped earth, I noticed two little girls running toward me hand in hand. I met them at the door, fearing a hasty summons, but my alarm was set at rest as the elder handed me a spray from the wild rosebush, brown, crisp, and tough with its long life and hard experience, not unlike what the little, soft brown hand that held them might be many years hence. I took the gift and turned to see if I had not some treasure for the child when the smaller girl thrust up her little fist before me. As I took it, she slowly opened the fingers and revealed one wee green leaf rumpled up in her warm, moist palm. Winter could not deny the child!

When the ice bound the streams and the great muddy Missouri in a motionless calm, and the bluffs were white with snow, then the children seemed like imps of activity. They secured blocks of ice and, mounted on these, they coasted down the hills at the risk of their necks and frostbites. A curved piece of wood with a string tied to one end made a favorite sled; a barrel stave was a great acquisition for this sport. The boy stands on the stick near one end, holding the string which is tied to the forward end, and having a stick in the other hand as a balancing pole, he scuds down the hill shouting and tumbling against trees, boys, or anything that happens to be in the way. It is astonishing, the steep pitches they will safely descend. Boys make sleds for the girls, but sometimes there are not enough of these to go around, and then anything serves a turn. As I was watching the children one bitter cold day, suddenly two girls shot by me; they were seated, one in the lap of the other, on the scoop of a shovel; four hands had tight grasp of the handle, and two legs stood out stiff on each side of it. It was a very successful shoot for quite a distance, and then, laughter overtaking the girls, they fell in a merry heap and rolled on down the hill into a deep snowbank.

Indian children, like all others, take fancies for queer articles. There was a small boy of whom his mother was very proud; she used to make for the little fellow gay jackets with shining buttons. One afternoon this boy, clad in all his splendor, entered the house of his uncle. The day was one of those in early spring when it is easy to lie down and let nature take its course, and so the uncle was taking a rest and turning over in his hand a white porcelain doorknob he had recently bought to adorn his little cabin, but which, from some cause, had proved to be an inferior article and had parted company with its shank. The child caught sight of the round, white, glossy thing and speculation filled his eyes. "Give it to me, won't you?" said the boy, without moving his gaze.

"This cost me money," replied the uncle, who loved a practical joke. "Why should I give it to you? You can buy it perhaps."

"I have no money," said the boy.

"Haven't you got anything you can give me for it?"

The boy looked very sober; evidently his possessions were limited. At last the uncle suggested, "You might give me your fine jacket?"

In an instant the boy was unbuttoning the brass buttons and twisting his arms out of his jacket. Then he threw it on his reclining uncle and, seizing the doorknob, he was off like a shot, out of the door into the sunlight. Everyone laughed and wondered what the child would do. No one, however, told of the transaction, but waited results, and the jacket was hung up on the back of the knobless door. For a day or two the boy and the knob were close companions and then the charm began to wane, and the knob went into his pocket to keep company with strings, nails, and all the odds and ends that only a boy can gather.

A few days later the father looked at the child and then, turning to his wife, said, "Where is the boy's jacket? He has not worn it for several days."

"My son, where is your jacket?" asked the mother.

"I gave it away," he replied, a touch of regret in his voice.

"To whom did you give it?" replied the mother.

"My uncle," said the boy, thrusting his hand in his pocket and grasping the doorknob.

"Your uncle! What did he want of it?" said the astonished mother.

"He made me give it to him, for this," and the child, with a rueful countenance, drew out the white knob, which had now lost its attractiveness.

Everybody laughed at the practical joke while the boy gathered in anger.

"He must give me back my jacket and take his thing, and, and, I'll thrash him!" exclaimed the child as he ran out with all speed to the cabin of his uncle. He soon returned with his jacket.

"Did you thrash him?" asked the father, laughing.

"I told him I wouldn't this time," said the boy, not doubting his ability to cope with the difficulty.

The uncle is a privileged character. He can play all manner of tricks on his nephews and nieces, which they can return, but nothing must be taken in ill part. No such familiarity exists between children and parents, or any other relation or friend, as with the uncle. Children are often on the lookout for these pranks and enjoy them on the whole.[4]

One evening an uncle brought his nephew the gift of a gun and the boy was delighted with the acquisition. He watched the uncle take it to pieces, and the little sister was equally intent in observing the operation. When the gun was apart the uncle looked up and said, "There it is! But you can't have any of it without dancing. You must dance for every piece!"[5]

"All right!" said the boy, hitching up his shoulders, and the uncle began to sing and beat his hands like the drum, the boy dancing vigorously. The music kept on for quite a while. At last it stopped and the uncle laid down the hammer, saying, "That is yours. Now you shall dance for the ramrod."

"All right!" said the boy, rising, for he had dropped on the ground to rest as the song ceased, and he began dancing again. He finally secured that article.

"Here's the barrel," said the uncle. "I can't let you have this unless your sister dances, too, and helps you."

"Come!" said the boy to the little girl, "Help me!" And the sister joined in the dance and so secured that piece.

When all were earned but the stock, the uncle took it up, saying, "This is the only piece I have left. We must have more dancing, someone else must dance. Grandmother must help you get this!" said the saucy uncle with glee.

The boy, breathless with excitement and dancing, went over to his grandmother, crying, "Come grandmother, help me!"

"I will," said the old woman, laughing and taking her place beside the children. She danced and laughed and kept up the courage of the hot, perspiring children until the gun was won and the lodge ringing with laughter at the manner of the winning.

There are duties as well as plays. The boys must look after the ponies, lend a hand in planting, keeping off the blackbirds and crows from the crops, and help to gather at the harvest time. The girls assist in the care of the younger children and gather wood and bring water for the mother.

Indian children are very fond of home; no threat is so severe as that a child will be taken away from its parents. Homesickness is a malady that besets the Indian during his entire life, and this peculiarity exercises considerable influence upon the career of the people and tends to make them clannish and averse to emigration.

The demarcation of child life comes at the time when the child is said "to have sense," that is, when he can remember his dreams and recall accurately events of the preceding year. His grandfather makes the examinations in this particular and decides whether or not the child's mind has become "white" or "light." As long as he cannot remember clearly "his mind is yet in the dark." At the period of "light" the time for religious training has arrived. This is generally about the twelfth year. The father makes a small bow and arrows for his son, which are not to be used during the fast about to take place. With prayerful hearts the parents smear the boy's head and face with moistened clay, in token of humility, and he is dismissed to seek a secluded spot where he is to remain, calling upon God by using the ritual chant which has been taught him for such occasions, until a vision appears or exhaustion drives him home. No one accosts the child or notices his departure; no one gives him counsel or direction; alone he goes forth to meet through physical privation the vision which will be to him a sort of patron saint or mediator through life. Arrived at a lonely place he seats himself upon the ground, draws his little blanket about him, and chants the following prayer; the meaning of the words is: "Mysterious Creator (or God), have compassion, for I am poor indeed."[6] [Ex. 1]

The word "Wakanda," used in the chant, is an old one and was not coined by the missionaries, although used by them; it signifies as nearly as can be expressed, "The power which can bring forth" or "to pass."[7]

Many a time have these child appeals been heard among the trees, for in case of trouble, or when something is greatly coveted, the child will retire and chant the prayer. Anyone chancing that way will give the little supplicant wide birth, for no one intrudes on devotions.

One day when the Fortieth Psalm was being read, at the passage "I am poor and needy yet the Lord thinketh upon me," an Indian turned toward me and said, "That is like our prayer that we sing when fasting. We are poor, men forget us, do not recognize us, but God does not forget or refuse to notice us."

At this period in life girls often make vows which influence their later life. Early in the spring when the first thunder is heard, religious ceremonies take place in several of the gentes, and individuals are apt to go out on the hills and pray. One afternoon there came a sudden and heavy peal of thunder, and shortly I heard a woman's voice chanting a mournful song. She was standing on a hill pouring forth her sorrowful soul in worship.

Score 1. Prayer Song for a Vision Seeker. Collection of Alice Cunningham Fletcher and Francis La Flesche, Smithsonian Institution, National Anthropological Archives (ms. 4558).

"When her mind became light" she had vowed to the thunder that she would give her firstborn child to the God. In the course of years a son was born and the mother was happy in the smiles and helplessness of the baby. Spring came on, and one day the thunder sounded; then the mother at once remembered her vow. Heavy-hearted she rose, taking her baby in her arms, and went out, following the trail that led to a high hill. When she reached the summit, she stood a moment and then laid the child upon the earth. The baby had been sleeping; the transfer from its mother's warm bosom to the cold, damp earth startled the infant, and as the mother turned, a pitiful wail was heard that rent her resolution; she caught up the child and fled breathless to her lodge. All that year she was a sad and fearful woman. Once again the spring bloomed, and the warning thunder sounded. The mother took her child and started toward the hill in obedience to her vow; the boy was larger now and heavier to carry, and her heart had grown heavier, too. She sat the little fellow down on the summit and turned away, not daring to look back. She had not gone far when she felt a pull at her skirt, and looking down she met the face of her laughing boy; he had toddled after her thinking his mother in play. Could it be that the Thunder God had given her back her son? A heavy peal rolled around the hill, but she could not drop the child from her arms, and again she fled home with the boy. She watched the son with a feeling akin to terror in the midst of her yearning love. In a few weeks he sickened and died, leaving the mother desolate. Then the lightning fell upon her and she lay senseless, with a blue jagged line down the entire length of the leg. She did not die, nor did any child ever come to call her mother again. She lived and voiced her sorrow in a song, and when the thunder sounded over the fresh grass and the happy flowers of the new year, that childless woman went out upon the hill and sang the requiem of a vow which her mother's heart would not let her fulfill.

NINETEEN

Hunting

Cold weather crept on, and the season for storytelling was at hand, for in summer the snakes are supposed to hear and make trouble. As we sat about the fire, myths, fables and stories of the hunt and the warpath filled the evenings, and many pages in my notebooks. The stories were often interspersed with songs, and sometimes these songs demanded a dance; on such occasions, the older men would call on the children to rise and do their share of the entertainment, and the little feet would respond with vim. The scenes were merry and at times full of touches of humor or pathos. Old and young of both sexes were always ready for these enjoyments.

The Indian story runs easily, is full of detail, and never interrupted with "he says" or "she says," for the masculine and feminine terminations being different, one can tell which is talking. Some of the men are capital storytellers; they change their voices for the male or female parts and for the different animals. This, added to their varied and dramatic gestures, makes it possible for one to follow the feeling of the narration even when comparatively ignorant of the language. Often, as I have sat in the midst of such a scene, I have recalled the popular impression of the stolidity of the Indian under all circumstances and have wondered how this impression came about; but later in my experience, when I have tried to show off my Indian friends to white people and failed utterly to open up the play of speech and expression, I have ceased to wonder. No oyster ever shut his shell tighter than can the Indian close out all sight of his relaxation from strangers and most white people. Ridicule is one of the Indian forms of punishment; this has tended to make the people abnormally self-conscious and to check the spirit of enterprise in the sense of branching out on experiments. It also makes them fear to venture on anything new before white people, knowing the misinterpretation and contempt which is felt toward the Indian by so many of the white race. How it came to pass that I was able to get behind the scenes, I do not know. I have often railed those with whom I was best acquainted for acting so differently when others of my race were present even though they knew the persons to be good friends. More than once I have received the laughing response, "Don't you know you are almost as good as an Indian?"

When I talked of past ceremonies and customs, only a few were ever present, and these men of position and probity, fitted to speak upon such topics of conversation. Even then the elder or more important persons would do the principal part of the talking. Such themes as the inaugurating of chiefs, the ceremonials of the hunt, the religious festivals, the honors and duties connected with war, the tribal organizations, and kindred subjects were never discussed in the presence of a company. They were not subjects of talk among the people, for they were believed in and carried out in life. The willingness of certain persons to discuss these topics with me came only after a tried experience. To some of the leading men I made known my wish to secure for preservation as much as possible of the past history of the Omahas, to prepare a faithful record of their traditions, myths, and customs while yet they remained in memory or practice. It was also understood that I would publish nothing without their knowledge and permission. The rich results of my research among them are largely due to their acquiescence in my plan and cordial cooperation.

One evening the father of the sister hostess and "the old man of the mountain" were talking with me of the hunting customs.

"I can't quite understand," I said, "why it was so grave a matter to be the director on the hunt."

"That man took upon him the whole responsibility of the lives of the people," answered the father.[1]

"Then all the tribes moved out on the summer hunt?" I asked.

"When the corn and beans had been hoed twice was the time for the people to move. This would be early in July."

"It was then the director was chosen, was it?"

"If a man aspired to the position of director he provided himself with three things: a flat-stemmed pipe having a bowl of the red pipestone, a piece of the side meat of the buffalo, and the sign of the office; this was a young sapling bent at the top (like a shepherd's crook), tied in that form by two thongs, and decorated with eagle feathers. Then he made a feast and invited the chiefs. If the man was deemed fitting he was appointed to the office. Should no person thus volunteer to be the director, the chiefs selected a man. Sometimes the man so selected declined the honor, he did not care to take the responsibility. Should no one be found, then the duty would fall upon some man in the subdivision of the Inkaesabba gens. The director controlled the movements of the tribe and selected the soldiers who officiated on the hunt. If there should be storms, sickness, attacks of war parties, or the tribe failed to find herds of buffalo, the director would be held responsible and considered as not being favored by God. In that case, the man would resign and the chief appoint another person to the office."

"I don't wonder that a man would shrink from the place, since he was held accountable for so many things he could not control," I exclaimed.

"The Indians consider that whatever happens to a man is in some way the result of his conduct or character. So if a man takes responsibility and misfortune comes to the people under him it is his fault. That is why Indians are slow to give advice and to direct other people. The man who does so must take the responsibility for the results, whatever they may be."

"That is a difficult standard," I said.

"There are many things hard in Indian customs. The council, which met to decide on the time of starting on the hunt and for listening to the director's plans, was hard on the chiefs. They had to be very careful."

"Tell me of that council."

"The crier or herald was sent out to call the chiefs together. The sacred tribal pipes were brought and filled by the keeper of the ritual; the chiefs gathered at the summons, wearing their buffalo robes with the hair outside and the garment arranged in the sacred manner. No feathers were worn or anything signifying war carried. After smoking the sacred pipes" (this ceremony was quite elaborate) "and when these had been cleansed and laid at rest, the chiefs remained in the position which they were obliged to maintain during this entire council; they sat with their robes drawn closely about them and their heads bowed. At length the principal chief, without raising his head, mentioned in low tones the term of relationship between himself and every chief present; then he reminded the men of the duties and obligations of the chiefs to the people and the benefit of all leaders being of one mind; he suggested to them that the time was near when they and their fathers were wont to move out in search of the animal which gave them life and clothing and that they were now gathered to search for the way which would lead the people in safety to the hunting grounds.

"The director was present, but he waited to hear what the chiefs would say. As I said, all the chiefs sat with their heads bowed, and each man was expected to review his life during the period since the last hunt. If during the year a chief had given way to anger, or used angry words or violent actions, he dared not speak in the council for fear that, because of his unchieftain-like conduct, disaster should fall upon his relations or the people. Only those chiefs who, after this self-examination, found that they had been faithful to their trust by their conduct ventured upon the responsibility of discussing a subject of such vital importance to the people as that before the council. When all who dared to do so had spoken, the time of departure on the hunt and the general direction to be taken were decided upon and proclaimed by the crier. After this was done each chief remained bowed and partook of the feast in silence out of the seven sacred bowls; then the men were free to leave. It was very hard work to sit, sometimes all day, with the robe tightly around one, and if it was hot, to feel the perspiration trickle over one's face and not dare to move!"

"Yes! but what impresses me is the requirements you demand of your chiefs. A chief can never make a slip and pass it by; he must never fail if he would be a leader, it seems."

"No, a chief must never forget the honor and solemnity of his calling; if he does, it brings disaster to the people."

"If our chiefs had lived up to the tradition of our fathers, we should not have been bought and sold by the white man," said the "old man of the mountain."

"As I think over the past," said the father, "while there is much that is foolish in Indian customs and traditions, there are some things that are good. I wish our young men would not throw away indiscriminately the teachings of their fathers. Little is really known about the Indians, judging from the conversations I have had with white men, those high in office, those who are sent out here, and also the ordinary settlers. There are men who have written about us and they are as foolish as anybody. They look upon the Indian as a queer sort of creature; they listen to traders and all sorts of Indians who tell nonsense, and the greater the nonsense, the more it is credited, I think. Then it is all published and people believe it! I have had such books read to me."

"I have read such, too, but one of these days the truth will get out," I replied.

"It will never get out through the politicians, or the men who fight the Indians and think the only good one is a dead one. That is what the white man says, I am told," said the old man.

"Not all say it," I answered, "and those who say or think it, whoever they may be, do it to their dishonor."

"I wonder why it never occurs to the white people to think that the Indian is a man," said the father. "Sometimes I wonder if they do not doubt that God made us!"

"Perhaps they believe our myths, that we came from the buffalo and elk and deer, and as they have killed off the game, they might as well destroy its descendants, the Indian," said the old man, with a satirical laugh.

"I have thought much over this thing," continued the father. "Every right of manhood is denied us; our ancient forms are broken; we are forced into the conditions of the white man, then we are deprived of everything good he possesses. No law protects us; we can make no appeal for justice, and we are prohibited from defending ourselves when our lives or property are taken from us; our land, the graves of our fathers and of our children we are not permitted to own. We are treated and talked to as though we had neither reason nor understanding. We are called savages, and yet the white men who call us such have done over and over again to us the savage acts that are charged upon the Indians. I have waited and hoped that the day would come when the Indian would be treated as a man. I have tried, as well as I could, to fit my children and help my people to live as the white man and to be friendly with all that is good; but I am growing old, and the clouds lie dark about me. I do not see from where help is coming."

I dreaded these talks; they made me sore and ill at ease. What right had I to be enjoying working out the sociology of the people, getting at their inner life and thought, when their sore troubles from the greed of my own race were so plainly discernible. Withhold my hand and do nothing for them? But what could I, a woman, do against this trend of wrong? To get rid of these wearying thoughts, I strove the harder at my ethnological work, but the thread was broken for this evening and we sat silent beside the waning fire.

Some nights after, as the father and my friend, the nervous man, sat round the comfortable blaze, I drew the conversation once more toward the hunting custom.

"When the tribe moved out on the hunt did everybody go? Was no one left in the village?" I asked.

"Sometimes," said the father, "the very old persons, and those who were too sick to travel stayed behind in the village; in that case several of the warriors remained to protect the people, but if possible all moved out. When we went on this hunt we camped in a circle, and every family pitched its tent with its gens. You know we have ten gentes in our tribe in five camps on the north half and five on the south half of the circle, the opening of which is to the east. The Sacred Tents are also set up, and all the sacred articles in their places."

"How many miles would the camp move in a day?"

"About fifteen miles was a good day's march. Sometimes we would not go so far, it would depend on the weather or the country. In very hot weather we would travel in the early morning and evening; occasionally we travel in the night."

"You must have made a long procession, there were so many of you."

"We used to spread out, but we kept well together. Over a thousand men, women, and children and nearly twice as many ponies and colts made quite a show," and he smiled as if at memories.

"You forget the dogs," said the nervous man. "What is an Indian camp without dogs?"

"Not a howling wilderness exactly," I suggested.

"They serve to carry things, and to eat," he continued. "Indian dogs are worth more than your dogs. Did the Sioux give you dog feasts?"

"Yes, but I don't like dog," I answered.

"Dogs are good. You eat oysters, I suppose," he inquired.

"Oh, yes."

"I'd as soon eat snakes," he retorted. Then he added, with his genial smile, "I'd like to take you on a hunt."

"I'd like to go, when shall we start?"

Both the men laughed and the father said, "I don't think you could bear the hardships."

"I'd try."

"Oh yes she could," said the other.

"Well," said the father, "we can't get up much of a hunt now; there's nothing but chickens to hunt here and the wolves are better at that than the rest of us."

"Tell us about your first hunt," I said to the nervous man.

"That was long ago," he responded. "I was young then; you don't expect me to remember so far back as that, do you?"

"Oh yes I do, grandfather!" I had fallen into the way of using the term of relationship in vogue in the family.

"Get some young man to tell you; he'll put in all sorts of things; but an old man like me—"

"Here he comes and now he shall tell the story," I said laughingly, for the son had entered and seated himself, asking, "What's that?"

"Grandfather is too old to remember his first hunt," I explained. "Poor old man! He is too old to work anymore. I wonder who can take care of his big farm?"

They all laughed, for he was a man in his prime, one of the most energetic persons on the reservation, and would compete with any white man at working.

"Well, if my grandfather is too old, I'm not. I'll tell you what I did on my first hunt," said the young man.

"The custom in our tribe is to make every boy break his own pony when he goes on his first hunt, independently I mean, not cared for as a little child. One day the people were all getting ready to move out when father lassoed a pretty animal that I had always admired. He threw the colt and put on a saddle and bridle; then, letting the little beast rise with this new rig on, he bade me mount. I didn't want to do it. The colt was a fiery little thing and was already very restive under the unwonted restraint. My father spoke again, telling the pony was to be mine after I had broken him, but I didn't move.

"'Mount!' said my father. Slowly I advanced. The colt ran one way as I came round the other. Father drew on the bridle and held the animal. I had made up my mind. So, grasping his mane in one hand, I swung myself into the saddle. Father let go and then the colt began to kick and rear, to jump and shake, but I stuck to him; at last he gave some sort of a jerk that broke the saddle girth and landed me over his head, and he ran. A young man who was nearby headed off the pony and brought him back—the colt protesting by twists and shakes of his head. Once more I mounted, to be dismounted a second time. Again he was caught and I was on his back only to be thrown again. I was getting mad, but mother was getting sorry. She ran to me where I was scrambling up and insisted on feeling my legs and arms to see if I was hurt. I was impatient of the delay. I was going to master the pony anyhow! I got on once more, and that time I stayed on. The little fellow lashed himself into a foam but he couldn't get rid of me. Then father led him between the tent poles which trailed behind a steady old horse, and there, fenced in, the pony and I rode all day, trying to get used to one another. He could not see his way to get out over the poles, and we were forced to agree. When the halt was called, the fun began again. The pony once more concluded to get rid of me. In his hurry he jumped over a nest of children, who were slung between tent poles, and roused the ire of any number of dogs. With them at his heels and me on his back, he was an object of mirth and terror to the camp. I couldn't hold him, he went where he liked; it was all I could do to stay on. At last he managed to get rid of me and then he was quiet and happy. I was mad and tired and felt like mounting him again, but father took the saddle off and turned him out with the other horses. The next day the colt jumped the poles. He had found out the trick of being fenced in. Two young men tied thongs to his bridle, and the pony was ingloriously led between two riders on that day. That night, while he was restless and tried to get rid of me, I dismounted myself; he didn't do it. By the third day he was a docile little horse and many a good ride he and I have had together. Oh, I forgot, my uncle gave me a pretty whip, the handle decorated with porcupine quills and it had a tassel of elk teeth. That was my first hunt."

"You don't seem to have hunted very much," I said, laughingly.

"I was a boy then, not more than thirteen years old. Boys don't hunt," he replied, a little nettled.

"He became one of the best hunters in the tribe," said the nervous man, "and that pony of his would do anything he wanted."

"I've no doubt of it, I've seen him ride. You look as if you grew on the horse," I said, turning to the young man.

"I don't jump up as if something pricked me every time the horse stepped, as the men do in the East," and he imitated the rising trot of the English school, to the uproarious laughter of the entire company.

"What do they do that for?" he asked of me.

"I am sure I don't know. The English use it and they are very fond of hunting," I replied.

"I'd like to see a man shoot buffalo riding that way," and again he mimicked the rising trot, the shooting of the gun, and the catastrophe to the rider, at which the company laughed again.

"It must be fun when you get to the hunting ground and all the people break away and chase the buffalo!" said I.

"Fun! do you know what happens to the man who should chase a buffalo herd without orders?" asked the young man.

"Get some game, I presume," was my reply.

The men smiled; then the father said, "No one can hunt unless the director permits it; if persons were allowed to do as they please, a few would scare away the herd and the people be left without food. The buffalo must be shared by all the tribe, not taken by a few persons."

"How do you manage to do that?" I asked.

"As we come near the hunting ground the director moves in advance, with the feathered staff of his office; no one dares precede that, and all orders are strictly enforced. The Sacred Pole and pack containing the white buffalo hide are carried near the front of the camp.[2] The director selects from among the sons of brave men twenty-five or thirty who are swift of foot and cautious of action and sends them out to seek for the herds. They must be careful and not surprise or startle the buffalo when they find them but return speedily to the camp, making certain signals when within sight of the people. As soon as these are seen the camp is halted and the old man, bearing the Sacred Pole, and the woman carrying the pack advance a little and await the approach of the young men. These whisper their tidings, being careful to understate the number of buffalo. The old man tells the director, and the tribe is ordered to move to a camping place near the herd. About fifteen soldiers are detailed to hold the hunters in check. When the camp is settled, silence is ordered; the women tie up the dogs, that they may not bark; and if the boys shout, they are whipped by the soldiers. The hunters make ready and mount their ponies. Two young men, naked but for the breechcloth, are each given an unstrung bow; one takes the pipe of the director, the others the staff of the office, and these start in advance of the hunters. The latter are divided into two parties and slowly follow, led by the soldiers, who have much to do to restrain the men and ponies and hold the force in check. Impetuous men who from excitement dart ahead are lashed across their naked breasts by the whips of the soldiers and often blood follows the strokes. When the two young men are seen to meet, then the buffalo are known to be surrounded. In a few moments the soldiers give the word, 'Go!' and with yells and shouts the hunters rush on all sides upon the bewildered buffalo. The two young men take the hearts and tongues from the first buffalo killed, and these are used in a feast held by the Hunga gens. This gens, you remember, has charge of the Sacred Tents containing the pole and pack."[3]

"I should think the men would resent being whipped by the soldiers," I remarked.

"Oh no! They dare not. One man who ventured to oppose his punishment was so severely whipped that he was paralyzed from the effects. If by any chance a man should accidentally scare a herd, he would run away from the camp and hide for a number of days to escape punishment, for whipping would follow such carelessness."

"We boys used to be sent out with the steady old ponies to bring in the meat," said the young man. "We used to have fun sometimes and get frightened, too. Once I was sent with my uncle to bring in his meat; he gave me all his clothing to keep while he entered the chase. That's the way the men do; we boys take care of the hunters' blankets and clothes. Well, I lost him. I looked and shouted; at last I saw a man all alone making signals. It was my uncle. I rode up to him, and he said he was looking for me. As he led the way to where his buffalo lay killed, we passed through a ravine; there we met a man and a buffalo bull and cow. The man told my uncle he had but one arrow left and he could not kill the cow, for every time he shot, the bull put himself between the cow and the man; he wanted my uncle to lend his gun, but my uncle said he couldn't spare his ammunition. He told the man to take the gun and to move around to the other side as if he were going to shoot the cow from that point; then my uncle would kill it from where he stood. The man started with the gun; the bull, which was full of arrows that had been shot at the cow, followed as before, trying to protect his mate from the man but leaving her uncovered on our side. Then my uncle sprung the bow and the cow lay dead, killed with the man's last arrow. When the bull saw the cow fall, his strength gave out, and he fell over and died too."

"That is a pitiful story."

"One has to have food; we were very hungry then," the young man replied.

TWENTY

Winter and War

Winter had come. The wind swept over the prairie, reared around the bluffs and in among the trees. The glare of the sun upon the snow almost blinded the eyes when one walked over the glistening crusts. On the edges of the wood were the two-by-two tracks of the rabbit or the marks of the softly stepping wolf. The latter now ventured nearer the dwellings, and one could sometimes catch the gleam of his red eyes as he prowled about hunting for food. The women passed rapidly to the creek, breaking the ice in order to dip up the family supply of water; there was no lingering, for there was no lurking lover seeking a word or glance. Everyone who could kept close to cover, and there was need. It was cold. The thermometer had dropped to a score or more below zero, and there was no sound save the wind lashing the trees and piling up the snow here and sweeping it away there, leaving bare the yellow disheveled grass, looking like the corpse of fair summer. The tent clothes were stiff with frost and cracked and groaned when they were touched. The log cabins were hot and fetid. The four-pane window was built tight in the wall and the door, if opened, let in the air that stung like needles. In the earth lodges, blankets were hung from the inner posts, narrowing the circle about the blazing fire, where one's face was scorched and one's back was like an icicle. Physical comfort was at its ebb. A strange solemnity came when night fell and the mercury was frozen. Should the fire fail, or should the fire break loose and destroy the dwelling, life could hardly be maintained without shelter in the direful cold. When dawn appeared, although there was no added warmth, there seemed to be, however, a better chance to battle with the silent force. Living with the Indian through these wintry days, sharing with him the storms that slay and the heats that wither, it was not so difficult to understand his silences, his outbursts, his reverence, and his superstitions. So little in his life was artificial that the year, in all its phases, took him and molded him close to nature, leaving him with little freedom to protest against his enslaver or chance for mental independence.

The Indian's religion is generally spoken of as a nature and animal worship, but careful inquiry and observation fail to show me that the Indian actually worships the objects which are set up or mentioned by them in his ceremonies. The earth, the four winds, the sun, moon, and stars, the stones, the water, the various animals are all exponents of a mysterious life and power encompassing the Indian and filling him with vague apprehension and desire to propitiate these and to induce them to friendly relations—not so much through the ideas of sacrifice as through more or less ceremonial appeals. More faith is put in ritual and a careful observance of forms than in any act of self-denial in its moral sense as we understand it. The claim of relationship is used to strengthen the appeal, since the tie of kindred among the Indians is one which cannot be ignored or disregarded.

A thoughtful Indian chief said to me, "Everything as it moves, now and then, here and there, makes stops. The bird as it flies stops in one place to make its nest and in another to rest in its flight. A man when he goes forth stops when he wills. So the god has stopped. The sun, which is so bright and beautiful, is one place where he has stopped. The moon, the stars, the winds he has been with. The trees, the animals, are all where he has stopped, and the Indian thinks of these places and sends his prayers there to reach the place where the god has stopped and to win help and a blessing."

The vague feeling after unity is here discernible, but it is like the cry of a child rather than the articulate speech of a man. To the Indian mind the life of the universe has not been analyzed, classified, and a great synthesis formed of the parts. To him the varied forms are all equally important and noble. A devout old Indian said, "The tree is like a human being, for it has life and grows, so we pray to it and put our offerings on it that the god may help us." In the same spirit the apology is offered over the slaughtered animal, for the life of the one is taken to supplement the life of the other: "that it may cause us to live," one formula expresses it. These manifestations of life, stopping places of the god, cannot therefore be accurately called objects of worship or symbols; they appear to be more like media of communication with the permeating occult force which is vaguely and fearfully apprehended. As a consequence, the Indian stands abreast with nature. He does not face it and hence cannot master or coerce it or view it scientifically and apart from his own mental and emotional life. He appeals to it but does not worship it.[1]

A blizzard blew without, the air was full of icy particles, one could not see two feet from the house; within on the floor lay a pile of snow blown through the keyhole, and all about the frame of the door was a molding of frost and snow. When one went out, a cord was tied about the person and an end fastened to the entrance so that he could find his way back, for in the blinding storm and numbing cold, persons are easily bewildered and men have died within a few feet of shelter. We were safely housed and seated about the fire; in the midst of comparative comfort we hoped that no poor traveler was caught in the tempest. To break away one's thoughts from present hardships, I ventured to talk of summer experiences. "It is pleasant to remember the green prairie, to think that seed time will come again, and the birds sing once more. Were you not always glad to have spring return?"

"Yes, winter is always hard at times," said the father.

"You have always raised corn?" I continued.

"We do not know the time when we did not have it, and beans and pumpkins beside."

"Did all the tribe plant in one place, like one large field?"

"No," he answered laughingly, "we never worked a field in common or owned anything in that manner until the government made us do so. Each family had its own patch of land and used it year after year."

"The women worked it, I suppose."

"Yes, each one selected her land. Some women were bright and chose the best lands. As long as a woman cultivated her patch, no one jumped her claim, as the white men do," he answered.

"A smart woman would get her crop in first," I suggested.

"No woman could plant," he replied, "until the keeper of the Sacred Tent sent around to each family a few kernels of red corn; these indicated that the time for sowing had come. The kernels were dropped in with the seed corn."

"Everything among the Indians seems to be regulated by some religious ceremony," said I.

"There are a great many ceremonies," remarked the father. "Almost every act is connected with one or another. All those pertaining to planting and hunting belonged to the two Sacred Tents in charge of the Hunga gens where the Sacred Pole and pack were kept."[2]

"Was anyone permitted to enter the Sacred Tents?" I asked.

"No one but those having charge," he answered.

"My sister ran in once," said a friend who was stormbound. "We were little children playing together, I was teasing her and she ran off to hide. I couldn't find her anywhere, and something put it in my head to peep in one of the Sacred Tents. There she sat. She laughed as she saw me. I took her out and carried her right home to mother and told her what had happened. Mother was troubled and led my sister away to the wife of the man who kept the tent, and the two women washed her and wiped her with artemisia" (wild sage).

"We boys," said the son, "used to be given extra horses to ride and drive. One day my friend and I planned to almost run into the old man who was carrying the Sacred Pole, just for fun; we did not mean to really touch him. We started up our horses, but they wouldn't go near the man. At last my ponies became excited and ran directly into him, nearly knocking him down. He was not hurt, but he was a little mad. I told him that I didn't mean to, and I didn't exactly mean to, either. When we got to camp that night my friend told of me to father. He said I ought to be more respectful and that I must take the horses to the old man and let him cleanse them. I did so and he sprinkled them with water and wiped them with artemisia. Father does not believe in those things, but he made me do it."

The father smiled but offered no comment.

"What would happen to a horse if it was not cleansed?" I asked.

"He would step into a hole and some disaster would befall both animal and rider," said the friend.

"I should like to have seen one of the thanksgiving festivals," I remarked after a pause.

"No one will ever see that ceremony again, it belongs to the past," answered the father. "The last man is dead who knew all of the ritual used in filling the sacred tribal pipes; they can never be filled again, and without them no tribal solemnity can take place. There are many old people who grieve over this loss and attribute to it all our troubles."

"I am glad I have seen it," said the young man. "I like to think over the history of my people. Of course it is meager compared to your history" (turning to me), "but there is a great deal that is interesting about it, and I think if the white people knew more about us and understood our customs better, they would treat us with more respect."

"That is not unlikely," I replied.

When the fire had been replenished, I asked the father if he would not tell me something of the thanksgiving festival. He complied, saying, "When we were within a few days' march of the village—usually the south side of the Platte River was the place selected—the tribe halted, a long tent was erected, families in each one of the gentes contributing tent poles, crotched sticks, and tent covers. This tent was erected at the western part of the tribal circle. In front of this long tent the white buffalo hide was opened and the Sacred Pole set up; behind the latter the sod was cut in a shape resembling the outline of an earth lodge, and the exposed soil mellowed. The crier called upon the families who were known to be well off to contribute the side meat of the buffalo. Anyone who refused to comply with this request would be subject to penalties; that is, he would step on something sharp, making a bad wound, or be struck by lightning, or some other disaster would befall him. These pieces of meat were laid in rows before the long tent and on each side of the pole. The fat from these offerings was prepared in a bowl and mixed with red paint. The man and woman in charge of the pole were dressed in new garments for the occasion, and the pole was anointed; the bunch of eagle down, which is bound to the pole, was opened and the woman shot arrows into it; the sacred songs were sung; gifts were brought; and the chiefs, who were gathered in the long tent, each laid out his bundle of reeds, each reed standing for a warrior in the gens of the chief.[3] Four images of grass were set up, and the brave men, clad in their war regalia, gathered on horseback and on foot and went through a sham battle, each man acting out his brave deeds."

"That was lively," said the young man, "just like the theatre, only it was out under the blue sky and the fresh breeze blowing in our faces. It was one of our ways of preserving tribal history. It was very exciting to see over a hundred warriors dashing about. We children used to crowd as near as we dared, and more than once I was nearly run over."

"After the battle was over," he continued, "then all the tribe, except the grave old men, had a great dance around a pole cut for this purpose and set up outside the tribal circle. Everybody was dressed in the best of clothing and ornaments. The two sacred pipes led the dance. Anyone who had done a very brave deed was permitted to dance in the reverse order to the rest of the people so as to be conspicuous—I suppose so that everyone should remember the brave deed thus commemorated."

"You know a woman," said the friend to me, "who always danced the opposite way from the other dancers. This is what she had done. One time when we were out on the hunt we were attacked by Sioux. The women and children made holes and hid in them. We were hard-pressed and at last we called to the women to take the children and flee to the timber while we could protect them. This woman started; when she was nearly to the woods she did not see her son so she ran back, right in the midst of the fighting, and found the boy and carried him safely away."

"Women are very brave," said the father. "One grandmother hid her children in a hole, but she did not have time to cover them up with brush and grass before the Sioux were upon her so she threw herself flat over the hole and lay as if dead. The Sioux came along and saw her and, not knowing whether she was dead, pierced her with his spear through the arm; the woman did not wince but lay there bleeding until he was gone, and so saved the children."[4]

"Did she die?" I asked.

"No, she lived many years. You know both of the grandchildren."

"Father told you that the men in the sham fights acted out their brave deeds, but a man is not the judge of his own honors," said the son.

"How is that?" I asked of the father.

"There are packs," he replied, "which are supposed to have the power of testing the truthfulness of a man's story about himself. These packs contain the skins of certain birds. The most noted of these packs is kept in the Sacred Tent of War, in charge of the Waejinste gens.* When a war party returns a day is set for conferring honors on the warriors. The chief and people gather; the keeper of the pack lays it on a pillow; the war party are arranged before it; one at a time the warriors step forward. A small stick is given to one of them; holding this in his hand over the pack he recounts his brave deed. At a signal from the keeper the warrior drops the stick; if it rests on the pack he has reported truly and can count the honor of the deed he has told; if the stick falls off he has not been accurate and the honor is lost."

"That is hard?" I exclaimed.

"It is the custom," he answered.

After the fire was built up afresh the friend remarked, "We have had many severe fights with the Poncas, Sioux, Pawnees, and Otoes. Peace would be made and broken, and then war would come again. My grandfather was in the great fight with the Pawnees."

"How did that come about?" I inquired.

"We were at peace with the tribe, but one day several of our ponies were stolen and tracked to the Pawnee village.[5] Four Omahas went to see the Pawnee chief about it. They told him that they did not believe he intended to break the peace but that some of the young men had probably

---

*The Sacred Tent of War, with its honor-giving and truth-testing pack, also the sacred shell and other articles pertaining to the war customs of the tribe and the powers vested in the chiefs, was placed in 1884 in the Peabody Museum of American Archaeology and Ethnology at Cambridge, Mass., by the consent of Wa-hue-nin-ga, its hereditary keeper. The act was without any spirit of iconoclasm but in recognition that the past was gone and the future demanded new methods and ideas. This instance is almost without parallel in the history of a tribe or people and the courage of the act cannot be fully appreciated unless one fully understands the sociology of the Omahas. [The Tent of War was kept by the Elk clan (*Wéžište* 'Angry Ones'); the last keeper was *Mųhįðįge* 'Lacks Knife'. The items associated with war customs were repatriated to the Omahas on August 14, 1989, at the annual tribal powwow. Ridington and Hastings, Blessing for a Long Time. —Eds.]

committed the theft and that if the ponies were returned, all would be forgotten. The story told by the leading Omaha who returned was a very strange one. Some of the Omahas think it could not be all true. The Pawnee chief was said to have treated the Omahas with great indignity, offering them vile things to drink. The men left, and on their way back the leader rent his blanket in twain, cut off all ornaments, and as he traveled he wept. Nearing the Omaha villages he took off his moccasins and in a pitiful plight entered his home, wailing. The people gathered and listened as he told the chiefs of the indignity put upon the men and how the Pawnee chief had refused to return the horses until the spring, when, he said, the Omahas should come bringing gifts, and then he would give them his other moccasin (meaning many gifts of horses). The leader replied to the chief that when the grass grew he would return with guns, powder, balls, and arrows. The people heard the story; a young warrior mounted his horse and rode around the village singing his death song, thus showing he would be ready to avenge this act of indignity. Other warriors joined him. All the winter the leader fasted and wailed; many other men did the same thing. The people gathered what they could for the traders and purchased ammunition. In the early spring the tribe started, men, women, and children. When they reached Shell Creek, only one day's march from the Pawnees, they built a large cache and buried their kettles, tent cloths, and other articles so that in case of defeat they could travel rapidly and no spoils would fall into the enemy's hands. Then they moved on a little and halted where the women and children should be safe. The plan was to attack the village just at daybreak. The leader gathered the warriors and told them that when the morning star rose, that would be the signal for the advance. The Pawnees lived on the Republican River in a stockaded village with only one entrance; a portion of the party were to aim to enter this unobserved, and the others to scale the wall and so burst upon the sleeping people from all sides. As the warriors were advancing, a Pawnee was seen approaching the village on horseback; two of the swiftest runners gave chase, but the man urged his pony to its utmost speed, shouting alarm as he rode, and reached the village before the attacking party could get there. The Omahas scaled the walls, fighting their way, and reached the inside of the enclosure. Some of them dug holes about the earth lodges and set fire to the interlining of straw, and the people who had huddled in the lodges were forced to run out to escape suffocation. As they appeared at the entrance they were shot down by men stationed for this purpose. It was a fearful battle. Many were killed on both sides, but the fight went on, for the leader had said to the man next in command, 'The battle must not stop until I am killed, for I cannot live. I cannot meet the faces of the women and see them point at me and hear them say, "He was the cause of the death of my brother, of my nephew."' When the leader fell the young men were called off and the battle ceased. The Omahas brought away their dead and many ponies, kettles, and valuable articles."

"There were seven Sioux in that fight and all were killed," added the father.

"How did they come to be there?" I asked.

"They were visiting the Omahas when the people moved out and desired to join them. Five of them were killed outright, two were wounded, one of them died on the way back, and the other when the Omahas reached the village."

"Did you bury your dead near the battlefield?" I inquired.

"No, they were all taken back and buried on the hills around the Omaha village."

"We have never made war on the white people, but we have fought for them," said the friend. "When the Pacific Railroad was being built several Omahas acted as part of the guard.[6] Some bad things happened about that time; I will tell you of one. Our men were sent to a camp a few miles north of the reservation to stay before they went west. Just as they were about to start, the sister and aunt of one of the men mounted their ponies to go and bid him goodbye. Near the camp they were set upon by five soldiers; the women defended themselves with their knives from the assault of the men; the soldiers fired and gashed the women; one had her teeth knocked out; they barely escaped with their lives, and one of the horses was killed."

"What was done about the outrage?" I asked.

"The agent wrote about it; the soldiers were arrested but they were released. The husband of one of the women was paid for the loss of the horse. That was all!"

"You know the woman," said the father, mentioning her husband's name.

"Is it possible that is how she lost her teeth, and she has not the full use of her arms—was that from her wounds?"

"Yes. It is very hard, for you know her husband is blind and she has to do double duty."

"And nothing was done to punish the men or provide for the women?" I asked again.

"Nothing," he replied. "Indians cannot appeal to the law."

"White people," said the young man, speaking in English, "are always blaming the Indians because they do not refrain from attacking women when at war. I have read some history and I do not find that the Indians are the only people who have done that thing. The white people are not guiltless of such actions even among their own people. If you live long enough among the Indians you will find out how white men treat Indian women. It is worse than dogs. I hope one of these days the Indian's side of the story will become known, for there are two sides to the history of this continent, the white man's side and the Indian's side. I know how clever the white man is, how he has turned the land of our fathers into a rich, prosperous country, and I am glad of it, but not of the way he has held down the Indians, cheating them, lying to them, killing them, and worse than all, debasing them, making paupers of them by rations and annuities, saying it is 'cheaper to feed the Indian than to fight him!' What does that mean? I think it means that it is easier for the white man to kill the manhood of the Indian than to take him by the hand, educate him, and show him how to live like a civilized man. The latter course takes Christianity; the former takes money only. It is easier to put one's hand in one's pocket than to put justice in one's soul."

The young man had risen during this speech and stood facing me as he arraigned my race. Defense there was none. As I sat there I wished the keen sorrow that pierced me might touch those who seem to forget humanity when the race line is crossed. Looking in the burning eyes of the speaker, I said, "It is all true, alas! What can I do to help it?"

"You can do much; everyone can do something; no one is without power to help. You have seen my people; they have taken you to their hearts, and they love you. Speak for them! You can do it, for you know them as no white person ever did before."

How the wind raved about the little house, shaking it until it seemed as though it must fall, while through every crack and crevice the cold thrust in its deadly darts. Terrible as was the storm, the subtle power of race hatred and indifference seemed more appalling, more difficult to encounter, and yet I was charged to do this thing!

TWENTY-ONE

Friends and Lovers

The sun shone brightly, the skies were clear, the hills were singing to the growing grass, the hepaticas and bloodroot blinked on the hillsides, for spring was here. One caught the stir of new life on every side; birds were caroling it, flowers nodding acquiescence to it, and the dancing eyes of youth and maidens revealing it.

Pursuing my way through a wooded dell, enjoying the genial air, the delicate green of the herbage, and the brook slipping over the brown leaves of last year's growth, my thoughts wandered far away to scenes that touched my life's young days. All at once I was recalled to the present by the wild cadences of a flute. I could not discern the player, but in a few moments I saw a flash from his mirror and then I knew I was not the only woman in the dell. "Oh," I thought, "it is as true of the Indian as of the pale Saxon. 'In the spring a young man's fancy lightly turns to thoughts of love'!"[1]

Not wishing to disturb the budding pleasures that were about me, I hesitated which way to go; while I stood irresolute, two girls came in sight. Their faces were merry and bright, their black braids shining, their voices blithe with the chatter of the intimate friendships of girlhood. They moved slowly to the creek, each one carrying her bucket for water. Down the hill on the other side of the brook came the gallants, for there were two of them. They stepped along with the conscious pride of youth. Their ornaments sparkled in the sunbeams and their gay blankets hung gracefully from one shoulder, revealing to the full their elastic figures. The girls did not look up, but dallied as they dipped in the stream. It was a pretty scene in which I found myself entrapped.

Suddenly one of the young men dropped on the grass, while the other with a light bound was at the creek and across it. The feminine position was flanked; would there be an unconditional surrender, I wondered. The girls by this time had turned and with their filled buckets were leaving the stream. A few steps more and the young man stood facing one of the maidens, shading his brow with a spray of artemisia. For a moment the two confronted each other; then the girl put down her bucket and turned sideways toward her lover. Her face was downcast and her moccasined foot busy brushing the tender grass. The young man was evidently quietly pleading his cause, and the girl was a not-unwilling listener; neither moved toward the other but maintained their first position some three or four feet apart. The girl's friend had passed on, set her bucket down, and dropped beside it, busying herself with botanical research; across the water on the hillside lay the friend of the young man; and up the ravine, hidden by the plum blossoms, I remained a surprised spectator while by the rippling brook two hearts were perchance mingling in a fate that stretched beyond this life. By and by the girl fumbled in her belt and drew out a little package. Opening it, a gay necklace fell about her fingers: this she shyly reached out to the young man, who took it gently from her hand. A moment more and the girl's friend said something; the young man gave one long look at the maiden that seemed to clothe her with consciousness; then he stepped to one side and leaped the brook. The two girls lifted their buckets and passed silently on without one backward glance. The youth flung himself down beside his friend and together they examined the necklace; finally they rose and ascended the hill. When they were near the top, I heard again the flute and listened as it grew fainter in the distance and gradually died away.

Once more I was alone, the scene in a life's drama was over and I turned to leave; just then a sound arrested my attention, and where the girl had passed there came an old wrinkled woman with prosaic tread carrying her bucket to fill. She went straight to the creek and dipped in the pail. A little bird sat swaying on a twig nearby and at that moment he piped out his notes of joy. The old woman sat down her burden and lifted her withered face to look at the songster; then she glanced about the sunny dell, passing her thin hands over her hair. Did something bring back the days when flutes sounded for her and lovers leaped the stream to whisper words of devotion while she stood and listened beside her brimming pail? Or did the song of the bird and the beauty of awakened nature plead with the immortal youth within her, that heritage of every human soul? Something in her face bred the thought and filled the dell with a charm that laid hold upon that which, having "primal sympathy, must ever be."

Friendship plays an important part in the lives of Indian men and women and often the intimacies begun in childhood extend to old age. The friendships among women have less of dramatic incident than those of the men, as the women are not so much exposed to the adventure of the hunt and warpath. I have seen instances of enduring kindness between women that came near being heroic. Some of these were between wives of the same man, and friendship under such trying circumstances is surely worthy of honor. Not all plural families were so fortunately adjusted, but I met everywhere a patience on the part of the woman that was surprising. Between masculine friends the relations are apt to be very close, and a man will cleave to his friend in peace and in war, following him in the face of the deadliest danger and avenging his death unmindful of all other claims. Friends are also confidants and few secrets are withheld from one's intimate, nor is the help of a friend refused, even in those matters we are wont to regard as belonging exclusively to private and personal affairs.[2]

One day as I sat busy with my notebook, while the daughter of the Indian whom I was visiting was working on her moccasin at my side, the dandy brother entered the lodge with a friend. They seated themselves and the brother began to open packs and take out his treasures. Evidently the young men were about to prepare for some festivity. After a time they brushed out their hair with a brush made of stiff grass and then the brother called his sister to dress his scalplock. She dropped her work and went over to him and he reclined so that she could easily reach his head. She unbraided the lock, straightened the parting, and braided it in a glossy, even, narrow braid of three strands. After her brother's lock was arranged she performed a similar service for his friend, then she returned to my side.

The young men proceeded to decorate each other's scalplocks with slides, ribbons, and beads. Next the paint was prepared in a hollowed dish and put on with a round, pointed stick; the partings were made red and the face colored in bands and dots of red, yellow, and green. This took much time, one young man painting the face of the other. Two or three hours were consumed in making the toilet. All this time the young men were talking over their private matters. They were close friends and confidants, and just now a delicate affair was being arranged between them. The friend was greatly smitten by the charms of a certain maiden, but his heart was faint, he could not win the fair lady.

"My friend, I can't speak to her," he said. "When I get a chance then my heart beats so fast that my mouth will not open. You must speak to her for me, and ask her to be kind to me."

"She is not my relation," returned the brother. "I have no more right to speak to her than you, and she might get angry."

"I do not think she would get angry, and I want you to help me. I cannot get her out of my mind."

After a period of quiet the brother said, "My friend, I will help you." Then he added, "I must think over what I shall say to her."

A silence followed, while the painting proceeded.

"When will you speak to her?" asked the friend, at length.

"I was going to see another person who let me speak to her last evening; she stopped at the creek; she liked to have me address her, and she gave me this match case," said the brother with animation.

"Be careful!" broke in the sister, as she bent over her work. "If a man tells of his favors the news flies!"

"I know when a girl likes me," retorted the brother, but he told no more tales that day.

A long pause ensued as the decoration proceeded. At the last the brother said, "I have thought how I will speak for you. I will step before her and say, 'Wait! I bring a message to you from one who has for many days been wishing to speak to you but hesitates because of his inferiority. He has at last begged me to speak to you in his behalf that you might listen kindly to him, even if your thoughts be in another direction when he comes to you to make known his wish. I myself am beneath your family and am not worthy of your notice, but the hopeless desires of my friend have touched my heart and have made me bold to come to you. My friend is one of many who desires to be of your people, even if it is to carry burdens and to take care of the animals belonging to your father. May it please you to speak kindly to my friend even if your heart declines him. Tomorrow as the sun goes down and the shadows of the hills are over the camp, and faces cannot be distinguished, the falling of a pole supporting the flaps of your tent shall be a signal that my friend is near and waits to see you. Pity him and come to him that he may open his heart to you.'"

During this long speech the toilet was suspended, the brother hesitating now and then to adjust the sentences but keeping his eyes fixed on his friend. When he had finished there was a pause before the friend answered gravely, "That will be very good. When you have opened the way for me, I shall speak to her myself."

"Let me say it over that I forget none of the words," said the brother. And again he repeated the address without changing a word. After a time he said, "You shall see me speak to her, but you must be hid. Should you show only the top of your head she would be angry with me."

"I will not be seen, I will watch," the friend replied.

At last the dressing was complete and the two gallants stood up, resplendent. The brother suddenly turned, saying, "I must perfume my blanket that I may be successful."

Opening a pack he took from thence some seeds, crushed them in his mouth, and blew them over his blanket; then putting the robe about him the two passed out of the tent.

Later when I stepped outside I saw the two young men on an elevation overlooking the tent of the maiden and in a position where they could make a rapid detour through a grove toward the creek and catch the girl as she went for water.

The tent pole must have fallen and the girl answered the signal, for in a few weeks the news spread that the two had eloped and were man and wife.

The creek or spring is the trysting place. The young girls go for water, never alone, but in pairs or groups or with an elder person. The young men haunt the favorable places for dipping up, lying hid in the grass until the wished-for damsel arrives; then the lover suddenly appears, accosts the girl, and she favors or frowns as her mood pleases. These secret meetings are all the opportunities the young people have of speaking together; and in spite of social bans and bars, they contrive to have a good many flirtations.

It is not unusual for a friend to prepare the way for his friend's courting. Once a young man quite gay and manly in his bearing stepped before a spirited girl and stopped her, as he pled for his friend in a manner similar to that already given. When he ended his speech the girl looked up, her eyes flashing, as she said, "I'll have nothing to do with your friend, or with you either!"

The young man hesitated a moment as if he was about to renew his suit; a dangerous movement of her water bucket made him leap to one side to escape a deluge.

There was a bachelor, the only one I knew of in the tribe, who was precise in all his ways, trim in dress, and scrupulously neat. Summer or winter he never missed his bath. He was also gifted with the sight of strange visions. He could see the dead and talk with them. He was accounted very holy. Although a dreamer, he was no idler; few men were more industrious and thrifty than he, or more exact in business. He was kind in word and act, and everyone respected him. Why he never married, no one but himself knew, but that he was not opposed to matrimony was to be inferred from his acts in behalf of others.

This man had two brothers; for some reason they were not attractive to the girls. Years passed on and the brothers could not win a wife. One day the bachelor said to one of the unsuccessful candidates, "I will help you get the girl you want." Great was the surprise of everyone when it was whispered that this Benedict had been seen at the creek as if courting; greater still was the astonishment of the girl to find herself addressed by this attractive but hitherto obdurate young man. The wooing sped prosperously and the elopement was planned. At the appointed time and place they met and together they rode to the lodge of one of his near relations, where the brother was already in waiting. The bachelor explained to the girl his disinterested conduct in winning her for his brother, and the girl, having compromised herself by running off with her supposed lover and being ashamed to return, concluded to accept the transfer and make the best of it. Leaving the couple to their odd honeymoon, he relapsed into his bachelor ways and the people were more surprised than ever at this turn of affairs. It was intimated that he had made use of charms potent with women in order to secure the girl and then hand her over so satisfactorily. Twice the bachelor courted, both times for his brother's benefit, and having settled the family in the matrimonial line, he washed his hands of it ever after.

The claims upon a girl in marriage by her potential relations oblige her to elope secretly with the young man of her choice if she is to be mistress of herself. Otherwise she must consent to be taken by a brother-in-law or married off by her parents to some influential old man. When the young couple, after their stolen interviews at the creek, determine on the final step, they agree to meet some evening; the youth generally rides to the lodge of the girl and, at a concerted signal, she slips out and they gallop off to one of his relations. In a day or two he takes her to his father's house, where she is received as the son's wife. By this act all other claims to the girl are cancelled, as far as marrying her is concerned; but gifts must be made to her parents and shared with her relations to ratify the act. In order to effect this, the father of the young man makes a feast and invites the girl's relations. When this invitation is accepted by them, and the presents received, the marriage is considered as settled, past all dispute. In the course of a few months the father of the bride generally presents her with gifts about equal in value to those he has received, and the young husband is expected to work for a year or two for his father-in-law. This latter claim is rigidly exacted and the father-in-law is often quite a tyrant over his son-in-law's affairs.

The custom prevails that no man can address directly or speak the name of his daughter-in-law, and a similar injunction is laid upon the young woman. Nor can a young man hold speech with his mother-in-law or mention her name. Some even avoid the presence of the other.

One rainy day a number of young men were visiting in a lodge. The old grandmother went out; when she returned, she snapped her blanket to shake off the drops, and one of the young men said, "Grandmother, how is the weather?"

"It drizzles," she replied.

"Oh hi," they shouted. "What have you done; that's your son-in-law's name!"

"I mean, it rains in gusts," she said, correcting herself.

"Why, that is his name too!" they cried. The old woman had given translations of the name.

"I tell you, the rain comes down in pieces," retorted the grandmother, determined to fly the mark this time, whereat all the young folk laughed and even the son-in-law joined. He was not able to pretend that he had not heard it.

When a girl is married off by her parents she is dressed in her best, mounted on a good pony well decked, and accompanied by four old men who fire guns and shout as they convey the bride-elect to the lodge of her husband, where the man receives her. He had already made large presents to the girl's father and relations. This kind of marriage is greatly derided by the young men, who say, "An old man can't win a girl, he can only win her parents."

When a young girl is asked in marriage a certain form is used; the identical words are not always repeated, but the general idea is the same. The young man is very humble; he disclaims all worthiness on his part of the honor of addressing her; he denies that he is her equal; he extols her, and her relations; he pleads his constancy. In wooing, the lover asks a boon of the maid in being his wife; he does not demand it as a right. If she assents, and darkness hides them from the curious gaze, he folds her in his arms, the draping of the blanket making it a classic picture.

The passages in my notebooks containing the expressions used in courtship read more like extracts from a novel of our grandmothers' time than gleanings from utterances of Indians. Much in the courtship of Indian women resembles the practice of our own race, and the carrying forward of the pleasures of the lovers into the daily life of marriage depends, there as elsewhere, upon individual character. I have seen many happy Indian families where affection twined all hearts closely together.

One can sometimes judge of the light by the depth of the shadow cast. An old man stood beside a young husband whose wife lay dead. The mourner sat wailing, holding the woman's cold hand and calling her by the endearing names that are not permitted to be uttered to the living. "Where shall I go, now you are gone! There is no place left for me!" he cried.

The old man looked earnestly at the sorrow-stricken one; at length he spoke: "My grandson! It is hard to lose one's mother, to see one's children die, but the sorest trial that can come to a man is to have his wife lie dead. My grandson! Before she came to you, no one was more willing to bring water for you. Now that she has gone, you will miss her care. If you have ever spoken harshly to her, the words will come back to you and bring you tears. No one is so near, no one can ever be so dear, as a wife; when she dies her husband's joy dies with her. My grandson, old men who are gone have taught us this. I am old. I have felt these things. I know the truth of what I say."

TWENTY-TWO

The Make-Believe White Men

A company of men and women gathered one evening under the trees. Someone had brought a supply of fresh corn to roast, so the sticks of the fire were drawn near together by twos, the coals raked between them, and the corn laid on the improvised rack. Its sweet odor during the cooking lent an additional aboriginal characteristic to the scene.

"Were you ever among the Mormons?" I was asked.

"No, were you?"

"They were among us while the government made us live near the agency at Bellevue.[1] They killed off the game and their cattle ate up our growing crops, so we were left without food."

"Brigham Young was a big man," said another speaker. "He had a gold chain running all over his front. He thought everybody was looking at him!"

"One thing I don't understand," remarked a third, "the white people say it is bad to have more than one wife. The Mormons are white, and they all had several wives at that time, and I am told they have still. Are the Mormons under the government?"

"Yes," I replied.

"Why doesn't the government talk to them about their wives as it talks to the Indian?"

"I don't know," I answered.

"They say God told them it is right to have many wives," said a new

304

speaker. "I don't like the way some of the men take and 'seal' women, as they call it.[2] I don't understand it. I married a Mormon woman, and she was a good woman; she tried to make a Mormon of me. I think she would have succeeded but a man had her sealed to him, and I wouldn't have a wife that way, so I left her. That was after the Mormons had gone to Utah. I went out there with her, from here."

The corn was ready for eating and everyone enjoyed the juicy ears.

"You have several ways of cooking corn?" I said to a woman near me.

She began counting them off on her fingers until she reached the number ten.

"This is the best way of any," said one, "because—we have it now!" And amid the laughter which followed this joke fresh ears were laid on.

"Where did you raise your corn when you first came up from Bellevue to this reservation?" I asked.

"The government broke the large field, you know, over at the agency, and every family could have a part of that to cultivate."

"Some of the tribe scattered after a short time," said a new speaker. "There were a few half-breeds living near Decatur, and not far from them on a wooded bottom was a little village. The people there were called 'the wood-eaters' because they cut timber for a living. There was one village near the Mission and we were called 'the make-believe-white-men' because the men built houses and farmed;[3] then there was the earth lodge village where the greater part of the tribe lived, and they were called 'the old folks'!" and everybody laughed.

"Our village was a fine affair!" said the nervous man. "We built a bridge, laid out roads, and each man erected his house. Our homes were not made of logs, they were grander; two were frame houses, the rest were of sawed lumber. We bought our shingles, windows, and hardware. We were not the best of carpenters but we knew how to hang doors so that they would creak, and each man learned to know the sound of his own door and every other man's door. As I lay in bed I would say, 'There goes my uncle's door; what makes him get up so early?'" Everybody enjoyed the jest of this early riser upon a man whose day generally began several hours later than the speaker's.

"Who put it in your head to plan your village as you did?" I asked.

"We had seen the white people, and that set us thinking and wanting to see what we could do, and he," indicating the father, "was our head chief and he helped us, for he had been East, and he believed in Indians becoming self-supporting," answered one of the men.

"Didn't some white person help you?" I questioned.

"Who was there to help us? We did it ourselves. We wanted to own our own things. We have never liked the tribal issue. We are not used to having things that belong to nobody. It is a bad plan, and I have found out, it is not the white man's way, but the government's way with the Indians."

"I will tell you something," said a new speaker. "We wanted to have our own things, as you have heard. We had little money; this man and this one," and he indicated a dozen or more, "each gave two dollars and with that we bought a plow. He," pointing to the father, "had oxen. We broke over one hundred acres and fenced it. We did all the work."

"We were the first to plant wheat and we raised corn, sorghum, and vegetables. We used to haul our crops on the ice to Sioux City and get money for them," added another.

"We had pigs too," said a third.

"I remember the first money I ever earned," began a thoughtful man. "It was at Bellevue. The missionary gave me some wood to chop. When it was done, he put some silver in my hand. I stood thinking how that silver had lain hid in the wood, and I had got it out by working. I thought it was good, so I worked more and more, and by and by I bought a horse with money I had earned. I thought it the best horse I had ever seen!"

"It was at Bellevue, too, that I first thought of work," said another man. "The white people had gathered about us. As I watched them, it seemed to me that everything around them glistened and I wondered how that could be. Then I saw that it came from the ground, and I determined that I would work the ground. I spoke to the agent and told him I wanted to work. 'That is good,' he said, but he did nothing to help me. Agents always have good words, but they do little, and I have come to the conclusion that their brains are not right!"

"That is the way with all white people who come from Washington," said a former speaker. "They gather the people together, tell them to work, and the white men do all the talking; they never come to our houses or to our farms and see how little we have to work with. No white person even entered my house except you and it sounded strange when you said you were going to see all of us. The men from Washington go to the agency and talk fine words and then go back and talk some more in Washington. I have heard them here and I have heard them there; they have no sense. We don't want anybody talking at us; we want our money and implements to work with. We can talk, too, but that won't raise a crop!"

"Tell me how it was that you men began to work at farming and so cut all these good women out of their rights," I asked.

"The game was gone, food could no longer be obtained in that way, it must come out of the ground, and it is a man's duty to supply his family with food," said an old man.

"I'll tell you when I first worked," said a large man. "I was my mother's only child; I used to lie and watch her work in the field. I said to myself, 'She does that to get food for you,' and then I determined not to let my mother work for me anymore, and I began to farm."

His mother, an old gray-haired woman, nodded her assent to this statement and said, turning to me, "He takes care of me now."

"Roaming over the country is as hard as working, and one gets little for it; but when one farms there is something in return for one's labor," said the man with the hard-working hands.

"They used to make me do the fighting," said "the old man of the mountain." "Whenever we have a new agent he has his own notions, and he changed all that the man before him had done. A new agent came while we were living in the village and he marked off the government farm in long strips and gave a strip to each family, and that worked badly."

"How?" I asked.

"Some people are lazy, and others, like my grandfather here, would prefer to work all day and all night too. By the new agent's plan the lazy folk had too much land and the ambitious men too little. It did not hurt the lazy man that his share was so large, but it did make it bad for the man who had not enough land. That seems to be the government's way, to make all Indians alike; it helps only the lazy ones."

"What did you have to fight about?" I inquired.

"That thing! The agent said he was going to cut up our farm in the same way. All but a few of our men worked there; those that did not had farms a little distance off. The men told me to watch at the bridge for the agent and stop him. One who spoke English stayed with me; all the rest were in the field at work. By and by the agent came along on his way to the mill. He did not stop. I waited to see him safe on the road back to the agency. Before long he returned, then he stopped. 'Where are the men?' he asked. 'Gone to the field,' I replied. 'You know,' said the agent, 'how I have fixed the field at the agency and made it look civilized, as the lands are where I came from?' 'I have heard about it and so have the men, and they have put me here to watch for you.' 'That is good,' said the agent. 'The people,' I continued, 'want me to tell you that you can do what you like at the agency, as that field belongs to the government, but it is different here. This field is our own and you are not to touch it.' His face turned very red as he said, 'I am the power here. I know more than you Indians, and I shall do as I think best.' 'You may at the agency, but not here!' He was angry and brought his whip down on his horse and was off."

"I never could see the use of agents," said a former speaker; "they do the Indians no good. They stay at the agency and when we ask them about our matters they seldom have the patience to answer us. We went once to an agent to find out about our money. You know, we are never allowed to know how our money is spent. It is not given us. We do not think that is a good way for us to understand something about money and what it can do. At our request to be told how much money had been expended and for what purposes, the agent said it would take too much time to find out, he was too busy. We told him that we understood he was placed over us to look after our affairs since we were not allowed to do so ourselves, and we thought it his duty to tell us of our funds. He said he had no time to look it up. We told him, one day we saw you drop a copper from your pocket, and we watched you get upon your hands and knees and search for it until you found it. We want to look after our coppers."

"I have thought about these things," said an earnest-faced man, "and this is my conclusion. The property the agent spends his time taking care of was nearly all, if not all of it, bought with our money, the money we received for our land. That property is ours, and it is not the government's, as the agent says, and as it is ours we ought not to be kept from our own things by a stranger. The agent is sent here that he may have money and men come here to make money; agents and they are alike. To them the Indian is not a man, to be treated as white men treat each other. White men think Indians know nothing. It is true we are not educated like the white man, but we can see and think, and we know a just from an unjust action."

"The farmers were no better," said another man.[4] "They would sometimes ride around on horseback, but we were not taught by them."

"We learned all we know watching the white farmers around the reservation. Sometimes our young men went out to work and they learned still more," said a third.

"That's true," said several voices.

"We have learned something from the shops and a little from the farmers. There have been a few men here who I think tried to help us, but most of the white men cared principally for the money, to some even five cents was dear!" said an old man.

"When at last after many years waiting the reservation was surveyed we were the first to select lands," said a former speaker. "We took down the houses in our village and put them up on our allotments. We began to feel like men, but it has been hard for us. Our ponies are small and weak; they are not strong enough to do heavy work. It seems sometimes as if, try as we may, we are always left in the winter!"

"We need implements. Without them and strong horses it is difficult to do a great deal more than when our women worked with the shoulder blade of an elk for a hoe," said another.

"Before I went on my land I was just a wild Indian, roaming over the country, looking for death," said the nervous man, and everyone laughed at this outburst.

"Now you roam over your sixty acres," suggested his neighbor.

"You do all your own work, too," I remarked.

"We have no one to help us if we send our children to school," said one.

"We used to be laughed at because our children went to the Mission," said another.

"You had no other schools then?" I suggested.

"No, not for many years. After a time the government opened a day school, and you know about the boarding school."

"Dear old Mission!" ejaculated a young man in English at my side. "I shall never love any place so well!"[5]

"There have been good men and women there and they have done much for our people. They put our boys in the shops to learn trades and taught our girls and women many things," said one of the group.

"I believe in education and want some of our boys to be lawyers!" said a thoughtful man.

"I'm going, for I must work tomorrow," said the nervous man, arising, and with a laugh at his zeal the company broke up.

TWENTY-THREE

The Schoolboys

The Mission of which the people had spoken deserved all they could say of it for it had done the lion's share in bringing the tribe forward to its present stage of advancement. Men and women have toiled there in the years gone by, leading unselfish and consecrated lives, and this labor of love still goes on.

The building is quaint and picturesque, reminding one of some old convent on the Rhine. It is an oblong stone structure, three stories high, surmounted by a belfry and void of all ornaments or any caprice of fancy within or without. It stands on a shallow terrace partway up the high wooded bluff that towers behind it and slopes steeply to the river bottom before it. The tall trees marshal themselves around the house, and the roses and shrubs, planted by gentle hands, cluster their blooms about its sturdy foundations.

On each side rise the heavily timbered bluffs; to the right the height is covered with Indian graves, and near the summit lies the Mission graveyard with its harvest of mounds, some marked by stones, others by flowers only. To the left a ravine dips between the hills and springs send a stream down to the flowing Missouri with its eddies, sandbars, and crumbling banks. To the east, beyond the river, stretch the rich bottomlands of Iowa, bounded in the distance by the bluffs that mark the limit of the valley. Looked at from the heights above or from the lowland by the river far to the south, the Mission presents a picture that lingers in the fancy and must dwell in the affection of one who has stayed there. The peal of the bell in the early morning, calling to prayers, hails the day with noble thoughts, and the call to the evening service comes like a benediction upon the gathering night.

The schoolroom is on the lower floor and also serves as a chapel. On Sunday, the boys, trim in their Sunday clothes, the girls in their fresh aprons and collars, cluster near the pulpit desk; the back part of the room is filled by the fathers, mothers, older brothers and sisters; the doorway too is crowded, and the windows opening upon the wide porch frame groups of faces. There is not room enough in the little chapel schoolroom for all who gather about the Christian workers who there uplift the standard that displaces self and substitutes the neighbor.

For twenty-eight years the Mission house has stood on its present site. It has seen the great bottom, where the agency shops and mills once stood and where the steamboat landed and brought news of the far-off world, break away and fall, acre by acre, into the restless Missouri. It has seen the children, it has trained them to grow to man's and woman's estate, many of them becoming thrifty workers and Christian parents. The changes wrought by the settling of the country around the reservation have left it stranded far from the present centers of activity. The railroad is now the highway of commerce and runs some fifteen miles to the westward, through the fertile valley of the Logan. This region presents claims to the farmer, rather than the broken woodlands of the bluffs. The old Mission is still alert for the good of the people and will find a way to meet the needs of a new generation.

Indian schoolchildren are full of tricks and pranks.[1] One day as I sat talking with some young folk who had been Mission scholars, their gleeful tales made it difficult for me to realize that I was not listening to the reminiscences of persons of my own race.

"I was the champion boy for securing holidays," said one young man. "One October day we were very tired of school; the air was brisk outside, and we boys wanted a run. So I said, 'When the teacher calls the class in the Fourth Reader, do all of you keep step with me and tramp as hard as you can.' I had previously loosened the stovepipe and I expected results. When the teacher called for the class I rose promptly and stepped out. All the boys followed, keeping time with me. The old floor shook and so did the stovepipe; then down it came, filling the room with smoke and soot. Everybody got a holiday that time!"

"We boys had to take care of the pigs," said another, "and he," pointing to the first speaker, "would run out just before school and loosen one of the bars and before long somebody would run in and shout, 'Send the boys, the pigs are out!' and then away we would run."

"How long it used to take us to catch the pigs!" added another, laughing.

"And how mad the girls were because they did not get out!" put in a third.

"You big fellows were awful hard on us smaller boys. I don't believe I got my Sunday cakes once a month!"

"Did they take them away?" I asked.

"I'll tell you," said the first speaker. "Every Sunday for lunch we had bread and butter and one round cake. We used to buy things with these. I bought an old gun lock, on which I could snap caps, for five cakes. Generally we only paid a half cake at a time, but sometimes I owed two boys and then, unless somebody owed me, I would have no cake at all. We always paid out our cakes first, before we ate anything. I owe some cakes yet! If I can ever buy any, I'll pay them."

"Do you remember that fellow who would not pay his debts?" said one. "He owed us three cakes and we danced about him every Sunday while he was eating the cake, singing, 'He owes me a cake! He owes me a cake!' and all the boys stood looking on and laughing at the delinquent."

"Yes, I remember, and he became so sick of it that he paid at last."

"I shall never forget when I first came to the Mission," said a tall young man. "I was a little fellow and didn't know anything. It was in the afternoon and I was put in the charge of a big boy who could speak English. He left me alone and by and by I found a small boy I knew. Just then the wife of the teacher came out of a room and smiled at us and took us into her room. How many things there were there! I didn't see what she could do with them! When her back was turned, the little boy pointed to a great black box and said, 'The teacher is to be buried in that and there is something inside that, when he punches it, makes a big groan.' I was so frightened at the box that when the lady showed me something, I couldn't look at it. Someone opened the door and I ran out as hard as I could and brought up against the big boy. He said we were all to go into the schoolroom; so he took me there and I sat beside him. Before very long the teacher came in and he had the great black box with him. He laid it down on the floor, then he raised the lid and slowly lifted out an awful-shaped thing, so I thought. I watched him take a stick and punch the thing. Sure enough, the big groan came, just as the little boy had said. I shook with terror and, thrusting my head in a desk, refused to come out!"

"How he used to make us sing to that bass viol!" said the first speaker, as soon as our laughter was over. "Don't you remember?" and he started up the song, the others joining:

Come along! Come along! Make no delay,
Come from every nation, come from every way,
For Uncle Sam is rich enough to give us all a farm.[2]

TWENTY-FOUR

Our Land

"Here's the paper," said my nervous friend. "You'll see it is just as the lawyer said, not a patent."

I unfolded the various wrappings that protected the long envelope and took out the clean and fresh document. It was a certificate of allotment signed by the commissioner of Indian affairs and stated that the person therein named was entitled to accept a certain quarter section and to be protected in his occupancy.

"It is not a patent and does not make you owner of the land specified," I said.

"Who then owns the land?" he asked.

"The government, I suppose."[1]

"We were sold this land, no one else ever lived on it. It was our father's home before it was ours. What right has the government to say it is not mine?"

"Because you are an Indian," I stated.

"Why don't you say a savage! That is what white people call us. It is a name no Indian recognizes. A white man may say what he likes and it is only because he is powerful that his words are heavy. Savage. What is a savage?"

"It used to mean a man who lived in the woods."

"Did the man who lived there call himself a savage?"

"No, he was called so by those who lived in cities."

"They were white men in the cities, were they not?" he asked.

"Yes, and so were the savages!"

"Ha! Then these were white savages?"

"Yes."

"Why are Indians called savages, they don't all live in woods."

"Because they are not civilized."

"Is being honest civilized?" he questioned.

"Yes, one way of being so," I answered.

"Then that is bad for the white man. Is telling the truth civilized?"

"I suppose so."

"Bad for the white man, again. Do all white men work?"

"Most of them do, I think," I replied.

"So do the Indians in their way, but everything is changed. Once I was a great hunter but the white men came and killed the game and I could no longer labor as did my forefathers. 'The land is left!' I said, and I watched the farmers and imitated them as well as I could. You know my farm and my crops. Now the white man wants to take away my land. Can a man live on air? The food God spread freely over the country is destroyed, the land is coveted; it is as though the white man said to me, 'You shall not have anything!' Is that civilized?"

"No, it is not," I answered.

"Where can an Indian turn for help? No one has ears in Washington. They have only eyes to see what is good for the white man, and hands to take it. We have asked many to help us. Our agents have written for us asking that we be sent strong papers for our land which the government promised in our treaties, but look! We have nothing," he said, holding up his certificate. "Any day soldiers may come to us, as to the Poncas, and drive us off our farms!"

He was deeply moved. "Listen! I will tell you something," he continued. "Not many years ago there came several men from Washington; they stopped at Decatur. We heard that they wanted to get our consent to sell our land and move to the Indian Territory. They sent for the chiefs. You know about chiefs. We of the young men's party talked to the tribe. Then the people told the chiefs that if they went down to see those white men everyone who did so would be held accountable. We would have done something severe to the chief who stirred. No one dared to go. Then the white men came up to the agency and three chiefs were brought there and it was told them that they had better consent to sell the land and go to the Territory, but they said, "We can't do this thing, we are not authorized; all the tribe must be present." The white men said they were in a hurry and that the chiefs could speak, as individuals and not officially, as to what they thought of the proposition. The chiefs declared they could say nothing. If they had spoken we would have punished them, and they knew it. So the white men went away. We know that our land is wanted by the white people, and they have many tricks by which to catch Indians!"

As he was talking several other men came in. One said, "I cannot sleep sometimes thinking of my land. If soldiers should come I could only stand looking at these hills."

"It is hard to work," said another, "when you know someone else has the power to take from you your home and thrust you into exile."

"As for me," remarked a third, "I am afraid to do any more breaking. The land is not mine and I may be working for some white man who will walk over my fields and reap from my labor. I wanted to build a house; I believed the agent; I cut logs; he let them rot; I could not get them sawed. Now I think if I had put up a house it would only have been one thing more for the white man to steal!"

"I have no house," said the man with the hard-working hands. "I cut good timber for my house. I hauled it to the mill. The agent said he must have a jail. He went down to the mill where the logs of the Indians lay and picked out the best. He took all of mine and built the blockhouse with it. I asked him why he did so. He said he picked out good material, he did not know whose it was."

"There is no law here or anywhere for Indians. White men kill us and go untouched. A new case of that kind happened not very long ago," said my nervous friend.

"At first I was afraid to break my land for the same reason as my nephew here," said a thoughtful man, "but when I became a Christian I believed God would help me. I went to work. You know my farm."

I had learned from experience that the chord of danger to his land vibrated in the heart of every man and woman in the tribe. No fireside was without the dreaded shadow of "removal." Its woeful presence among the people haunted me day and night; it waylaid me at every turn; I could not study for the weariness of it. I knew the men were right about the promise in their treaties to give them patents for I had examined these at the agency. Slowly the resolve was getting possession of me that I must do something toward righting their wrongs. As I listened to the speakers, suddenly, and before I fully realized the import of the words, I was saying, "Call all the men together who have worked. I will need them, and God helping me I will help you!"

Leaving my friends I went out to walk alone on the bluffs and to think of what was before me, for it became clear that I had entered upon a battle that would outlast my life.

The men gathered as requested. I prepared a petition on a single page of my notebook asking the government to grant patents to the signers because by their work they had practically homesteaded their farms and desired to transmit to their children the benefits of a permanent home. The men listened and said, "It is good." I went on to explain, "Every man who signs this paper must give me a statement of his work: how many years he has farmed, how he obtained the materials to build his house, how he earned the money to buy his door and windows and any articles he may possess. I must also see his farm and crops, for all we put on this paper must be exact."

"Tell the government to give land to those who work, that we may not be held back by the men of our tribe who do not care for the future," interrupted one of the men present.

"Say that we will keep on asking for patents and will never give up until we get them," said my nervous friend.

Two months were spent collecting the statistics that were afterward condensed and transmitted to Washington as an appendix to the petition. The document addressed to the Senate left the reservation on the last day of the year 1881. As the mail carried the petition over the reservation line the Christian Indians held a meeting for prayer asking that the Divine Power might touch the hearts of the congressmen to grant the request now speeding toward them.[2]

All the winter I was busy planning how to help the people to meet the future that I believed would be theirs. Better houses were needed to insure better homes. The young married couples should be brought into educated companionship in order to work and record social reforms and to institute a new order of society. The Indians marry young and after marriage several years are before them wherein they can study with benefit. As they are already joined, if they are educated together the risk of a boy with some training marrying an untutored girl is avoided. In order to test the feasibility of this plan of teaching married people I gathered a few young couples about me and the long evenings were spent over slates and geographies, the latter serving the purposes of readers. The interest in study spread; young people and those of mature age were touched with the desire to learn and were added to the class. My efforts were cordially seconded by a sweet-souled woman at the Mission. The number of students increased and at last the Mission opened a night school, and for weeks the chapel schoolroom was crowded and the Mission corps severely taxed by the extra labor. The agency school caught the infection and a prosperous night school was started there. Some ambitious young men attended both schools, which were held on alternate nights.

The zest for study did not abate the interest in the expected "words from Washington." As the winter waned, men rode miles to ask if the longed-for words had come. Spring loosened the brooks and the stir of life was in the air. Watching and winter were possible companions, but the pulses of spring demanded action.

In my ignorance I was surprised at the silence regarding the petition, which, I learned, had been received at Washington. Finally a day came when I could wait no longer. I bade my friends goodbye, saying they would not see me until I had good news to tell. Men, women, and children gathered to bid me farewell, and alone I started to study a new phase of Indian affairs.

Of my three-months' stay at the capital; of the noble men and women who, when they heard direct from the people of their wrongs and needs, rallied to help set the crooked things straight; of the obstacles overcome, the misapprehensions cleared away, it would take too long to tell. On August 7, 1882, the president signed the bill giving the Omahas their lands individually, the patent to be held in trust for twenty-five years, the United States acting as guardian.[3]

I was among the Indians when the telegram was forwarded telling of the president's assent. We were once more under the oak, the good news traveled quickly over the reservation, and men and women gathered about me. Pathetic speeches were made and manly hopes expressed. At the close of the impromptu meeting an old woman arose and advanced toward me, lifting her hands in the sign of thanks, and blessed me on behalf of the Indian mothers, who were no longer threatened with homelessness.

Before many weeks I was again turning eastward, this time accompanied by thirty-six Omahas, boys and girls on their way to Carlisle Training School in Pennsylvania and young married couples on their way to Hampton Institute, Virginia.[4] The young couples were to go to school and to live in cottages, each couple keeping house, thus learning civilized home life by an experience never to be forgotten.

Every child brought off the reservation to an outside school has to pass a strict physical examination. The girls of my party were unfortunate and there was much weeping among rejected ones. I therefore failed to get the complement of girls, but there were more than enough of boys ready to fill their vacant places and I returned to take them and fill up the number. When we arrived at Carlisle the superintendent looked at the surplus boys. His generosity rose to the emergency. He obtained permission to keep them if I could raise the money for their support for a single year. Generous persons had already defrayed a part of the traveling expenses for the children. The task of securing this money kept me past a few months, but it was done.[5] During all my work on behalf of the Omahas I had been cordially seconded by the Indian Department, the secretary of the interior, and I received from the Indian commissioner a letter of thanks.

The experiment has proved successful. Ladies connected with the Woman's National Indian Association and its auxiliaries have raised money and loaned it to these young couples on their return to the reservation to build themselves houses on their farms.[6] Two such houses stand today, and others are going up. These educated, properly housed families set an example of civilized Christian homes and form the nucleus of a new society.

TWENTY-FIVE

Starting Afresh

In the spring of 1883 the secretary of the interior sent me as a special agent to carry out the provisions of the bill in which I was so deeply interested. An educated Omaha accompanied me as my clerk.[1] During all the work which followed, the agent and his corps of assistants lent me cordial and generous aid.

The people were mainly living in the bluffs, where the land was unequal in value for farming. They were also far from market and too much isolated from the white settlers for any rapid progress in new ideas. I had long urged their going to the Logan Valley, near the railroad. Some had made selections there, but the fear of losing their land caused them to hesitate to settle.

As soon as my new tent was completed by the Omaha women and my camp outfit secured, I started with my clerk and an Indian matron for the western portion of the reservation. My tent was pitched on an elevation overlooking the Logan Creek and commanding a view for many miles in every direction. The slope back of the tent to the stream was a terrace of flowers and the green, unbroken, rolling prairie in spring was resonant with the song of birds. The Indians gathered about me; the surveyor's tent was set up and before many days the white people over the line were filled with curiosity as to what the sudden encampment could mean.

Early every morning we would start. The surveyor's white horses were to the front, and about his wagon and my own vehicle circled over a hundred Indians on horseback, their lariats trailing and snapping the flowers as the rope skipped along the ground. It was a picturesque scene and one full of activity and hope. When a tract was selected, the corners were established, the township, range, section, and subdivision noted on my field book and marked on the plats. We had but one set of plats and the surveyor improvised copies of the township plats on the skirts of his long waterproof map. There were often contested sections of land. Some of these claims were easily adjusted, others had to be referred to a later day for fuller investigation than was possible in the field.

The land west of the railroad was to be appraised and opened for settlement after such Indians as chose had made their selection. It was necessary to attend to this portion of the allotments as rapidly as possible and the Indians found it difficult to move speedily in so important a matter. Rains set in and, wrapped in my waterproof, I rode miles trying to get these selections settled. The Logan Creek had to be crossed and recrossed. The stream was deep and rapid and the banks of black mud were covered with a coarse grass. I often had to be carried down by an Indian and placed in the boat to be poled over. There was no way of getting my wagon across except by making a wide detour of several miles to reach a bridge south of the reservation. Work on both sides of the creek demanded two wagons if one would not lose time. Walking was dangerous on account of the rattlesnakes.

One day I was carried down to the boat and while I was crossing, some Indians took a light wagon to pieces and floated it over, the horses swimming alongside. After the vehicle was put together again and the horses harnessed we got in and drove off. Many men joined us on horseback. We dashed about looking at different sections. The railroad had to be crossed. It was ditched on each side and the sleepers stood high on the roadbed. The horses were not the most tractable. One called Black Pawnee was noted for his will and independence; he was a saddle horse and resented the harness. I suggested I would rather walk down the ditch and climb over the rails and sleepers, but the Indians were anxious to save me fatigue, so down we went the almost perpendicular pitch, but the wagon doubled on the horses like a jackknife and I landed on or under Black Pawnee. In an instant two or three Indians had pulled me out of the reach of his restless heels. I was somewhat cut about the head and torn in clothing, but after a few repairs and bathing and bandaging we went on.

Before long we came to a bad gully; I was allowed to walk this time. The wagon was got safely down and through the bog and stream, but without rubber boots I could not pass the place. A young Indian caught me up in his arms and carried me over both bog and stream, his feet often sinking ankle-deep in the soft black mud. When I climbed into the wagon my notebook was not to be found. The stream was crossed and search made in every direction, but in vain. The record of several weeks' work was gone. My nervous friend, fearing some fresh calamity had overtaken me in the gully, hastened to learn the cause of my delay. I told my trouble and that I feared the book was in the stream that flowed rapidly to the Logan. He walked the middle of the creek. I followed as well as I could on the bank. At last he disappeared at a bend of the stream but soon returned in triumph. The book had caught on a snag; the rubber bands had held it closed and only the covers were soaked. It served me during all the work and remains as a souvenir of that day of mishaps.

Men would come before sunrise and shout to me outside of the tent and sunset would not abate their ardor. My matron and clerk used to scold the people because they gave me so little chance for rest. One morning we were roused when it was hardly day by a man running up and insisting upon the surveyor's going at once to a certain piece of land. The Indian had had a son born after midnight and the father had sped without delay some fifteen miles to secure for this son of the family the possession of real estate.

The weather grew intensely hot and every night storms swept over the prairies, the rain falling so rapidly that the water stood nearly an inch deep. It became a part of the night work to rise and shift the papers to protect them from the wet, for no one could tell from which quarter the storm would strike. Each morning we looked to see whose tent had been swept away.

"I don't like a regular diet of cyclones for breakfast," said the surveyor, after a fortnight's experience of these visitations.

When the good land within a radius of six miles or more of my tent was taken, we moved to another locality. Thus the summer days sped and the work advanced. A difficult matter demanded an immediate hearing. A tent was erected for the meeting and both parties and their witnesses gathered. The evidence was all taken in writing and some white men who were involved were at first inclined to dispute the right or capacity of a woman to attend to such business, but as the trial advanced they became orderly and attentive. The Indians learned something of what constituted evidence. The entire day was consumed and much surprise was manifest when the people found that I must first transmit the evidence and my decision to Washington for approval or disapproval before they would hear from the case.

Directions had been given for the removal of my tent on the day of this trial to a certain creek some ten miles distant. As I stepped into the wagon to go on to the new location I noticed heavy clouds rolling up rapidly. There was no shelter for many miles and no escape from the storm. After a few miles the rain fell in torrents and the lightning was striking all about us. My faithful driver and his steady ponies braced themselves to the task before us. It was a fearful scene; the heavens were black, the lightning gashing the clouds and bolt after bolt falling on each side of us, frightening the ponies. There was no hole in the bottom of the wagon to let off the rain. The box became full and we sat ankle-deep in the splashing water.

"There's an Indian lives in a hollow not far from here who has tools; I can borrow an auger and let out this water. It is enough to kill you!" said my companion.

In time we drew up to the cabin and I was lifted out, dripping, and made welcome. The women dried me as well as they could while the men worked to empty the wagon. The storm abated and it was nearly dark. We must hasten to reach our tent, wherever that might be. As we rode, the night gathered in blackness. At length we halted and my companion stood up and listened; after several minutes a faint sound was heard and then all was still again.

"That was thrumming from the tent poles," he said as he sat down and gathered up the reins. We drove on, following the direction of that one slight signal. At last we reached the place where our belongings lay on the wet grass. The matron was greatly distressed for she had no wood to make a fire, owing to the lateness of her arrival and the thick darkness. She had labored to preserve the bedding from the rain, for which we were duly thankful; so, making a supper of such cold food as we happened to have, and glad to get off some of my wet clothing although there was no chance of drying it, I rolled myself in my blankets for sleep.

Sometime in the night I was wakened by a terrible gust and peal of thunder. The tent was swaying.

"Get up and hold on to the tent," cried my clerk. "It will be terrible to lose shelter in this storm; it is the worst we've had!"

The matron was doing her best, and I struggled while the wind tore the tent cloth out of my hands. Then came a flash that seemed to take my heart away and as soon as the thunder subsided, I said, "That struck near here; I hope the horses are not killed!" In the grey dawn the horses were seen standing as if stunned and not many feet from the tent the grass lay burned to a crisp. I gathered some and kept it.

The region where my tent now stood was in the thick of the heathen and non-progressive element. The people were opposed to schools, to every sort of advancement, and were of the class most apt to be seen about an agency. They hated my work. To show them the folly of their ways was a difficult task, requiring patience and a constant remembrance of the demands of the future upon these belated men overtaken by days they knew not.

Each morning the matron used to set up four crotched poles and tie to these a red comforter as an awning. Under this shade I carried my camp table and chairs, spread out the plats, and examined locations before going out to look at selections of land. The men who gathered about me at this place were a motley crew and rather troublesome to deal with, but they improved as the work went on. The ponies used to be very curious about the crowd grouped around my table and would jump along with their hobbled feet and peer over the shoulders of the men trying to make out what was going on.

One clear, warm day I heard a voice singing. Looking in the direction of the sound I saw an old man clad in a blanket only, which was gathered about his loins. Everyone paused to listen to him. He sat apparently unconscious of observation, chanting the allegory which had been given to the people by a chief who died forty years ago, foretelling the coming of the white men, the obliteration of the Indians' past, and bidding his people make ready for the change and possess their land that they might not perish. "It has come true! Go to the woman. Your chief has forewarned you!" he cried, then rose, folded his blanket about him, and vanished over the hill.

The days of storm and sunshine came and went. The fieldwork was nearly done when suddenly I found myself unable to rise and fire such as I had never known raging through my veins. For days I battled with disease while the storm continued to rage about the tent.

"She will die," I heard an Indian say.

"She must be got to shelter, or she certainly will not live," my clerk replied.

I was too ill to direct or protest when the tent cloth was raised by my pallet and I was lifted carefully and put in the wagon. The horses, already harnessed, were fastened to the vehicle and strong arms held me as I was driven over the hills and through creeks some twelve miles to the Mission. The thunder rolled and the rain fell as I reached the kindly haven where I was put to bed and the death struggle began. Every kindness possible was bestowed upon me by the missionaries, the government officials, and the Indians. After a month I was carried down and laid on a mattress and driven a dozen miles or more to the agent's house and placed in his large parlor, and everything was done for me that generosity and friendliness could devise during the long months that I lay helpless; haply, my mind was clear and I could use my hands. It was thought I must die, so I promised the Indians I would work for them until the last. Ministered by a faithful woman and the unfailing attention of the agent and his wife, and with my trusty clerk's desk by my bed, I began the second stage of my work.

All the papers for the Indians to sign that were to be sent to Washington, and receipts for the same to be left with the Indians, were to be made out. Evidence of claims put forward by mixed-bloods and others to Omaha lands was to be taken. Many councils and trials were held about my bed during the weeks when death and work raced with each other.

"Pain cannot kill your care for us; you make us wonder," said an old man as he stood by me. "If you die, what will become of us? No one else will care for us and protect us."

Flowers were never forgotten as long as a bit of green could be found. One winter day a young Indian entered my room bearing a bowl of wild honey. Handing it to me he said, "I watched the bees last fall and saw where they had filled a hollow log. I thought the honey would taste good to you in winter." He added, "I left enough for the bees, you need not fear they will be hungry!"

More than once Indians came and leaned over me, taking my hand, and gazed at me in silence. One said: "You do not look like the same woman who used to be around among us; all this change has come because you have tried to help us!"

Kind friends in the East made it possible for me to provide some of the families with needed articles. About Christmas time the money was expended for lamps, clocks, chairs, underclothing, and other garments. My friend who told his story in the earth lodge received the gift of a lamp. "You have made it light when the sun is gone!" he exclaimed and fell on his knees by my bedside and prayed earnestly that my life might be spared. It was not uncommon for the Christian Indians to kneel by my sickbed and many of them sent me word that they and their children prayed daily for my recovery.

The non-progressive Indians had been told by one of their magicians that he had put a worm in me and that I would not be able to go on with my work. Great was their amazement to find me as determined when in my bed as when on my feet. One man who was much moved by my misfortune said, "I can take out the worm that makes you sick. To do so will make the man who put it in you angry, but you are our friend and I do not like to see you suffer. So I will do it for you!"

I was forced to decline his generous offer and so lost a rare chance for ethnological study by being the subject of an exorcism; to have accepted would have hurt my progressive friends.

Before the snows were gone I was again laid in the bottom of an easy wagon, bolstered by pillows and attended by Indian friends. I started ten miles south to the physician's house, who was in charge of the Omahas, that I might be nearer the place where large councils of the tribe must be held to give a full hearing to certain claimants. The roads were washed away and more than once we had to turn into icy fields on the side hills.

My Indian friends manned the wheels to prevent the wagon swinging around on the horses and causing an accident to me. No baby was ever more closely watched than was I during this ride. Men leaned over from their horses and adjusted my wrap or veil to keep off the wind. Arrived at the house, I spent several weeks enjoying a gracious hospitality and in taking evidence and holding tribal councils and gathering in a few refractory men who would not take any land. "Allot them in the air!" said some irate Indians.

English names were given to all allottees and I declared that the last child born and allotted must be called Benjamin, be it boy or girl.[2] One day a ruddy-faced man who was married to a thrifty Omaha woman came in.

"Is it too late for 25-8?" he asked.

"That depends upon where you want to make a change. I am just beginning to number the allotments in that township," I answered.

"I don't want to change. I have a son and I want to show you the forty acres I'd like my boy to have," he said with apparent pride.

"That is all right," I replied as I looked at the square he pointed out. "What is the child's name?" I had in mind my resolution.

"Benjamin!"

I laughed, and he looked embarrassed until I explained the cause of my mirth, when he too enjoyed the joke.

"He's named for his grandfather and great-grandfather," said the man.

"A foreordained thing, evidently," I exclaimed, and the child proved to be the Benjamin of the tribe.

Finally, the last claim was discussed and submitted; the last change made to benefit newly married pairs by bringing their two eighty acres together; the last allotment entered on plat and book; the last comparing done on the registry to be transmitted to Washington and on the copy to remain at the agency. The long struggle was over, involving so much for all of us.

The people were on their feet but nothing more; for it became clear that, important as is the assigning of the land individually, it is only preparing the way for the Indians' long, slow battle with a dependence begotten of ignorance and the agency system, together with a native unwillingness to assume responsibility. But loosed from his past, striving timidly toward a place among a strong, powerful race that holds out no welcoming hand, the progressive Indian stands in the midst of an isolation that would daunt any man to face. He must fight injustice and learn by his sorrows how to use the keen blade of the law in his own defense when that weapon shall be placed in his hands. He must acquire English and suffer his mother tongue to die; a hard sacrifice to make, but if he would survive, it must be made. The stress of a many-sided life is upon him: the winds, the water, the trees, and the animals must become his servants, not his companions as in the olden time. He is called to the supreme test of all manhood, to lay down what he thinks is his life that he may win it. The present and the next generation must suffer much; there is no escape; they stand in the gap and are called to combat their own inherent disabilities and a race prejudice that will not and cannot abate until the equalizing seal of citizenship is placed upon the Indian.

TWENTY-SIX

The Sacred Pipes

Of all the articles associated with religious ideas, none among the Omahas were claimed as God-given but the sacred pipes. The originals do not exist, nor are they ever mentioned. The form and the power of the pipes lie in the symbolism set forth in the secret ritual wherein the articles to be used, the order in which they are "tied" upon the pipes, the explanation of their meaning given, the regulations to be observed in the ceremonials connected with the pipes, the order of the ritual songs given and explained, and the tie of relationship established by the pipes and its obligations defined. Hundreds of these pipes have been "tied" during the centuries and many exist at the present day. Only a man who by his character, attainments, and gifts to others is invested with the knowledge of this secret ritual can "tie," or make these pipes, for his own or another's use.[1] Great reverence is shown them and more than once I was told that should their form be imitated in corn husk, the pipes would still be honored.

One of the trusty men of the tribe who knew the ritual said to me: "These are the oldest pipes among our people. They were with us when we lived far to the east. They are older than the flat-stemmed pipes with the bowl of red pipestone, the sacred tribal pipes. The latter are for the chiefs, the former for the people. Everyone derives benefit from these, the poor as well as those in authority. These are the true sacred pipes."

The stem is of ash and round, the hole through its length is made by fire. Seven spans of the thumb and forefinger is the length of a sacred pipe.

The stem is painted green to symbolize the clear sky and verdant earth. Along its length is a straight groove painted red; the streamers of red and those of the white hairs of the rabbit, as also the head of the red-headed woodpecker, typify the rising sun. There is no bowl; the head of a peculiar duck is thrust on the stem; the breast of the duck supports a tuft of owl feathers. A fan-shaped arrangement of eagle feathers descends from the stem. On the tobacco pouch of bladder, on the two gourd rattles, and on the unblemished ear of white corn bound to a feathered stick, the sign of the four winds—a circle with four projections—is painted in green. These and the pipes are carried in the skin of a wildcat from which the claws have not been removed.[2]

Elaborate ceremonies attend the pipes when they are carried by a company under the direction of a leader who must be a man well approved and offered to a man of another gens or tribe who is also required to be well considered. It is a great honor to be offered the pipes; it indicates appreciation of a man's character. Gifts are carried by the visitors, who receive horses from the man and his relations who accept the pipes. The gifts, in order to be counted to a man's honor, must be given to others who need them, for the Indian record of wealth is that of what a man has given away and not that which he has hoarded. Ritual songs accompany the ceremonies and vary in rhythm and feeling in different parts of the rite. The secret ritual is given by the leader to the man who receives the pipes over the head of one of his younger children. The child's head is covered with eagle down painted red. The child is called "Hunga," the Ancient One. In one part of the ceremony the leader says to the man who has received the pipes and who is called son, "My son! You have bestowed many gifts upon me (referring to the horses received). These will soon perish but that which I give you will remain with you forever (referring to the ritual). The words which I give you are worth more than gifts and they are sought after by many persons. If you keep these words your path in life shall be straight as this groove upon the pipe. Travel along this straight path of peace and justice, turn not aside from it and the day shall be bright with you."

After my long season of illness some of the tribe opened to me the meaning of these pipes, which long ago Marquette[3] declared to be marvelous in their power and influence. A pair of pipes was "tied" and presented jointly to me and the young Omaha, my clerk. I was permitted to learn the songs. The people loved to linger and look at the pipes as they hung framing the east window of my room. An old man said as he sat gazing at them: "The fierce birds on the pipes, and the wildcat, never lose their prey. These animals give their power to bring peace, good feelings, and gifts to the poor. The pipes can subdue the anger of the worst man and make him at peace with his enemy. We bless with the corn, for the corn gives us food and life, and we paint on the articles the symbol of the clear sky and four winds, which hold up the sky and give strength."

"My grandfather knows the ritual," said another man. "He would take the pipes and pray by them and his prayers were always answered. This may seem hard to believe but it is true. Some of the ritual songs ask for fair weather; when they are sung the sun shines. This too is strange, but it is true. The red streamers on the pipes mean the dawn, the day is coming, light and peace are coming, and with them good hearts and gifts for the poor, who are in need."

After talking much of the pipes an Omaha said, his face glowing: "All things bear their part in the pipes; the birds, the animals, the fruits of the earth, the trees, and men share in the blessing. The pipes are of God!"

Several of the leading men agreed to exemplify portions of the ceremonial connected with the sacred pipes that I might better understand the rite. I was to meet the people for the first time since my illness and I had provided food for about fifty persons. The feast and ceremony were to be held in a large earth lodge whither the invited guests made their way in the early twilight. When I saw the numbers of persons flocking in, my housewifely thoughts took alarm, fearing there would not be food enough. I whispered to my friend, the former head chief, and asked if the entrance could not be closed to prevent the mishap I feared. He looked at me kindly and said: "No. They can come. The pipes are free to all," adding after a pause, "Do not fear for the feast; the servers will understand."

I watched over two hundred men, women, and children gather. In the distance, I heard the sound of the ritual song of approach; it grew more distinct and soon the two men swaying the pipes and a third holding the wildcat skin, corn, and crotched stick between the other two were seen slowly moving along the passageway that formed the entrance to the lodge.

The fire was blazing brightly as the men made their way by the south to the west, moving in slow, rhythmic steps, singing as they came. At the west they halted and sang the song of laying down the pipes, moving them in a circling movement, as an eagle hovers over its nest before alighting. At the close of the third song the one who carried the cat skin spread it on the ground on a clean blanket and placed the crotched stick ready for the pipes to rest upon and stood the corn in front between the skin and the fire. During the fourth song the pipes circled lower and lower until with the last cadence they rested upon the skin, the mouthpieces crossing each other on the crotched stick. They placed the rattles under the fan-shaped feather pendants and the men sat down behind the pipes.

At the first sound of the song of approach and until the pipes were laid at rest, silence was observed, but after a decorous pause the company resumed their merry chatter.

The space between the pipes and the fire is never crossed or entered except when a man advances to make a gift to the pipes. All other parts of the lodge are free of access.

A half-dozen women gathered to the northeast and south of the fire, and preparations for the feast began. As this was an informal gathering, women did the cooking. At a formal feast only meat is served, the cooking is done by men, and gravity is observed in every particular, quite unlike the present merry scene.

It is difficult to convey the picturesqueness of the scene: the leaping flames cast dancing shadows, while strong lights caught on colors, glinted on ornaments, brought out the rich hues of the faces, with their bright eyes, glossy hair, and white teeth. Merry laughter and a genial sense of happiness pervaded the lodge. The women about the fire rolled out the dough on boards partly resting in the lap and partly on the ground. The children chased in and out and about their mothers. The pots bubbled over the blaze; the piles of round cakes of fried bread grew taller and taller and the coffeepots sent out savory puffs. Bustle and cheer touched everyone, even the irrepressible puppy that would not be banished.

When the food was ready, two or three of the leading men made grave speeches referring to the sacredness of the pipes and the love and reverence felt toward them. Their hearts were sorrowful because the pipes were taken up informally, but they had consented for a good reason and in no spirit of disrespect. When the speaker had finished, I was lifted to my feet and, leaning on my crutches, expressed my appreciation of their act and also my pleasure that this first meeting after my long illness should be in the presence of these sacred pipes, which made us all one in peace and brotherhood.

The wood was piled on the fire and the flames leaped up, lighting the ribbed dome of the lodge until it shone like polished ebony. The three men arose, and with the ritual song and movements, took up the pipes, the skin, and other articles. Then, slowly wheeling to the left, they began the circuit of the lodge facing the people, singing and moving with slow, rhythmic steps as before, waving over the heads of the assembled men, women, and children the pipes, in the blessing of peace and fellowship, and the people, as the pipes passed them, caught up the strain and a wave of song followed the pipes. The firelight touched the brilliant colors of the streamers and the fan-shaped pendants cast wing-shaped shadows and made it seem as though the pipes were attended by a phantom bird. Four songs were sung in making one passage around the lodge. At the close of each song the people gave thanks. Four times the pipes passed before they were laid to rest with the ritual formalities. A joyful solemnity pervaded the scene and stirred me deeply.

A friend who had been for two years in mourning for a dearly loved son, a lad of great promise and fine character, took this occasion, as a delicate tribute of friendship toward me, to lay aside his mourning. When the pipes were spread, he stepped into the consecrated space between the pipes and the fire and said: "Shall these pipes of our fathers pass unheeded about the fire and our hearts lie cold?" Then in a few pathetic words he gave a horse to a man who had just met with sorrow and a number of articles of food and clothing to aged and poor persons.

An old man made a stirring speech, thanking the donor in behalf of those whom he had remembered, bidding him welcome once more among the people. Then the pipes were praised and the young exhorted to worthy actions. Meanwhile, an old man had passed out of the lodge and I heard his voice ringing through the night air as he sang of the generous deeds of my friend.

A man belonging to the subdivision of the gens having in charge the sacred tribal pipes advanced to the space in front of the pipes, leading his little boy about four years old. This man and his son were clad in citizen's dress, for he and his family are entirely committed to "the white man's way." This fact added to the pathos of his act. "The pipes," he said, "were in the care of my fathers. My son is born into their rights. Now we do not often see these pipes." Tears filled his eyes and with breaking voice, he added, "I want my boy to touch the pipes of his fathers once again!" Taking a little stick the child held in his hand, the father threw it into my lap. It was the gift of a pony. I transferred the gift to the pipes that it might feed the hungry.

Gifts equal to two hundred dollars have been made to the aged and poor through the pipes now in my possession which have only been taken up informally, showing how sincere is the regard felt toward them and the lesson they teach.

"We do not know why these pipes are made as they are," said an Omaha to me. "Our fathers have left them to us, and we have taken them up. They are very old, generations and generations have possessed them. Other customs have died out, but these pipes have lived. Solid rocks have been broken, iron has been worn out and thrown away, but these frail pipes are not broken or worn out or thrown away! They give life and homes to the poor. Many people have been made happy by them. The pipes are made for all; all are helped by them because they are of God!"

Many times I was charged with the sacredness of the trust imposed upon me in being permitted to present these pipes to the knowledge of the white race. I have been reminded that in their presence no angry word may be spoken or vengeful thought cherished, nor may they be lightly handled. Never before, so far as I can learn, have these sacred pipes been suffered to leave the Indians. Indians from the north and the south have looked at them as they hang in my eastern home and have said: "We have heard that the Omahas had given you these pipes and our hearts are sad to see our sacred articles in the hands of strangers." [Ex. 2]

"Do not be sad," I have replied. "These pipes are still on their mission of peace and fellowship; they have only traveled a little farther to teach the white man that the Indian should be a brother."

Score 2. Sacred Pipe Song. Collection of Alice Cunningham Fletcher and Francis La Flesche, Smithsonian Institution, National Anthropological Archives (ms. 4558).

"It is well. We are content!" is the invariable reply.

God speed the day when both races may join in this sacred song of the pipes:

> Beautiful as is the cloudless sky and verdant fruitful earth,
> It is not so good as peace and fellowship among men.

Appendix

Fletcher's 1881 Field Sketches

Alice Fletcher's 1881 field notebooks include sixty-three sketches, inventoried by Francis La Flesche in the listing that follows. Of the sketches, forty-two appear in book 1 and twenty-one in book 2. The notebooks also include occasional rough drawings or diagrams in the context of ethnographic descriptions, which are not included in the list. La Flesche used Fletcher's notations on the sketches to provide titles for them. The date he compiled the list is not known but was probably after Fletcher's death in 1923.

The original lists are in the Fletcher and La Flesche Collection, Smithsonian Institution, National Anthropological Archives, box 12. Note that in book 1 La Flesche combined the first two drawings under number 1 and gave the number 16 to two drawings (present 17 and 18). We have corrected those numbering errors.

The present publication of the manuscript "Life Among the Indians" reproduces twenty-two sketches from book 1 and fifteen sketches from book 2. We selected all the sketches that can be positively identified with subjects in her manuscript, and because the notebooks are more comprehensive than the manuscript, we also selected a variety of additional sketches to give readers a sense of their diversity. The repetitiveness of the subject matter confirmed our decision not to publish all the sketches. Of the sixty-three on La Flesche's list, 45 percent are of Fletcher's camp-sites; 8 percent are of landscapes or botanical specimens; 22 percent are of Euro-American houses, settlements, or agency buildings; and 25 percent are of Indian activities, artifacts, or portraits.

Some general observations may be made about Fletcher's field sketches. They are done in hard pencil on the pages of her notebooks, which are as thin as tissue paper. None are fully finished drawings. Fletcher may have used some of the sketches as a way of interacting with others; this is clearly suggested by her comments about the profile she drew of Wajepa (fig. 3). Moreover, in this first fieldwork Fletcher may have sketched as a means of grounding herself in the alien environment of the plains and of adjusting to camping, which for her was a new and intimidating experience. By making these drawings she may have sought to control her environment by depicting it, no matter how sketchily. By 1882 Fletcher was more comfortable with fieldwork and her notebooks include far fewer drawings of her field camps and scenery and many more drawings of Indian ceremonies, notably of the Sioux Sun Dance. It is also likely that Fletcher planned to use these sketches as mnemonic devices to help her remember activities, ceremonies, and events that at the time may have overwhelmed her senses (for example, "Soldier Creek. An Indian death scene," fig. 28).

Our captions for Fletcher's field sketches always include, in quotation marks, the transcribed handwritten notes on the face of the sketches, together with any relevant additional information from La Flesche's list or the notebooks themselves. Note that most of the field sketches published in the present volume have been improved and enhanced by Noel Elliott to bring out the original pencil lines and to eliminate as far as possible paper discoloration and writing on the reverse of the paper. He has increased contrast and eliminated dirt and smudges on most of the field sketches. Thus, anyone ordering these images from the National Anthropological Archives will not get the results shown in this book.

Fig. 32. "Ma-he-ga-tha-be-ga, Sandstone. Oct. 21, 1 P.M. North wind blowing storm threatening." Alice Fletcher and Susette La Flesche Tibbles are pictured in the foreground wearing bonnets. The Omaha name is *Mąhį gasábe egą́* 'Darkened Stone'. Original field sketch (Fletcher, 1881 Notebook 2, 65) enhanced. Smithsonian Institution, National Anthropological Archives (ms. 4558).

Fig. 33. "Ne-da-ge-ne-nes-ga-the—Not cooked or furnished well. Headwaters Ponca River Oct. 22, 1881, 5:30 P.M." The Omaha name seems to be *Nida-ži nįsnįska* 'Raw Spring'. Original field sketch (Fletcher, 1881 Notebook 2, 67–68) enhanced. Smithsonian Institution, National Anthropological Archives (ms. 4558).

Fig. 34. "Ta-tae-wa-gish-ka—Deer creek. Headwaters of the Keyapaha." October 22–23, 1881. "The hills were the buttes of Fort Randall. I sketched them at Keyapaha, we sighted them this morning. They are now on the other side of us" (Fletcher, 1881 Notebook 2, 129). A dried plant sample that Fletcher had collected was affixed to this drawing but disintegrated before the image was photographed. La Flesche's list spells the name "Ta-tae-wa-gish-ma." The Omaha name is *Ttá·xti wačʰíška tʰe* 'Deer Creek'. Original field sketch (between pp. 50 and 51) enhanced. Smithsonian Institution, National Anthropological Archives (ms. 4558).

Fig. 35. "Ma-ne-ka-snah. Only earth or clay or mud: The hills the Ponka woman saw Oct. 24, 1881. 2:30 P.M." La Flesche's caption reads, "Ma-ne-ka-snah, Pa-he-shua-be." The Omaha name seems to be *Mą ðikka šna ppahé·mąšiadi* 'Bare Earth Mountain'. Original field sketch (Fletcher, 1881 Notebook 2, 134) enhanced. Smithsonian Institution, National Anthropological Archives (ms. 4558).

Fig. 36. "Oct. 25, 26, 27. Where camped on Stony Pt. Mo. [Missouri] river Ft. Randall—D.T." "Sketched our camp at a little distance—nothing to be seen but tent top & wagon hoops—the grass taller than I am. A perfect day, warm and delightful. Everybody in a better mood" (Fletcher, 1881 Notebook 2, 141). Original field sketch (between pp. 145 and 146) enhanced. Smithsonian Institution, National Anthropological Archives (ms. 4558).

Abbreviations

BAE   Bureau of American Ethnology

HAINM   *Handbook of American Indians North of Mexico*. Edited by Frederick Webb Hodge. Bureau of American Ethnology, Bulletin 30. 2 vols. Washington DC, 1907, 1910.

HNAI   *Handbook of North American Indians*. Edited by William C. Sturtevant. Vol. 4, *History of Indian-White Relations*, edited by Wilcomb E. Washburn. Washington DC: Smithsonian Institution, 1988.

NAA   National Anthropological Archives, Smithsonian Institution, Washington DC

NARA   National Archives and Records Administration, Washington DC

Peabody Museum Records   Peabody Museum of Archaeology and Ethnology Records, 1851–1968. Ms. no. UAV 677.38. Harvard University, Cambridge MA.

PMAR   *Annual Reports of the Trustees of the Peabody Museum of American Archaeology and Ethnology Presented to the President and Fellows of Harvard College*. Cambridge MA.

345

Notes

Introduction

1. Henry L Dawes served in the U.S. Senate from 1875 to 1892. He was the principal author and promoter of the Severalty Act of 1887, which provided for the allotment of land to individual Indians, to be held in trust by the federal government for twenty-five years. The Indians would be recognized as U.S. citizens; the result would be the breakup of the tribes and the dissolution of the reservations. Dawes's papers are preserved in the Library of Congress; the finding aid notes that Electa Dawes's primary life work was that she "kept her husband informed of happenings in his district."

2. For a list of original sources documenting Fletcher's early fieldwork, see "Sources Documenting Fletcher's Fieldwork among the Omahas and Sioux."

3. Fletcher, "Elk Mystery or Festival. Ogallala Sioux" (1884), treats the Elk Society in greater detail.

4. Note that "manly progress" is not a gendered concept. Fletcher, as a follower of social evolutionary theory in anthropology, assumed that American Indians were in the "childhood" of development and needed to be helped to attain "manhood," that is, adulthood, by rising from primitive society to civilization.

5. Comparison of "Life among the Indians" with Fletcher and La Flesche, *Omaha Tribe* (1911), reveals other correlations:

    Chapter 16, "The Young Mother," explaining kinship terms and social relations, cf. *Omaha Tribe*, 313–17; on ability to understand baby talk, cf. *Omaha Tribe*, 328.

    Chapter 18, "Child Life," on a child's first haircut and receiving new moccasins, cf. *Omaha Tribe*, 118–22, including ritual songs, and 327–28.

    Chapter 20, "Winter and War," on incident of war with the Pawnees, cf. *Omaha Tribe*, 406–8.

Chapter 21, "Friends and Lovers," on friendship, cf. *Omaha Tribe*, 318–19; on courting and stories related to it, cf. *Omaha Tribe*, 324–25, which includes courtship songs; story of grief at death of wife, cf. *Omaha Tribe*, 327.

Chapter 24, "Our Land," concerning the petition Fletcher wrote on behalf of some of the Omahas for land patents, cf. *Omaha Tribe*, 636–41.

6. Joseph La Flesche, recognized as an Omaha tribal leader before 1866, headed the Citizens' Party, the faction that advocated assimilation. His group lived in a village known by the traditionalists as the Village of Make-Believe White Men, because their houses were like those of white settlers. La Flesche, *Middle Five* (1900), xvi. See the discussion of Joseph La Flesche as a cultural intermediary in Tong, *Susan La Flesche Picotte* (1999), 13–25. Through accommodation and adaptation La Flesche sought to bridge the political and cultural gaps between the Omaha tribal ways and those of Euro-American society. He believed that the only way to meet the changing cultural pressures was through formal education. He was also a staunch supporter of temperance and of Christianity.

Francis La Flesche, who became Fletcher's protégé and coauthor, was a son of Joseph La Flesche. Born in 1857, he was raised by his father to follow a Euro-American lifestyle. Educated at the Presbyterian Mission School on the Omaha Reservation, he accompanied his sister Bright Eyes on Standing Bear's 1878–79 tour of eastern cities. His experience interpreting for Standing Bear prepared him for his subsequent collaboration with Fletcher. Fletcher, "La Flesche, Francis," HAINM (1907, 1910), 1:751–52. Francis was considered one of the best interpreters on the reservation. During the investigation of the Ponca removal by a special Senate committee in the spring of 1880, led by Senator Samuel J. Kirkwood of Iowa, Francis acted as official interpreter. Then in June 1881, through the influence of Kirkwood, who was appointed secretary of the interior in March 1881 (but resigned in April 1882), Francis was appointed as a copyist in the Office of Indian Affairs in Washington DC. Green, *Iron Eye's Family* (1969), 43, 54, 175.

7. Susette, a daughter of Joseph La Flesche, was also known by the English translation of her Omaha name, Bright Eyes. Born in 1854, she was educated at the Presbyterian Mission School on the Omaha Reservation, then attended the Elizabeth Institute in New Jersey from 1869 to 1875. Having received an

excellent education in English and literature, she returned to the Omaha Reservation and taught in a government day school. In 1878–79 she accompanied the Ponca chief Standing Bear on his tour of eastern cities, together with her brother, Francis, and Thomas Henry Tibbles, a newspaper editor who arranged the tour. She and Tibbles married in July 1881 and subsequently lived in Lincoln, Nebraska, until her death in 1902. Fletcher, "Bright Eyes," HAINM (1907, 1910), 1:165–66; Green, *Iron Eye's Family*, 47–48, 64–66.

8. Rosalie, who was also educated at the Presbyterian Mission School on the Omaha Reservation, aided Fletcher with many of her research projects. She admired Fletcher and the name *Fletcher* was continued among her descendants for several generations. Green, *Iron Eye's Family* (1969), 54–65.

9. Elliott, *Culture Concept* (2002), xxvi–xxvii.

10. This was the period of anti-Mormon polygamy hysteria. Ann Eliza Young, one of Brigham Young's many wives, offered a sensational insider's account of polygamy in *Wife No. 19* (1876). She followed the publication of her book with a lecture tour. Our thanks to Nicole Tonkovich for pointing out this reference.

11. The monthly magazine *Wide Awake*, edited by Ella Farman and published by D. Lothrop and Company, Boston, first appeared in 1875–76, perhaps in conjunction with the Centennial year. Directed at young readers, its contents included serial stories, short stories, poems, sketches of great men (contemporary and historical), and articles on important branches of industry, children's etiquette, and music; in addition, it included "entertaining and illustrated original papers concerning every-day life of the animal kingdom, and the men, women and children of strange countries" (vol. 1, no. 6, 1875).

12. NAA, Fletcher–La Flesche Collection, box 1, folder "Incoming Correspondence," March 16, 1882.

13. Frederic Ward Putnam (1839–1915) was one of the first museum anthropologists in the United States. He became curator of the Peabody Museum of American Archaeology and Ethnology at Harvard University in 1875 and served in that capacity until 1909; he was also the Peabody Professor of American Archaeology and Ethnology from 1886 to 1909. Biographical information from inventory of F. W. Putnam Papers, Harvard University. See also Darnell, *And Along Came Boas* (1998), 118–23; Dexter, "F. W. Putnam's Role" (1980); and Hinsley, "Museum Origins of Harvard Anthropology" (1992).

14. Fletcher to Putnam, June 27, 1886, Peabody Museum Records, box 7, folder "1886 A–I".

15. Putnam Papers, Harvard University, box 6, folder "1881–1890 F."

16. Scribner's to Fletcher, May 10, 1886, and June 4, 1886, Archives of Charles Scribner's Sons, Princeton University Library, letter books #164 and #211, ms. CO101, series 15, subseries F, vol. 11. The letters from Fletcher are not in the archive.

17. Dawes Papers, Library of Congress, box 10.

18. Fletcher diary, 1887, NAA, Fletcher-La Flesche Collection, box 12A.

19. Peabody Museum Records, box 7, folder "1887 D–F."

20. Joseph Henry to Charles Rau, December 10, 1864, cited in Hinsley, *Smithsonian and the American Indian* (1994), 37.

21. Fletcher diary, Monday, May 23, 1887, NAA, Fletcher-La Flesche Collection, box 12A. Jean Margaret Davenport Lander was one of the founding directors of the Women's Anthropological Society of Washington and a longtime member of the Literary Society; Elizabeth Blair was a vice president of the Women's Anthropological Society. "Women's Anthropological Society," 1889.

22. Fletcher to Putnam, July 3[, 1887], Putnam Papers, Harvard University, box 6, folder "1881–1890F."

23. Jane Gay was a close friend of Fletcher who accompanied her in 1888 when she allotted the Winnebago Reservation and during the summers of 1889–92 when she allotted the Nez Perces. According to Frederick E. Hoxie and Joan T. Mark (introduction to *With the Nez Perces* [1981], xxvi), Fletcher and Gay had attended the same girls' school in Brooklyn when they were growing up, but they do not document that connection. See Tonkovich, *Allotment Plot* (2012). Tonkovich believes that Gay and Fletcher met in Washington DC in the mid-1880s; she found no documentation of an earlier school connection.

    The first mention of Jane Gay in Fletcher's extant diaries is in the entry for May 8, 1888: "Miss Gay here." NAA, Fletcher-La Flesche Collection, box 12A. For scholarly insight into Gay's life, see Tonkovich, "Lost in the General Wreckage" (2003); and Tonkovich, *Allotment Plot* (2012).

24. Gay to Putnam, March 18, 1891, Putnam Papers, Harvard University, box 9. We wish to thank Nicole Tonkovich for pointing out this letter to us.

25. Elliott, *Culture Concept* (2002), 108.

26. Fletcher, *Camping with the Sioux* (2001).

27. Fletcher, "Shadow or Ghost Lodge: A Ceremony of the Ogallala Sioux" (1884). As another example, Fletcher, "White Buffalo Festival of the Uncpapas" (1884) parallels sections of chapter 12, "A Religious Festival."

28. Fletcher, "The Elk Mystery or Festival. Ogallala Sioux" (1884), 280n3.

29. *Century Illustrated Monthly Magazine*, formerly *Scribner's Monthly*, began publication in 1881 with a subscriber base of 125,000 readers. It was a popular literary illustrated magazine that, according to the first issue, would include studies of history and cover issues of morals, religion, politics, literature, and life. "Century Magazine" (1881).

Fletcher published the following articles in *Century Magazine*: "On Indian Education and Self-Support" (May 1883); "Personal Studies of Indian Life: Politics and 'Pipe-Dancing'" (January 1893); "Indian Songs: Personal Studies of Indian Life" (November 1893–April 1894); "Hunting Customs of the Omaha: Personal Studies of Indian Life" (September 1895); "Tribal Life among the Omahas: Personal Studies of Indian Life" (January 1896); and "Home Life among the Indians: Records of Personal Experience," (June 1897).

Kamala Visweswaran observes, "Ethnological pamphlets produced at the world's fairs and articles written for the popular press were normative rather than unique, and analysis of the writings of early women anthropologists proves it difficult to distinguish the articles that appeared in the *American Anthropologist* or the *Journal of American Folklore* from those appearing in more popular fora" ("'Wild West' Anthropology and the Disciplining of Gender" [1998], 90).

30. Cushing, "My Adventures in Zuni," 26:1 (1883): 28; 25:2 (1882): 205–7.

31. Fletcher was very aware of the similarities in research style between Cushing and herself. On April 24, 1900, at the memorial meeting of the Anthropological Society of Washington, following Cushing's death, she made the following comments:

> My acquaintance with Mr. Cushing dates from the spring of 1882. He had come to Washington with some of his Zuni friends on his first return East from his ethnologic researches in the Southwest. I was also just from my studies in the homes of the Indians in the Missouri valley, having left them to plead before Congress the cause of a tribe that was threatened with the loss of its ancestral lands. Mr. Cushing and I, all

unknown to each other, had been doing our work in the same manner, both going to live with the natives, accepting the natural conditions and merging ourselves, as far as possible, with the people, that we might learn their social organization, customs and religious rites. (McGee et al., "In Memoriam" [1902], 367)

32. Hinsley, *Smithsonian and the American Indian* (1994), 196, makes this point in his discussion of Cushing but goes on to describe how Cushing's presence was also a disruptive factor in Zuni Pueblo.

33. A letter from Mary Copley Thaw dated October 1, 1890, establishing the Thaw Fellowship, and Putnam's acceptance of it on behalf of the Peabody Museum, dated December 2, 1890, are reproduced in Harvard College, *Annual Reports of the President and Treasurer*, 1891, 208–9.

34. Fletcher to Putnam, July [1887], Putnam Papers, Harvard University, box 6, folder "1881–1890F."

35. Fletcher, "Notes on Certain Beliefs Concerning Will Power" (1897), 331.

36. This observation about Cushing was made in Hinsley, *Smithsonian and the American Indian* (1994), 196.

37. Fletcher, *Indian Education and Civilization* (1885).

38. Fletcher, *Indian Education and Civilization* (1885), 9–10.

39. Tylor, "How the Problems of American Anthropology Present Themselves" (1884), 550.

40. "Victorian ideas of feminine purity enabled nineteenth-century women anthropologists to work independent of men on the frontier because they were considered morally superior and thus desexualized." Visweswaran, "'Wild West' Anthropology and the Disciplining of Gender" (1998), 97–99. Visweswaran considers Fletcher's "evangelical ethnography" as enabled by a form of Victorian maternalism (98–101). Also see Jacobs, *White Mother to a Dark Race* (2009).

41. Mark, *Stranger in Her Native Land* (1988), 6–13.

42. Croly, *History of the Woman's Club Movement* (1898), 27.

43. Welch, "Alice Cunningham Fletcher" (1980), 17.

44. Association for the Advancement of Women, *Annual Report for 1881*, 7.

45. Caroline H. Dall described a visit with Fletcher on January 11, 1885. Dall wrote in her journal, "I heard for the first time—the terrible story of her life. It was

for her bread that she first sought employment at the Peabody Museum and as a lecturer" Dall Collection, Massachusetts Historical Society.

46. Welch, "Alice Cunningham Fletcher" (1980), 19.

47. These titles are from a circular that she sent to Maj. John Wesley Powell in a letter dated August 10, 1881. NAA, Records of the BAE, Correspondence, Letters Received 1879-88, box 60.

48. Fletcher to Secretary S. F. Baird, October 2, 1879, Smithsonian Archives, Record Unit 28, Secretary 1879-1882, Incoming correspondence, box 10, folder 8; Baird to Fletcher, October 8, 1879, Smithsonian Archives, Record Unit 33, reel 112, vol. 86, p. 316.

49. *Boston Daily Advertiser*, "Life among the Omahas: A Descriptive Lecture" (1882) (p. 2, col. D). In April 1887 she gave a benefit talk in Washington DC for the Homeopathic Free Dispensary titled "A Visit to Alaska and the Aleutian Islands"; the entrance fee was fifty cents. *Washington Post*, April 19, 1887.

50. Fletcher to Putnam, December 30, 1890, Peabody Museum Records; letter transcribed by Nicole Tonkovich; we were unable to locate the original.

51. For the history of the Bureau of Ethnology (after 1897, Bureau of American Ethnology), see Hinsley, *Smithsonian and the American Indian* (1994).

52. See Hoxie, *Final Promise* (1984), 20-21, 25-29, 76-77. Hoxie summarizes, "Alice Fletcher's career offers a clear example of the power of social evolutionary theory in late nineteenth-century America" (27). See also Fletcher, "Civilization," HAINM (1907, 1910), 1:301-2.

53. Fletcher to F.W. Putnam, September 9, 1879, Peabody Museum Records, box 2, folder "1879 F-J."

54. Dexter, "F. W. Putnam's Role" (1980), 185-86, quoting an announcement printed in 1878 at the opening of the new museum building.

55. The first American PhD in anthropology at Harvard was awarded to George A. Dorsey in 1894 and, like the great majority of doctoral degrees offered at Harvard, it was based on archaeological fieldwork, not ethnology or linguistics. Darnell, *And Along Came Boas* (1998), 121, 171. John G. Owens never received a graduate degree; he died while conducting anthropological fieldwork in Honduras. Hinsley, *Smithsonian and the American Indian* (1994), 134-35.

56. Fletcher diary, Monday, May 22, 1885, NAA, Fletcher–La Flesche Collection, box 12A: "Dined at Mrs. Stevenson with Mrs. Teller, Miss Skull [*sic*, Scull], talked of atlas, & of forming Anthropological Society for ladies."

Matilda "Tilly" Coxe Stevenson began her career in anthropology as the "volunteer coadjutor in ethnology" of her husband, Col. James Stevenson, who was associated with the Hayden Geological Survey of the 1870s. During her early fieldwork Stevenson was one of the first anthropologists to study the lives of women and children. After her husband's death in 1888 she became the first woman to be hired by the BAE, originally to put her husband's papers in order and subsequently to continue his research. She published extensively on Sia and Zuni Pueblos, returning again and again to do field-work. Issac, "Re-observation and the Recognition of Change" (2005). Stevenson also helped survey archaeological sites in the Southwest; her interest in preserving those sites from vandalism meshed with Fletcher's interests and was one of the projects they worked on together.

In 1887–88 Fletcher and Stevenson, as representatives of the Women's Anthropological Society and the American Association for the Advancement of Science, lobbied Congress for passage of a bill (which failed at that time) to declare several ruins, including Mesa Verde, national parks. Parezo, "Matilda Coxe Stevenson" (1993), 60. As Stevenson's biographer observes, "Stevenson and Fletcher apparently never became intimate friends, however, despite their professional association in Washington." Miller, *Matilda Coxe Stevenson* (2007), 190.

Harriet Bruce Teller was the wife of Senator Henry M. Teller, who was secretary of the interior in 1885.

Miss Scull was Sarah Amelia Scull, a teacher of ancient history and mythology in a private girls' school in Washington DC, originally called the Mount Vernon Seminary (opened in 1875). Scull was the first corresponding secretary of the Women's Anthropological Society. Mount Vernon Seminary became Mount Vernon Junior College in 1969 and then became part of the George Washington University in 1996.

See brochure on the "Organization and the Constitution of the Women's Anthropological Society, Founded 1885, Washington, D.C.," NAA, Records of the Anthropological Society of Washington, box 17, Publications and Photographs, ms. 4821.

57. Fletcher diary, Saturday, January 25, 1890, NAA, Fletcher–La Flesche Collection, box 12A: "At office in a.m./Election at W. Anthro. Soc./Elected Presid."

58. The Poncas were arrested and released on habeas corpus, and the resulting

trial, which they won, allowed them to remain in Nebraska. See Mathes and Lowitt, *Standing Bear Controversy* (2003). For a view of how the press handled the Ponca affair, see Coward, *Newspaper Indian* (1999), 196–223.

59. Tibbles, *Buckskin and Blanket Days* (1957), 236–37; see also Green, *Iron Eye's Family* (1969), 62.

60. Peabody Museum Records, box 4, folder "1881 C–F."

61. In February 1881 Fletcher had a serious fall on ice, which severely limited her activities. See Fletcher to Putnam, March 22, 1881, Peabody Museum Records, box 4, folder "1881 C–F."

62. Fletcher to Carr, August 3, 1881, Peabody Museum Records, box 4, folder "1881 C–F."

63. Fletcher to Powell, August 10, 1881, NAA, Records of the BAE, Correspondence, Letters Received, 1879–1888, box 60.

64. Fletcher to Putnam, August 10, 1881, Peabody Museum Records, box 4, folder "1881 C–F."

65. Fletcher to Mallery, August 23, 1881, NAA, Records of the BAE, Correspondence, Letters Received, 1879–1888, box 60.

66. His Omaha name was *Wajé·pʰa* 'Herald' or 'Crier'; he was known in English as Ezra Freemont. In Fletcher's earlier writings she spells her Omaha companion's name as Wajapa; later she systematizes it to Wajepa. Both spellings thus appear in this publication.

67. Gaha's Omaha name apparently was *Gahé* 'Combed' or 'Neat'.

68. Dorsey, *Ꞔegiha Language* (1890), 1.

69. Joseph La Flesche had two wives. His principal wife was Mary Gale, whose name is usually given as Hinnuagsnun 'The One Woman'. The name is in the Iowa-Otoe language, *Hį·nų e gašną* 'Only One Who Is the Eldest Daughter'. They had four daughters, Susette "Bright Eyes," Rosalie, Marguerite, and Susan. His second wife was Tainne; her name is Omaha, *Ttą́į ðį* 'Becoming Visible', referring to the new moon. She was also known as Elizabeth Esau and as Lizzie La Flesche. She and Joseph had two sons and a daughter: Francis, Lucy, and Carey. Because Joseph La Flesche converted to Christianity he deemphasized his relationship with his second wife and removed her from the family circle, although he continued to support her. This must have affected Francis and created in him a feeling of marginality. See Smith, "Francis La Flesche and the World of Letters" (2001), 583–85. However, respecting

his father's commitment to assimilation, Francis also embraced a Euro-American lifestyle.

Susette, Marguerite, and Susan attended a boarding school in Elizabeth, New Jersey. Marguerite, Susan, Lucy, and Carey all went to Hampton Industrial and Agricultural Institute at Hampton, Virginia, a school started after the Civil War for the education of emancipated blacks, which opened its doors to Indians in 1878. Susan La Flesche graduated from the Women's Medical College of Pennsylvania in Philadelphia and became a medical doctor. Susette La Flesche was a public speaker, lecturer, and teacher. Marguerite La Flesche became a teacher. For more information on the La Flesche family, see Green, *Iron Eye's Family* (1969); and Tong, *Susan La Flesche Picotte* (1999).

70. Francis La Flesche, "Alice C. Fletcher's Scientific Work," 1923 draft, in NAA, Fletcher–La Flesche Collection, box 15. This is the same text as the foreword published in the present volume.

71. Spotted Tail was murdered on August 15, 1881. Hyde, *Spotted Tail's Folk* (1961), 299–300.

72. Inexplicably, Fletcher identifies Asanpi (*Asáŋpi*) 'Milk' as the chief of the "Ogallala Indians." Fletcher, *Camping with the Sioux* (2001), October 11, 1881. This is certainly an error. There were two men at this time known as Asanpi. One, an Oglala, was born about 1851 and had a wife named Holy Woman (Pine Ridge Reservation Census, 1890, U.S. Indian Census Schedules, NARA, RG 75). No children are listed for this couple. In 1881 he would have been only about thirty. The other man named Asanpi was a Brule Sioux who was fifty-eight years old as of June 1891 (Rosebud Agency Census, 1891, U.S. Indian Census Schedules, NARA, RG 75), which would have made him about forty-eight when Fletcher met him. In her notebook Fletcher says that Asanpi was about forty-five years old. In her notebook entry for October 14, 1881, Fletcher gives the name of Asanpi's wife as Was-ta-we (*Waštéwiŋ*) 'Good Woman'. The 1887 Rosebud Agency census confirms that the wife of the Brule chief Asanpi was named "Good Woman" and that the couple had three children living with them: two daughters, Brown Over and Gets There First, and one son, Grown in a Day; at the time of Fletcher's visit the girls would have been ages nine and eleven and the boy, age one.

In her notebook Fletcher mentions that Milk himself had visited Carlisle

School. *Camping with the Sioux* (2001), October 11, 1881. Information on Daniel Milk was provided by Barbara Landis, Cumberland County Historical Society, Carlisle PA. For Carlisle students, see Bell, "Telling Stories Out of School" (1998); and Bell and Landis, "Carlisle Indian School Student Record Database."

73. Compare the chapter "The Welcome" to the account of Asanpi's feast in Fletcher, *Camping with the Sioux* (2001), October 11, 1881.

74. Fletcher, *Camping with the Sioux* (2001), October 19, 1881.

75. 1881 notebook, entry for October 23, NAA, Fletcher-La Flesche Collection, box 11. Although a transcription of most of this notebook is found online, there are pages and paragraphs omitted from the online version. This paragraph is one of them.

76. Fletcher and Tibbles had numerous disagreements over the years. See Mark, *Stranger in Her Native Land* (1988), 124–34. In his account of their travels, written in 1905, Tibbles translated the Omaha name given to Fletcher by Wajepa, *Mąší·ha ðį* 'Moving on High' (referring to the soaring of an eagle) as "Highflyer" (Tibbles, *Buckskin and Blanket Days* [1957], 239). *Webster's Dictionary* defines *highflier* as "an uncompromisingly orthodox or doctrinaire person," which doubtless perfectly characterizes Tibbles's opinion of Fletcher.

77. Fletcher, *Camping with the Sioux* (2001), October 30, 1881. For Major Sanders, see Heitman, *Historical Register and Dictionary of the United States Army* (1903), 858. A letter of December 5, 1881, from U.S. Indian Inspector C. H. Howard to Commissioner of Indian Affairs Hiram Price mentions a report by Major Sanders written at the time Fletcher was traveling with him that recommended to Gen. Alfred Terry the removal of the military from Cheyenne River Agency and the firing of an interpreter for drunkenness. Records of the Bureau of Indian Affairs, NARA, RG 75, Letters Received, 1880–1907, 1881–21246.

78. Col. George L. Andrews, Twenty-Fifth Infantry, was assigned to Fort Randall in May 1880; the regiment consisted of white officers and African American enlisted men. See Greene, *Fort Randall on the Missouri* (2005), 126.

79. John P. Williamson (1835–1917) was a Presbyterian missionary at Yankton Agency; see Barton, *John P. Williamson* (1919).

80. Stephen R. Riggs (1812–83) and his son Alfred L. Riggs (1837–1916) were Congregationalist missionaries to the Santee Sioux. S. R. Riggs's *Tah´-koo*

Wah-kań (1869) contains detailed ethnographic material on the Sioux; Fletcher would have been familiar with it. For biographical sketches see Washburn, *History of Indian-White Relations* (1988), 679–80.

81. D. A. Goddard, editor of the *Boston Daily Advertiser* and a prominent Indian rights advocate. Mark, *Stranger in Her Native Land* (1988), 107.

82. Fletcher to Putnam, November 7, 1881, Peabody Museum Records, box 4, folder "1881 C–F."

83. Fletcher to Jane Smith, November 14, 1881, Peabody Museum Records, box 4, folder "1881 C–F."

84. Fletcher to Powell, November 16, 1881 (letter no. 832), NAA, Records of the BAE, Correspondence, Letters Received 1879–1888. The sad event in the nation to which Fletcher refers was the shooting of President James Garfield on July 2, 1881; he died on September 19, 1881.

85. Fletcher, *Camping with the Sioux* (2001), October 1, 1881.

86. Mark, *Stranger in Her Native Land* (1988), 69.

87. U.S. Congress, *Memorial of the Members of the Omaha Tribe* (1882).

88. For Morgan, see Hoxie, *Final Promise* (1984), 72, 160.

89. Fletcher to John Morgan, December 31, 1881, NAA, Fletcher–La Flesche Collection, box 2, folder "Outgoing Correspondence 1873–1883."

90. Fletcher told Powell that she wanted to go to escape the severe Nebraska winter. Fletcher to J. W. Powell, November 16, 1881, NAA, Records of the BAE, Letters Received, 1879–1887, box 69.

91. Fletcher to Putnam, February 4, 1882, Peabody Museum Records, correspondence, box 4.

92. Her address was given as 229 West 23rd St., New York, on numerous letters to Putnam of this time, including one dated April 15, 1882. Peabody Museum Records, correspondence, box 4.

93. Mark, *Stranger in Her Native Land* (1988), 73–77.

94. NAA, Fletcher–La Flesche Collection, box 30, folder "Other Tribes Quapaw-Zuni."

95. The Fletcher manuscript relating to this trip is titled "Going Home with the Indians," NAA, Fletcher–La Flesche Collection, box 6.

96. Fletcher, "Sun Dance of the Ogalalla Sioux" (1883). An account of this event from McGillycuddy's perspective appears in McGillycuddy, *McGillycuddy, Agent* (1941), 167–75. The public performance of the ceremony was banned by

the government from 1882 until 1934. Prucha, *Great Father* (1984), 2:646–47, 951–52.

97. Hampton Normal and Industrial School at Hampton, Virginia, was a vocational school founded after the Civil War for the education of emancipated blacks. Capt. Richard Henry Pratt was in charge of seventy-two Plains Indian prisoners of war held at Fort Marion, Florida, from 1875 to 1878. Through Pratt's efforts, seventeen of the released prisoners entered Hampton to further their education. In 1879 Pratt opened Carlisle Indian Industrial School in Carlisle, Pennsylvania, which he headed through 1904. Pratt, *Battlefield and Classroom* (1964).

98. *Morning Star*, October 1882, 34.

99. Fletcher, "On Indian Education and Self-Support" (1883), 315.

100. In PMAR 18–19, 3:5 and 6 (1887): 388, Fletcher is listed as a special assistant. Although Rubie S. Watson has suggested that Fletcher's position was unpaid (Watson, "Introduction" [1994–95]), there is a note in Harvard College, *Annual Reports of the President and Treasurer*, that "in 1882 . . . there was also received toward the salary of an assistant, and in aid of Miss Fletcher's researches among the Indians . . . $550" (1891: 210). That Fletcher was remunerated for her work in 1882, or at least her expenses were being paid, seems clear, and that remuneration came from donations to the museum by individuals who wished to further her work. PMAR 16–17, 3:3 and 4 (1884): 156.

101. Fletcher to Mrs. Dawes, November 24, 1882, Dawes Papers, Library of Congress.

102. About half of the unallotted land would be reserved for children who would be born during the twenty-five-year trust period; the other half would be opened to non-Indian settlers.

103. Fletcher to Putnam, May 1, 1883, Putnam Papers, Harvard University, box 5.

104. Letter to Commissioner of Indian Affairs, June 25, 1884, Records of the Bureau of Indian Affairs, NARA RG 75, Letters Received, 1884-13244.

105. Fletcher to Caroline H. Dall, September 7, 1883, Dall Collection, Massachusetts Historical Society, box 8, folder 22, item 22; Fletcher to Caroline H. Dall, July 20, 1884, Dall Collection, Massachusetts Historical Society, box 9, folder 4, item 29.

106. In a deposition given on July 2, 1925, by Francis La Flesche, at the time that Alice Fletcher's will in his favor was being contested, he made the follow-

ing statement: "In 1883 while making the allotments [for the Omaha Tribe] just referred to Alice C. Fletcher became seriously ill and was attended and brought back to health partly by aid [of the] affiant [Francis]. Thereafter, affiant and Alice C. Fletcher both living in Washington became exceedingly close friends, Alice C. Fletcher taking towards affiant the attitude of a mother. She had been all her life deeply interested in Indian work and Indian Affairs." NAA, Fletcher–La Flesche Collection, box 13, folder "Biography & Memorabilia."

107. Fletcher to Caroline Dall, January 20, 1884, Dall Collection, Massachusetts Historical Society, box 9, folder 1, item 24.

108. La Flesche, "Alice C. Fletcher" (1923).

109. Fletcher and La Flesche, *Omaha Tribe* (1911), 376–77; Fletcher to Putnam, May 13, 1884, Peabody Museum Records, box 5, folder "1884 C-F."

110. Boyd, *Boyd's Directory*, the city directory, gives the address of the Temple Hotel as 604 and 606 Ninth Street NW. The first entry for Fletcher as a resident of the Temple Hotel in *Boyd's Directory* is not until 1887, when she is inexplicably listed as a clerk in the Interior Department. However, in a letter to Putnam dated June 16, 1884, Fletcher wrote that she arrived home "last Sunday & am closing up my work"; this letter gives the Temple Hotel as the return address. Peabody Museum Records, box 5, folder "1884 C-F Fletcher Letters." There is some uncertainty about the date. On June 25, 1884, Fletcher submitted her final report on Omaha allotments, a process that began May 12, 1883, and ended with the final distribution of allotment certificates on June 8, 1884; that letter has a return address of Omaha Agency, Nebraska. Records of the Bureau of Indian Affairs, NARA, RG 75, Letters Received, box 197, item 1884-13244. In any case, the evidence suggests that Fletcher was renting rooms at the Temple Hotel before La Flesche moved into it on September 15, 1884, when he began paying rent to Mrs. La Fetra, the proprietor. La Flesche diary, NAA, Fletcher–La Flesche Collection, box 16; Boyd, *Boyd's Directory* (1884).

111. Fletcher to Putnam, July 28, 1884, Peabody Museum Records, box 5, folder "1884 C-F."

112. This was the first professional paper presented by La Flesche. Smith, "Francis La Flesche and the World of Letters" (2001), 587. His diary for September 9, 1884, reads, "Miss F. and I read our papers to a large audience. They were well received!" 1884 diary, NAA, Fletcher–La Flesche Collection, box 16.

113. Fletcher, "Lands in Severalty" (1885), 661, 663.

114. The Lake Mohonk conferences began in 1883 under the leadership of Albert K. Smiley, whom President Hayes had appointed to the Board of Indian Commissioners in 1879. Smiley owned a resort hotel on Lake Mohonk, New York, where the conferences were held each fall. The Lake Mohonk reformers promoted change in Indian policy, fostering education and industrial training to prepare Indians to become self-supporting, abolishing the ration system, and allotting Indian lands in severalty—all with the goal of giving Indians full rights of American citizenship. The conference proceedings for the first twenty years were published as an appendix to the *Annual Report of the Board of Indian Commissioners*. HAINM (1907, 1910), 1:928–29. See also Gilcreast, "Smiley, Albert K." (1988).

The Board of Indian Commissioners had been formed in 1869 to oversee budgetary matters concerned with Indian affairs. Board members served without salary and were responsible to and under the direction of the president of the United States. They exercised joint control over Indian appropriations with the secretary of the interior. By 1882, however, the board members' activities were limited to inspection visits to Indian agencies. The board was abolished in 1933. Berthrong, "Nineteenth-Century United States Government Agencies" (1988), 260; Hunt and Brown, *Brevet Brigadier Generals in Blue* (1990), 671.

115. [Lake Mohonk Conference], *Second Annual Address* (1884), 24.

116. [Lake Mohonk Conference], *Second Annual Address* (1884), 6.

117. [Lake Mohonk Conference], *Second Annual Address* (1884), 26.

118. Fletcher wrote to Putnam, December 11, 1885, "I have had some composite photographs taken of Omahas male & female, that was very troublesome, but they are good. I hoped to enclose them to you but they are not yet in. I have also some of the Sioux, I thought to use the latter in an article, the former in the Omaha work. What do you say?" Peabody Museum Records, box 5, folder "1885 F–J." In 1886 she published the Sioux photographs in Fletcher, "Composite Portraits of American Indians," but she does not seem to have published the Omaha photographs.

119. The sketches of boys' symbolic haircuts are reproduced in Fletcher and La Flesche, *Omaha Tribe* (1911), 145–89.

120. Fletcher to Putnam, June 6, 1884, Peabody Museum Records, box 5. On June 17, 1884, Fletcher wrote to Jane Smith (Putnam's secretary), "I've sent the

biggest kind of a prize to the museum in the belongings of one of the Sacred Tents of the Omahas." Peabody Museum Records, box 5.

121. Ridington and Hastings, *Blessing for a Long Time* (1997), 24.

122. Fletcher, "Report of Alice C. Fletcher" (1885).

123. Fletcher, *Historical Sketch of the Omaha Tribe* (1885).

124. Fletcher, *Indian Education and Civilization* (1888).

125. "Proceedings of the Section of Anthropology," *Science* 6:136 (1885): 233.

126. Fletcher, "Average Day in Camp among the Sioux" (1885) and " Evening in Camp" (1885). Part of the text of the Sioux article is nearly identical in content to chapter 10 in the present volume, "Journeying with the Indians."

127. [Address on treaty keeping], *Proceedings of the Third Annual Meeting of the Lake Mohonk Conference of Friends of the Indian Held October 7 to 9, 1885* (Philadelphia: Sherman, 1886), 46.

128. Reported in the *New York Times*, November 21, 1885.

129. For a discussion of the issues involving citizenship and allotment that led to the breach between Fletcher and Tibbles, see Boughter, *Betraying the Omaha Nation* (1998), 106-14.

130. La Flesche had been married twice, to Omaha women. The first marriage was in 1877 but his wife died the next year. The second was in 1879 but the couple separated when he moved to Washington in 1881 and divorced in 1884. Mark, *Stranger in Her Native Land* (1988), 308.

131. Goddard to Welsh, August 2, 1886, Historical Society of Pennsylvania, Indian Rights Association Papers, Incoming Correspondence, box 2, series 1A.

132. Fletcher to Armstrong, April 11, 1886, Hampton University, Indian Education Correspondence. For discussion of the relationship between Fletcher and Tibbles, see Mark, *Stranger in Her Native Land* (1988), 129-34.

133. Fletcher's attendance in New Haven was reported in the *New York Times*, July 22, 1886.

134. Fletcher to Putnam, November 19, 1886, January 17 and 25, 1887, Peabody Museum Records, box 7, folder "1886 A-I" and "1887 D-F."

135. Boyd, *Boyd's Directory*, lists Alice C. Fletcher as a resident of the city from 1887 to 1888 and 1893 to 1923.

136. Fletcher, "Crowning Act" (1887).

137. For the text of the Dawes Act, see Prucha, *Documents of United States Indian Policy* (2000), 170-73.

138. Fletcher, "Crowning Act" (1887).

139. Fletcher, "Home Building among the Indians" (1885); also reported in Women's National Indian Association, *Annual Report* (November 17, 1885):

> Indian Home-Building . . . recommended for adoption at this our Annual Meeting . . . provided for by designated gifts only . . . nothing is better adapted to secure these homes than Miss Alice C. Fletcher's admirable plan for helping young Indian pairs. . . . The plan Miss Fletcher has successfully inaugurated is to lend to the Indian pair a sufficient sum of money, say $300 to $400, with which to build their little home, the money to be returned by them in small annual payments, thus stimulating and helping without pauperizing them, and this plan is the one commended by our Board. (13)

140. Bland and Bland, "Miss Fletcher Sadly Disappointed" (1887). The article probably was written by T. A. and M. C. Bland, the editors of *Council Fire*. The conference referred to was the Annual Conference of the Board of Indian Commissioners, which met on January 6, 1887, in Washington DC. The Riggs House was a popular hotel located across the street from the Treasury Building.

141. Fletcher, "Letter to General Whittlesey" (1889).

142. Prucha, *Documents of United States Indian Policy* (2000), 182–84.

143. Quotations from Fletcher, "Experiences in Allotting Land" (1892); see Fletcher, "Land Tenure," HAINM (1907, 1910), 1:756, "Camping and Camp Circles," HAINM (1907, 1910), 1:197, "Property and Property Right," HAINM (1907, 1910), 2:308.

144. Fletcher, "Experiences in Allotting Land" (1892), 28.

145. Fletcher diary, Monday, August 23–Thursday, September 9, 1897, NAA, Fletcher–La Flesche Collection, box 12A. In a letter to Smiley, September 21, 1897, Fletcher specifically says that she was returning to visit the Omahas after a seven-year absence. Smiley Family Papers, Haverford College Library.

146. La Flesche, "Indian Allotment" (1900), 77–78.

147. Fletcher and La Flesche, *Omaha Tribe* (1911), 640.

148. Kelly, "United States Indian Policies" (1988), 72.

149. Mead, *Changing Culture of an Indian Tribe* (1932), 46–47, 52–53.

150. From the 1880s through the first decade of the 1900s, single woman scientists were caught between "mutually exclusive stereotypes: as scientists they

were atypical women and as women they were unusual scientists." Appropriate behavior and roles were closely linked with an individual's gender. Rossiter, *Women Scientists in America* (1982), xv–xvi. In general women had few opportunities in the scientific research institutions of this period. Those who did receive support were often the relatives of the men in charge; single women were at an even greater disadvantage. Rossiter, *Women Scientists in America*, 60.

151. Fletcher to Smith, November 14, 1881, Peabody Museum Records, box 4, folder "1881 c–f." The "Mrs. Smith" to whom Fletcher refers is Erminnie Adele Smith, who in 1878–79 did fieldwork among the Tuscaroras in Canada. In 1879, at the meeting of the American Association for the Advancement of Science, she had the distinction of giving the earliest recorded anthropological paper by a woman before a learned society in the United States. In 1885 she became the first woman anthropologist to publish in *Science*. She died in 1886. See Lurie, "Women in Early American Anthropology" (1966). In 1880 Smith hired John Napoleon Brinton Hewitt, a part–Tuscarora Indian, to help her with her study of the Tuscarora language. After her death he took over her work, which led to his long career with the BAE. Saunders-Lee, *In Memoriam* (1890), 48; Swanton, "John Napoleon Brinton Hewitt" (1938).

152. Fletcher wrote to Putnam, May 13, 1884, "I will excavate about the side of an old village of lodges which is beyond the memories of old Omahas and tradition says once was the village of the Arickerees. I have the interest and permission of the Indian on whose land the site lies to dig. He thinks I will find much." Peabody Museum Records, box 5, folder "1884 c–f." See Putnam, "Serpent Mound of Ohio" (1890), 872.

153. Fletcher to Putnam, July 31, 1892, Peabody Museum Records, box 12.

154. Fletcher, "Composite Portraits of American Indians" (1886).

155. Fletcher to Putnam, February 13, 1895, Putnam Papers, Harvard University, box 9.

156. William Henry Holmes to Fletcher, February 27, 1903, NAA, Fletcher-La Flesche Collection, box 2, folder "Incoming Correspondence." For Fletcher's articles in *Handbook of American Indians North of Mexico*, see the bibliography.

For the politics regarding Smithsonian pressure to publish the *Handbook of American Indians North of Mexico*, which was "a model of nineteenth-century popular science—a generation late" and was thought at the time to be "a practical manual for congressmen and constituents," see Hinsley, *Smithsonian and the American Indian* (1994), 156–58, 252, 282–83.

157. Visweswaran observes, "The central contradictions of Victorian evolutionism can then be simply stated: if the status of women was seen to be the measure of civilization, why was it that white women were denied the vote, rights to property, and independence in a range of social activities, when 'primitive' Native-American women might have rights to property, a say in ritual practice and considerable social freedom?" "'Wild West' Anthropology and the Disciplining of Gender" (1998), 109. Jane E. Simonsen suggests that late nineteenth-century Euro-Americans' perception of American Indian women's work as being of lower status primarily reflects the way in which women's work was viewed in their own society. *Making Home Work* (2006), 10–11.

158. Fletcher, "Letter to General Whittlesey" (Sept. 20, 1888). Eliphalet Whittlesey was a member of the Board of Indian Commissioners from 1874 to 1900.

159. Mark, *Stranger in Her Native Land* (1988), 47, quoting Francis La Flesche.

160. Fletcher to Putnam, May 22, 1891, Putnam Papers, Harvard University, box 9.

161. Fletcher to Putnam, October 19, 1894, Peabody Museum Records, box 13, "Curator's Correspondence, 1894."

162. Mary Thaw and her late husband, William Thaw, had been helping fund Fletcher's research at least since 1883. In a letter to Putnam of January 20, 1883, Fletcher wrote, "Mr. Thaw while I was in Pittsburg insisted upon my accepting a gift from him by which I could come here & work up my notes with Frank." Peabody Museum Records, box 5, folder "1883—D–F."

However, negotiations with Mrs. Thaw were not always easy. On June 18, 1890, Fletcher wrote to Putnam, "Mrs. Thaw still makes her offer to me, but she seems inclined to control my whereabouts etc. suggesting that I live with a 'charming old maid' dau.[ghter] or sis[ter] of a Presbyterian minister. Now I am not inclined to old maids nor to the blue atmosphere & I fear I should find myself in theological troubles all around. I want to devote myself to sciences not to any doxy. As matters stand I shall try & keep Mrs. Thaw happy, but stick to my Gov't work for the present." Again, on August 1, 1890, Fletcher wrote to Putnam,

I hope Mrs. Thaw will make her gift one to extend beyond my lifetime, for if I should be so unfortunate as to live to be old, I should be troubled at it & if I should die before I get my present notes worked out I should regret that there would be no way for them to be carried out to completion. I think too it is asking too much of you to put me there for my lifetime & not leave the place to be filled by a worthier person when I drop off. So with all my heart I wish that Mrs. Thaw, who has done so generously toward me, would carry her feeling farther & let her act benefit science in the future. (Fletcher to Putnam, June 18 and August 1, 1890, Peabody Museum Director's Records, Harvard University, box 2, folder 1)

163. Fletcher diary, January 14, 1892, NAA, Fletcher-La Flesche Collection, box 12A.

164. Fletcher diary, August 8, 1892, NAA, Fletcher-La Flesche Collection, box 12A: "Applying for money to build a room to F[rancis]"; August 16, 1892, "F[rancis] to 214 First. S.E."

165. Mead and Bunzel, Golden Age of American Anthropology (1960), 227.

166. Visweswaran, "'Wild West' Anthropology and the Disciplining of Gender" (1998), 93.

167. Fletcher, "Ethics and Morals," HAINM (1907, 1910), 1:441–42.

168. Fletcher to Carr, August 31, 1881, Peabody Museum Records, box 4, folder "1881 C-F."

169. Fletcher, "Indian Speech" (1899), 426; Visweswaran, "'Wild West' Anthropology and the Disciplining of Gender" (1998), 117n37.

170. Fletcher, "Indian Woman and Her Problems" (1899), 174.

171. Fletcher to Commissioner of Indian Affairs, June 25, 1884, Records of the Bureau of Indian Affairs, NARA, RG 75, Letters Received, box 197, item 1884-13244.

172. Hoxie, Final Promise (1984), 1–9.

173. Hoxie, Final Promise (1984), 30.

174. Fletcher to Putnam, February 24, 1881, Peabody Museum Records, box 4, folder "1881 C-F"; Tibbles, Buckskin and Blanket Days (1957), 236.

175. Hoxie, Final Promise (1984), 34.

176. Quoted in Mark, Stranger in Her Native Land (1988), 268.

177. Boughter, Betraying the Omaha Nation (1998), 118, blames Fletcher's maternalism for the disaster of Omaha allotment; Jacobs, White Mother to a Dark Race (2009), focuses on Fletcher's role in championing boarding schools;

Tonkovich, *Allotment Plot* (2012), focuses on her role in policy development and specifically in allotting the Nez Perce reservation.

178. Fletcher, "Phonetic Alphabet of the Winnebago Indians" (1890); Fletcher, "Indian Messiah" (1891).

179. Fletcher, "Hae-thu-ska Society of the Omaha Tribe" (1892), 143-44.

180. La Flesche, in fact, had worked on Omaha songs with James Owen Dorsey during 1878-80, and he continued to collect song texts himself. Some of the songs in Fletcher and La Flesche, "A Study of Omaha Indian Music" (1893), such as the children's song "Follow My Leader," were no doubt from his childhood memory. See Deloria, *Indians in Unexpected Places* (2004), 191.

181. George Miller arrived on May 15, 1888, and Fletcher returned with him to Hampton on May 23, 1888. Fletcher diary, NAA, Fletcher-La Flesche Collection, box 12A.

182. *Federal Cylinder Project* (1984), 62-66.

183. [Putnam], "Sixteenth Report of the Curator" (1884), 178.

184. Fletcher, "Quillwork," HAINM (1907, 1910), 2:341-42.

185. Bailey, *Osage and the Invisible World* (1995), 17; Smith, "Francis La Flesche and the World of Letters" (2001), 582. Short portions of "Life among the Indians" appear in La Flesche, *Middle Five* (1900), suggesting the interrelatedness of Fletcher's and La Flesche's work. For example, compare the account of pranks played by Omaha schoolboys in order to be let out of the classroom in chapter 23 of Fletcher's manuscript with La Flesche, *Middle Five*, 97-98.

186. Fletcher to Putnam, October 10, 1907, Putnam Papers, Harvard University, box 15.

187. Fletcher, "'Wawan,' or Pipe Dance of the Omahas" (1884).

188. Fletcher, "Import of the Totem" (1898), 297.

Foreword

1. *Tte-są* 'White Buffalo' (literally, *są* signifies 'pale') was a chief among the Omahas in the early nineteenth century. Bradbury, *Travels in the Interior of America* (1819), 89-90.

2. See Bradbury, *Travels in the Interior of America* (1819).

3. *Mąší·ha ðį* 'Moving on High', referring to the flight of an eagle. Wajepa was a member of the *Tteppá'itʰaži* 'They Don't Touch Buffalo Heads' (Eagle People) subclan of the *Ðáttada* 'On the Left [Side]' clan. The name he chose for

Fletcher was a common one; in his subclan, nine women bore the name. Fletcher and La Flesche, *Omaha Tribe* (1911), 168.

4. *Ttą́wą* 'Village'.

5. *Wábaha* 'Travois, Litter'.

6. *Húðuga* 'Camp Circle'.

1. Over the Border

1. Fletcher set out from Omaha on September 16, 1881, in an army ambulance, painted yellow and marked "U.S.," that was provided for her use by Gen. George Crook, commanding officer at Fort Omaha. The driver was a soldier named Baker. Fletcher was accompanied by Susette La Flesche Tibbles and her husband, Thomas Henry Tibbles. In an earlier draft Fletcher designated the conveyance as an "ambulance" but in revising changed it to "wagon."

2. Florence, Nebraska. Fletcher, 1881 Notebook 1, September 16. Florence was annexed by the city of Omaha in 1917.

3. The woman was Mrs. Smith, who was originally from Pennsylvania but had lived in Nebraska for thirty years. Fletcher, 1881 Notebook 1, September 16.

4. Hunt, *Worth and Wealth* (1856).

5. The Homestead Act of 1862 allowed individuals to claim 160-acre tracts of land but required that the land be improved by cultivating it and building a house on it.

6. The cabin was near Redbird City, Nebraska. Fletcher, 1881 Notebook 1, October 4.

7. The "amateur soldiers" were the Nebraska State Militia.

8. Fort Randall (1856–92) was located on the west bank of the Missouri River in Dakota Territory, just north of the Nebraska border. In May 1880 the post was garrisoned by the Twenty-Fifth Infantry (African American); they served there until November 1881. Greene, *Fort Randall on the Missouri* (2005), 126.

9. Near Newcastle, Nebraska; Fletcher recorded the woman's name as Hugho. Her parents were from New York but she had emigrated to Michigan, then Iowa, and finally to Nebraska. Fletcher, 1881 Notebook 1, September 23.

10. On October 10 Fletcher's party entered the Great Sioux Reservation. Fletcher, 1881 Notebook 1.

2. Reporting

1. Fletcher reported to the agency on October 12, the day after her arrival at Rosebud Agency. Fletcher, 1881 Notebook 1, 169–73. John Cook was appointed agent at Rosebud in 1880 and served until 1884. Hill, *Office of Indian Affairs* (1974), 177.

2. Gen. George Crook, at Fort Omaha. Fletcher struck out this sentence in revising the manuscript; those deletions that seemed to us to be substantive have been restored and placed in square brackets.

3. Probably Daniel Milk, a student at Carlisle Indian School. See introduction, note 72.

4. This scene is a literary device. In fact, the military driver took Fletcher to the Omaha Reservation; she arrived at Rosebud in the company of the Tibbleses, three Omahas (Wajepa, Buffalo Chip, and the latter's wife, Gaha), a Sioux scout whose name Fletcher gives as The Eagle but whom Tibbles called Thigh, and the scout's wife. Fletcher, 1881 Notebook 1, October 10; Tibbles, *Buckskin and Blanket Days* (1957), 255–56.

3. The Welcome

1. Fletcher's host at Rosebud was Milk (*Asáŋpi*), the leader of a Brule band. Fletcher, however, identified him as Oglala. Fletcher, 1881 Notebook 1, October 11.

4. The Chief's Entertainment

1. The chief was the younger Spotted Tail. His father, the leading chief of the Brules, had been murdered on August 5, 1881. Hyde, *Spotted Tail's Folk* (1961), 299–300.

2. Fletcher described the dance in "Indian Songs" (1894), 421–22; that account confirms that the dance was held in the camp of young Spotted Tail.

3. Fletcher witnessed the Omaha or Grass Dance, the primary social dance of the Sioux. Certain men who had won war honors were allowed to "dance the tail," that is, the last portion of the song. Densmore, *Teton Sioux Music* (1918), 468–73. Fletcher was told that the Sioux borrowed this dance from the Omahas in 1859. Fletcher, 1881 Notebook 1, October 14.

5. The White Man's Shadow

1. Prairie turnips, or *pommes blanches* (*Psoralea esculenta*). See Gilmore, "Uses of Plants by the Indians" (1919), 92–93.

2. Compare Fletcher, "Home Life among the Indians" (1897), 254.

3. Wajepa (Ezra Freemont), one of Fletcher's Omaha traveling companions, told her that since the white people came to Omaha country, the original buffalo grass was being crowded out by bluejoint, which the Omahas called "red grass," that had been introduced by the whites. Fletcher, 1881 Notebook 1, September 24.

4. A portion of the Northern Cheyennes were removed to Indian Territory in 1877; the next year they fled north to rejoin their relatives in Montana. The group under Dull Knife was captured by the army and imprisoned at Fort Robinson, Nebraska. They escaped on January 9, 1879, and more than half of the 149 Cheyennes were killed by the soldiers. See Sandoz, *Cheyenne Autumn* (1953); and Powell, *People of the Sacred Mountain* (1981), 2:1153–1213.

6. An Outline Chapter

1. In nineteenth-century ethnology the term *gens* (plural *gentes*) designated patrilineal social groups that recognized descent (that is, membership in the group) though the male line; *clan* designated matrilineal social groups that recognized descent through the female line. While the Omahas were patrilineal, the Sioux were in fact bilateral: an individual might belong to the social group (band) of either the father or mother, the choice being made by residence. The Sioux lacked some of the characteristics of unilineal societies; for example, they did not have distinctive symbols (totems) or stocks of personal names associated with social groups. See DeMallie, "Kinship" (1998), 330–39.

2. Like the Omaha gentes, the Sioux bands had their regular places within the camp circle. The following description of the arrangement of places within a tipi appears in revised form in Fletcher, "Home Life among the Indians" (1897), 252–53.

3. Fletcher's description here fits more closely with the Omahas than the Sioux, among whom chieftainship was less formalized and less of a religious status.

4. Among the Sioux there were several men's societies whose members are usually referred to as soldiers. They encouraged one another to perform feats of

valor against the enemy and to give to the poor and served at times as police to maintain order, particularly during camp moves and buffalo hunts. See Wissler, "Societies and Ceremonial Associations" (1912), 25–36.

7. The Indian Woman

1. A version of the discussion of women's ownership of property (tent, horses) as well as the etiquette of sitting appears in revised form in Fletcher, "Home Life among the Indians" (1897), 253.

8. The Woman's Society

1. The society was called *kat'éla* and was found in every band; all its members were married women. Fletcher, 1881 Notebook 1, October 14; 1881 Notebook 2, October 15. Wissler, "Societies and Ceremonial Associations" (1912), 75–76, reports that only women whose husbands or male relatives had performed brave deeds in war were eligible to join. Fletcher, however, says that membership was based on the character of the woman, not the position of her husband.
2. This was Milk's wife, whose name was Good Woman (*Waštéwiŋ*). Fletcher, 1881 Notebook 2, October 15.
3. "At the close of one movement the women shout wa-wa-wa, which we supposed to be the Indian man's cry." Fletcher, 1881 Notebook 2, October 15.
4. In her notebook Fletcher wrote, "I heard a queer shouting that grew nearer and nearer and in a moment a man with his hair cut short and naked, all but his shirt, appeared at the opening of the tent wailing and crying." The deceased was his mother, who had recently been the woman's society's drum keeper. Fletcher, 1881 Notebook 2, October 15.

9. Acting out a Vision

1. This material on vision seeking and the Elk Society enactment is elaborated on in Fletcher, "Elk Mystery or Festival: Ogallala Sioux" (1884). Fletcher witnessed the ceremony at Pine Ridge in 1882 and credited information to Blue Horse and Little Bull. Fletcher, 1882 Notebook of Sioux Fieldwork, 133–34.
2. Other accounts of the Elk Society are given in Wissler, "Societies and Ceremonial Associations" (1912), 85–88; and Densmore, *Teton Sioux Music* (1918), 293–98.
3. Here and elsewhere Fletcher's use of *reeds* apparently refers to willow shoots.

10. Journeying with the Indians

1. This account of moving camp and settling into a new camp was incorporated in Fletcher, "Average Day in Camp among the Sioux" (1885), 285–86.

11. Natives and Visitors

1. The ceremonies that followed the sudden death of the man named Kick, a member of Standing Elk's camp at Rosebud Agency, occurred on October 17, 1881. Fletcher, 1881 Notebook 2.

12. A Religious Festival

1. A fuller account, incorporating the material in this chapter, appears in Fletcher, "White Buffalo Festival of the Uncpapas" (1884). Fletcher recorded the information about this ceremony in 1882 while visiting Sitting Bull's camp at Fort Randall, Dakota Territory, where the chief and his people were being held as prisoners of war. She credits One Bull, Touch the Sky, Sitting Bull, Four Horns, and Black Bear for information.

13. The Ghost Lodge

1. This material on the Ghost Lodge is elaborated on in Fletcher, "Shadow or Ghost Lodge: A Ceremony of the Ogallala Sioux" (1884). Fletcher witnessed the ceremony at Pine Ridge on June 26, 1882. Fletcher, 1882 Notebook of Sioux Fieldwork, 190–210.
2. Here, for the Sioux, the appropriate term for the social group is *band* rather than *gens*.
3. The man's name was Black Bear. Fletcher, 1882 Notebook of Sioux Fieldwork, 145.
4. By *reeds*, Fletcher means willow rods.

14. Beef versus Men

1. Fletcher and her party left Rosebud Agency October 19, 1881, heading for Fort Randall to visit Sitting Bull. Fletcher, 1881 Notebook 2.
2. A reference to the forced removal in 1877 of the Poncas from Nebraska to Kansas, and ultimately to Oklahoma. See Wishart, *Unspeakable Sadness* (1994).
3. Fletcher attended Sunday service at the Episcopal church at Rosebud. Fletcher, 1881 Notebook 2, October 16.

4. Fletcher witnessed the beef issue at Rosebud Agency. Fletcher, 1881 Notebook 2, October 17. At the Sioux agencies, army officers from the nearby military posts were assigned to serve as official witnesses to the issuing of cattle.

15. Among the Omahas

1. Fletcher, accompanied by Susette La Flesche Tibbles and Thomas Henry Tibbles, first entered the Omaha Reservation on September 18, 1881, in a military ambulance provided by General Crook at Omaha. Fletcher, 1881 Notebook 1, September 18.

2. On their way to Rosebud Reservation, Fletcher's party stopped at the home of Susette's parents, Joseph and Mary Gale La Flesche.

3. The three daughters mentioned here are Susette, Rosalie (who married Edward Farley), and Marguerite (who married Charles Picotte and, after Picotte's death, Walter Diddock). Green, *Iron Eye's Family* (1969), 64, 132, 144.

4. The grandmother was the mother of Mary Gale La Flesche, named Nicomi; the "oldest grandmother" was Nicomi's sister, Madeline Wolfe. Green, *Iron Eye's Family* (1969), 123.

5. The Old Man of the Mountain was a celebrated formation in the White Mountains of New Hampshire that resembled a jagged profile of a man's face.

6. The Poncas' land had inadvertently been included in the territory of the Sioux as defined in the 1868 treaty. In August 1881, while visiting Washington, Red Cloud agreed that if the Poncas wished to return from the Indian Territory, they could reoccupy their old territory. See Olson, *Red Cloud and the Sioux Problem* (1965), 274–75.

7. This group formed after the signing of the 1854 treaty; it was made up of young men who wished to farm and live like white men. Fletcher and La Flesche, *Omaha Tribe* (1911), 633.

8. Under the 1854 treaty the Omahas sold their hunting grounds in Nebraska to the United States, retaining only a three-hundred-thousand-acre reservation; the monies for this land sale were to be paid over forty years. Fletcher and La Flesche, *Omaha Tribe* (1911), 623. For the treaty text, see Kappler, *Indian Affairs* (1904), 2:611–14.

9. In the parlance of Indian affairs, agents identified themselves as "fathers" of their Indian "children." The president of the United States was the "great father."

10. This occurred in 1866; Joseph La Flesche later returned to the Omaha Reservation and continued to be a leader of the Citizens' Party until his death in 1889.

11. "Soldiers" were officers appointed by the tribal council to carry out their collective decisions. Fletcher and La Flesche, *Omaha Tribe* (1911), 209-10.

12. Robert Burns (1759-96), from "To a Louse," in Burns, *Poems and Songs* (1909-14).

16. The Young Mother

1. The Presbyterian Mission on the Omaha Reservation was founded in 1857. Fletcher and La Flesche, *Omaha Tribe* (1911), 627.

2. It was a common nineteenth-century misconception that Canadian French was a patois, since it differed from the French spoken in France. In fact, Canadian French is different because it represents an older version of the language, unaffected by the linguistic reforms that followed the French Revolution.

3. William Wordsworth (1770-1850), "Ode: Intimations of Immortality from Recollections of Early Childhood," in Quiller-Couch, *New Oxford Book of English Verse* (1955), 626-33.

4. Joseph Blanco White (1775-1841), "To Night," in Quiller-Couch, *New Oxford Book of English Verse* (1955), 685.

5. This dialogue about kin terms appears in Fletcher, "Home Life among the Indians" (1897), 257-59. It is an ingenious way of explaining the principles that underlie the Omaha system of kinship, in which some terms are applied across generations. For a thorough discussion of Omaha kinship, see Barnes, *Two Crows Denies It* (1984).

6. A similar account appears in Fletcher, "Home Life among the Indians" (1897), 255.

17. An Indian's Story

1. The pipestone (catlinite) quarry, now Pipestone National Monument, is located in southwestern Minnesota.

2. See the discussion of migrations in Fletcher and La Flesche, *Omaha Tribe* (1911), 70-81. For the village on Omaha Creek, see O'Shea and Ludwickson, *Archaeology and Ethnohistory of the Omaha Indians* (1992).

3. Fletcher had studied the prehistoric mounds of the Ohio Valley and delivered popular lectures on the topic.

18. Child Life

1. Fletcher, "Glimpses of Child Life among the Omaha Indians" (1888), 115, says that the child was named on the fourth day after birth; in "Home Life among the Indians" (1897), 254, she says the child was named when four or five days old.
2. This material on infants and early childhood is included in revised form in Fletcher, "Home Life among the Indians" (1897), 254–56.
3. The ceremony and the boys' haircuts are described in Fletcher, "Glimpses of Child Life among the Omaha Indians" (1888), 115–18; Fletcher, "Home Life among the Indians" (1897), 255–56; and Fletcher and La Flesche, *Omaha Tribe* (1911), 117–18, 327–28. Fuller descriptions of the ceremony appear in Fletcher, " Significance of the Scalp Lock" (1898), 439–50; and in Fletcher, "Indian and Nature" (1915), 471–72. The hair-cutting ceremony is also described in Fletcher, "Child and the Tribe" (1915), 569–72.
4. A similar description of the role of the uncle appears in Fletcher, "Home Life among the Indians" (1897), 259–60.
5. The account of this incident is included in Fletcher, "Home Life among the Indians" (1897), 259–60.
6. This song appears in Fletcher, *Indian Story and Song* (1900), 29.
7. See Fletcher, "Wakonda," HAINM (1907, 1910), 2:897–98.

19. Hunting

1. This chapter presents a popularized account of the buffalo hunt. A fuller version appears in Fletcher, "Hunting Customs of the Omaha" (1895); the most detailed account is in Fletcher and La Flesche, *Omaha Tribe* (1911), 275–82. The "father" who told Fletcher about hunting customs was Joseph La Flesche.
2. Fletcher presents an account of the Sacred Pole and the rituals associated with it in "Sacred Pole of the Omaha Tribe" (1896). There she reports the death of Joseph La Flesche and notes that some of the Omahas attributed it to his role in divulging the ritual of the Sacred Pole (274).

3. For details concerning the Sacred Tents, see Fletcher and La Flesche, *Omaha Tribe* (1911), 221.

20. Winter and War

1. The preceding three paragraphs appear in Fletcher, "The Elk Mystery or Festival: Ogallala Sioux" (1884), 276n1.
2. For details of the Sacred Tents, see Fletcher and La Flesche, *Omaha Tribe* (1911), 221.
3. The *reeds* were probably willow rods.
4. See Fletcher, 1881 Allotment Notebook 2, November 14, 2–3.
5. A more detailed version of this story appears in Fletcher and La Flesche, *Omaha Tribe* (1911), 406–8.
6. The Union Pacific Railroad began construction west of Omaha in 1865. Billington, *Westward Expansion* (1974), 556.

21. Friends and Lovers

1. Most of this chapter appears in slightly revised form in Fletcher, "Leaves from My Omaha Notebook" (1889).
2. The material on friendship and courting behavior and the story of the bachelor finding wives for his brothers appears in slightly revised form in Fletcher and La Flesche, *Omaha Tribe* (1911), 318–27.

22. The Make-Believe White Men

1. Council Bluffs Agency, which had responsibility for the Omahas and other tribes, was established in 1836 and in 1839 agency buildings were constructed at Bellevue, Nebraska. In 1856 a separate agency was established for the Omahas on the west bank of the Missouri near Decatur, Nebraska. Hill, *Office of Indian Affairs* (1974), 51, 122. The Mormon emigrants, numbering some twelve thousand people, spent the winter of 1846–47 on the west bank of the Missouri across from Council Bluffs, near the Omahas. The Latter-Day Saints, under the leadership of Brigham Young, left in spring 1847 for their future home in Utah. Billington, *Westward Expansion* (1974), 458.
2. "Sealing" is a religious ceremony in the Church of Jesus Christ of Latter-Day Saints that binds one individual to another beyond death, for eternity.
3. The Village of the Make-Believe White Men was constructed by Joseph La

Flesche and his followers. See Fletcher and La Flesche, *Omaha Tribe* (1911), 633.

4. "The farmers" presumably were agency employees hired to instruct and aid the Omahas in their agricultural pursuits.

5. The Presbyterian Mission boarding school functioned from 1857 to 1868; from 1869 to 1878 the agency experimented with day schools; then in 1879 the mission school reopened and took over the work of the day schools. Milner, *With Good Intentions* (1982), 173, 182.

23. The Schoolboys

1. Many of the pranks described here are included in La Flesche, *Middle Five* (1900), 96-103.

2. Jessie Hutchinson Jr.'s "Uncle Sam's Farm" became a popular song that encouraged homesteading. Hutchinson, *Uncle Sam's Farm* (1850).

24. Our Land

1. Fulfilling provisions of the treaties of 1854 and 1865, the Omahas received allotments of land in severalty in 1869-70. These patents, however, did not guarantee ownership of land and the Omahas feared that, as with the Poncas, the government would remove them to Indian Territory. Milner, *With Good Intentions* (1982), 160-81. Fletcher, at the request of Joseph La Flesche and fifty-two other Omaha men, sent a petition to Washington on December 31, 1881, to request that individual members of the Omaha tribe be granted title to their lands. As a result, the Omahas' lands were allotted in 1883.

2. Printed as U.S. Congress, *Memorial of the Members of the Omaha Tribe* (1882). The petition was signed by fifty-three Omaha men.

3. *U.S. Stat.* 22:341; reprinted in Kappler, *Indian Affairs* (1904), 1:212-14.

4. While in the East Fletcher met Richard Henry Pratt, a military officer who had been in charge of the Indian prisoners (mostly Cheyennes, Kiowas, and Comanches) who were incarcerated at St. Augustine, Florida, from 1875 to 1878. After they were released, Pratt arranged to have seventeen of them enrolled at Hampton Normal and Agricultural Institute in Virginia, with more enrolling in subsequent years. In 1879 Pratt founded the Carlisle Indian School in an abandoned army barracks in Pennsylvania. See Pratt, *Battlefield and Classroom* (1964).

5. The *Easthampton (MA) News and Easthampton Enterprise*, November 17, 1882, reported that Fletcher had been "telling the story in different parts of the country to collect money for the work. The Payson Sunday school contributed $50 and a collection of $42 was taken at the lectures."

6. Fletcher's essay "Home Building among the Indians" (1885), describing the education of young Indian couples at Hampton, was published as a leaflet of the Women's National Indian Association, Philadelphia, in 1885.

25. Starting Afresh

1. See Fletcher, "Lands in Severalty" (1885). Francis La Flesche served as her allotment clerk.

2. In the Bible, Benjamin was the youngest son of Jacob and Rachel. Genesis 35:18.

26. The Sacred Pipes

1. Fletcher's full report on the Pipe Dance appears in "'Wawan,' or Pipe Dance of the Omahas" (1884), which includes songs with musical notation. Portions of this chapter appear in revised form in Fletcher, "Personal Studies of Indian Life: Politics and 'Pipe Dancing'" (1893). Also see Fletcher and La Flesche, *Omaha Tribe* (1911), 376-77.

2. The "peculiar duck" was a mallard. Fletcher and La Flesche, *Omaha Tribe* (1911), 376. The tobacco pouch was made of a buffalo bladder. Fletcher, "'Wawan,' or Pipe Dance of the Omahas" (1884), 310.

3. Father Jacques Marquette, S.J. (1637–75), missionary to the Indians in New France, wrote around 1670 that the Sioux "chiefly adore the Calumet." Thwaites, *Jesuit Relations* (1899), 191, 193.

Sources Documenting Fletcher's Fieldwork among the Omahas and Sioux, 1881-82

Fletcher's Notebooks

1. Notebook 1, "Field Diary—1881" (September 17–October 14); Notebook 2, "Field Diary—1881" (October 15–November 2). Fletcher and La Flesche Collection, NAA, box 11.

2. "Omaha Field Diaries, 1882–1885, 1895, 1898." Fletcher and La Flesche Collection, NAA, box 20. This notebook has on its cover a label, "3/vii.B.14d," and the pages are numbered 1–167 and 262–386, with the intervening ninety-three pages blank.

3. 1881 Allotment Notebook. Fletcher and La Flesche Collection, NAA, box 3. A notebook relating to the allotment of land to the Omahas has on its cover a label, "5/[?] 15/Nov. 14, 1881/ about allot," and the pages are numbered 1–194.

4. "Going Home with the Indians," 1882; also a draft manuscript based on the notebook. Fletcher and La Flesche Collection, NAA, box 6.

5. Notebook of Sioux Fieldwork, 1882, with pages numbered 1–243 but no identifying notation on the cover. Fletcher and La Flesche Collection, NAA, box 30.

   All the notebooks include interviews, ethnological observations, and linguistic notes. The notebook entries are mainly undated but include significant ethnological observations of Omaha and Sioux life, many folktales, and notes concerning books and articles Fletcher was reading while in the field, as well as letters dictated to her by the Indians she met, imploring her to appeal to government officials on their behalf to secure title to their lands.

The Omaha allotment notebook also includes personal information about individuals and their families, houses, farms, animals owned, and land in use. The field notebooks used in this project were transcribed by Scherer with the help of numerous interns.

Partial Typewritten Transcript of the 1881 Notebook

This transcript was presumably made by Francis La Flesche after Fletcher's death (see Mark, *Stranger in Her Native Land*, 362). The original is in the Fletcher and La Flesche Collection, NAA, box 12; it was scanned and made available online by the NAA in November 2001 (Fletcher, *Camping with the Sioux*, http://www.nmnh.si .edu/naa/fletcher/fletcher.htm).

Fletcher's "Life among the Indians"

The manuscript printed in this volume, an account in two parts: part 1, "Life among the Sioux" (fourteen chapters), and part 2, "The Omahas at Home" (twelve chapters). The originals are preserved in the Fletcher and La Flesche Collection, NAA, box 7.

Thomas Henry Tibbles's Account

Tibbles's account of his travels with Fletcher in 1881 is included in his memoirs, written in 1905. The book was published in 1957 as *Buckskin and Blanket Days: Memoirs of a Friend of the Indians*, edited by Theodora Bates Cogswell, long after Tibbles's death in 1928. He devotes five chapters to Fletcher's field trip: "Guests of the Ponca Tribe," "On Our Way," "Pipe-Dancing the Sioux," "We Look Before and After," and "Sitting Bull Welcomes Us."

Bibliography

Manuscript Collections

Hampton University, Hampton VA
> Museum Archive: Indian Education Correspondence

Harvard University, Cambridge MA
> Frederic Ward Putnam Papers. Ms. no. HUG 1717.xx.
> Peabody Museum of Archaeology and Ethnology Records, 1851–1968. Ms. no. UAV 677.38.
> Peabody Museum Director's Records, 1870–1923. Ms. no. 38–22, 41–47, unaccessioned.

Haverford College Library, Special Collections, Haverford PA
> Smiley Family Papers, 1885–1930.

Historical Society of Pennsylvania, Philadelphia
> Indian Rights Association Papers.

Library of Congress, Washington DC
> Henry L. Dawes Papers.

Massachusetts Historical Society, Boston
> Caroline H. Dall Collection. Ms. no. N-1082.

National Archives and Records Administration, Washington DC
> Records of the Bureau of Indian Affairs. RG 75.
> Records of the Office of the Secretary of War. RG 107.
> U.S. Indian Census Schedules. Rosebud Agency, 1887, 1891. Pine Ridge Reservation, 1890. RG 75, M595, roll 427.

Princeton University Library, Manuscript Division, Princeton NJ
> Archives of Charles Scribner's Sons, 1786–2003. Ms. no. C0101.

Smithsonian Institution, Washington DC

National Anthropological Archives

Alice C. Fletcher and Francis La Flesche Collection. Ms. no. 4558.

Anthropological Society of Washington Records.

Records of the Bureau of American Ethnology, Correspondence Files.

Records of the American Anthropological Association.

Smithsonian Archives, Washington DC

Records of the Secretary of the Smithsonian.

Southwest Museum of the American Indian, Los Angeles

Charles Fletcher Lummis Manuscript Collection, 1879–1928.

Frederick Webb Hodge Manuscript Collection.

Publications

Alexander, Hartley B. "Francis La Flesche." *American Anthropologist* 35:2 (1933): 328–31.

American Folk-Lore Society. "Second Annual Meeting of the American Folk-Lore Society." *Journal of American Folk-Lore* 4:12 (1891): 1–12.

Association for the Advancement of Women. *Annual Report for 1881.* Boston: Cochrane and Sampson, 1882.

Babcock, Barbara A., and Nancy J. Parezo. *Daughters of the Desert: Women Anthropologists and the Native American Southwest, 1880–1980; An Illustrated Catalogue.* Albuquerque: University of New Mexico Press, 1988.

Bailey, Garrick A., ed. *The Osage and the Invisible World: From the Works of Francis La Flesche.* Norman: University of Oklahoma Press, 1995.

Barton, Winifred W. *John P. Williamson: A Brother to the Sioux.* New York: Fleming H. Revell, 1919.

Barnes, R. H. *Two Crows Denies It: A History of Controversy in Omaha Sociology.* Lincoln: University of Nebraska Press, 1984.

Bell, Genevieve. "Telling Stories Out of School: Remembering the Carlisle Indian Industrial School, 1879–1918 (Pennsylvania)." PhD diss., Stanford University, 1998.

Bell, Genevieve, and Barbara Landis. "Carlisle Indian School Student Record Database." 1997–present. (Contains a template of data found in NARA RG 75, file 1377.) Electronic database in the possession of Bell and Landis.

Berthrong, Donald J. "Nineteenth-Century United States Government Agencies." In Washburn, *History of Indian-White Relations,* 255–63, HNAI, vol. 4, 1988.

Billington, Ray Allen. *Westward Expansion: A History of the American Frontier*. 4th ed. New York: Macmillan, 1974.

Bland, T. A., and M. C. Bland, eds. "Miss Fletcher Sadly Disappointed." *Council Fire* 10:2 (1887): 27.

Boston Daily Advertiser. "Life among the Omahas: A Descriptive Lecture by Miss Alice C. Fletcher—the Manners and Customs of the Tribe." December 14, 1882.

Boston Daily Globe. "Mrs. Thaw Will Aid Helen Keller: Blind Scholar to Have Half of Fellowship Fund." April 21, 1923. ProQuest.

Boughter, Judith A. *Betraying the Omaha Nation, 1790-1916*. Norman: University of Oklahoma Press, 1998.

Boyd, W. H., ed. *Boyd's Directory of the District of Columbia*. Washington DC: W. H. Boyd, 1884-1934.

Bradbury, John. *Travels in the Interior of America in the Years 1809, 1810, and 1811. . . .* 2nd ed. London, 1819. Reprinted in *Early Western Travels, 1748-1846 . . .* , ed. Reuben Gold Thwaites, vol. 5. Cleveland: Arthur H. Clark, 1904. Page numbers refer to the Thwaites edition.

Burns, Robert. *Poems and Songs*. The Harvard Classics, vol. 6. New York: P. F. Collier and Son, 1909-14. Accessed May 5, 2010, www.bartleby.com/6/.

"The Century Magazine." *Century Illustrated Monthly Magazine* 23:1 (1881): 143-44.

Coward, John M. *The Newspaper Indian: Native American Identity in the Press, 1820-90*. Urbana: University of Illinois Press, 1999.

Croly, J. C. *The History of the Woman's Club Movement in America*. New York: Henry G. Allen, 1898.

Cushing, Frank Hamilton. "My Adventures in Zuni." *Century Magazine* 25:2 (1882): 191-208; 25:4 (1883): 500-512; 26:1 (1883): 28-48.

Darnell, Regna. *And Along Came Boas: Continuity and Revolution in Americanist Anthropology*. Amsterdam: John Benjamins, 1998.

———. "The Development of American Anthropology, 1879-1920: From the Bureau of American Ethnology to Franz Boas." PhD diss., University of Pennsylvania, 1970.

Deloria, Philip Joseph. *Indians in Unexpected Places*. Lawrence: University Press of Kansas, 2004.

DeMallie, Raymond J. "Kinship: The Foundation for Native American Society." In *Studying Native America: Problems and Prospects*, ed. Russell Thornton, 306-56. Madison: University of Wisconsin Press, 1998.

DeMallie, Raymond J., and Douglas R. Parks. "George A. Dorsey and the Development of Plains Indian Anthropology." In *Anthropology, History, and American Indians: Essays in Honor of William Curtis Sturtevant*, ed. William L. Merrill and Ives Goddard, 59–74. Smithsonian Contributions to Anthropology, no. 44. Washington DC: Smithsonian Institution, 2002.

Densmore, Frances. *Teton Sioux Music*. Smithsonian Institution, Bureau of American Ethnology, Bulletin 61. Washington DC, 1918.

Dexter, Ralph W. "F. W. Putnam's Role in Developing the Peabody Museum of American Archaeology and Ethnology." *Curator* 23:3 (1980): 183–94.

Dorsey, Rev. James Owen. *The Ȼegiha Language*. Contributions to North American Ethnology, vol. 6. Washington DC, 1890.

Elliott, Michael A. *The Culture Concept: Writing and Difference in the Age of Realism*. Minneapolis: University of Minnesota Press, 2002.

The Federal Cylinder Project: A Guide to Field Cylinder Collections in Federal Agencies. Vol. 1, *Introduction and Inventory*. Washington DC: American Folklife Center, Library of Congress, 1984.

Fletcher, Alice C. "Adai," "Adornment," "Agency System," "Aguacay," "Ahouerhopihein," "Akasquy," "Amediche," "Anadarko," "Analao," "Anamis," "Anoixi," "Aranama," "Arhau," "Arikara," "Arkokisa," "Arthur, Mark," "Avavares," "Avoyelles," "Bright Eyes," "Buffalo," "Caddo," "Caddoan Family," "Cahinnio," "Camping and Camp Circles," "Campti," "Chaquantie," "Chaui," "Choye," "Civilization," "Coaque," "Dolls," "Doustioni," "Dramatic Representation," "Dreams and Visions," "Earth Lodge," "Ethics and Morals," "Etiquette," "Eyeish," "Fasting," "Feasts," "Furniture," "Governmental Policy," "Grass House," "Hair Dressing," "Higos," "Imaha," "Irrupiens," "Kabaye," "Kadohadacho," "Karankawa," "Keremen," "Kiabaha," "Kitkehahki," "La Flesche, Francis," "Land Tenure," "Legal Status," "Mariames," "Masks," "Mayeye," "Mento," "Meracouman," "Mourning," "Music and Musical Instruments," "Nacaniche," "Nacisi," "Nanatsoho," "Natasi," "Natchitoch," "Ointemarhen," "Onapiem," "Oratory," "Orcan," "Orientation," "Panequo," "Pawnee," "Pehir," "Peinhoum," "Peissaquo," "Penoy," "Petao," "Piechar," "Pitahauerat," "Poetry," "Property and Property Right," "Quillwork," "Skidi," "Soldier," "Spichehat," "Tattooing," "Trading Posts," "Tsera," "Tyacappan," "Wakonda," "War and War Discipline," "Yatasi," "Yguases." In *Handbook of American Indians North of Mexico*, ed. Frederick Webb Hodge. Bureau of American Ethnology, Bulletin 30. 2 vols. Washington DC, 1907, 1910.

——. "An Average Day in Camp among the Sioux." *Science* 6:139 (1885): 285-87.

——. "Camping among the Sunflowers." *Wide Awake* 18:3 (1884): 204-8.

——. *Camping with the Sioux: Fieldwork Diary of Alice Cunningham Fletcher*. 2001. Smithsonian Institution, National Anthropological Archives (http://www.nmnh .si.edu/naa/fletcher/).

——. "The Carlisle Indian Pupils at Home." *Wide Awake* 18:2 (1884): 141-44.

——. "The Child and the Tribe." In *Proceedings of the National Academy of Sciences*, no. 1, 569-74. 1915.

——. "Composite Portraits of American Indians." *Science* 7:170 (1886): 408 and illus.

——. "The Crowning Act." *Morning Star* 7 (March 1887): 1.

——. "The Elk Mystery or Festival. Ogallala Sioux." PMAR 16-17, vol. 3, no. 3-4 (1884): 276-88.

——. "An Evening in Camp among the Omahas." *Science* 6:139 (1885): 88-90.

——. "Experiences in Allotting Land." In *Proceedings of the Tenth Annual Meeting of the Lake Mohonk Conference of Friends of the Indian*, ed. Martha D. Adams, 24-29. 1892.

——. "Extracts from Miss Fletcher's Letters." *Morning Star* 3:3 (1882): 1.

——. "Glimpses of Child Life among the Omaha Tribe of Indians." *Journal of American Folk-Lore* 1:2 (1888): 115-23.

——. "Hae-thu-ska Society of the Omaha Tribe." *Journal of American Folk-Lore* 5:17 (1892): 135-44.

——. *Historical Sketch of the Omaha Tribe of Indians in Nebraska*. Washington DC: Judd and Detweiler, 1885.

——. "Home Building among the Indians." *Leaflets of the Women's National Indian Association*. 1885.

——. "Home Life among the Indians: Records of Personal Experience." *Century: A Popular Quarterly* 54:2 (1897): 252-63.

——. "Hunting Customs of the Omaha: Personal Studies of Indian Life." *Century: A Popular Quarterly* 50:5 (1895): 691-702.

——. "The Import of the Totem." *Science* 7:4 (1898): 296-304.

——. "The Indian and Nature." In *Proceedings of the National Academy of Sciences*, no. 1, pp. 467-73.

———. "The Indian and the Prisoner." *Southern Workman and Hampton School Record* 17:4 (1888): 45.

———. *Indian Education and Civilization: A Report Prepared in Answer to Senate Resolution of February 23, 1885.* 48th Cong., 2d sess., February 23, 1885, S. Ex. Doc. 95, serial 2264. Special Report, U.S. Bureau of Education. Washington DC: Government Printing Office, 1888.

———. "The Indian Messiah." *Journal of American Folk-Lore* 4:12 (1891): 57–60.

———. "Indian Songs: Personal Studies of Indian Life." *Century: A Popular Quarterly* 47:3 (1894): 421–32.

———. "Indian Speech." *Southern Workman and Hampton School Record*, 28:2 (1899): 426–28.

———. *Indian Story and Song from North America.* Boston: Small, Maynard, 1900.

———. "The Indian Woman and Her Problems." *Southern Workman and Hampton School Record* 28:5 (1899): 172–76.

———. "In Memoriam: Frank Hamilton Cushing." *American Anthropologist*, n.s., 2:2 (1900): 367.

———. "Lands in Severalty to Indians; Illustrated by Experiences with the Omaha Tribe." In *Proceedings of the American Association for the Advancement of Science, Thirty-Third Meeting, held at Philadelphia, Penn., September, 1884*, 654–65. 1885.

———. "Leaves from My Omaha Notebook." *Journal of American Folk-Lore* 2:6 (1889): 219–26.

———. "Letter to General Whittlesey." In *Proceedings of the Sixth Annual Meeting of the Lake Mohonk Conference of Friends of the Indian, Held September 26, 27, and 28, 1888*, ed. Isabel C. Barrows, 7. 1888.

———. "Letter to General Whittlesey. South Fork of Clearwater, Nez Perce Agency, Idaho, Sept. 17th." In *Proceedings of the Seventh Annual Meeting of the Lake Mohonk Conference of Friends of the Indian*, ed. Samuel J. Barrows, 13–14. 1889.

———. "Notes on Certain Beliefs Concerning Will Power among the Siouan Tribes." *Science* 5:113 (1897): 331–34.

———. "On Indian Education and Self-Support." *Century; A Popular Quarterly* 26:2 (1883): 312–15.

———. "Personal Studies of Indian Life: Politics and 'Pipe-Dancing'." *Century: A Popular Quarterly* 45:3 (1893): 441–56.

——. "The Phonetic Alphabet of the Winnebago Indians." In *Proceedings of the American Association for the Advancement of Science for the Thirty-Eighth Meeting, Held at Toronto, Ontario, August 1889*, 354–57. 1890.

——. "The Registration of Indian Families." In *Proceedings of the Eighteenth Annual Meeting of the Lake Mohonk Conference of Friends of the Indian*, ed. Isabel C. Barrows, 73–76. 1900.

——. "The Religious Ceremony of the Four Winds or Quarters, as Observed by the Santee Sioux." *PMAR* 16–17, vol. 3, no. 3–4 (1884): 276–88.

——. "Report of Alice C. Fletcher to the Honorable Commissioner of Indian Affairs." In *The Indian Bureau at the New Orleans Exposition*, 8152–8154. Washington DC, 1885. Reprinted in *The Native Americans Reference Collection: Documents Collected by the Office of Indian Affairs*, pt. 1, *1840–1900* (microfilm). Bethesda MD: University Publications of America, 1991.

——. "The Sacred Pole of the Omaha Tribe." In *Proceedings of the American Association for the Advancement of Science for the Forty-Fourth Meeting, Held at Springfield, Mass., August–September 1895*, 270. 1896.

——. "The Shadow or Ghost Lodge: A Ceremony of the Ogallala Sioux." *PMAR* 16–17, vol. 3, no. 3–4 (1884): 296–307.

——. "The Significance of the Scalp-Lock: A Study of Omaha Ritual." *Journal of the Anthropological Institute of Great Britain and Ireland* 27 (1898):436–50.

——. "The Sun Dance of the Ogalalla Sioux." In *Proceedings of the American Association for the Advancement of Science, Thirty-First Meeting, Held at Montreal, Canada, August, 1882*, vol. 30, 580–84. 1883.

——. "Tribal Life among the Omahas: Personal Studies of Indian Life." *Century: A Popular Quarterly* 51:3 (1896): 450–62.

——. "Tribal Structure: A Study of the Omaha and Cognate Tribes." In *Putnam Anniversary Volume: Anthropological Essays Presented to Frederic Ward Putnam in Honor of His Seventieth Birthday, April 16, 1909*, ed. Franz Boas, et al., 253–67. New York: G. E. Strechert, 1909.

——. "The 'Wawan,' or Pipe Dance of the Omahas." *PMAR* 16–17, vol. 3, no. 3–4 (1884): 308–33.

——. "The White Buffalo Festival of the Uncpapas." *PMAR* 16–17, vol. 3, no. 3–4 (1884): 260–75.

Fletcher, Alice C., aided by Francis La Flesche. "A Study of Omaha Indian Music." In *Archaeological and Ethnological Papers of the Peabody Museum, Harvard Uni-*

versity, vol. 1, no. 5, 7–152. Cambridge MA: Peabody Museum of American Archaeology and Ethnology, 1893.

Fletcher, Alice C., and Francis La Flesche. *The Omaha Tribe*. In *Twenty-Seventh Annual Report of the Bureau of American Ethnology for the Years 1905-6*. Washington DC, 1911.

Gates, Merrill E. "Mohonk Indian Conferences." In *Handbook of American Indians North of Mexico*, ed. Frederick Webb Hodge, 1:928–29. Bureau of American Ethnology, Bulletin 30. Washington DC, 1907.

Gilcreast, E. Arthur. "Armstrong, Samuel Chapman, 1839–1893." In Washburn, *History of Indian-White Relations*, 618–19, HNAI, vol. 4, 1988.

———. "Smiley, Albert K., 1828–1912." In Washburn, *History of Indian-White Relations*, 685, HNAI, vol. 4, 1988.

Gilmore, Melvin R. "Uses of Plants by the Indians of the Missouri River Region." In *Thirty-Third Annual Report of the Bureau of American Ethnology*, 43–154. Washington DC, 1919.

Green, Norma Kidd. *Iron Eye's Family: The Children of Joseph La Flesche*. Lincoln: Johnsen Publishing, 1969.

Greene, Jerome A. *Fort Randall on the Missouri, 1856-1892*. Pierre: South Dakota State Historical Society Press, 2005.

Harvard College. *Annual Reports of the President and the Treasurer of Harvard College*. 1891, 1929.

Harvard University. *Fund and Gift Supplement to the Financial Report for the Fiscal Year 1988-1989*. Cambridge MA: Harvard University.

Heitman, Francis B. *Historical Register and Dictionary of the United States Army, from Its Organization, September 29, 1789, to March 2, 1903*. Vol. 1. Washington DC: Government Printing Office, 1903.

Hill, Edward E. *The Office of Indian Affairs, 1824-1880: Historical Sketches*. New York: Clearwater Publishing, 1974.

Hinsley, Curtis M. "The Museum Origins of Harvard Anthropology, 1866-1915." In *Science at Harvard University: Historical Perspectives*, ed. Clark A. Elliott and Margaret W. Rossiter, 121–45. Bethlehem PA: Lehigh University Press; London: Associated University Press, 1992.

———. *The Smithsonian and the American Indian: Making a Moral Anthropology in Victorian America*. Washington DC: Smithsonian Institution Press, 1994.

Howard, E. A. [Annual report, Spotted Tail Agency, Nebraska.] In *Annual Report of the Commissioner of Indian Affairs to the Secretary of the Interior for the Year 1875.* Washington DC, 1875.

Hoxie, Frederick E. *A Final Promise: The Campaign to Assimilate the Indians, 1880-1920.* Lincoln: University of Nebraska Press, 1984.

Hoxie, Frederick E., and Joan T. Mark. Introduction to *With the Nez Perces: Alice Fletcher in the Field, 1889-92,* ed. E. Jane Gay. Lincoln: University of Nebraska Press, 1981.

Hunt, Freeman. *Worth and Wealth: A Collection of Maxims, Morals and Miscellanea for Merchants and Men of Business.* New York: Stringer and Townsend, 1856.

Hunt, Roger D., and Jack R. Brown. *Brevet Brigadier Generals in Blue.* Gaithersburg MD: Olde Soldier Books, 1990.

Hutchinson, Jessie, Jr. *Uncle Sam's Farm: Words and Music.* Boston: Geo. P. Reed, 1850.

Hyde, George E. *Spotted Tail's Folk: A History of the Brulé Sioux.* Norman: University of Oklahoma Press, 1961.

Issac, Gwyneira. "Re-observation and the Recognition of Change: The Photographs of Matilda Coxe Stevenson (1879-1915)." *Journal of the Southwest* 47:3 (2005): 411-55.

Jacobs, Margaret D. *White Mother to a Dark Race: Settler Colonialism, Maternalism, and the Removal of Indigenous Children in the American West and Australia, 1880-1940.* Lincoln: University of Nebraska Press, 2009.

Kappler, Charles J., comp. and ed. *Indian Affairs: Laws and Treaties.* Vol. 1, *Laws.* Washington DC: Government Printing Office, 1904.

——, comp. and ed. *Indian Affairs: Laws and Treaties.* Vol. 2, *Treaties.* Washington DC: Government Printing Office, 1904.

Kelly, Lawrence C. "United States Indian Policies, 1900-1980." In Washburn, *History of Indian-White Relations,* 66-80, *HNAI,* vol. 4, 1988.

La Flesche, Francis. "Alice C. Fletcher." *Science* 58:1494 (1923): 115.

——. "An Indian Allotment." In *Proceedings of the Eighteenth Annual Meeting of the Lake Mohonk Conference of Friends of the Indian,* ed. Isabel C. Barrows, 77-78. 1900.

——. *The Middle Five: Indian Schoolboys of the Omaha Tribe.* Boston: Small, Maynard, 1900.

[Lake Mohonk Conference.] *Second Annual Address to the Public of the Lake Mohonk Conference, Held at Lake Mohonk, N. Y., September, 1884, in Behalf of the Civiliza-*

tion and Legal Protection of the Indians of the United States. Philadelphia: Executive Committee of the Indian Rights Association, 1884.

Lurie, Nancy Oestreich. "Women in Early American Anthropology." In *Pioneers of American Anthropology*, ed. June Helm, 32–42. Seattle: University of Washington Press, 1966.

Mark, Joan. *A Stranger in Her Native Land: Alice Fletcher and the American Indians*. Lincoln: University of Nebraska Press, 1988.

Mason, Otis T. "Woman's Share in Primitive Culture." *American Antiquarian* 11 (1889):1–13.

Mathes, Valerie Sherer, and Richard Lowitt. *The Standing Bear Controversy: Prelude to Indian Reform*. Urbana: University of Illinois Press, 2003.

McGee, W. J., et al. "In Memoriam: Frank Hamilton Cushing." *American Anthropologist*, n.s., 2:2 (1902): 354–80.

McGillycuddy, Julia B. *McGillycuddy, Agent: A Biography of Dr. Valentine T. McGillycuddy*. Stanford CA: Stanford University Press, 1941.

Mead, Margaret. *The Changing Culture of an Indian Tribe*. New York: Columbia University Press, 1932.

Mead, Margaret, and Ruth Leah Bunzel, eds. *The Golden Age of American Anthropology*. New York: G. Braziller, 1960.

Miller, Darlis A. *Matilda Coxe Stevenson: Pioneering Anthropologist*. Norman: University of Oklahoma Press, 2007.

Milner, Clyde. *With Good Intentions: Quaker Work among the Pawnees, Otos, and Omahas in the 1870s*. Lincoln: University of Nebraska Press, 1982.

Morgan, Lewis Henry. *Ancient Society; or Researches in the Lines of Human Progress from Savagery through Barbarism to Civilization*. New York: Henry Holt, 1877.

New York Times. "To Help the Red Men: Speeches before the Indian Rights Convention at New-Haven." November 21, 1885 ProQuest.

———. "Word for the Indians: The Indian Rights Association Meets at Newport." July 22, 1886. ProQuest.

Olson, James C. *Red Cloud and the Sioux Problem*. Lincoln: University of Nebraska Press, 1965.

O'Shea, John M., and John Ludwickson. *Archaeology and Ethnohistory of the Omaha Indians: The Big Village Site*. Lincoln: University of Nebraska Press, 1992.

Parezo, Nancy J. "Matilda Coxe Stevenson: Pioneer Ethnologist." In *Hidden Schol-*

ars: Women Anthropologists and the Native American Southwest, ed. Nancy Parezo, 38–62. Albuquerque: University of New Mexico Press, 1993.

Peabody Museum of American Archaeology and Ethnology. *Eighteenth and Nineteenth Annual Reports (1885–1886) of the Trustees of the Peabody Museum*, vol. 3, no. 5–6 (1886).

Powell, Father Peter J. *People of the Sacred Mountain: A History of the Cheyenne Chiefs and Warrior Societies, 1830–1879; with an Epilogue, 1969–1974*. 2 vols. San Francisco: Harper and Row, 1981.

Pratt, Richard H. *Battlefield and Classroom*. Edited by Robert M. Utley. New Haven CT: Yale University Press, 1964.

Prucha, Francis Paul, ed. *Documents of United States Indian Policy*. Third ed. Lincoln: University of Nebraska Press, 2000.

———. *The Great Father: The United States Government and the American Indians*. 2 vols. Lincoln: University of Nebraska Press, 1984.

Putnam, F. W. "The Serpent Mound of Ohio." *Century: A Popular Quarterly* 39:6 (1890): 871–88.

[Putnam, F. W.] "Sixteenth Report of the Curator." PMAR 16–17, vol. 3, no. 3–4 (1884): 159–206.

Quiller-Couch, Sir Arthur, ed. *The New Oxford Book of English Verse, 1250–1918*. New ed. New York: Oxford University Press, 1955.

Ridington, Robin, and Dennis Hastings (In'aska). *Blessing for a Long Time: The Sacred Pole of the Omaha Tribe*. Lincoln: University of Nebraska Press, 1997.

Riggs, Stephen Return. *Tah́-koo Wah-kaṅ; or, The Gospel among the Dakotas*. Boston: Congregational Publishing Society, 1869.

Rossiter, Margaret W. *Women Scientists in America: Struggles and Strategies to 1940*. Baltimore: Johns Hopkins University Press, 1982.

Sandoz, Mari. *Cheyenne Autumn*. New York: McGraw-Hill, 1953.

Saunders-Lee, Sara L. *In Memoriam: Mrs. Erminnie A. Smith, 1837–1886*. Boston: Lee and Shepard, 1890.

Simonsen, Jane E. *Making Home Work: Domesticity and Native American Assimilation in the American West, 1860–1919*. Chapel Hill: University of North Carolina Press, 2006.

Smith, Sherry Lynn. "Francis La Flesche and the World of Letters." *American Indian Quarterly* 25:4 (2001): 579–603.

Swanton, John R. "John Napoleon Brinton Hewitt." *American Anthropologist* 40:2 (1938): 286–90.

Thwaites, Reuben Gold, ed. *The Jesuit Relations and Allied Documents: Travels and Explorations of the Jesuit Missionaries in New France, 1610–1791*. Vol. 54, *Iroquois, Ottawas, Lower Canada, 1669–1671*. Cleveland: Burrows Brothers, 1899.

Tibbles, Thomas Henry. *Buckskin and Blanket Days: Memoirs of a Friend of the Indians*. Edited by T. B. Cogswell. Garden City NY: Doubleday, 1957.

Tong, Benson. *Susan La Flesche Picotte, MD: Omaha Indian Leader and Reformer*. Norman: University of Oklahoma Press, 1999.

Tonkovich, Nicole. *The Allotment Plot: Alice C. Fletcher, E. Jane Gay, and Nez Perce Survivance*. Lincoln: University of Nebraska Press, 2012.

———. "'Lost in the General Wreckage of the Far West': The Photographs and Writings of Jane Gay." In *Trading Gazes: Euro-American Women Photographers and Native North Americans, 1880–1940*, ed. Susan Bernardin, Melody Graulich, Lisa MacFarlane, and Nicole Tonkovich, 33–70. New Brunswick NJ: Rutgers University Press, 2003.

Tylor, Edward B. "How the Problems of American Anthropology Present Themselves to the English Mind." *Science* 4:98 (1884): 545–51.

U.S. Congress. *Memorial of the Members of the Omaha Tribe of Indians, for a Grant of Land in Severalty*. 47th Cong., 1st sess., January 11, 1882, S. Misc. Doc. 31, serial 1993.

Visweswaran, Kamala. "'Wild West' Anthropology and the Disciplining of Gender." In *Gender and American Social Science: The Formative Years*, ed. Helene Silverberg, 86–123. Princeton NJ: Princeton University Press, 1998.

Washburn, Wilcomb E., ed. *History of Indian-White Relations*. Vol. 4 of *Handbook of North American Indians*, ed. William C. Sturtevant. Washington DC: Smithsonian Institution, 1988.

Washington Post. "The Anthropological Society: Interesting Papers Read by Miss Alice Fletcher and Prof. Homes." January 4, 1899. ProQuest.

———. "Famous Lake Mohonk: Picturesque Spot Where the Indian's Friends Meet." October 9, 1904. ProQuest.

———. "Indian Association Elects Officers." January 7, 1905. ProQuest.

Watson, Rubie S. "Introduction: Alice Fletcher." In *Three Generations of Women Anthropologists*, 3–8. Cambridge MA: Peabody Museum, Harvard University, 1994–95. Published in conjunction with an exhibition at the Tozzer Library.

Welch, Rebecca Hancock. "Alice Cunningham Fletcher, Anthropologist and Indian Rights Reformer." PhD diss., George Washington University, 1980.

Wishart, David J. *An Unspeakable Sadness: The Dispossession of the Nebraska Indians*. Lincoln: University of Nebraska Press, 1994.

Wissler, Clark. "Societies and Ceremonial Associations in the Oglala Division of the Teton-Dakota." In *American Museum of Natural History Anthropological Papers*, vol. 11, no. 1 (1912): 1–99.

"The Women's Anthropological Society." *Science* 13:321 (1889): 240–42.

Women's National Indian Association. *Annual Report of the Women's National Indian Association*. Philadelphia, 1885.

Young, Ann Eliza. *Wife No. 19; or, A Life in Bondage: A Full Exposé of Mormonism*. Hartford CT: Dustin, Gilman, 1876.

Chronological Listing of Works Cited by Alice C. Fletcher

1882. "Extracts from Miss Fletcher's Letters." *Morning Star* 3:3, p. 1.

1883. "On Indian Education and Self-Support." *Century; A Popular Quarterly* 26:2, pp. 312–15.

1883. "The Sun Dance of the Ogalalla Sioux." In *Proceedings of the American Association for the Advancement of Science, Thirty-First Meeting, Held at Montreal, Canada, August, 1882*, vol. 30, pp. 580–84.

1884. "Camping among the Sunflowers." *Wide Awake* 18:3, pp. 204–8.

1884. "The Carlisle Indian Pupils at Home." *Wide Awake* 18:2, pp. 141–44.

1884. "The Elk Mystery or Festival. Ogallala Sioux." PMAR 16–17, vol. 3, no. 3–4: 276–88.

1884. "The Religious Ceremony of the Four Winds or Quarters, as Observed by the Santee Sioux." PMAR 16–17, vol. 3, no. 3–4, pp. 276–88.

1884. "The Shadow or Ghost Lodge: A Ceremony of the Ogallala Sioux." PMAR 16–17, vol. 3, no. 3–4, pp. 296–307.

1884. "The 'Wawan,' or Pipe Dance of the Omahas." PMAR 16–17, vol. 3, no. 3–4, pp. 308–33.

1884. "The White Buffalo Festival of the Uncpapas." PMAR 16–17, vol. 3, no. 3–4, pp. 260–75.

1885. "An Average Day in Camp among the Sioux." *Science* 6:139, pp. 285–87.

1885. "An Evening in Camp among the Omahas." *Science* 6:139, pp. 88–90.

1885. *Historical Sketch of the Omaha Tribe of Indians in Nebraska*. Washington DC: Judd and Detweiler.

1885. "Home Building among the Indians." *Leaflets of the Women's National Indian Association*.

1885. "Lands in Severalty to Indians; Illustrated by Experiences with the Omaha Tribe." In *Proceedings of the American Association for the Advancement of Science, Thirty-Third Meeting, held at Philadelphia, Penn., September, 1884*, pp. 654–65.

1885 [1991]. "Report of Alice C. Fletcher to the Honorable Commissioner of Indian Affairs." In *The Indian Bureau at the New Orleans Exposition*, pp. 8152–8154. Washington DC. Reprinted in *The Native Americans Reference Collection: Documents Collected by the Office of Indian Affairs*, pt. 1, *1840–1900* (microfilm). Bethesda MD: University Publications of America.

1886. "Composite Portraits of American Indians." *Science* 7:170, p. 408 and illus.

1887. "The Crowning Act." *Morning Star* 7 (March), p. 1.

1888. "Glimpses of Child Life among the Omaha Tribe of Indians." *Journal of American Folk-Lore* 1:2, pp. 115–23.

1888. "The Indian and the Prisoner." *Southern Workman and Hampton School Record* 17:4, p. 45.

1888. *Indian Education and Civilization: A Report Prepared in Answer to Senate Resolution of February 23, 1885*. 48th Cong., 2d sess., February 23, 1885, S. Ex. Doc. 95, serial 2264. Special Report, U.S. Bureau of Education. Washington DC: Government Printing Office.

1888. "Letter to General Whittlesey." In *Proceedings of the Sixth Annual Meeting of the Lake Mohonk Conference of Friends of the Indian, Held September 26, 27, and 28, 1888*, ed. Isabel C. Barrows, p. 7.

1889. "Leaves from My Omaha Notebook." *Journal of American Folk-Lore* 2:6, pp. 219–26.

1889. "Letter to General Whittlesey. South Fork of Clearwater, Nez Perce Agency, Idaho, Sept. 17th." In *Proceedings of the Seventh Annual Meeting of the Lake Mohonk Conference of Friends of the Indian*, ed. Samuel J. Barrows, pp. 13–14.

1890. "The Phonetic Alphabet of the Winnebago Indians." In *Proceedings of the American Association for the Advancement of Science for the Thirty-Eighth Meeting, Held at Toronto, Ontario, August 1889*, pp. 354–57.

1891. "The Indian Messiah." *Journal of American Folk-Lore* 4:12, pp. 57–60.

1892. "Experiences in Allotting Land." In *Proceedings of the Tenth Annual Meeting of the Lake Mohonk Conference of Friends of the Indian*, ed. Martha D. Adams, pp. 24–29.

1892. "Hae-thu-ska Society of the Omaha Tribe." *Journal of American Folk-Lore* 5:17, pp. 135–44.

1893. "Personal Studies of Indian Life: Politics and 'Pipe-Dancing'." *Century: A Popular Quarterly* 45:3, pp. 441–56.

1893. "A Study of Omaha Indian Music" (aided by Francis La Flesche). In *Archaeological and Ethnological Papers of the Peabody Museum, Harvard University*, vol. 1, no. 5, pp. 7–152. Cambridge MA: Peabody Museum of American Archaeology and Ethnology.

1894. "Indian Songs: Personal Studies of Indian Life." *Century: A Popular Quarterly* 47:3, pp. 421–32.

1895. "Hunting Customs of the Omaha: Personal Studies of Indian Life." *Century: A Popular Quarterly* 50:5, pp. 691–702.

1896. "The Sacred Pole of the Omaha Tribe." In *Proceedings of the American Association for the Advancement of Science for the Forty-Fourth Meeting, Held at Springfield, Mass., August–September 1895*, p. 270.

1896. "Tribal Life among the Omahas: Personal Studies of Indian Life." *Century: A Popular Quarterly* 51:3, pp. 450–62.

1897. "Home Life among the Indians: Records of Personal Experience." *Century: A Popular Quarterly* 54:2, pp. 252–63.

1897. "Notes on Certain Beliefs Concerning Will Power among the Siouan Tribes." *Science* 5:113, pp. 331–34.

1898. "The Import of the Totem." *Science* 7:4, pp. 296–304.

1898. "The Significance of the Scalp-Lock: A Study of Omaha Ritual." *Journal of the Anthropological Institute of Great Britain and Ireland* 27, pp. 436–50.

1899. "Indian Speech." *Southern Workman and Hampton School Record*, 28:2, pp. 426–28.

1899. "The Indian Woman and Her Problems." *Southern Workman and Hampton School Record* 28:5, pp. 172–76.

1900. *Indian Story and Song from North America*. Boston: Small, Maynard.

1900. "In Memoriam: Frank Hamilton Cushing." *American Anthropologist*, n.s., 2:2, p. 367.

1900. "The Registration of Indian Families." In *Proceedings of the Eighteenth Annual*

Meeting of the Lake Mohonk Conference of Friends of the Indian, ed. Isabel C. Barrows, pp. 73–76.

1907, 1910. "Adai," "Adornment," "Agency System," "Aguacay," "Ahouerhopihein," "Akasquy," "Amediche," "Anadarko," "Analao," "Anamis," "Anoixi," "Aranama," "Arhau," "Arikara," "Arkokisa," "Arthur, Mark," "Avavares," "Avoyelles," "Bright Eyes," "Buffalo," "Caddo," "Caddoan Family," "Cahinnio," "Camping and Camp Circles," "Campti," "Chaquantie," "Chaui," "Choye," "Civilization," "Coaque," "Dolls," "Doustioni," "Dramatic Representation," "Dreams and Visions," "Earth Lodge," "Ethics and Morals," "Etiquette," "Eyeish," "Fasting," "Feasts," "Furniture," "Governmental Policy," "Grass House," "Hair Dressing," "Higos," "Imaha," "Irrupiens," "Kabaye," "Kadohadacho," "Karankawa," "Keremen," "Kiabaha," "Kitkehahki," "La Flesche, Francis," "Land Tenure," "Legal Status," "Mariames," "Masks," "Mayeye," "Mento," "Meracouman," "Mourning," "Music and Musical Instruments," "Nacaniche," "Nacisi," "Nanatsoho," "Natasi," "Natchitoch," "Ointemarhen," "Onapiem," "Oratory," "Orcan," "Orientation," "Panequo," "Pawnee," "Pehir," "Peinhoum," "Peissaquo," "Penoy," "Petao," "Piechar," "Pitahauerat," "Poetry," "Property and Property Right," "Quillwork," "Skidi," "Soldier," "Spichehat," "Tattooing," "Trading Posts," "Tsera," "Tyacappan," "Wakonda," "War and War Discipline," "Yatasi," "Yguases." In *Handbook of American Indians North of Mexico*, ed. Frederick Webb Hodge. Bureau of American Ethnology, Bulletin 30. 2 vols. Washington DC.

1909. "Tribal Structure: A Study of the Omaha and Cognate Tribes." In *Putnam Anniversary Volume: Anthropological Essays Presented to Frederic Ward Putnam in Honor of His Seventieth Birthday, April 16, 1909*, ed. Franz Boas, et al., pp. 253–67. New York: G. E. Strechert.

1911. *The Omaha Tribe* (with Francis La Flesche). In *Twenty-Seventh Annual Report of the Bureau of American Ethnology for the Years 1905–6*. Washington DC.

1915. "The Child and the Tribe." In *Proceedings of the National Academy of Sciences*, no. 1, pp. 569–74.

1915. "The Indian and Nature." In *Proceedings of the National Academy of Sciences*, no. 1, pp. 467–73.

2001. *Camping with the Sioux: Fieldwork Diary of Alice Cunningham Fletcher*. Smithsonian Institution, National Anthropological Archives (http://www.nmnh.si.edu/naa/fletcher/).

Index

Carlisle Indian Industrial School, 31, 40, 67, 320, 356n72; founding of, 38, 359n97, 369n3 (chap. 2), 377n4 (chap. 24); and *Morning Star* (newspaper), 40, 53. *See also* education

"The Carlisle Indian Pupils at Home" (Fletcher), 7

Carlisle Indian School. *See* Carlisle Indian Industrial School

Carlisle Training School. *See* Carlisle Indian Industrial School

Carr, Lucien, 9, 22, 28, 40, 59; Fletcher's letters to, 26–27, 47, 63–64

Cemetery Hill (*Mįxe ppahé*). *See* Hill of the Graves (Me-ha-pach-he)

census: of 1850 (U.S.), 18; of 1884 (of Omaha tribe undertaken by Fletcher), 42; of 1890 (Pine Ridge Reservation), 356n72; of 1890 (U.S.), 68; of 1891 (Rosebud Agency), 356n72

Century Co., 10

Century Illustrated Monthly Magazine (magazine), 13, 14, 63, 351n29

ceremonies, 11, 41, 160–61, 186, 210, 270–72, 285, 287–89; exorcism, 327; Fletcher's respect for, 12; Four Winds (Santee), 40; and haircuts of children, 264, 265, 375n3 (chap. 18); Hunkpapa White Buffalo, 40, 206–11; thanksgiving, 288–89; welcome, 138; and willow rods, 185, 221, 288, 371n3 (chap. 9), 372n4, 376n3 (chap. 20). *See also* dances; death customs; feasts; Ghost Lodge; religion; sacred pipes

Charles Scribner's Sons, 8, 350n16

Cheyenne River Agency (Sioux), 357n77

Cheyennes, 71, 377n4 (chap. 24). *See also* Northern Cheyennes

chiefs, 99, 240, 275–77, 316–17; and corruption, 238–39; and hunting councils, 275–76; selection of, 4, 99, 159–60, 370n3 (chap. 6); and war parties, 290–91. *See also* social institutions, Indian

child-rearing, 7, 149, 164, 181–82, 262–72

children, 139–40, 177, 198, 226–27, 251; and baby boards, 173, 263; and clothing, 148–49, 181–82, 267–68; and discipline, 149, 198–99, 256; duties of, 269; and games, 181, 198, 265–67; and hair, 148, 264–65, 375n3 (chap. 18); and naming practices, 262–63, 375n1 (chap. 18); and navel cord cases, *174*; and pranks, 267–69, 312–14; and rites of passage, 269–72; and the sacred pipes ceremony, 331, 335; and tent positions, 132, 158–59; and travel, 189, 191, 192, 195, 197. *See also* education

Christianity, 67, 293, 318, 327, 355n69; and the Congregational Mission, 29, 32, 92–93; and Episcopalian services, 224, 372n3 (chap. 14); and missionaries, 33, 52, 223–24, 226, 306, 357nn79–80; and the Presbyterian Mission School, 37, 38, 39, 243, 244, 309–14, 319, 348nn6–7, 349n8, 374n1 (chap. 16), 377n5. *See also* religion

Dawes, Henry L., 1, 3, 49, 50, 66, 67, 68, 347n1
Dawes Act of 1887, 10, 47, 50, 52–55, 57, 61, 67, 347n1; amendments to the, 56. *See also* reform movement
Dawes Severalty Act. *See* Dawes Act of 1887
Dawson, N. H. R., 15
death customs, 180, 205, 302–3, 334; and animals, 202, 203, 204, 215, 216; and criers, 213, 214, 218; and feasts, 216, 219; Ghost Lodge, 4, 12, 40, 212–21, 372nn1–2 (chap. 13); and gifts, 202, 203, 204, 213, 215, 217–18, 219–21; and hair, 202, 213, 214, 215, 219, 221; and kinship, 218, 372n2 (chap. 13); and nakedness, 33, 180, 371n4; and painting, 201, 213, 214. *See also* religion
Decatur NE, 305, 316, 376n1 (chap. 22)
De Groffs, Edward, 54, 55
Dexter, Ralph, 22
Diddock, Marguerite La Flesche. *See* La Flesche, Marguerite
Diddock, Walter, 373n3
discrimination, anti-Indian, 107, 108–9, 112, 182–83, 228–30, 277–78, 315–17; and the media, 3; and white agents and traders, 4–5, 199–201, 225–26, 240
D. Lothrop and Company, 7, 349n11
dogs, 33, 163, 119–20, 122, 131, 151, 203, 204, 215, 219, 223, 248, 258, 279–80, 282. *See also* animals
"The Domestic Alien." *See* "Life among the Indians" (manuscript)

Dorsey, George A., 22, 353n55
Dorsey, James Owen, 21, 367n180
dress. *See* clothing
Dull Knife, 65, 370n4 (chap. 5)

The Eagle. *See* Thigh
earth lodges, 5, 42, 61, 71, 233, 240, 253–58, 259, 261, 284, 288, 291, 305, 327, 332. *See also* tents (tipis)
Easthampton (MA) News and East-hampton Enterprise, 378n5
education, 74, 182, 226, 234, 238, 325; in Alaska, 52, 53; and assimilation, 5, 21, 29, 69, 348n6; and boarding schools, 69–70, 309–10, 355n69, 366n177, 377n5; and the Carlisle Indian Industrial School, 31, 38, 40, 67, 320, 356n72, 359n97, 377n4 (chap. 24); Fletcher's studies of Indian progress in, 15, 48–49, 67, 366n177; and the Hampton Industrial and Agricultural Institute, 40, 51, 71, 320, 355n69, 359n97, 377n4 (chap. 24), 378n6; and the Presbyterian Mission School, 37, 38, 39, 243, 244, 309–14, 319, 348nn6–7, 349n8, 374n1 (chap. 16), 377n5; and reform, 47, 53–54, 319, 361n114. *See also* children
E-la-hon-h, Mary, 39
Elizabeth Institute, 348n7, 355n69
Elk dreamer, 40
Elk Society, 4, 13, 184, 185–87, 347n3, 371n1 (chap. 9). *See also* vision seeking
Episcopal Church (Rosebud Agency), 372n3 (chap. 14)

Esau, Elizabeth. *See* Tainne (Mrs. Joseph La Flesche)

ethnography, 4–7, 12–13, 32, 35, 49, 59–60, 72–74, 122; and anonymity of subjects, 6; and Frank Hamilton Cushing, 13–14, 351n31; methods of, 10–11; and music, 71. *See also* anthropology; ethnology

ethnology, 14, 20, 21, 22, 24, 39–41, 47–48, 59, 67–72, 83, 107; and kinship, 370n1 (chap. 6). *See also* anthropology; ethnography

etiquette, Indian, 4, 11, 149–50, 158, 196; sitting, 164–65, 371n1 (chap. 7). *See also* social institutions, Indian

"An Evening in Camp among the Omahas," 49

Farley, Edward, 235, 236, 243, 373n3

Farley, Rosalie La Flesche (Mrs. Edward Farley). *See* La Flesche, Rosalie

Farman, Ella, 349n11

farming, 65, 163, 182, 314, 377n2 (chap. 23); and implements, 200–201, 225, 227, 260–61, 306, 309; and Indian agents, 306, 307–8, 309, 377n4 (chap. 22); and the Omaha, 36, 57, 238, 240, 248, 305, 307–8, 309, 316, 318, 373n7. *See also* land ownership

Fassett, Samuel Montague, 50

"the father." *See* La Flesche, Joseph (Iron Eyes)

feasts, 11, 187, 197, 258, 305; and children, 149, 262; and death customs, 216, 219; and dishes, 4, 171; dog, 203, 279; and marriage, 301; meaning of, 170; and religious festivals, 184, 209, 216, 219, 332, 333; to welcome Fletcher, 31, 33, 130–33, 134, 135; and the woman's society, 4, 169–70, 171, 173, 178–79. *See also* ceremonies; dances

"feeding system." *See* rations, government

Fletcher, Alice, vi, 19, 38, 44, 341; academic articles of, 12, 15, 41, 43, 49, 60, 70–71, 363n139; advocacy of, for Indians, 14, 15, 32, 35–39, 40, 49, 50, 58, 63, 64–65, 67, 68, 69, 70, 73, 293–94, 318–20, 326–29, 377n1 (chap. 24); in Alaska, 52, 53, 54, 55; on allotment failure, 55–57; and allotment policy, 21, 38–39, 40, 47, 55–57, 64, 69, 318, 319–20, 366n177, 377nn1–2 (chap. 24); and allotment work, 41–42, 56, 67–68, 321–29, 350n23, 360n110; and anonymity of subjects, 6, 74; and anthropological studies, 21–22, 24, 35, 47–48, 59–61, 62–65, 72–75, 361n118; and artifacts, 22, 43, 44, 45, 46, 48, 49, 52, 69, 72, 361n120; birth of, 17; and the Bureau of Indian Affairs, 48; and camping, 31, 87, 89, 90, 91, 92, 93–95, 109, 114, 115, 116, 122–23, 190–96, 222–23, 321, 323, 324–25, 344; collaboration of, with Francis La Flesche, 5, 29, 39, 58, 71, 72–73, 348n6, 367n180, 367n185; at the Congregational Mission (Santee Reserva-

373n9; and Fletcher's illness, 326;
George W. Wilkinson, 41, 42; John
Cook, 6, 31, 119, 120-22, 369n1
(chap. 2); Nathan C. Meeker, 65;
and traders, 238
"Indian problem (Indian Question),"
55, 60, 65-66, 140
Indian Rights Association, 49, 52
"Indian Songs" (Fletcher), 351n29,
369n2 (chap. 4)
"Indian Speech" (Fletcher), 64
Indian Territory, 69-70, 92, 153, 316-
17, 370n4 (chap. 5); Poncas'
removal to, 24, 36, 65, 67, 69, 94,
223-24, 234, 348n6, 354n58, 372n2
(chap. 14), 373n6, 377n1 (chap. 24)
Iowas, 71, 87

Jackson NE (Cut River Bluff), 87
Jackson, Sheldon, 53, 54, 55
Jenks, Lucia Adeline (Mrs. Thomas
Fletcher). See Fletcher, Lucia Ade-
line Jenks (Mrs. Thomas Fletcher)
jewelry, 168, 171, 175. See also clothing
Johnson, Lem, 112
Jones, Miss. See Smith, Mrs. (Miss
Jones)

Kansas (tribe), 253
kat'éla. See woman's society
Keene, James William, 54, 55
Keyapaha, 342
Kick, 201-2, 203, 204-5, 372n1 (chap.
11)
kinship, 4; and clans, 156-57, 370n1
(chap. 6); and death customs, 218,
372n2 (chap. 13); and gens, 156-59,

160, 164, 218, 262-65, 278, 290,
370n1 (chap. 6), 372n2 (chap. 13);
and naming practices, 156, 158,
262-63; and the Omaha, 4, 156,
249-50, 262-65, 267-69, 278, 301,
374n5; and pranks, 267-69; and
tent positions, 158-59, 370n2
(chap. 6). See also social institutions, Indian
Kirkwood, Samuel J., 84, 348n6
Kostromentinoff, George, 54, 55

La Flesche, Francis, 14, 49, 90,
355n69, 359n106; and allotments,
41, 57-58, 321, 325, 378n1 (chap.
25); birth of, 348n6; collaboration
of, with Fletcher, 5, 29, 39, 58, 71,
72-73, 348n6, 367n180, 367n185;
education of, 348n6; marriages of,
51, 362n130; in the Office of Indian
Affairs, 39, 348n6; The Omaha
Tribe, 5, 58, 72-73, 347n5; and publication of Life among the Indians,
11; and ritual objects, 43, 44, 45,
48, 72, 332; scholarly papers of, 43,
94, 360n112; speaking tour of, 24,
25, 348nn6-7; in Washington DC,
43, 52, 62, 360n110
La Flesche, Joseph (Iron Eyes), 6, 43,
241, 289-90, 292, 348n7, 373n2;
and assimilation, 14, 29, 348n6,
355n69; birth of, 87; and Christianity, 355n69; death of, 375n2 (chap.
19); on education, 238; on farming,
286-87; on Fletcher, 61, 87; on
hunting, 274-79, 281-82, 375n1
(chap. 19); and land ownership, 35,

Literary Society, 350n21

Little Big Horn River, 3

Little Bull, 371n1 (chap. 9)

Livingston Ranch, *113*

Ma-choo-e-see-sa, *114*

Mąchú isisi ('Grizzly Moving Around'). *See* Ma-choo-e-see-sa

Ma-he-ga-tha-be-ga (Sandstone), *341*

Mąhi gasábe egą ('Darkened Stone'). *See* Ma-he-ga-tha-be-ga (Sandstone)

Mallery, Garrick, 28

Ma-ne-ka-snah (Only earth or clay or mud), *343*

"manly progress," 5, 230, 347n4. *See also* social evolutionary rhetoric

Mą ðikka šna ppahé·mąšiadi ('Bare Earth Mountain'). *See* Ma-ne-ka-snah (Only earth or clay or mud)

Mark, Joan: *A Stranger in Her Native Land*, 17, 68, 69

Marquette, Jacques, 331, 378n3

marriage customs, 164, 319; and gifts, 250–51, 301, 302; and kinship, 156, 157, 250, 301; Omaha, 5, 250–51, 299, 301–3; and polygyny, 6, 147–48, 250–51; and separation, 164. *See also* courtship customs

Mason, Otis T., 16

McGillycuddy, Valentine T., 40

Mead, Margaret, 58–59, *63*

medicine, 4, 161, 185, 194–95, 212, 240. *See also* social institutions, Indian

"medicine men," 161, 194–95, 212. *See also* religion

Meeker, Nathan C., 65

Me-ha-pach-he (Hill of the Graves), *89*

men's roles, 163, 167–68, 169, 206, 209, 210, 297; and child-rearing, 263–64; and farming, 163; and honors, 4, 157, 160, 212, 260, 289–90, 369n3 (chap. 4); and hunting, 161–62; and societies, 184; and vision seeking, 183–87; and the woman's society, 172, 371n1 (chap. 8). *See also* social institutions, Indian; women's roles (Indian)

Meriam Report of 1928, 58

Mesa Verde, 353n56

The Middle Five (La Flesche), 72, 367n185

"Mike," 108–9

Milk (Sioux chief). *See* Asanpi (Milk, Brule)

Milk, Daniel, 31, 122, 140–41, 150, 193, 194–95, 222, 369n3 (chap. 2); on discrimination, 153–54, 182–83, 199, 200, 356n72; on treaties, 151–52

Miller, George, 71, 367n181

missionaries, 33, 52, 223–24, 226, 306, 357nn79–80. *See also* Christianity

mission schools, 5, *53*; Presbyterian Mission School, 37, *38*, *39*, 243, 244, 309–14, 319, 348nn6–7, 349n8, 374n1, 377n5. *See also* education

moccasins, 11, 31, *116*, 127, 129, 146, 160, 165–67, 169, 199–200, 263, 291; and ceremonies, 264, 265; as gifts, 184, 209, 217, 218, 220, 221, 264. *See also* clothing

Morgan, John T., 36

Morgan, Lewis Henry, 21

Mormons, 304–5, 349n10, 376n1 (chap. 22); and "sealing" ceremony, 305, 376n2 (chap. 22). *See also* religion

Morning Star (newspaper), 40, 53. *See also* Carlisle Indian Industrial School

Mosquito Camp. *See* Oo-hay-a-ta (Mosquito Camp)

Moundbuilders (mounds), 20, 375n3 (chap. 17)

music, 60–61, 71, 118, 325–26, 367n180; and children, 247, 270, 271, 272, 314; and courtship, 295, 296; and dances, 176, 177, 178; and religion, 11, 270, *271*; and the sacred pipe ceremony, 11, 331, 333, *336*. *See also* dances

nakedness, 208, 210, 282; and death customs, 33, 180, 371n4. *See also* clothing

naming practices, 4, 5, 156, 158; of the Omahas, 5, 48, 262–63, 328, 375n1 (chap. 18). *See also* social institutions, Indian

navel cord case, *174*

Nebraska State Militia, 109, 368n7

Ne-da-ge-ne-nes-ga-the (Not cooked or furnished well), *341*

"the nephew." *See* Milk, Daniel

Newcastle NE, 110–12, 368n9

Nez Perces, 60; and land allotments, 56, 67, 68, 350n23, 366n177

Nicomi (mother of Mary Gale La Flesche), 235–36, 373n4

Nida·ži nįsnįska ('Raw Spring'). *See* Ne-da-ge-ne-nes-ga-the (Not cooked or furnished well)

Niobrara River, 94, 95

Northern Cheyennes, 65, 69, 370n4 (chap. 5). *See also* Cheyennes

"Notes on Certain Beliefs Concerning Will Power" (Fletcher), 15

Office of Indian Affairs, 39, 67, 348n6

Oglala Sioux Ghost Lodge. *See* Ghost Lodge

"old man of the mountain," 236, 237, 240, 241, 274, 277, 307, 373n5

Old Smoke, *97*

Oliver, Emily, 32

Omaha NE, 84, 85, 105, 252, 368n1

Omaha Act of 1882, *50*

Omaha Agency, *xii*, 41, 87, 360n110

Omaha Club, *203*

Omaha Dance (Grass Dance), 71, 141–45, 369nn2–3 (chap. 4). *See also* dances

Omaha Herald, 24

Omaha Mission. *See* Presbyterian Mission School

Omaha Pipe Dance ("Wawa*n*"), 42–43, *44, 45, 46,* 67, 72, 331–36, 378n1 (chap. 26). *See also* dances; sacred pipes

Omaha Reservation, 29, 35, 38–39, 57, 66–67, 234–51, 254–61, 295; and corruption, 239, 240, 241–42; creation of the, 36, 85, 252; and earth lodges, 253–58, 259; Fletcher's arrival at, 85–86, 233–36, 369n4 (chap. 2), 373n1; Presbyterian Mis-

sacred pipes, 11, 275–76, 330–36, 378n3; descriptions of, *44, 45, 46,* 330–31, 378n2 (chap. 26); and the Omaha Pipe Dance (Wawa*n*), 42–43, *44, 45, 46,* 67, 72, 331–36, 378n1 (chap. 26). *See also* ceremonies

Sacred Pole, 48, 72, 282, 287, 288, 289, 375n2 (chap. 19)

Sacred Tents of War, 48, 49, 72, 278, 282, 287, 290, 361n120

Sanders, William Wilkins, 32, 357n77

Santee Four Winds ceremony, 40. *See also* ceremonies

Santee Mission. *See* Congregational Mission (Santee Mission)

Santee Sioux, 29, 33, 40, 59, 85, 92–93, 357n80

Santee Sioux Reservation, 29, 32, 33–34, 40, 86, *110. See also* Santee Sioux; Sioux

scalplocks, 123, 129, 142, 148, 181, 226, 297–98. *See also* hair

School of American Archaeology, 60

School of Anthropological Research. *See* School of American Archaeology

Science (magazine), 49, 60, 364n151

Scribner's Monthly. See Century Illustrated Monthly Magazine (magazine)

Scull, Sarah Amelia, 353n56

Seventh Annual Lake Mohonk Conference. *See* Lake Mohonk conferences

Severalty Act of 1887. *See* Dawes Act of 1887

sewing, 7, 140, 146, 147, 163, 167, 168–69, 172–73, 182, 243, 245, 262; and porcupine quills, 72, 127, 165, 167, 176, 178, 220, 254, 281. *See also* clothing

Sia (Zia) Pueblo, 353n56

Simonsen, Jane E., 365n157

Sioux, 29, 31, *174,* 370n2 (chap. 6); and the Black Hills, 11, 152; and chieftainship, 4, *99,* 159–60, 370n3 (chap. 6); and children, 67, 92–93, 122, 148–49, 158–59, 164, 173, *174,* 181–82, 198–99, 226–27; and clothing, 72, 146–47, 148–49, 160, 165–69, 173, 180, 181–82, 196, 219, 220; dances, 33, 70–71, 141–45, 161, 169–72, 173, 175–80, 185–87, 369nn2–3 (chap. 4), 371n3 (chap. 8); discrimination against, 3, 4–5, 182–83, 200, 225–26, 228–30; and dog feasts, *203,* 279; Elk Society, 4, 13, 184, 185–87, 371n1 (chap. 9); and feasts, 31, 33, 130–33, *134,* 135, 169–70, 171, 178–79, 187, 197, *203,* 209, 216, 219; Ghost Lodge, 4, 12, 40, 212–21, 372nn1–2 (chap. 13); and hair, 129, 141, 168, 171, 181, 213, 214, 215, 219, 221; and the Hunkpapa White Buffalo ceremony, 40, 206–11; and hunting customs, 138, 150–51, 206; and kinship, 4, 156–59, 164, 218, 370n1 (chap. 6), 372n2 (chap. 13); and land ownership, 138, 199, 237, 347n1; and marriage customs, 147–48, 156, 157, 164; men's society, 370n4 (chap. 6); and naming practices, 4, 156, 158; and the Omaha

Dance (Grass Dance), 71, 141–45, 369nn2–3 (chap. 4); and painting (of face and hair), 129, 142, 168, 171, 175, 185, 196–97, 208, 213, 214; physical characteristics of, 47–48, 60, 145, 361n118; and religion, 4, 13, 40, 152–53, 160–61, 183–87, 206–11, 371n1 (chap. 9); Sun Dance, 40, 41, 72, 340, 358n96; and tents (tipis), 4, 124–27, *128*, 141–42, 183, 188–89, 190–91, 192–93; and traveling methods, 188–97; and vision seeking, 183–87, 371n1 (chap. 9); and war, 85, 162, 289, 290, 292; on white men, 150–54, 164, 199, 200–201; and the woman's society, 171–73, 175–80, 371n1 (chap. 8); and women's roles, 4, 7, 61, 163–65, 169, 188–89, 190–91, 371n1 (chap. 7)

Sioux City IA, 244, 260, 306

Sitting Bull, 33, 206, 208, 372n1 (chap. 12), 372n1 (chap. 14); and the Hunkpapa White Buffalo ceremony, 40, 372n1 (chap. 12); as prisoner of war, 32, *207*. *See also* chiefs

Smiley, Albert K., 361n114

Smith, Erminnie Adele ("Mrs. Smith"), 59, 364n151

Smith, Jane, 33–34, 59–60, 361n120

Smith, Mrs. (Miss Jones), 106–7, 368n3

Smithsonian Institution, 9, 14, 20; and the Bureau of [American] Ethnology, 21, 27, 28, 34–35, 52, 61, 74; National Anthropological Archives, 3, 11

social evolutionary rhetoric, 21, 57, 63–64, 72, 329, 353n52; and "manly progress," 5, 230, 347n4; and reform, 3, 43. *See also* anthropology

social institutions, Indian, 155–56; and chief's role, 4, 159–60, 370n3 (chap. 6); etiquette, 4, 11, 149–50, 158, 164–65, 196, 371n1 (chap. 7); and inheritance, 157; and medicine, 4, 161, 212; men's honors, 4, 157, 160, 212, 260, 289–90, 369n3 (chap. 4); naming practices, 4, 5, 48, 156, 158, 262–63, 328, 375n1 (chap. 18); and soldiers, 160, 240, 282, 370n4 (chap. 6), 374n11. *See also* kinship; religion; women's roles (Indian)

sod houses, 112–13. *See also* houses

"soldiers" (in Indian society), 160, 240, 282, 370n4 (chap. 6), 374n11. *See also* social institutions, Indian

songs. *See* music

Sorosis, 18, *19*

Southern Workman (magazine), 56, 64. *See also* Hampton Industrial and Agricultural Institute

Spotted Tail, 31, 356n71, 369n1 (chap. 4)

Spotted Tail (Young Spotted Tail), 31, *125*, *126*, *127*, 137–45, *228*, 369n1 (chap. 4); and dance given for Fletcher, 33, 140–45, *143*, 369nn2–3 (chap. 4). *See also* chiefs

Standing Bear, 65, 66, 94–95, *95*, *96*, *97*, *98*; speaking tour of, 24, *25*, 65, 348nn6–7. *See also* chiefs

In the Studies in the Anthropology of North American Indians Series

A Grammar of Creek (Muskogee)
Jack B. Martin

A Dictionary of Creek / Muskogee
By Jack B. Martin and Margaret McKane Mauldin

Wolverine Myths and Visions: Dene Traditions from Northern Alberta
Edited by Patrick Moore and Angela Wheelock

Ceremonies of the Pawnee
By James R. Murie
Edited by Douglas R. Parks

Households and Families of the Longhouse Iroquois at Six Nations Reserve
By Merlin G. Myers
Foreword by Fred Eggan
Afterword by M. Sam Cronk

Archaeology and Ethnohistory of the Omaha Indians: The Big Village Site
By John M. O'Shea and John Ludwickson

Traditional Narratives of the Arikara Indians (4 vols.)
By Douglas R. Parks

A Dictionary of Skiri Pawnee
By Douglas R. Parks and Lula Nora Pratt

Osage Grammar
By Carolyn Quintero

They Treated Us Just Like Indians: The Worlds of Bennett County, South Dakota
By Paula L. Wagoner

A Grammar of Kiowa
By Laurel J. Watkins with the assistance of Parker McKenzie

To order or obtain more information on these or other University of Nebraska
Press titles, visit www.nebraskapress.unl.edu.